CREATING HIGH PERFORMANCE TEAMS APPLIED STRATEGIES AND TOOLS FOR MANAGERS AND TEAM MEMBERS

Creating High Performance Teams is an accessible and thorough new introduction to this key area of business education. Written by teams experts Ramon J. Aldag and Loren W. Kuzuhara, this book provides students with both a firm grounding in the key concepts of the field and the practical tools to become successful team managers and members. Built on a solid foundation of the most up-to-date research and theory, the chapters are packed with case studies, real-world examples, and tasks and discussion questions, while a companion website supports the book with a wealth of useful resources for students, team members, and instructors.

Centered around an original model for high performance teams, topics covered include the following:

- Building and developing effective teams
- Managing diversity
- Fostering effective communication
- Team processes—meetings, performance management
- Dealing with change and team problems
- Addressing current issues—virtual teams, globalization

With its combined emphasis on principles and application, interwoven with the tools, topics, and teams issues most relevant today, *Creating High Performance Teams* is perfectly placed to equip upper-level undergraduate and MBA students with the knowledge and skills necessary to take on teams in any situation.

Ramon (Ray) J. Aldag is a professor in the Department of Management and Human Resources at the Wisconsin School of Business, University of Wisconsin–Madison, USA. He holds the Glen A. Skillrud Family Chair in Business.

Loren W. Kuzuhara is a teaching professor in the Department of Management and Human Resources at the Wisconsin School of Business, University of Wisconsin–Madison, USA.

CREATING HIGH PERFORMANCE TEAMS

Applied Strategies and
Tools for Managers and Team Members

RAMON J. ALDAG AND LOREN W. KUZUHARA

Routledge
Taylor & Francis Group

NEW YORK AND LONDON

First published 2015
by Routledge
711 Third Avenue, New York, NY 10017

and by Routledge
2 Park Square, Milton Park, Abingdon, Oxon, OX14 4RN

Routledge is an imprint of the Taylor & Francis Group, an informa business

Library of Congress Cataloging-in-Publication Data
Aldag, Ramon J., 1945–
    Creating high performance teams : applied strategies and tools for managers and team members / Ramon J. Aldag and Loren W. Kuzuhara.
        pages cm
    Includes bibliographical references and index.
    1. Teams in the workplace.   2. Organizational behavior.   I. Kuzuhara, Loren W.   II. Title.
    HD66.A43 2015
    658.4'022—dc23
    2014025765

ISBN: 978-0-415-53491-8 (hbk)
ISBN: 978-0-415-53841-1 (pbk)
ISBN: 978-0-203-10938-0 (ebk)

Typeset in Sabon & Frutiger
by Apex CoVantage, LLC

For my wife, Deborah Douglas; our children, Kat Aldag,
Lizzie Aldag Carley, Drew Douglas, and Wyn Douglas; our daughter-in-law,
Shahree Douglas; our son-in-law, Eli Carley Olson; our grandson,
Anthony Fazzari; and our bichon frise, Lily.
RAMON J. ALDAG

For my wife, Lavina, my son, Daniel, and my daughter, Carolyn.
LOREN W. KUZUHARA

BRIEF CONTENTS

CONTENTS

FIGURES

Chapter 5: Managing Team Diversity

Chapter 6: Fostering Effective Communication in Teams

Chapter 7: Facilitating Team Processes

Chapter 8: Managing Change in Teams

Chapter 9: Dealing with Team Problems

Chapter 10: Teams: Evaluating Team Effectiveness

Chapter 11: The New Teams: Virtual, Global, Connected, and Self-Managing

Chapter 12: Designing and Implementing Team-Based Organizations

Chapter 13: Teams Summary and Integration

A VISUAL TOUR OF
CREATING HIGH PERFORMANCE TEAMS

Pedagogical Features

Creating High Performance Teams possesses a number of features that are designed to engage students, enhance understanding of key concepts, and facilitate the development of skills for effective team leadership and membership.

The High Performance Teams Model

The High Performance Teams Model provides a basic integrated conceptual framework that organizes the overall chapter topics covered in the text. It shows the sequence of phases in which a team is formed, developed, and enhanced through an ongoing process of evaluation and continuous refinement of the team system. This framework is useful in that it emphasizes that teams must be structured and managed as a system and that a systematic process is needed in order for team leaders and members to be effective.

Learning Objectives

Each chapter begins with a set of Learning Objectives, which note the things the student should be able to do after reading the chapter. These objectives provide both an introduction to the chapter's content and a checklist to ensure that the student has subsequently focused on all key issues.

Teams in the News

This feature provides examples of news stories from major publications and websites that illustrate a wide variety of team issues from fields such as business, sports, and health care. These stories help students see the relevance of team concepts, strategies, and tools as they affect the functioning and effectiveness of teams in the workplace. Many of these news stories also illustrate useful strategies that team leaders use to develop their teams.

TEAMS IN THE NEWS: The Chilean Mine Disaster[1]

The Chilean Mine Disaster offers a dramatic example of the power of team leadership and teamwork under conditions of tremendous time pressure, threat, and stress. On the afternoon of August 5, 2010, more than 700,000 metric tons of rock collapsed, blocking the central passage to the tunnels in the San José copper-gold mine in Chile's Altacama Desert. A second earthquake followed two days later. 33 men were trapped deep underground, their location and condition

Team Scholar

Team Scholar profiles present interviews with academicians who are experts on team management and discuss what these experts have learned through their research in the field. These profiles help students not only understand the empirical research that is the foundation for much of the existing knowledge on team functioning and effectiveness but also learn about scholars' views on the status and future directions of team research.

TEAM SCHOLAR

Astrid C. Homan, University of Amsterdam

Astrid C. Homan (Ph.D., 2006, University of Amsterdam) is an assistant professor of work and organizational psychology at the University of Amsterdam. Her research interests include team diversity, team processes, team performance, subgroup salience, leadership, and diversity beliefs. She is particularly interested in determining how to harvest the potential value in diversity. Her work is published in outlets such as the *Journal of Applied Psychology, Journal of Personality and Social Psychology, Organizational Behavior and Human Decision Processes,* and *Academy of Management Journal.*

1. What sparked your interest in diversity in work groups?
    My first interest related to group processes, as I wondered why some groups are productive and efficient, whereas other groups are not. I quickly found that the composition of the group (on any dimension) was a strong predictor of the processes that occurred within the group. As our societies and organizations get more and more

Team Management Coach

This feature presents interviews with individuals who have experience with leading and/or working on various types of teams and describes what they have learned about team management as a result. Many interviewees offer specific guidance to students regarding the actions they can take to become more effective team leaders and members.

TEAM MANAGEMENT COACH

Cody Candee, Finance Leadership Rotational Program, Intuit

We all know that many college students dislike working in teams in class projects. What would you like to say to current students about the importance of learning how to work in a team?

Working in teams is an inevitable part of life. When you're in the work force, you'd better be ready for it. Nearly every employer in a job interview will assess your teamwork skills and ask you questions like "Tell me about a time when you had to work with others towards a shared goal" or "Tell me about a time when you overcame a disagreement with a team member." When interviewing, you are going to want as many examples as you can to demonstrate your team working abilities. You'll be constantly working with people in your job, and employers want to know that you've learned how to handle different scenarios.

Which specific experiences did you have during your college years that were the most helpful in enabling you to learn how to develop and lead a team effectively?

In college, I was involved in various student organization leadership roles that really proved valuable for developing team leadership skills. I would say I learned more from these nonclassroom experiences than anything else in college. I was very active in Delta Sigma Pi professional business fraternity with roles of president, chancellor, and vice president of chapter development. Being in a role where I had to lead others helped me develop various skills such as public speaking, running meetings, motivating the unmotivated, and balancing everything else that a college student has going on.

What advice would you give current students about what they should do now to develop their skills in working and leading teams in preparation for working in a real-world job after graduation?

I highly recommend to anyone to jump at the opportunity of being president of a student organization. You'll learn so much and really grow as a person. I think it's also really important for student organization officers to add their own goals to the role rather than just doing what the officer before them did. Being able to say you've achieved "xyz" in a role—and that it wasn't done before—shows great initiative and that goes a long way in job interviews (not to mention the skills you gained along the way). I'd also strongly recommend getting internship experience as soon as possible and more specifically one that will give you the opportunity to have ownership of your work and see direct results (as opposed to simply helping out in the office).

Other Chapter Features

Additional text materials, while not included in every chapter, are provided as appropriate. These include "Teams Videos," "Teams Research" (highlighting recent research on chapter topics), and "That's Interesting" (noting teams-related issues that may strike students as surprising and thought-provoking).

Summary and Integration

Each chapter ends with a useful set of key points and practical takeaways that help reinforce the points and connect the dots between different chapter concepts.

Student Companion Website

The Student Companion website offers a variety of additional resources to stimulate student interest in teams, deepen their understanding of key concepts and models, and develop targeted team management skills. First, there are interactive learning activities, including practice quizzes and *Jeopardy*-style game grids with questions organized in a fun and engaging format. Second, there are numerous links to

- news articles from popular business publications (e.g., the *Wall Street Journal*, *Fortune*, and *Business Week*);
- practitioner-oriented books;
- videos profiling teams in the workplace and interviews with team managers and leaders;
- websites on team issues and opportunities for student involvement (e.g., case competitions, student organizations) that will develop teamwork skills;
- case studies that illustrate common challenges facing team leaders in the workplace;
- additional experiential and skill practice exercises;
- assessment tools for evaluating team effectiveness; and
- self-assessments for enhancing student understanding and awareness of personality factors and students' roles in leading and managing teams effectively.

In addition, the website provides instructors with a full PowerPoint presentation for each chapter as well as an extensive test bank.

Visit the Student Companion website at www.routledge.com/cw/aldag

My Team Journal

This feature on the text website gives students an opportunity to document their thoughts and reflections on the material and exercises completed in each chapter. Doing so will enable students to relate what they are learning from each chapter to past and present experiences on teams as well as to their future job and career goals in an organization after graduation.

Key Words and Glossary

Throughout the text you will find key terms in bold. Those terms are included and defined in the Glossary. Other significant terms are in both bold and italics.

CHAPTER 1

Teams
Opportunities and Challenges

Learning Objectives

After reading this chapter, you should be able to do the following:

1. Identify and discuss the reasons why team management skills are important for your job and career success after graduation.
2. Identify and discuss the differences between a work group and a team.
3. Compare and contrast different types of work teams that are used in organizations and their respective advantages and disadvantages.
4. Identify and describe the general characteristics of effective teams.
5. Identify and describe the common problems with teams.
6. Identify and describe the elements of a high performance team framework and discuss its practical implications for team management.

· ·

Team Management and Why It Matters

Most of us have participated in teams whether it was working at a summer job in college, on a painting crew, or as a server in a restaurant; doing volunteer work; or taking on summer internships while in college. And of course, most of us have been part of many group projects throughout our college careers. Some of these experiences may have been positive, but others may have been characterized by loafing on the part of some team members, leaving you to do a large part of the project on your own, personality conflicts in deciding how to complete a project, and challenges associated with trying to schedule meetings and coordinate project completion.

Because most of us have had at least some experience working in teams, there is a tendency to feel that we already know everything there is to know about working in and leading teams in a professional work environment. There is also a tendency to believe that obtaining a good GPA is all we need to do to prepare ourselves for a successful job and career after graduation. Further, we may fear that working in teams can put our GPA at risk since our grade depends on the contributions of others who may not be as motivated or as capable of contributing to the creation of a team project that will earn an "A."

In reality, the ability to work in a team will be critical for your career success. Moreover, a lack of teamwork skills can potentially derail your career. Consider the case of Steve Sinofsky, the architect of Microsoft's Windows 8 operating system, who abruptly left the company in November 2012 shortly after the product's release. While many in the company viewed Sinofsky as a brilliant technician, his reputation for being abrasive and noncollaborating undermined his chances of being considered as a candidate for CEO.[1]

Working in teams in organizations can vary in many ways. For example, consider the following team situations from individuals' actual experiences and think about how you would handle them as a team leader:

I was the member of a team in which I had a very different perspective of how to get things done with another team member. This led to arguments between us about nearly [every] aspect of the project. Meanwhile, other members of the team were either apathetic or unwilling to speak up and take a side on issues because they did not want to rock the boat. The individual with whom I was having issues with sent e-mails to other members of the team alleging that I was pushy and not a team player.

I worked for a car dealership doing detail work and new vehicle prep and the teams were extremely ineffective. We would receive orders/instruction from two owners, the service manager, and technicians, all of whom had different demands and expectations. Along with poor communication, there was also poor follow-up and evaluation of the team's work.

I was a part of a team when I worked at a YMCA summer camp in Minnesota. We were charged with the task of creating a skit for the whole camp. My group consisted of many people who were unlike each other, and our group lacked cohesiveness. The group had no icebreaking activities, and it was evident that group members felt awkward contributing in front of others.

I was on a team that was supposed to create a marketing plan for a company. The other members of the team did not care about the project so they did not respond to e-mails or voice mail messages to set up meetings, and they either did not complete their assigned work on time or they turned in work that was unacceptable. About a week before the deadline for the project, the other four members of the team basically bailed out on me and left the completion of the project for me to do on my own.

I was on the executive board for a student organization. Our team mostly communicated via e-mail. Roles and assigned duties were not established, so sometimes things weren't addressed ahead of time. Deadlines that were set for team members were not properly enforced, and many protocols that seemed like common sense weren't established, so the exec team wasn't as efficient as it could have been.

These scenarios show there are no quick or easy solutions to the kinds of team problems you are likely to encounter in your job.

TEAMS IN THE NEWS: "Google Management Award Winner Learns How to Keep a Team Together"

This article describes how Farzad "Fuzzy" Khosrowshahi, an award-winning project leader at Google, devotes a significant amount of time to the development of a strong team. Why does he do this? The reason is that engineers at Google can switch between projects at their discretion. This makes it critical for Farzad to develop and manage a project team that engages team members and motivates them to want to remain with the team in the future. Team development is also important in order for Farzad to recruit the best and brightest people to join his project team in the future. What does Farzad do to enhance his effectiveness as a team leader? First, he gives his team members 2 weeks a year to pursue any projects in which they are interested. He also has developed key skills that enable him to communicate effectively with his team members, including how to negotiate, how to give feedback, and how to deal with performance issues.

Source: J. Walker, "Google Management Award Winner Learns How to Keep a Team Together," *Wall Street Journal*, July 4, 2012. http://professional.wsj.com/article/SB10001424052702303410404577466881997151146.html.

Recent research shows that teamwork skills are critical for an individual's future job success. The 2012 Job Outlook survey conducted by the National Association of Colleges and Employers (NACE) identified the qualities that employers value most in college graduates. The ability to work in a team was ranked as the number one quality, with nearly 80% of employers indicating that they value this attribute when hiring. Figure 1-1 shows a partial listing of other highly rated qualities.

Ability to:	Weighted average rating*
work in a team structure	4.60
verbally communicate with persons inside and outside the organization	4.59
make decisions and solve problems	4.49
obtain and process information	4.46
plan, organize, and prioritize work	4.45
analyze quantitative data	4.23
master team-related technical knowledge	4.23
demonstrate proficiency with computer software programs	4.04
create and/or edit written reports	3.65
sell or influence others	3.51

Figure 1-1

Qualities That Employers Seek on a Job Candidate's Resume[1]

*5-point scale, where 1 = Not important; 2 = Not very important; 3 = Somewhat important; 4 = Very important; and 5 = Extremely important

[1]"Job Outlook: The Candidate Skills/Qualities Employers Want." National Association of Colleges and Employers, October 26, 2011. http://www.naceweb.org/s10262011/candidate_skills_employer_qualities/

In addition, most business professionals who have relevant experience feel that working in teams is not only part of their jobs but also critical for their career success. The interviews with two business professionals profiled in this chapter offer thoughts about the importance of teamwork and advice for developing effective team management skills. The first interview is with Cody Candee, a recent college graduate who was a strong leader during his time as an undergraduate business student. The second interview featured later in this chapter is with Al Johnson, a more experienced business professional.

TEAM MANAGEMENT COACH

Insights and Advice

Cody Candee, Finance Leadership Rotational Program, Intuit

We all know that many college students dislike working in teams in class projects. What would you like to say to current students about the importance of learning how to work in a team?

Working in teams is an inevitable part of life. When you're in the work force, you'd better be ready for it. Nearly every employer in a job interview will assess your teamwork skills and ask you questions like "Tell me about a time when you had to work with others towards a shared goal" or "Tell me about a time when you overcame a disagreement with a team member." When interviewing, you are going to want as many examples as you can to demonstrate your team working abilities. You'll be constantly working with people in your job, and employers want to know that you've learned how to handle different scenarios.

Which specific experiences did you have during your college years that were the most helpful in enabling you to learn how to develop and lead a team effectively?

In college, I was involved in various student organization leadership roles that really proved valuable for developing team leadership skills. I would say I learned more from these nonclassroom experiences than anything else in college. I was very active in Delta Sigma Pi professional business fraternity with roles of president, chancellor, and vice president of chapter development. Being in a role where I had to lead others helped me develop various skills such as public speaking, running meetings, motivating the unmotivated, and balancing everything else that a college student has going on.

What advice would you give current students about what they should do now to develop their skills in working and leading teams in preparation for working in a real-world job after graduation?

I highly recommend to anyone to jump at the opportunity of being president of a student organization. You'll learn so much and really grow as a person. I think it's also really important for student organization officers to add their own goals to the role rather than just doing what the officer before them did. Being able to say you've achieved "xyz" in a role—and that it wasn't done before—shows great initiative and that goes a long way in job interviews (not to mention the skills you gained along the way). I'd also strongly recommend getting internship experience as soon as possible and more specifically one that will give you the opportunity to have ownership of your work and see direct results (as opposed to simply helping out in the office).

It is apparent that working in teams was an integral part of Condee's work experiences and success in his job and other professional activities. Moreover, getting involved in activities such as student organizations and obtaining experience working in and leading teams is also critical for developing team management skills.

As we've said, many students maintain a negative attitude toward working in teams. However, most students also possess a keen interest in acquiring the knowledge and skills that will help them obtain a good job after graduation. It is also clear from the business professionals' comments included in subsequent features that development of team management skills both as a leader and a team member is critical. We ask you to accept the challenge of investing yourself in a learning process to develop your team management skills.

Maximizing the Value of This Text for Your Career Success

Our goal in this text is to help you to lay a strong foundation for understanding key team management frameworks, concepts, and principles. We also hope that you will develop insights about how to apply that knowledge to become a more effective team member and leader. In the short term, much of what you will learn from this book will help you identify actions to enhance the effectiveness of group projects in your classes or in your role as a member or leader of student organizations. In the longer term, your team management knowledge and skills will enhance your capacity to work effectively as part of a work unit or project team. Further, we hope such knowledge and skills will apply to any type of organization, whether in investment banking, public accounting, consumer products, health care, or other industries.

We encourage you to view your development as a partnership in which you can always feel free to contact us (see the text website for our contact information). Let us know if you have questions about how to make the content of this book more beneficial to you in terms of your involvement in student organizations and other activities as well as in your future job and career. Remember, the more time and effort you invest in learning as much as you can about team management from this book, the more you will get out of it.

In addition, we strongly recommend that you view the resources on the text website as an integral component of your learning process. We have attempted to keep the chapters focused and concise by discussing core team concepts and issues here while placing the more interactive and experiential activities on the website. The student resources on the website include practice mastery questions for every chapter, webinars on selected topics, links to recent articles about teams, skills practices, self-assessments, case studies, and experiential exercises. Please be sure to bookmark www.routledge.com/cw/aldag so that you can easily go to the website on a regular basis.

In particular, we recommend that you consider using the "My Team Journal" feature on the text website to document your thoughts and reflections on the material and exercises you complete in each chapter. This will help you relate what you are learning with your past and present experiences in teams as well as with your future job and career goals.

Skills Practice 1.1 on the text website provides an opportunity for you to reflect on your learning goals regarding team management and to identify some actions for achieving these goals.

Differences between Groups and Teams

Students often ask whether a **group** and a **team** are the same thing. While it is common for students and even business professionals to use the terms interchangeably, they are in fact different. Figure 1-2 summarizes characteristics of groups and teams. Two factors are especially noteworthy.

First, in a team, mutual accountability is a differentiating trait. That is, in a team individual members feel a sense of responsibility for meeting expectations regarding their own duties and responsibilities and also for overall team success. Many students complain that when they are working on group projects, the work is divided so that each individual is responsible for one part of the project. However, when individual members' contributions are aggregated to form the final report, each member only reviews his or her section. As a result, the different parts of the project are interdependent but lack mutual accountability. This causes the individuals to act as a group, generally damaging performance.

Another differentiating characteristic of a team is that when team meetings are held, team members are encouraged to engage in open-ended discussion of issues, and there is a process for active problem solving that includes all team members. The key here is that a team uses an inclusive process in which everyone can brainstorm ideas and solutions, their ideas

Figure 1-2

Characteristics of Groups and Teams[1]

Characteristic	Working Group	Team
Leadership	Strong, clearly focused	Shared leadership roles
Accountability	Individual	Individual and mutual
Purpose	Same as the broader organizational mission	Specific team purpose that the team itself delivers
Work Products	Individual	Individual and collective
Performance	Sum of the individual bests of team members	Greater than the sum of individual bests of team members; a team is more than the sum of its parts
Meeting Goal	Efficiency	Open-ended discussion and active problem solving
Focus of Meeting Process	Discussion, decisions, and delegation	Discussion, decisions, and real working together
Measurement of Effectiveness	Indirectly by its influence on others	Directly by assessing collective work products

[1]Adapted from J. R. Katzenbach, & D. K. Smith. "The Discipline of Teams." *Harvard Business Review*, July-August, 2005, pp. 164.

are discussed, and there is an attempt to work together to develop an appropriate solution to an issue or problem. In a group, the emphasis during meetings is much more on clearly defining the issues included on an agenda and going through the agenda in the most efficient manner possible. Group members are generally not encouraged to offer their input on issues, and there is little or no joint discussion of how to develop solutions to problems. Sometimes this is an issue with group projects in that members are concerned most with getting through the agenda in the most efficient manner, and discussion of issues and how to solve specific problems is viewed as an annoyance and a distraction.

TEAMS IN THE NEWS: "The Last Best Hope of Teamwork"

The U.S. Women's National Soccer Team was credited with creating "soccer mania" in the United States during its inspiring performance at the 2011 Women's World Cup in Germany. Although the team came up just short of the championship, losing to Japan in the penalty shootout after ending regulation play in a tie, the U.S. women's soccer team has been held up as an example of teamwork at its best. When a team member is asked how she made a great play, she typically gives credit to her teammates.

Collectively, the team is known for its gritty style in which every member plays hard and never gives up. Goalkeeper Hope Solo was ostracized by her teammates for making comments that were critical of the team's coach at the 2007 World Cup after he decided to play another goalie in a semifinal game that the United States ended up losing 4–0. Finally, the team plays with a sense of purpose that is to promote women's soccer rather than just winning games. Together, these attributes are part of the reason why many people view the U.S. women's soccer team as an example of exceptional teamwork.

Source: M. Futterman, "The Last Best Hope of Teamwork," *Wall Street Journal.* http://professional.wsj.com/article/SB100014240527023036787045764422307 50997082.html.

Types of Teams in Organizations

Work teams can come in a variety of forms depending on the nature of the work to be performed and the team objectives. It is important to understand which type of team is most appropriate for achieving a specific objective. A variety of factors, including characteristics of the team members, the task, the style of the team leader, and the culture of the larger organization, help determine the appropriate team type for various objectives. Figure 1-3 displays a summary of team types and their characteristics.

Figure 1-3

Comparison of Types of Work Teams

Team Characteristics	Functional Teams	Cross-Functional Teams	Self-Managing Work Teams	Process Improvement Teams	Problem Solving Teams	Virtual Teams
Composition	Composed of individuals from within a common function (e.g., finance, marketing, etc.)	Composed of individuals from multiple functions in an organization (e.g., finance, marketing, engineering, manufacturing, etc.)	Typically composed of individuals who possess responsibilities related to managing an overall product or service business unit.	Typically composed of individuals who possess relevant knowledge and experience related to a specific key business process.	Typically composed of individuals who possess relevant knowledge and experience related to resolving an undesirable condition or level of performance.	Composed of individuals who are asked to collaborate on a task or project in which they will have little or no face-to-face interaction.
Objective	To bring together individuals with relevant knowledge and experience to handle operations or to achieve objectives related primarily to a single functional area.	To bring together and to leverage relevant knowledge and experience from individuals working in multiple functional areas in order to enhance the efficiency, quality, and user satisfaction of the process (such as new products and customer service).	To empower members of a team to take full responsibility for designing and managing all aspects of operations for a specific product or service unit without a formal team leader.	To bring together and to leverage the knowledge and experience of individuals who can evaluate a process and identify and implement opportunities to enhance its efficiency, effectiveness, and performance.	To bring together and to leverage the knowledge and experience of individuals who can analyze a problem, identify its root cause, and identify and implement opportunities to enhance its efficiency, effectiveness, and performance.	To enable individuals who are separated by physical distance to work together in order to achieve a desired objective.

Figure 1-3

(continued)

Team Characteristics	Functional Teams	Cross-Functional Teams	Self-Managing Work Teams	Process Improvement Teams	Problem Solving Teams	Virtual Teams
Advantages	Expertise from a single functional unit is concentrated on the team Similarities in perspectives may increase group cohesion and reduce conflict Issues may be resolved more efficiently	All relevant perspectives and experience related to the task are represented in the team producing a more holistic perspective Problems or issues related to various functional areas are identified early and resolved by the team Team members develop a more in-depth understanding of the role of other functional units in achieving an objective The team's process increases the likelihood that different functional areas will be aligned with each other in producing a deliverable	Team members feel empowered to take responsibility for making decisions needed to achieve the objectives of the team Team members often feel more motivated to perform their jobs and more committed to achieving the team's objectives	Enables qualified individuals who understand a process to work together in a systematic manner in order to identify bottlenecks in a target process and to redesign it to enhance efficiency and effectiveness, to increase customer satisfaction, and to reduce costs Has the potential to achieve dramatic improvements in process efficiency, effectiveness, and performance	Enables qualified individuals who understand the target problem to work together in a systematic manner in order to identify root causes and to implement changes to enhance the performance level in terms of key metrics Has the potential to achieve dramatic improvements in key areas of performance for a unit or organization	Enables workers who are separated by any physical distance to be able to work together on a key task or problem Can reduce costs associated with travel, accommodations, etc., that would be incurred if the team was not virtual

Figure 1-3

(continued)

Team Characteristics	Functional Teams	Cross-Functional Teams	Self-Managing Work Teams	Process Improvement Teams	Problem Solving Teams	Virtual Teams
Disadvantages	Blind spots associated with other functional perspectives not being considered	Potential for greater conflict, at least initially, between members with different perspectives and priorities	Some workers are not comfortable being empowered because it is different and/or they lack the skills needed to be successful under this approach

Some managers and executives resist the idea of allowing teams to be self-managing due to issues of trust and control | Requires team members to possess an understanding of basic process improvement and quality tools that they may or may not have

Process improvement training may be needed that can be costly | Requires team members to possess an understanding of problem-solving tools that they may or may not have

Problem-solving training may be needed that can be costly | Can be more difficult to develop effective working relationships between team members given little or no face-to-face contact

Communications technologies are needed to support the team's meetings and activities that may not always be available

It can be more challenging for leaders of virtual teams to motivate and engage their direct reports

The potential for miscommunication among team members is higher |

10

This listing of team types is representative rather than exhaustive. Other types of teams include task forces (study an issue and make recommendations to management), committees (meet to plan, execute, and evaluate ideas for addressing a specific area of focus, such as safety or wellness), advisory teams (serve as sounding boards by providing feedback to managers or leaders regarding strategic and operational issues), and project teams (typically formed to work together for a relatively short time to complete a task).

Another key point is that the teams in organizations are often hybrids of two or more team types. For example, a customer service team that is composed of individuals from different units of a company, including marketing, human resources, and information technology, is also a **cross-functional team,** because multiple functions are represented, and a **virtual team,** because team members work in different geographic locations in the company.

TEAMS VIDEO: "Burberry CEO Talks Teamwork"

Angela Ahrendts, CEO of Burberry PLC, the British designer of luxury apparel and accessories for women and men, believes that teamwork is critical to the company's ability to drive innovations in products, service, strategy, and operations. The company's process for selecting teams includes a careful consideration of the requirements of the task and the relevant skills and expertise of potential team members regardless of their positions in the company. Once a team is formed, it is empowered to do what is necessary to achieve its objective but is also given support by the company's executive committee. The company has also formed a Strategic Innovation Council composed of professionals under 30 years old who brainstorm ideas for new products. These ideas are shared with the executive committee, composed of seasoned veterans who are approximately 50 years old, so that they can execute the ideas from the Strategic Innovation Council. Finally, employees and managers place a strong emphasis on overcommunicating with one another about fundamental issues such as "Where are we going?" and "What do you need from me in order to be successful?" This promotes a strong team culture in the company that enable it to sustain its competitive advantage of innovation. (Follow this link to view the video: http://live.wsj.com/video/burberry-ceo-talks-teamwork/5A36C6AD-91FC-4898–8B9B-666660092F25.html/.)

Characteristics of Effective Teams

Students and business practitioners often ask, "What makes a team effective?" Here are some examples of highly effective teams. Can you identify recurring themes?

When I worked for Omni Glass & Paint as a painter's assistant, we had a very effective team. Different teams were required to perform different jobs, and it was very effective because of the enormous amount of communication between team members, individual teams, and project managers. It was also effective because our team project managers were always there to answer our questions about specifications and/or desired methods.

The most effective team was for a team project for one of my business classes. We were effective because everyone participated and clearly communicated to one another and this lead to a productive teaming environment. Communication is key, especially with a larger team, to make sure everyone is on the same page with each other and is able to accomplish all of the work well.

The most effective team that I have been a part of was a math group my freshman year. We were put into teams of four and had two group projects that we had to complete throughout the year. Each one of our members had extremely different personalities that "constructively clashed." We all brought different perspectives to the table that helped create a successful atmosphere which earned us A's on both the projects.

Skills Practice 1.2 on the text website focuses on the use of mindmapping as a tool for creating a visual representation or a personal theory of the elements of an effective team.

In subsequent chapters, we will address this issue in great depth. As an initial response to this question, let's consider some of the best-known team management frameworks.

The Scholtes Team Model

Peter Scholtes identified the following ten traits that are associated with effective teams:[2]

1. **Clarity in team goals.** Effective teams have clearly defined goals for themselves and maintain a strong focus on these goals throughout their work processes.
2. **Improvement plan.** Effective teams embrace the concept of continuous improvement in their work processes and formulate a formal plan for evaluating their functioning and enhancing their effectiveness.
3. **Clearly defined roles.** Effective teams formulate clearly defined roles for each member of the team and communicate them to members so that every member of a team has a clear understanding of his or her own role as well as those of other members of the team. It may seem that this would be a basic issue that is a no-brainer for teams to handle, but

it turns out that it is one of the most common reasons why a team may not be functioning effectively.

4. **Clear communication.** Effective teams establish and maintain open channels of communication between team leaders and team members and between team members. As Angela Ahrendts, the Burberry CEO profiled in the earlier feature, stated in her video interview, it is critical to overcommunicate to promote and to sustain effective teams.

5. **Beneficial team behaviors.** The members of effective teams are more likely to engage in behaviors that support other members of the team as well as the overall team in relation to achieving its objectives. The U.S. women's soccer team profiled in the feature included earlier in the chapter is a good example of a group of individuals who engage in behaviors that support and reinforce the importance of teamwork.

6. **Well-defined decisions about procedures.** Effective teams develop a formal approach for handling issues and making decisions. That is, they decide how they want to decide.

7. **Balanced participation.** Effective teams work to ensure that all members are engaged in meetings, decisions that need to be made, and the overall workflow of the team's activities.

8. **Established ground rules.** Effective teams establish basic rules early in their existence to communicate expectations for appropriate team member behavior and performance.

9. **Awareness of group process.** Members of effective teams develop a capacity to monitor, reflect on, and evaluate the team's process and dynamics. This enables the team to discuss issues related to its functioning and to continuously enhance its **effectiveness**.

10. **Use of the scientific approach.** Effective teams use tools to collect data to analyze problems, generate problem solutions, make decisions, and enhance effectiveness.

The Scholtes Team Model provides a profile of highly effective teams. It demonstrates that creation of an effective team requires addressing structural factors, such as clear goals, ground rules, and roles, as well as process and people factors, such as communication, positive team behaviors, and awareness of the team's process.

The Hill and Anteby Model for Analyzing Teams

Figure 1-4 shows the Linda Hill and Michel Anteby Teams Model.[3] The model has two important aspects. First, it views a team as a system. Second, it sees alignment among the elements of the team as the key to enhancing team effectiveness. The concept of a team as a system indicates that a team is composed of multiple interrelated factors. This holistic view of a team recognizes that we cannot just focus on managing one element of a team in order to maximize performance; all elements must be managed concurrently so they are consistent and mutually supportive. We'll present examples of alignment and misalignment after we describe the elements of the model.

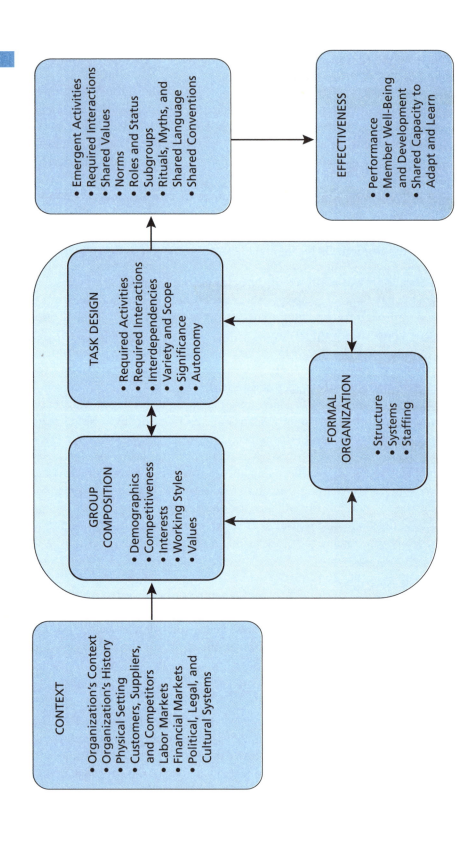

Figure 1-4

The Hill and Anteby
Model

CONTEXT

- Organization's Context
- Organization's History
- Physical Setting
- Customers, Suppliers, and Competitors
- Labor Markets
- Financial Markets
- Political, Legal, and Cultural Systems

GROUP COMPOSITION

- Demographics
- Competitiveness
- Interests
- Working Styles
- Values

TASK DESIGN

- Required Activities
- Required Interactions
- Interdependencies
- Variety and Scope
- Significance
- Autonomy

FORMAL ORGANIZATION

- Structure
- Systems
- Staffing

- Emergent Activities
- Required Interactions
- Shared Values
- Norms
- Roles and Status
- Subgroups
- Rituals, Myths, and Shared Language
- Shared Conventions

EFFECTIVENESS

- Performance
- Member Well-Being and Development
- Shared Capacity to Adapt and Learn

The Effectiveness box on the right side of the model is the bottom-line focus. Effectiveness includes all relevant performance outcomes and critical measures of team success. Some outcomes may relate to the overall team and its business objectives, such as productivity, efficiency, customer satisfaction and service, and product quality. Others, such as engagement, task satisfaction, motivation, and retention, relate more to individual team member attitudes and performance. The Effectiveness element of the model suggests that it should be your goal to align all the other elements of the model to support the performance outcomes that matter to you.

The second part of the model, Design Factors, is the core of the team system. Design Factors encompass Group Composition, Task Design, and Formal Organization. Group Composition includes demographic and other factors such as age, gender, education, generational characteristics, personality, work style, and work preferences. An effective team leader (and team member) needs to understand that he or she will need to be aware of these idiosyncrasies and adapt to them. This can be especially difficult when there is a need to get buy-in from team members of diverse backgrounds for a team objective.

The Task Design factor refers to characteristics of the tasks to be performed by team members and their respective roles on the team. For example, are the team's tasks primarily varied or routine? Do team members have the autonomy to make their own decisions about how to perform their tasks, or do they require direct supervision and oversight from the team leader? Are the tasks viewed as being important to the company, customers, and/or another stakeholder group? Do team members work independently in performing their tasks, or do they need to work together to get the job done? Finally, Formal Organization refers to the overall structures, systems, and processes that enable the team to function. This would include human resource processes such as recruiting, hiring, training, performance evaluation, and compensation as well as core work processes such as planning, executing, and evaluating.

The next factor, Leadership Style, refers to the approach the team leader adopts to coordinate the Group Composition, Task Design, and Formal Organization factors. For example, your leadership style could be task oriented, focusing on directing team members about what to do and how to do it. Or, it could be more relationship oriented, focusing on encouraging and motivating team members to exert appropriate effort toward a desired goal.

The Context factor includes relevant factors in the larger organization in which a team exists as well as the external environment of the organization. Both factors are important since a team clearly does not exist in a vacuum. Organizational factors include elements of its strategic plan (vision, mission, strategic objectives) and the nature of its business, among others. External environmental factors include such things as the legal and regulatory environment, customers, competitors, suppliers, and economic conditions. Team leaders need to monitor the context of their teams and identify appropriate courses of action to adapt to emerging opportunities and challenges.

The last factor in the team system is the Group Culture. Essentially, this is the collective personality of the team in terms of its norms, values, rites and ceremonies, narratives, and assumptions. Team leaders must work to ensure that the Group Culture is in alignment with the Design Factors and the Effectiveness outcomes and measures. For example, if one of a team's objectives is to excel in product innovation, then it is critical that the Group Culture embraces values, beliefs, and norms that are consistent with being innovative.

Now that we have discussed each of the elements of a team system, let's work through a few examples. Read the following brief team scenarios and answer the accompanying questions to test your understanding of the model and its basic application.

Example 1: The members of a customer service team at a credit card company need to possess superior knowledge of the company's financial products as well as excellent interpersonal skills for dealing with customers on the phone. However, many of the customer service representatives possess very weak interpersonal skills, and their knowledge of the company's products is limited. Based on the Hill and Anteby Teams Model, which two elements of the team system are misaligned?

ANSWER: There is a misalignment between Group Composition and Task Design factors because the team members lack the knowledge and skills required for their jobs.

Example 2: The product development team at a beverage company is focusing on implementing a process for developing more sugary soda products although the company is focusing more on moving into healthier, non-soda products. Based on the Hill and Anteby Teams Model, which two elements of the team system are misaligned?

ANSWER: There is a misalignment between the Formal Organization and Context factors because the team's strategic focus on sodas is misaligned with the company's strategic focus on healthier beverages.

Example 3: A quality improvement team at a computer manufacturer seeks to reduce product defects as its key measure of success, but its team mentality and value system still emphasize reducing manufacturing costs. Based on the Hill and Anteby Teams Model, which two elements of the team system are misaligned?

ANSWER: There is a misalignment between the Group Culture and Effectiveness factors because the team's new performance measure (product defects) is not aligned with its Group Culture that still emphasizes reducing manufacturing costs.

Practical Implications of the Hill and Anteby Model

The Hill and Anteby Teams Model is useful for diagnosing the functioning of a team and identifying opportunities to enhance its effectiveness. The keys to applying this model are these:

1. Assess each of the factors in the model and identify the key issues associated with each factor.
2. Evaluate the degree of alignment between the factors in the model. Alignments in the model should be viewed as team strengths to build on, whereas misalignments are opportunities for improvement.
3. Identify actions that you can take to change team factors to enhance the degree of alignment within the overall team.

John Maxwell's "17 Indisputable Laws of Teamwork"

John Maxwell developed a set of 17 key team success factors, shown in Figure 1-5.[4]

These laws show that effective team management requires a comprehensive approach. For example, winning teams need proactive, results-oriented members, shared values and goals, an effective measurement system, clearly defined responsibilities, mutual trust, and good leadership. Not surprisingly, Maxwell's laws partially overlap with elements of the Scholtes Team Model, adding to confidence in their use.

Law of Significance – One is too small a number to achieve greatness	**Law of Compass –** Vision gives team members direction and confidence	**Law of Identity –** Shared values define the team
Law of the Big Picture – The goal is more important than the role	**Law of the Bad Apple –** Rotten attitudes ruin a team	**Law of Communication –** Creating positive change in an organization requires communication. Effective teams have teammates who are constantly talking and listening to each other
Law of the Niche – All players have a place where they can add the most value	**Law of Countability –** Teammates must be able to count on each other when it matters	**Law of the Edge –** The difference between two equally talented teams is leadership
Law of Mt. Everest – As the challenge escalates so does the need for teamwork	**Law of the Price Tag –** A team fails to reach its potential when it fails to pay the price	**Law of Dividends –** Investing in the team compounds over time
Law of the Chain – The strength of a team is impacted by its weakest link	**Law of the Scoreboard –** The team can make adjustments when it knows where it stands	**Law of High Morale –** When you're winning nothing hurts
Law of the Catalyst – Winning teams have players who make things happen	**Law of the Bench –** Good teams have great depth	

Figure 1-5

Maxwell's "17 Indisputable Laws of Teamwork"

TEAM MANAGEMENT COACH

Insights and Advice

Al Johnson, president and chief coaching officer, Inspiratude Coaching Solutions

What did you learn about being an effective team member while in college?

To be an effective team member, I've learned that the following are three keys to success:

Be engaged. Just attending meetings or reading meeting minutes is not enough to drive success—ironically, more than a few of my business partners have thought this was the ticket to success. Being engaged is critical.

Be aligned on the vision. Many times you end up on a team because your manager delegated his or her spot to you, or you are volunteered because you have experience or knowledge the team needs. To be an effective team member, knowing what the team is trying to accomplish is key. Start with the ends in mind.

Be a team player. Every large cross-functional team I have been on has had at least one member who was more interested in personal gain rather than the gain of the larger team. Success in teams is driven by the greater good, not the mighty, selfish one. If I complete a task early, I ask if I can help others with theirs. Similarly, being a team player means knowing when to ask for help. If I'm falling behind on my work and that could hurt the team, raising my hand for help early benefits not just me, but the greater team.

It's also important to know what each team member can contribute and/or wants to get out of being on my team. I know that peers and subordinates are more likely to be able to roll up their sleeves and get tactical work done for me.

I would also contend that knowing where to go for information on the team is critical. Though senior leaders may be present, your line-level team members may have the most accurate account of processes and/or customer accounts.

What advice would you give current students about what they should do now to develop their skills in working and leading teams in preparation for real-world jobs after graduation?

I would advise current students to truly understand why working in teams is important. People tend to do/practice those things that they have a clear understanding of. Don't just work in a team because it's part of course instructions; seek to understand why working in a team is valuable.

Once teamwork at its core is understood, I would challenge students to learn how to actively listen and respect others. These seem like commonsense things to do, but they become increasingly important if you are going to work well in a team environment.

Next, I would challenge students to remember the step forward, step back philosophy. As you engage with your team, be sure to step forward and speak when you can add value. At the same time, be sure you step back and listen when necessary as well. Sharpening your active listening skills is a sure way to succeed in teams. Recognize that you will not always like what you hear and that others will not always agree with you. Along with contributing and listening comes the need to respect what others say and/or feel.

Last, I would encourage current students to enroll in a course on teamwork. One of my favorite classes of all time was the undergraduate organizational behavior course I took that emphasized teamwork; it remains one of the most actionable courses for me to this day. So much of what I thought was pure theory then, I recognize as practical information now.

No one person can go it alone in life. Those who don't value and embrace teamwork should consider going into business for themselves where they can call all the shots on their own. But chances are great that even if you go into business for yourself, you won't be able to totally escape having to work with others—after all, business is about profitable growth and obtaining customers, and customers enable your growth and are perhaps your biggest asset.

American Society for Quality's International Team Excellence Criteria[5]

The **American Society for Quality (ASQ)**[6] is the world's largest professional association for students, academics, and business professionals who are interested in enhancing the quality of the work processes, products, and services of all types of organizations. ASQ offers the International Team Excellence Award (ITEA) Program to promote and recognize team performance excellence. The program evaluates the effectiveness of **problem-solving** and **process improvement teams** using formal criteria that ASQ has developed. To participate, each team prepares an application describing how the team satisfies the criteria for performance excellence. Teams of trained examiners then evaluate the applications.

Teams receiving the highest scores are recognized at ASQ's annual World Conference on Quality and Improvement. Win or lose, each team benefits from feedback about its application that can be used to enhance its future effectiveness. Many teams go on to apply for the award in future years.

Five criteria are used to evaluate team excellence in the ITEA Program:

- Team project selection/purpose
- Current situation analysis
- Solution development
- Project implementation and results
- Team/project management and project presentation

Team Project Selection/Purpose

- (1A) Explain the methods used to choose the project. (Provide specific examples of techniques and data used.)
  - Describe the types of data and/or quality tools used to select the project, and why they were used.
  - Explain the reasons why the project was selected.
  - Describe the involvement of potential stakeholders in project selection.

- (1B) Explain how the project supports/aligns with the organization's goals, performance measures, and/or strategies.
  - Identify the affected organizational goals, performance measures, and/or strategies.
  - Identify the types of impact on each goal, performance measure, and/or strategy.
  - Identify the degree of impact on each goal, performance measure, and/or strategy, and explain how this was determined.

- (1C) Identify the potential stakeholders and explain how they may be impacted by the project.
  - Identify potential internal and external stakeholders and explain how they were identified.
  - Identify the types of potential impact on stakeholders and explain how these were determined.
  - Identify the degree of potential impact on stakeholders and explain how this was determined.

Current Situation Analysis

- (2A) Explain the approach/process the team used to identify the potential root causes/improvement opportunity(ies).
  - Describe the methods and tools used to identify possible root causes/improvement opportunities.
  - Describe the team's analysis of data to identify possible root causes/improvement opportunities.
  - Describe how or if any of the stakeholders were involved in identifying the possible root causes/improvement opportunities.

- (2B) Describe how the team analyzed information to identify the final root cause(s)/improvement opportunity(ies). (Include any appropriate validation.)
  - Describe the methods and tools used to identify the final root cause(s)/improvement opportunity(ies).
  - Describe the team's analysis of data to select the final root cause(s)/improvement opportunity(ies).
  - Identify the root cause(s)/improvement opportunity(ies) and explain how the team validated the final root cause(s)/improvement opportunity(ies).

Solution Development

- (3A) Explain the methods used to identify the possible solutions/improvement actions.
  - Describe the methods and tools used to develop possible solutions/improvement actions.
  - Describe the team's analysis of data to develop possible solutions/improvement actions.
  - Indicate the criteria the team decided to use in selecting the final solution(s)/improvement action(s).

- (3B) Explain how the final solution(s)/improvement action(s) was/were determined.
  - Describe the methods and tools used by the team to select the final solution(s)/improvement action(s).
  - Describe the team's analysis of data to select the final solution(s)/improvement action(s).
  - Describe the involvement of stakeholders in the selection of the final solution(s)/improvement action(s).

- (3C) Explain the final solution(s)/improvement action(s), validation, and the benefits expected to be realized by implementing the team's solution(s)/improvement action(s).
  - Describe the final solution(s)/improvement action(s) and explain how the team validated the final solution(s)/improvement action(s).
  - List the types of tangible and intangible benefits that are expected to be realized by implementing the team's solution(s)/improvement action(s).
  - Explain how the team used data to justify the implementation of the team's solution(s)/improvement action(s).

Project Implementation and Results

- (4A) Explain how buy-in/agreement was achieved for implementation.
  - Indicate the types of internal and external (if applicable) stakeholder involvement in implementation.
  - Describe how various types of resistance were identified and addressed.
  - Explain how stakeholder buy-in was ensured.

- (4B) Explain the approach used by the team to implement its solution(s)/improvement action(s) and to ensure the results.
  - Describe the plan developed by the team to implement its solution(s)/improvement action(s).
  - Describe the procedure, system, or other changes that were made to implement the solution(s)/improvement action(s) and to sustain the results.
  - Describe the creation and installation of a system for measuring and sustaining results.

- (4C) Describe the results achieved.
  - Identify the types of tangible and intangible results that were realized.
  - Explain how the project's results link with the organization's goals, performance measures, and/or strategies.
  - Describe how results were shared with stakeholders.

Team/Project Management and Project Presentation

- (5A) Explain how the team members were selected and how they were involved throughout the project.
- (5B) Explain how the team was prepared to work together in addressing the project.
- (5C) Explain how the team managed its performance to ensure it was effective as a team.
- (5D) The team will also be judged on the clarity and organization of its presentation.

The ITEA Program has been credited with helping teams in a variety of organizations in the United States as well as around the world to pursue and to achieve performance excellence. The ITEA Program website also includes case studies of winning teams from the competition.[7]

Common Problems with Teams

Most of us could easily generate a list of negative experiences we have had working in teams and the reasons why these teams were ineffective and/or unsuccessful. These would likely include problems with ineffective communication between team members, poor planning and organization in relation to the team's work process, problem team members who were abrasive or unwilling to do their fair share of the work, procrastination, negative attitudes about the team, and so on.

Five Dysfunctions of a Team

Patrick Lencioni's **Five Dysfunctions of a Team Model**, shown in Figure 1-6, offers a useful framework to identify some major causes of ineffective teams.[8] The five dysfunctions build on one another starting from the bottom of a pyramid.

1. **Absence of trust.** This occurs when team members are unwilling to open up and to learn to develop effective working relationships with each other. There is a lack of familiarity with each other, and team members are unable to recognize and accept their personal weaknesses and vulnerabilities. These conditions contribute to a lack of trust in the culture of the team and are the foundation for creating other team dysfunctions.
2. **Fear of conflict.** Due to the lack of trust that prevails on the team, there is an unwillingness to deal with problems and issues in an open and frank manner. Team members are guarded in what they say to others

Figure 1-6

The Five Dysfunctions of a Team

and often cannot be direct in expressing concerns to other team members about their performance. This dysfunction extends to team meetings, where members cannot debate an issue among themselves. This makes it difficult for the team to thoroughly discuss important issues or to evaluate options for effectively addressing a problem.

3. **Lack of commitment.** As a result of the lack of constructive conflict in the team's process for working together and making decisions, there is also a failure to achieve the level of buy-in from all team members necessary to support the effective implementation of a team's decisions. This condition increases the likelihood that the team will not be successful in executing its decisions or plans, which can undermine the overall effectiveness and performance of the team.

4. **Avoidance of accountability.** Due to a lack of buy-in for a specific course of action, decision, or objective, team members are likely to engage in behaviors that are counterproductive or misaligned with team goals. Team members are also less likely to hold each other responsible for meeting deadlines or fulfilling their commitments.

5. **Inattention to results.** The first four dysfunctions culminate in creating a team where members do not feel they are part of a cohesive unit or committed toward achievement of collective goals. This results in suboptimal team performance.

The Five Dysfunctions of a Team Model provides some useful practical takeaways. First, it emphasizes the importance of investing in team-building activities that enhance trust among team members as the foundation for building a strong team. Scheduling team activities where members can spend time together in a positive setting (such as an off-site retreat) while interacting with each other can be very effective. Engaging in **icebreaker** activities that require some basic sharing of personal information (e.g., personal interests, hobbies) can also help to build trust among team members. Second, teams need to actively foster constructive conflict in their discussions of issues and when making key decisions about the team's approach for achieving its goals. Finally, a team needs to work actively to ensure that all members have the opportunity to provide input regarding decisions in order to get everyone on the same page regarding team objectives and approaches for achieving them.

Skills Practice 1.3 on the text website focuses on conducting research on the Internet to identify an example of a work team and the factors that are related to its effectiveness.

An Integrated Model for High Performance Teams

This chapter has provided a basic understanding of types of teams, conceptual frameworks of teamwork, characteristics of effective teams, and common problems in teams. It also made the case that developing a more systematic and strategic approach to leading and working in teams will aid your career success.

Figure 1-7 presents a High Performance Teams Model that reflects our view of effective teams and shapes the organization of later chapters. The model views team management as a system to be built and a process to be actively managed. It also recognizes that there are two distinct but complementary perspectives of team management—one from the perspective of the

Figure 1-7

The High Performance
Teams Model

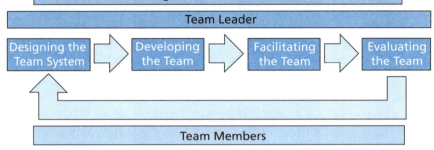

team leader, who is responsible for planning, organizing, coordinating, and evaluating the functioning of the overall team, and the other from the perspective of the team member, who performs various tasks to support team objectives, works with other team members, and reports to the team leader.

Skills Practice 1.4 on the text website involves the conduct of interviews with a team leader and team members to better understand the perspectives of team leaders versus team members. In addition, Skills Practice 1.5 on the text website provides an opportunity to analyze team-development issues based on the movie *Miracle*, which tells the story of the 1980 U.S. Olympic men's hockey team that won the gold medal despite huge odds against it.

Summary and Integration

Based on this chapter, the key takeaways for effective team management include the following:

Teamwork skills are one of the top skills that employers look for when evaluating applicants for jobs. Given this, it is critical for students to further develop their teamwork skills while they are in school in preparation for jobs with real world organizations after graduation.

Groups and teams are not the same thing. Sometimes working in a group can produce acceptable task performance. However, when a task is challenging, complex, and interdependent, then a team is needed.

Effective teams share many common attributes, including a clearly defined goal, formal roles for team members, an effective communication system, balanced participation of team members, and a system for evaluating the effectiveness of the team in order to drive continuous improvements in the system.

Teams need to be managed as systems of interrelated elements. The goal of a team leader is to assess alignment between elements of a team system and to take appropriate action to strengthen alignment between elements of the system.

Notes

1 A. Vance and D. Bass, "Why Steven Sinofsky Really Left Microsoft," *Bloomberg Business Week*, November 15, 2012. http://www.businessweek.com/articles/2012–11–12/microsoft-shows-its-windows-chief-the-door.

2 P.R. Scholtes, B.L. Joiner, and B.J. Streibel. *The Team Handbook* (Oriel: Madison, WI, 2003).

3 L. Hill, & M. Anteby, *Analyzing Work Groups* (Boston, MA: Harvard Business School Publishing, 2006).

4 J. Maxwell, *The 17 Indisputable Laws of Teamwork: Embrace Them and Empower Your Team* (Nashville, TN: Thomas Nelson, 2001).

5 American Society for Quality (ASQ), "2014–15 International Team Excellence Award Process," ASQ 2015 World Conference on Quality and Improvement. http://wcqi.asq.org/team-competition/index.html.

6 American Society for Quality (ASQ), "Home Page." http://asq.org/index.aspx.

7 American Society for Quality (ASQ), "International Team Excellence Award," 2014 World Conference on Quality and Improvement, May 5–7, 2014. http://wcqi.asq.org/team-competition/case-studies.html.

8 P. Lencioni, *The Five Dysfunctions of a Team* (San Francisco, CA: Jossey-Bass, 2002).

Bibliography

American Society for Quality (ASQ). "Home Page." http://asq.org/index.aspx

American Society for Quality (ASQ). "2014 International Team Excellence Award Video Highlights," May 5–7, 2014. http://wcqi.asq.org/team-competition/video-highlights.html

American Society for Quality (ASQ). "International Team Excellence Award," 2014 World Conference on Quality and Improvement, May 5–7, 2014. http://wcqi.asq.org/team-competition/case-studies.html

American Society for Quality (ASQ). "2014–15 International Team Excellence Award Process," ASQ 2015 World Conference on Quality and Improvement." http://wcqi.asq.org/team-competition/index.html

Hill, L., & Anteby, M. *Analyzing Work Groups* (Boston, MA: Harvard Business School Publishing, 2006).

Katzenbach, J.R., & Smith, D.K. "The Discipline of Teams," *Harvard Business Review*, July–August, 2005, pp. 162–171. http://professional.wsj.com/article/SB10001424052702303678704576442230750997082.html

Lencioni, P. *The Five Dysfunctions of a Team* (San Francisco, CA: Jossey-Bass, 2002).

Maxwell, J. *The 17 Indisputable Laws of Teamwork: Embrace Them and Empower Your Team* (Nashville, TN: Thomas Nelson, 2001).

National Association of Colleges and Employers. "Job Outlook: The Candidate Skills/Qualities Employers Want," National Association of Colleges and Employers, October 2, 2013. http://www.naceweb.org/s10022013/job-outlook-skills-quality.aspx

Scholtes, P. R., Joiner, B. L., & Streibel, B.J., *The Team Handbook*. 3rd ed. (Madison, WI: Oriel, 2003).

Vance, A., & Bass, D. "Why Steven Sinofsky Really Left Microsoft," *Bloomberg Business Week*, November 15, 2012. http://www.businessweek.com/articles/2012–11–12/microsoft-shows-its-windows-chief-the-door

Walker, J. "Google Management Award Winner Learns How to Keep a Team Together," *Wall Street Journal*, July 4, 2012. http://professional.wsj.com/article/SB10001424052702303410404577466881997151146.html

WSJ Video. "Burberry CEO Talks Teamwork," *WSJ* Live, March 20, 2012. http://live.wsj.com/video/burberry-ceo-talks-teamwork/5A36C6AD-91FC-4898-8B9B-666660092F25.html

Designing the Team System

CHAPTER 2

Learning Objectives

In this chapter we focus on the Designing the Team System component of our High Performance Teams Model. After reading this chapter, you should be able to do the following:

1. Identify and describe the key elements of an effective team system.
2. Develop a team charter to define the scope and objectives of a team.
3. Develop a Gantt chart that specifies a timeline for the completion of a team project or objectives.
4. Develop a role responsibilities matrix that shows the individual and shared responsibilities of members of a team to support the achievement of team objectives.
5. Develop a team dashboard that provides a team with a measurement system for evaluating its effectiveness and performance.

Designing a Team System

Step back and consider your experiences working in teams in classes, internships, student organizations, jobs, and elsewhere. If you compare the highest-performing against the lowest-performing teams, which factors explained the difference in performance? Some factors students mention include that everyone had a team spirit, carried their weight by completing their part of the project, and got along well with each other.

While many factors can contribute to the success of a team, a great team starts with a strong structural foundation in terms of having clearly defined objectives and scope for its task, a systematic process and timeline for achieving its objectives, clearly defined roles for each team member, and a formal measurement system that is used to evaluate and to improve performance.[1] Moreover, it is important for an effective team to possess all of these structural elements in order to perform at a high level; it is also critical that these elements are managed and coordinated as part of an integrated system.

Having this **team system** is an example of demonstrating a strong commitment to how a team gets work done, one of the five elements of a team discipline shown to be associated with high performance teams.[2] This system is the focus of this chapter. Specifically, we discuss how a team can create a team charter for defining the scope of a project, a Gantt chart for laying out a visual timeline for completing a project, a role responsibility matrix for defining the respective responsibilities of each team member, and a team dashboard for evaluating the performance of a team. Together, these tools aid process clarity, which has been shown to enhance **team potency** (the degree to which the group feels strong and influential) and team performance.[3]

Development and use of these tools is an important element of team proactivity. **Team proactivity**—taking charge, remaining adaptive, and avoiding passivity—is critical to team innovation and performance.[4]

Developing Team Scope and Objectives: The Team Charter

The foundation of a great team is a clear sense of objectives and an appropriate scope. While it may seem obvious that every team would have a clear sense of what it is seeking to accomplish, you may be surprised at the number of team members who do not know what their team is focused on. In college, the experience of many students with group projects is that their professors provide them with a lot of structure to define the requirements and parameters for assignments. However, for the types of projects that most teams complete in real-world organizations, the appropriate scope is not clear.

One of the basic tools for defining the objective and scope of a team project is the **team charter**.[5] The charter is a document developed by a team leader, usually with input from team members. Figure 2-1 provides a basic example of a team charter.

Basic Elements of a Team Charter
The elements of a team charter are as follows:

1. **Team name.** The *final* name you selected for your team.
2. **Date.** The date that the team charter is being created.
3. **Team member information.** This includes the appropriate information needed about team members.
4. **Name of team sponsor.** This is the name, position title, and contact information of the primary person you are working with at the organization being studied for your project.
5. **Name of team mentor.** This is the individual who is responsible for providing general advice and counsel for the team.
6. **Purpose/objectives of the project.** This specifies what you are trying to accomplish by completing your project.
7. **Scope of the project.** This specifies the parameters of your project (e.g., which issue, work unit/organization you will include in your analysis).
8. **General schedule/meeting days and times.** The schedule describes the team's basic plan for meetings in terms of when meetings will be held, how often, length, time, locations, and so on.
9. **Deliverables.** These are the key outcomes that the team will provide to the sponsor and mentor.

> **TEAM WORDS OF WISDOM**
>
> "You can design and create, and build the most wonderful place in the world. But it takes people to make the dream a reality."
>
> WALT DISNEY

Figure 2-1

Sample Team Charter

Team Name: Team Zeta
Date: 10/1/14
Team Member Information

Name	Contact Information
Don Peterson	E-mail: dpeterson@stateu.edu Phone: 231-987-1213
Beth Lundgren	E-mail: blundgren@stateu.edu Phone: 242-234-1912
Caitlin Roth	E-mail: croth@stateu.edu Phone: 237-128-9763
Dennis Stevenson	E-mail: dstevenson@stateu.edu Phone: 323-129-0012
Linda Gonzalez	E-mail: lgonzalez@stateu.edu Phone: 224-406-0249
Kristen Wolf	E-mail: kwolf@stateu.edu Phone: 453-765-2327
Gina Chang	E-mail: gchang@stateu.edu Phone: 782-239-0231

Team Sponsor(s)

Name(s)	Position Title	Contact Information
Samuel Robertson	Director	E-mail: srobertson@companyx.com Phone: 327-209-1820
Nicole Bright	Assistant Director	E-mail: nbright@companyx.com Phone: 327-209-1821

Team Mentor(s)

Name	Position Title	Contact Information
Jane Hoffman	Professor, Business	E-mail: jpreston@stateu.edu Phone: 432-444-4434
Weston O'Brien	Teaching Assistant	E-mail: wobrien@stateu.edu Phone: 432-444-4435

Project Objectives

1. Hold seminars and events on financial literacy that can provide meaningful information and experiences for participants.
2. Hold at least two large events where we can reach out into the community and educate individuals.
3. Grow the membership of the organization to increase reach and knowledge of the vision.

Project Scope

This project is limited to targeting students, faculty, and staff in the university community and the immediate surrounding community. The project will focus on issues related to financial literacy.

General Plan for Team Meetings (time, location, frequency, process)

For the general team meeting, we will have an hourly weekly meeting on Tuesday from 4:30 pm to 5:30 pm. There will always be an agenda for the meeting. The team leader will always play the role of facilitator and every member will have a chance to play the role of timekeeper and scribe.

Figure 2-1

(continued)

Deliverables

- Planning and execution of events on financial literacy
- Summary report with recommendations for future implementation
- Presentation of report to director, assistant director, and staff

Measures of Success

- Grade on the project
- Completion of the project by the deadline
- Client satisfaction with the project
- Program participant satisfaction

Project Communication Plan

Date	To Whom (Sponsor, Mentor, Client)	Method	Accountability
Bi-Weekly	Teaching Assistant	In person	Full Team
Bi-Weekly	Assistant Director	E-mail or Skype	Team Leader
Monthly	Director	E-mail or Skype	Team Leader
Monthly	Professor	In person	Full Team

Additional Required Resources (financial, equipment, information)

Funding, posters, handouts, copies of program materials, room reservation fees, refreshments for events

Milestones

- Every Monday, the start of a new week, is a key milestone
- Every monthly check-in meeting with the Director and Professor
- One week before the project deadline

Project Charter – Terms of Agreement

Signatures

Team Name: Team Zeta

Team Leader Signature
There is no formal leader for the team.

Team Member Signatures	**Team Mentor(s) Signatures**
Don Peterson	Jane Hoffman
Beth Lundgren	Weston O'Brien
Caitlin Roth	
Dennis Stevenson	**Team Sponsor(s) Signatures**
Linda Gonzalez	Sam Robertson
Kristen Wolf	Nicole Bright
Gina Chang	

10. **Measures of success.** These are the specific and quantifiable measures that the team will use to evaluate the effectiveness of its process and outcomes.
11. **Communication plan.** This indicates with whom (e.g., sponsor, mentor) the team will be communicating during the project, the media used to communicate (e.g., e-mail, reports, meetings), and the dates and times when these communications will take place.

12. **Additional resources needed.** This includes additional financial, equipment (computer, photocopying, etc.), and information needed to complete the project.
13. **Key milestones.** These refer to significant dates for the team's progress on the project. These may include completing the project proposal, completing data collection related to the project, reaching the halfway point in the project, and completing the project.
14. **Signatures.** This page (often the last page) includes the names and signatures of all team members.

Procedure for Developing a Team Charter

In order to create a team charter, it is important to use a systematic approach that includes all members of the team.[6] The basic steps are as follows:

1. **Define the objective(s) of the project.** The team leader should organize a meeting with members of the team to discuss and agree on the key objective(s) for the project. This is the foundation for the development of the overall charter. Objectives should be specific, difficult, and realistic—and should specify a completion date.[7]
2. **Define the parameters of the project.** Once the objective is in place, the team leader should discuss boundary issues related to the project in terms of which issues are within the scope of the project and which issues are outside the scope of the project. For example, if the objective of a project is to evaluate the loyalty of a company's customer base, the discussion of parameters could include whether to examine data for all customers or just customers who meet certain demographic requirements (age, geographic location, etc.).
3. **Define the supporting elements of the charter.** The team leader and members should then walk through the completion of the rest of the sections of the charter in order to address a variety of related issues, including a communication plan, team meeting process, and so on.
4. **Validate the charter.** The team should conduct a check of the overall charter to ensure that everyone is in agreement about its appropriateness.

Practical Guidelines for Using a Team Charter

1. **Share the final charter with all members of the team and its stakeholders.** Once the team charter is finalized, the leader should share it with all members of the team, its mentors, and any other stakeholders (e.g., internal or external customers, suppliers, members of senior management). Doing so will help to get everyone on the same page in terms of understanding the objectives and parameters of the project. If the team has a Web space (e.g., website, Google Doc), the charter should be posted in this area as an ongoing resource that can be easily accessed.
2. **Use it as a reference point in developing the team's planning and tasks.** In many teams, the charter becomes a fundamental document used to drive the creation of a timeline for completing the team's work (discussed in the next two points) and for monitoring and evaluating the ongoing activities of the team. Essentially, the team charter becomes the anchor to help ensure that a team remains focused on in-scope issues

and activities and does not suffer from the project creep that occurs when the focus of a team's activities starts to gradually drift from its original objectives and parameters.

3. **Link the charter to team meeting agendas.** One specific approach for maintaining a focus on a team's objectives and parameters is to include the charter with the development and distribution of all meeting agendas. This makes it easy for the team to reference it during discussions of issues and when making key decisions.

4. **Evaluate and update the charter as needed.** Some students express concern that using a team charter creates a rigid work process and stifles creativity. Actually, a team charter can and should be evaluated by the team leader, team members, and potentially other stakeholders to ensure that it continues to reflect an appropriate focus for the team and its use of human and financial resources. If the situation has changed in terms of the team's needs or objectives or the needs of its stakeholders, then the charter should be revised and updated. If this is done, it is important to again deploy the guidelines discussed previously for using team charters.

Skills Practice 2.1 on the text website focuses on illustrating the steps in the development of an actual team charter for a given work project.

TEAM SCHOLAR

Greg Stewart, University of Iowa

Greg L. Stewart is the Henry B. Tippie Research Professor of Management and Organizations at the University of Iowa. He serves as the Team and Formative Evaluation Core leader in the Veterans Health Administration VISN 23 PACT Demonstration Laboratory. He is a fellow of The Society for Industrial and Organizational Psychology and the American Psychological Association. Professor Stewart received a BS from Brigham Young University and a PhD from Arizona State University. He has published numerous articles related to designing work teams and team leadership. His research articles have appeared in leading academic journals including *Journal of Applied Psychology, Personnel Psychology, Academy of Management Journal, Organization Science, Journal of Management, Human Relations*, and *Human Resource Management Review*. He also served as an associate editor for the *Journal of Management*, and he has done consulting and training work with numerous organizations.

Based on your research, what do you think are some of the most important findings regarding the impacts of team design features on team performance?

I think there are three critical aspects to team design: task structure, composition, and leadership. The first aspect concerns how teams approach their work tasks. Teams working on creative tasks benefit from having members work together closely (high interdependence) coupled with substantial freedom for the group to determine its course of action (high autonomy). Teams working on more routine tasks are more effective when they have limited autonomy and moderate interdependence, such as on an assembly line.

The second aspect of design is team composition. You have to get the right people on the team. Some traits such as conscientiousness are universally important, suggesting that teams are best when all members are conscientious. The effects of other traits, such as extraversion, depend on teammates. Having all team members be extraverted results in too many people trying to take charge. Having too few extraverts results in problems getting organized and setting goals. Teams with a mix of extraverts and introverts perform best.

The third design aspect of leadership represents both formal and informal influence. Although it can initially be difficult, teams benefit over time from having empowering leaders who guide and assist rather than direct and control. This leadership role can be difficult to enact. For example, I am currently doing work with health care teams where we find that medical doctors have difficulty shifting their leadership from a commanding to an empowering approach.

What do you see as some of the most important emerging issues regarding teams?

I think one of the most important issues is gaining a better understanding of how teams evolve and change over time. We generally do research that captures a snapshot of things like design features. Of course, this fails to capture much of what is important. For example, team composition frequently changes as individuals quit and new members are included. This process of turnover affects coordination and alters the mix of individual traits included within the team. Teams with more frequent changes find it more difficult to adapt and perform at a high level than stable teams. Teams may also change their task structure when new members join a team. Understanding how such effects play out over time is one emerging issue that I think will be important to assess in the future.

Another emerging issue is gaining a better understanding of status and skill differences in teams. Much of our current research assumes that team members are interchangeable. However, in many settings this is simply not true. An example where I am currently doing research is outpatient health care, where medical care is often delivered by teams consisting of a doctor, a registered nurse, a licensed practical nurse, and a clerk. Each member of the team brings unique skills, and as suggested earlier, there is a traditional hierarchy that often impedes cooperation and teamwork. In such cases, truly understanding the team requires a clear picture not only of each individual but also of his or her specific role and its demands.

Developing a Team Project Timeline: Gantt Chart

After a team has established a charter, it now has the first piece of the infrastructure needed to build a high performance team. The next component of the system that is needed is a formal timeline for completing a project. One of the most common types of project timelines is a **Gantt chart**,[8] named after Henry Gantt, one of the original developers of the tool. Gantt charts are useful in that they show the relationship between tasks that need to be performed and time, typically measured in weeks or months. Figure 2-2 presents an example of a basic Gantt chart for a 4-month project involving the design of a new product.

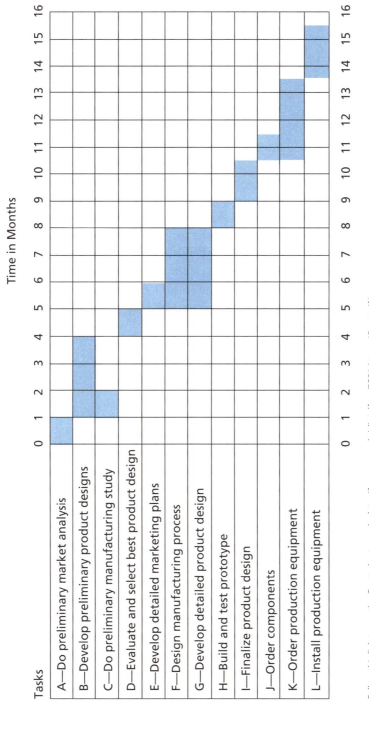

Follow this link to see the Gantt chart sample: http://home.snc.edu/eliotelfner/333/pictures/Gantt.gif/.

Figure 2-2

Sample Gantt Chart

Benefits of a Gantt Chart

Benefits to using a Gantt chart include these:

1. **Making the project time line visual.** Tools that make a plan, tasks, or a process visual facilitate interpretation. With a Gantt chart, teams can see the flow and interrelationships between various tasks in the context of the overall parameters of a project. In addition, the visual format is very intuitive.
2. **Facilitating communication between team leaders, team members, and stakeholders.** Once a Gantt chart has been created, it can be shared with team members and stakeholders. Like a charter, a Gantt chart puts everyone on the same page in terms of understanding the plan for completing a project and the status of a project at any given point in time.
3. **Sequencing tasks in relation to time.** Linking tasks with specific blocks of time helps to foster a process mentality and approach among team members and provides specific targets for when each task should be completed.
4. **Enabling checks of planned versus actual progress.** This is one of the most valuable aspects of using a Gantt chart. For each block of time in the chart, the team leader can evaluate the degree to which tasks that were planned to be completed were actually completed. For example, if one of the tasks to be completed in a given week was to administer a customer survey, but this was not completed, then the Gantt chart shows that it was not completed because the cell for that task is left blank. If the task was completed, then the cell is completely shaded in to reflect this fact.

Procedure for Developing a Gantt Chart[9]

Developing a Gantt chart requires all members of a team to engage in a systematic process that is as inclusive as possible. The basic steps are as follows:

1. **Identify your ultimate objective(s) for the team's project.** This is what a team is seeking to achieve, or the deliverable or outcome of its work process. For example, one objective could be, "To launch a social media strategy for the company's new line of computer peripherals by Quarter 3, 2015." Document your team objective(s) in a Gantt chart worksheet.
2. **List the tasks needed to complete the team project.** The team should then identify the tasks needed to achieve the objectives of the project. This should be as specific and complete a list as possible. Once the tasks are identified, they should be sequenced in the order in which they should be completed. This will create a process for the team. These tasks should then be listed in the proper order on the Gantt chart worksheet.
3. **Estimate the number of units of time (e.g., days, weeks, months) required to complete the tasks in the Gantt chart.** The cells that correspond with the unit of time allocated for each task should be outlined (not shaded in). For example, Figure 2-3 shows an example of a portion of a Gantt chart that includes the planning for a number of tasks. In this example, the focus in October 2014 is to meet to develop the team charter. How-

Figure 2-3

Sample Gantt Chart
Set-Up

Tasks	October 2014	November 2014	December 2014	January 2015	February 2015	March 2015
Meet to develop Team Charter	☐					
Communicate Charter with all stakeholders		☐				
Assign responsibilities to team members		☐				
Complete Phase 1		☐	☐	☐		
Complete Phase 2					☐	☐

ever, in November 2014, the team is planning to complete the communication of its charter to its stakeholders and assign responsibilities to team members. It also plans to work on completing phase 1 of its project from November 2014 through January 2015 and then work on phase 2 from February through March 2015.

A variety of Web-based interactive Gantt charts are now available for use by project teams. These provide considerable flexibility and offer, for example, dynamic linking to detailed project tasks, communication and activity streams, and document attachments.[10]

Practical Guidelines for Using a Gantt Chart

Once the structure of a Gantt chart has been established, it is important to implement some key strategies that will ensure that the tool contributes to the success of a team.

1. **Distribute the Gantt chart to the team and its stakeholders.** As is the case with the team charter, the Gantt chart should be shared with all members of a team and its stakeholders to ensure that everyone is on the same page with the planned timeline. It is also helpful for the team leader to walk through the chart with the team to address any questions that members may have about it.
2. **Include the chart with all meeting agendas.** This helps to promote a process focus on a team and maintains a high level of awareness of a team's plan for completing its objectives. Team leaders should add "Review of Gantt Chart" as a discussion item on every meeting agenda to ensure that the chart is built into the evaluation and coordination of the team's process.
3. **Conduct PvA (Planned versus Actual) comparisons of planned tasks completion versus actual levels of achievement.** At each team meeting, the Gantt chart should be reviewed in terms of where the team should be in completing various tasks (planned tasks) relative to the degree to which these tasks have actually been completed (actual task completion). If a team has successfully completed an entire planned task, the entire cell for that task should be shaded in to reflect this fact. If less than 100% of the task was completed, then only that portion of the cell should be filled in. A visual representation of PvAs enables a team to identify gaps in completing tasks. When a gap is identified, then a team can formulate a specific action for eliminating it. Alternatively, a team can choose to modify the task, break it down further into other tasks, or modify the time allocated for its completion.
4. **Update the chart as necessary** As indicated earlier, a Gantt chart should be evaluated, revised, and updated by a team as necessary. A common misconception is that a Gantt chart makes the team's process rigid and inflexible. Keep in mind that this tool is designed to capture and represent a team's plan for completing a project as a roadmap for success.

Skills Practice 2.2 on the text website shows the steps that are required in the development of an effective Gantt Chart that provides a visual timeline for completing the tasks associated with a project.

Insights and Advice

Stephanie Johnson, business analyst, Target Corporation

You have been a frequent user of Gantt charts in your work on teams. Why is this tool so beneficial to you?

I find a Gantt chart to be a very functional tool for teamwork because it lays out very visually the steps of the project. It's also a great tool for prioritizing tasks as you can see what needs to be finished before another step can be started. By taking the time to set up a Gantt chart with your team you can gather feedback and input from all members and be sure everyone is on the same page with regards to the timing and action of the project. My teams also enjoyed tracking our progress as we went and being able to note and celebrate accomplishments along the way.

What are the strategies that you use to design and use Gantt charts effectively in your work on teams?

Creating a Gantt chart is a team activity. After the project goal has been defined, I like to sit down with my team and discuss the steps necessary to achieve our goal. After making the list, we start discussing sequence and timing. By the end of the process we have an outline of the entire project. By using the Gantt chart we can easily divide out roles and tasks and denote who is responsibility for each step. After the Gantt chart is finalized, you can send it out to each team member so everyone has a copy. I like to put time aside in each team meeting to go over the Gantt chart, track progress and see if any bottlenecks or timing issues are arising so we can, as a team, proactively combat the issue. It also gives each team member a platform to share his or her progress with the team and garner any feedback to improve the project overall. Last, it's a great way to track and recognize accomplishments of the team!

What advice would you give to students about the importance of teamwork in organizations and what they can do to develop teamwork skills while they are still in school in preparation for working in teams in the future?

Students should seek out opportunities to work in teams, whether by taking classes with a large group project component, getting involved in student organizations and committees, looking for internships that foster a team culture or even by getting involved with campus intramurals. Putting yourself in a team environment will expose you to different ways teams can work and give you experience on what went well and what you could do differently the next time a project arises. Getting these experiences early and often will help you develop as both a team player and a leader and shape experiences that you can use in interviews or apply to teamwork in organizations.

Developing a Role Responsibilities Matrix

What Is It?[11]

While the team charter provides a formal definition of the objectives and scope of a project and the Gantt chart provides a timeline for completing a project, an effective team system also requires a formal specification of the responsibilities of each member of the team. A Gantt chart identifies the tasks that need to be performed and when they need to be performed, but it does not indicate who is accountable for completing each task. If team members are not given specific role responsibilities, they are likely to

Figure 2-4

Sample Role Responsibilities Matrix for a Fund Raising Project

| | Team Members | | | | | |
Tasks	Courtney Bates	Marianne Vasquez	Megan Williams	Drew Anderson	Wesley Chang	Nicole Dougherty
Developing Prospective Donor Lists	X					X
Reserving Rooms and Conference Space for Events	X		X			X
Developing and Maintaining Budget		X			X	X
Recruiting and Training Volunteers for Events		X		X		X
Handling Promotions for the Events			X			X
Handling Event Operations	X	X	X	X	X	X

experience role conflict and role ambiguity, to be discussed in Chapter 3.[12] This is where a tool called a role responsibilities matrix becomes useful. Figure 2-4 shows a basic role responsibilities matrix.

The **role responsibilities matrix** shows which tasks that need to be completed have been assigned to different team members, as shown with an "X" in various cells. The tasks can be identified based on those listed in the team's Gantt chart. Initially, Nicole Dougherty has responsibility for all of the tasks. This would be typical for an individual who is a coordinator or leader. Other team members have one or more responsibilities that define their roles on the team. This matrix can be expanded as much as needed to accommodate as many team members and tasks as are associated with the completion of a project.[13]

Benefits of a Role Responsibilities Matrix

The main benefit of a role responsibilities matrix is that it provides a visual summary of all required tasks that need to be completed and of who is accountable for completing them. It shows which tasks are the responsibilities of a single team member versus those tasks that are shared responsibilities for two or more individuals. In fact, once a role responsibilities matrix has been created, it is possible to list all of the responsibilities for each team member in a separate document called a role or position description.

Procedure for Developing a Role Responsibilities Matrix

The basic steps in the process for creating a role responsibilities matrix include the following. Figure 2-5 shows the basic template that can be used to lay out the matrix.

1. Schedule a meeting to solicit all team member input in the development of the role responsibilities matrix.
2. List all team members in a table, with each team member's name in a separate column.
3. List all the tasks that need to be performed by the team in the rows of the table.
4. **Make decisions about which tasks, if any, are going to be the sole responsibility of one team member.** Indicate responsibility for these tasks by placing an "X" in the cell for the appropriate team member.
5. **Make decisions about which tasks, if any, are going to be shared responsibilities between two or more team members.** Indicate responsibility for these tasks by placing an "X" in the cells for the appropriate team members. Consider whether there are any tasks for which all team members should be responsible. Some tasks, such as evaluating proposals or plans, may be appropriate as things for which all team members should be accountable.
6. **Discuss the overall draft of the matrix as a team and finalize the document.**

Practical Guidelines for Using a Role Responsibilities Matrix

The following supportive actions can enhance the effectiveness of a role responsibilities matrix:

1. **Share the finalized matrix with the team's members and stakeholders and link the matrix to the team's charter and Gantt chart.** Taking these

Figure 2-5

Role Responsibilities
Matrix Template

Team Members

Tasks

steps will help to provide the specificity and clarity of accountabilities needed to ensure that team members follow through on their responsibilities and that they feel a sense of ownership for the tasks assigned to them. This will promote a team system mentality among team members so that they can develop a holistic perspective of the team.

2. **Use the matrix to evaluate the performance of team members in successfully completing their assigned tasks.** If the team has a performance evaluation process, then the role responsibilities matrix should be used to identify the criteria for evaluating the performance of team members and as the basis for formulating performance improvement plans for team members based on the results of their performance evaluations.

3. **Reevaluate the appropriateness of the matrix on a regular basis** to ensure that it is still up to date and reflective of what team members need to be doing to support the team in achieving its overall objective.

Skills Practice 2.3 on the text website focuses on the steps that need to be taken to create a role responsibilities matrix that shows individual and shared responsibilities for each task associated with a project.

TEAMS IN THE NEWS: Teamwork at the Mayo Clinic

The Mayo Clinic is an integrated nonprofit medical practice based in Rochester, MN, that specializes in treating difficult cases. It focuses on the combination of medical practice, education, and research in treating a wide range of health care needs. One of the distinctive features of the approach used at the Mayo Clinic is that it employs a team-based approach to diagnosing medical cases. This is done by having physicians and other staff members engage in daily rituals in which everyone shares information about patients, debates various options for treatment, and makes decisions about the best approach for handling various cases. The clinic also uses information technology and various work systems to support the learning and collaboration of staff members by making key information accessible to them on a timely basis. This team approach that prevails at the Mayo Clinic is a major reason why it has earned the reputation for being one of the best medical care centers in the world.

Source: D. McCarthy, K. Mueller, and J. Wrenn, "Mayo Clinic: Multidisciplinary Teamwork, Physician-Led Governance, and Patient-Centered Culture Drive World-Class Health Care." http://www.commonwealthfund.org/Publications/Case-Studies/2009/Aug/Mayo-Clinic-Multidisciplinary-Teamwork-Physician-Led-Governance-and-Patient-Centered-Culture.aspx.

Developing a Team Dashboard

What Is a Team Dashboard?[14]

Imagine that you are in your car leaving your apartment to drive to work. The dashboard can tell you how much gas you have, your speed, the number of miles you have traveled, and so on. It can also give you alerts that there is a problem with the functioning of your automobile in terms of low tire pressure, low gas, or an overheating engine. Similarly, a dashboard can be used by team leaders and members to evaluate their team's functioning. Figure 2-6 shows an example of a dashboard from the Virginia Department of Transportation.

Figure 2-6

Sample Team Dashboard

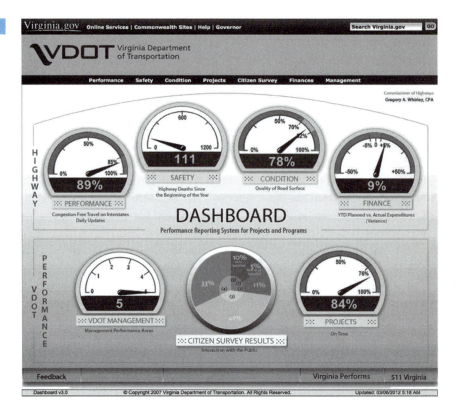

Benefits

Benefits associated with the use a **team dashboard** include the following:

1. **Dashboards emphasize the importance of measurements.** Management experts such as W. Edwards Deming and Peter Drucker are known to have emphasized the importance of measurement in the evaluation and management of business and organizational processes with quotes such as, "You can't manage what you can't measure." A team dashboard enables a team to create and use a performance measurement system for itself, not just one for the overall company. It enables a team to obtain ongoing data about its functioning and effectiveness for the performance metrics that it feels are most important.

2. **Dashboards help focus all team members on a common set of performance metrics.** Doing so helps a team to learn to speak a common language because all members of the team are focusing on and talking about the same key measures of success (e.g., reducing costs, increasing productivity). This is especially beneficial if the composition of a team is cross-functional, composed of individuals who work in different functional units of an organization, such as engineering, law, finance, human resources, marketing, and others.

3. **Dashboards enable a team to focus on both process and outcomes in evaluating its effectiveness and performance.** Generally speaking, many teams focus on outcomes or results (e.g., productivity, efficiency) as the primary indicators of effectiveness and performance.

However, it also valuable to monitor and evaluate process indicators (such as adherence to the project plan and implementation of key actions by designated deadlines) as they are the means through which the team achieves desired ends. In addition, these process and outcome indicators can identify red-flag or out-of-bounds conditions. These indicate when an undesirable condition or result has occurred that requires attention and potentially corrective action by a team. For example, if a team has used more than 90% of its financial resources, or may be late in reaching a milestone and thus impact a key deadline, the dashboard can help to draw attention to these conditions for the team.

Procedure for Developing a Team Dashboard

1. **There are four key principles for guiding the development of a team dashboard:**[15]

   a. The measurement system should focus on helping the team, not senior management, to enhance its effectiveness and performance.
   b. Members of the team should be empowered to create their own measurement system.
   c. If a team's process and activities are cross-functional, then the measurement system should also reflect this cross-functional emphasis.
   d. The team should adopt no more than 5–7 key measures to prevent diluting its focus.

2. **The first step in creating a team dashboard is to solicit input from all team members regarding the performance metrics that they feel are most relevant to the objectives of the team.** Reviewing the team's charter and Gantt chart will be useful in identifying appropriate process and outcome measures.

3. **The team should discuss the potential metrics identified in the first step and make decisions about which metrics to include in the actual dashboard.** The general rule of thumb is to limit the number of measures to fewer than fifteen in total.

4. **Once the metrics have been identified, the team should create a gauge for each metric similar to the one shown in** Figure 2-7. The team should then create a scale for the gauge that reflects the primary range of values for the metric. Then the team should identify performance thresholds that define the "green zone," "yellow zone," and "red zone" on the scale for that gauge. Scores within the green zone would be considered by the team to reflect good performance for that performance metric while scores within the yellow zone would reflect an area of concern: performance on that metric should be monitored closely for potential action in the future. Scores in the red zone reflect poor performance and require corrective action by the team. Think of this system as being like the scale for monitoring your total cholesterol. Generally, a score less than 200 is considered to be a green zone score, a score from 200–239 is a yellow zone score, and a score of 240 or above is a red zone score.[16]

Figure 2-7

Team Dashboard Gauge
for Cholesterol

Red Zone	Yellow Zone	Green Zone
Scores in Range 240 or above	Scores in Range 200–239	Scores in Range 200 or below

5. **Finalize the performance gauges and thresholds for green, yellow, and red zones.** The team should discuss each metric and evaluate its appropriateness as an indicator of the team's performance. One important consideration before finalizing any performance gauge is to ask the question, "Would any given score on a particular gauge cause the team to change its behavior about how it performs its work?" If the answer is "no," then the team should reconsider using that performance gauge as it is of limited value if it cannot change the decisions or actions of the team.

Practical Guidelines for Using a Team Dashboard

To implement a team dashboard, the following steps should be taken:

1. **Integrate the discussion and use of the team dashboard with the other elements of a team system (charter, Gantt chart, role responsibilities matrix).** The other parts of the team system provide the structural foundation for a team in terms of defining its objectives, structure, and process; the team dashboard helps the team to evaluate its effectiveness and performance on an ongoing basis using empirical data.
2. **Identify methods (e.g., surveys, production reports) and sources of data (e.g., databases, customers) to obtain the data needed to report results for each performance metric at appropriate time intervals (e.g., weekly, monthly, annually).** Care must be taken to ensure that the data collected are reliable (consistent) and valid (accurate). If this is not the case, decisions made based on the data may be misinformed and biased.
3. **Schedule regular team meetings to discuss and evaluate the performance of the team on its key metrics.** The team should formulate action plans to focus on leveraging and enhancing green-zone results, moving yellow-zone results into the green zone, and moving red-zone results out of the critical range of scores.

Skills Practice 2.4 on the text website illustrates the steps involved in creating a team dashboard measurement system that provides a visual representation of the key performance indicators that can be used to evaluate the functioning of a team.

Summary and Integration

Based on this chapter, the key takeaways for effective team management include the following:

The foundation of an effective team is a formal, integrated system that includes a team charter, a Gantt chart, a role responsibilities matrix, and a team dashboard.

The development of an effective team system is based on a team charter that specifies the objectives and scope of the team's project.

The Gantt chart gives a team a formal time line for completing a project.

A role responsibilities matrix lays out the individual and shared responsibilities of each team member so that the role or set of duties and responsibilities for each team member is clear.

Finally, a team dashboard provides a team with a measurement system that it can use to evaluate its effectiveness and performance using empirical data.

Notes

1 For a meta-analysis of relationships between team design features and team performance, see G.L. Stewart, "A Meta-Analytic Review of Relationships between Team Design Features and Team Performance," *Journal of Management*, 2006, *32(1)*, pp. 29–55.

2 J.R. Katzenbach & D.K. Smith, "The Discipline of Teams, "*Harvard Business Review*, March-April 1993, pp. 111–120.

3 J. Hue & R.C. Liden, "Antecedents of Team Potency and Team Effectiveness: An Examination of Goal Process Clarity and Servant Leadership," *Journal of Applied Psychology*, 2011, *96(4)*, pp. 851–862. To learn more about team potency and related constructs, see A.D. Stajkovic, D. Lee, & A.J. Nyberg, "Collective Efficacy, Group Potency, and Group Performance: Meta-Analyses of Their Relationships, and Test of a Mediation Model," *Journal of Applied Psychology*, 2009, *94(3)*, pp. 814–828.

4 See, for example, H.M. Williams, S.K. Parker, & N. Turner, "Proactively Performing Teams: The Role of Work Design, Transformational Leadership, and Team Composition," *Journal of Occupational and Organizational Psychology*, 2010, *83(2)*, pp. 301–324; and, K. Strauss, M.A. Griffin, & A.E. Rafferty, "Proactivity Directed toward the Team and Organization: The Role of Leadership, Commitment and Role-Breadth Self-Efficacy," *British Journal of Management*, 2009, *20(3)*, pp. 279–291.

5 Mind Tools, "Team Charters: Getting Your Teams Off to a Great Start." http://www.mindtools.com/pages/article/newTMM_95.htm. For the importance of team charters in enhancing the effectiveness of global business teams, see V. Govindarajan & A.K. Gupta, "Building an Effective Global Business Team," *MIT Sloan Management Review*, 2001, *42(4)*, pp. 63–71. For a discussion of the value of team charters in increasing student-learning team effectiveness, see P. Hunsaker, C. Pavett, & J. Hunsaker, "Increasing Student-Learning Team Effectiveness with Team Charters," *Journal of Education for Business*, 2011, *86(3)*, pp. 127–139.

6 S.D. Anthony, M.W. Johnson, J.V. Sinfield, & E.J. Allman, *Innovator's Guide to Growth* (Boston, MA: Harvard Business Press, 2009).

7 We will discuss the goal-setting literature in subsequent chapters. Much of this literature is based on decades of theory and research by Edwin Locke and Gary Latham. For excellent overviews, see E.A. Locke & G.P. Latham, "Building a Practically Useful Theory of Goal Setting and Task Motivation: A 35-Year Odyssey," *American Psychologist*, 2002, *57(9)*, pp. 705–717; and, E.A. Locke & G.P. Latham, eds., *New Developments in Goal Setting and Task Performance* (New York: Routledge, 2013).

8 Gantt.com, "What Is a Gantt Chart?" http://www.gantt.com/index.htm.

9 W. Clark & H.L. Gantt, *The Gantt Chart, a Working Tool of Management* (Charleston, SC: Nabu Press, 2010).

10 For links to a variety of Web-based interactive Gantt charts go to A. Augustine, "Interactive Gantt Charts for Project Teams: Online and Real-Time Collaborative Project Scheduling." http://collaboration.about.com/od/projectmanagement/tp/Interactive-Gantt-Charts-For-Project-Teams.htm.

11 P.R. Scholtes, B.L. Joiner, & B.J. Streibel. *The Team Handbook* (Madison, WI: Oriel, 2003).

12 J.R. Rizzo, R.J. House, & S.I. Lirtzman, "Role Conflict and Ambiguity in Complex Organizations," *Administrative Science Quarterly*, 1970, *15(2)*, pp. 150–163. For a recent discussion of the impact of team role stress on team learning and performance, see C. Savelsbergh, J.M.P. Gevers, & B.I.J.M. van der Heijden, "Team Role Stress: Relationships With Team Learning and Performance in Project Teams," *Group & Organization Management*, 2012, *37(1)*, pp. 67–100.

13 For a recent discussion of a form of role responsibilities matrix, see Y. Yin, S. Qin, & R. Holland, "A Role-Based Design Performance Measurement Matrix for Improving Design Performance," First Cambridge Academic Design Management Conference, September 7–8, 2011.

14 C. Meyer, "How the Right Measures Help Teams Excel," *Harvard Business Review*, May-June 1994, pp. 95–103.

15 Ibid.

16 *Web*MD, Cholesterol & Triglycerides Health Center, "Understanding Cholesterol Numbers." http://www.webmd.com/cholesterol-management/guide/understanding-numbers.

Bibliography

Anthony, S.D., Johnson, M.W., Sinfield J.V., & Allman, E.J. *Innovator's Guide to Growth* (Boston, MA: Harvard Business Press, 2009).

Augustine, A. "Interactive Gantt Charts for Project Teams: Online and Real-Time Collaborative Project Scheduling." http://collaboration.about.com/od/project management/tp/Interactive-Gantt-Charts-For-Project-Teams.htm

Clark, W., & Gantt, H.L. *The Gantt Chart, a Working Tool of Management* (Charleston, SC: Nabu Press, 2010).

Govindarajan, V., & Gupta, A.K. "Building an Effective Global Business Team," *MIT Sloan Management Review*, 2001, *42(4)*, pp. 63–71.

Hue J., & Liden, R.C. "Antecedents of Team Potency and Team Effectiveness: An Examination of Goal Process Clarity and Servant Leadership," *Journal of Applied Psychology*, 2011, *96(4)*, pp. 851–862.

Hunsaker, P., Pavett, C., & Hunsaker, J. "Increasing Student-Learning Team Effectiveness with Team Charters," *Journal of Education for Business*, 2011, *86(3)*, pp. 127–139.

Katzenbach, J.R., & Smith, D.K. "The Discipline of Teams," *Harvard Business Review*, March-April 1993, pp. 111–120.

Locke, E.A., & Latham, G.P. "Building a Practically Useful Theory of Goal Setting and Task Motivation: A 35-Year Odyssey," *American Psychologist*, 2002, *57(9)*, pp. 705–717.

Locke, E.A., & Latham, G.P., eds. *New Developments in Goal Setting and Task Performance* (New York: Routledge, 2013).

McCarthy, D., Mueller, K., & Wrenn, J. "Mayo Clinic: Multidisciplinary Teamwork, Physician-Led Governance, and Patient-Centered Culture Drive World-Class Health Care." http://www.commonwealthfund.org/Publications/Case-Studies/2009/Aug/Mayo-Clinic-Multidisciplinary-Teamwork-Physician-Led-Governance-and-Patient-Centered-Culture.aspx

Meyer, C. "How the Right Measures Help Teams Excel," *Harvard Business Review*, May-June 1994, pp. 95–103.

Mind Tools. "Team Charters: Getting Your Teams Off to a Great Start." http://www.mindtools.com/pages/article/newTMM_95.htm

Rizzo, J.R., House, R.J., & Lirtzman, S.I. "Role Conflict and Ambiguity in Complex Organizations," *Administrative Science Quarterly*, 1970, *15(2)*, pp. 150–163.

Savelsbergh, C., Gevers, J.M.P., & van der Heijden, B.I.J.M. "Team Role Stress: Relationships With Team Learning and Performance in Project Teams." *Group & Organization Management*, 2012, *37(1)*, pp. 67–100.

Scholtes, P.R., Joiner, B.L., & Streibel, B.J. *The Team Handbook* (Oriel: Madison, WI, 2003).

Stajkovic, A.D., Lee, D., & Nyberg, A.J. "Collective Efficacy, Group Potency, and Group Performance: Meta-Analyses of Their Relationships, and Test of a Mediation Model," *Journal of Applied Psychology*, 2009, *94(3)*, pp. 814–828.

Stewart, G.L. (2006). "A Meta-Analytic Review of Relationships between Team Design Features and Team Performance," *Journal of Management*, 2006, *32(1)*, pp. 29–55.

Strauss, K., Griffin, M.A., & Rafferty, A.E. "Proactivity Directed toward the Team and Organization: The Role of Leadership, Commitment and Role-Breadth Self-Efficacy," *British Journal of Management*, 2009, *20(3)*, pp. 279–291 and Williams, H.M., Parker, S.K., & Turner, N. "Proactively Performing Teams: The Role of Work Design, Transformational Leadership, and Team Composition," *Journal of Occupational and Organizational Psychology*, 2010, *83(2)*, pp. 301–324.

Yin, Y., Qin, S., & Holland, R. "A Role-Based Design Performance Measurement Matrix for Improving Design Performance," First Cambridge Academic Design Management Conference, September 7–8, 2011.

Building and Developing the Team

Learning Objectives

After reading this chapter, you should be able to do the following:

1. Choose a team size.
2. Identify guidelines for effectively staffing the team.
3. Define the team's assignment.
4. Plan the team effort.
5. Recognize and employ the power of norms.
6. Understand helpful and harmful team roles.
7. Identify the stages of group development, including important differences across the stages.
8. Take steps to build team spirit.

. . . .

IN CHAPTER 2 WE DISCUSSED VARIOUS STRUCTURAL ELEMENTS OF effective teams, including a team charter, Gantt chart, role responsibilities matrix, and performance dashboard. In this chapter, we discuss key factors that add to this structural foundation to build and develop effective teams. These include choosing team size and membership, defining the team's assignment, planning the team effort, managing the team through the stages of group development, and building team spirit.

Choosing a Team Size and Members

A basic issue facing teams is the selection of its members, which requires decisions about both team size and the mix of members. When a team is formed, there is often a tendency, to borrow a line from the classic film *Casablanca*, to "round up the usual suspects." Instead, it is important to pay careful attention to the size and composition of the team.

Selecting a Team Size

How big should a team be? We'll start with the bottom line: choose a five-person or seven-person team unless there are compelling reasons to do otherwise.

Any team with fewer than five members has its own unique set of problems. The smallest team, with two members, is called a *dyad*. People in dyads tend to be anxious and uncomfortable. Members are reluctant to give opinions and constantly ask for opinions. If the two members can't reach an agreement, there may be a stalemate, the team may break up, or one member may force the other to give in. Three-person teams, *triads*, have a special problem:

if there is disagreement, the split is two to one. While people generally don't like to be on what might be considered to be the losing side, it is especially upsetting to be an isolate, the *only* so-called loser. In a triad, the member in the minority is *always* an isolate. Because of this, either one member is very unhappy, or coalitions constantly have to shift, with associated tension and political activity. Four-person and six-person teams can lead to stalemates or power plays if the team is equally split—this is a problem with any even-sized group, but an even split is less likely as teams get larger.

TEAMS IN THE NEWS: "Computer Programmers Learn Tough Lesson in Sharing"

We've said that people in dyads tend to be uncomfortable and anxious. Such discomfort is seen in this *Wall Street Journal* article on the practice of pair programming in high-tech firms. With pair programming, two computer programmers share one desk and one computer. One person—the driver—controls the keyboard and types in code. The other—the navigator—monitors design and scans for bugs. The 175 engineers at software development firm Pivotal Labs pair all day, every day. In theory, paired coders can catch software errors and are less likely to waste time surfing the web. However, relationships are often tense—clashes may arise over working habits—and annoyances ranging from personal hygiene to feet on the shared desk can pile up. One manager said, "There's a joke that pairs, like fish and house guests, go rotten after three days."

Source: J. Walker, "Computer Programmers Learn Tough Lesson in Sharing," *Wall Street Journal*, August 27, 2012, p. A1.

When a team has more than seven people, team management becomes much more difficult. For instance, there are increased coordination problems, and some members may be tempted to engage in **social loafing**.

THAT'S INTERESTING! The Magical Number 7, Plus or Minus Two

The fact that teams seem to have severe problems once they have more than seven members is a reflection of a more general finding regarding our cognitive and perceptual limitations. In 1956 George Miller published an article (one of the most influential over coming decades) with surprising results. Miller wrote that, "I have been haunted by a number . . ." He showed that across a remarkable range of human capacities we seem to be unable to distinguish more than seven (plus or minus two) distinct levels of things such as tones, points on scales, taste intensities, loudness, and visual position. Beyond seven levels, our reactions become confused and erratic. So, whenever we're dealing with more than seven levels of a perceptual dimension (sight, hearing, taste, smell, or whatever), we're likely to have trouble making meaningful distinctions.

Source: G. A. Miller, "The Magical Number Seven, Plus or Minus Two: Some Limits on Our Capacity for Processing Information," *Psychological Review*, 1956, *63(2)*, pp. 81–97.

Figure 3-1

Effects of Team Size

Team Size						
2 (Dyad)	**3 (Triad)**	**4**	**5**	**6**	**7**	**>7**
Tense	Coalition formation	Danger of a 2-2 split	Ideal unless many inputs are needed	Danger of a 3-3 split	Ideal if many inputs are needed	Coordination problems
Little sharing of opinion	Minority is an isolate	If 2-2 split, stalemate or power play		If 3-3 split, stalemate or power play	Some co-ordination problems	Deperson-alization
Fragile	Shifting coalitions					Lack of cohesiveness

When might you want to use groups larger or smaller than five or seven members? Quite simply, there are times when the problem or task isn't important enough to involve five members, or five people simply aren't available. Conversely, there may be political reasons for involving more than seven people, or the problem or task may demand broad participation because of its great complexity. However, the problems associated with large teams are so great that we encourage you to do all you can to keep teams small. This may require breaking the team into subteams, or using techniques (such as the nominal group technique, which we'll discuss later in the chapter) that restrict the degree of member interaction and thus the related problems. Figure 3-1 summarizes some effects of team size.

Staffing the Team

The team's composition can have a major impact on how well it achieves its goals and how satisfied its members feel. In Chapter 5 we discuss how team composition, including member diversity, personalities, and cross-cultural differences, can be taken into account when forming teams. Here, we provide some general guidelines.

Strategies for Forming Effective Teams

- **Vary team membership across tasks**. When "the usual suspects" are given the responsibility for all key decisions and activities, others feel excluded. And, those always included may feel overwhelmed. Also, different perspectives and expertise are needed for different tasks.
- **Ensure availability of key information, skills, and other resources**. Don't wait until the team members have been selected to determine what the team needs to effectively accomplish its goals. Of course, not all key information, skills, and resources have to reside within the team itself. However, it is important that team members have access to needed inputs. Here, interpersonal ties may be important. *Strong ties* are links between family members, close friends, or colleagues. *Weak ties* are

links between acquaintances or even friends-of-friends. Perhaps surprisingly, weak ties have been shown to be especially important. Those sharing strong ties tend to move in the same circles, so they often have similar information. Weak ties, conversely, are with acquaintances that tend to know people we don't, so they provide more novel information.[1]

- **Ensure participation of affected parties.** Those who will be impacted by the team's outcomes who can participate in the team's activities are more likely to be able to identify with the team decision or other outcome and to be more enthusiastic in accepting and implementing it. This does not mean that those parties have to be directly involved in making the final decision. Instead, it means that their inputs should be solicited, fully considered, and respected.
- **If you will not be leading the team, appoint a task-oriented leader with sufficient power to keep the team on track.** It is a mistake to think that team members resent structure and guidance. Instead, while concern for people is a critical leadership skill, concern for the task is also necessary.
- **Consider varying membership over the course of the task.** Just as it is important to vary team membership across tasks, it may also be useful to vary membership *within* tasks. For example, over the course of a task it may be useful to involve different members in defining the problem, generating alternative solutions, making a choice, and implementing the decision.

General Electric is one company that makes heavy use of action forums. **Action forums** are broadly inclusive corporate meetings that involve key players from management, the factory floor, and even outside suppliers and customers. By bringing these players together, action forums lead to faster and better decisions and help ensure the commitment of those who will implement the decisions. Companies as far away as Japan are developing action-forum approaches to their organizations.[2]

In the Team Management Coach feature, Michael Bailen, who manages the recruiting team at Zappos, the world's largest online shoe store, discusses steps Zappos takes to develop its employees and encourage collaboration, creativity, and entrepreneurship. Zappos, noted for its superior customer service, is one of *Fortune*'s "100 Best Companies to Work For."

Insights and Advice

Michael Bailen, corporate recruiter, Zappos

Mike Bailen has been with the Zappos family since March of 2010. After graduating from the University of Wisconsin–Madison with a bachelor of business administration degree in human resources and psychology, he worked as a corporate recruiter for American Family Insurance in Madison, WI. After leaving the frozen tundra, he headed out west to join the Zappos family as a recruiter. Since then, he moved on to create the Zappos summer internship program and currently manages the recruiting team. He loves the challenge of

TEAM MANAGEMENT COACH

finding candidates that are fun and a little weird, and that can help drive the Zappos culture forward.

What steps does Zappos take to develop superior talent?

Talent management is a top priority for Zappos. We know that talent can come from any level in the organization. That's why it's important for top management to remain accessible and approachable. Our top executives sit in the same open cubical arrangement as our other employees, and don't get any special perks or treatment. They make it a priority to get to know employees outside of the conventional office setting where it's easier and more conducive for brainstorming new ideas.

We do many things to help our employees develop their careers. We have a Pipeline division that offers a variety of classes, from technical skills to soft skills. These classes are built into employees' expectations and progression plans.

Employees are also encouraged to seek new opportunities within Zappos. We post all our positions to our internal employees so they have an opportunity to apply for a new career. We also have a Z'Apprentice program. A Z'Apprentice is basically an internal internship that lasts for 90 days. In the Z'Apprenticeship, employees get regular feedback on their performance and this can lead to a permanent position within the team.

How does Zappos encourage employees to collaborate?

We want all departments to collaborate and strengthen relationships. This starts right when employees start with Zappos. Each employee, regardless of position, goes through four weeks of call center training. This is a great opportunity for employees from all departments to get to know each other. This orientation and introduction to Zappos helps create tight cross-departmental bonds.

What does Zappos do to encourage employee entrepreneurship and creativity?

Entrepreneurship and creativity are among the strengths and skills that will be in most demand in the next five years. At Zappos, many great ideas come from what is called the ZFrogs process. When employees have new and innovative ideas they can make a pitch to ZFrogs, a kind of venture capitalist group made up of our top executives. If the ZFrogs like what they hear, they'll provide resources to make sure the person's or team's idea can be implemented.

Defining the Team's Assignment

Defining the team's assignment involves specifying—preferably, in writing—the team's purpose, responsibilities, and needs. Answers to the following questions make up the team's assignment.

- **What is the issue with which the team must deal?** What is its scope?
- **What is the team's responsibility?** To perform a specific task? To make a decision? To exchange information?
- **What are the constraints on the group?** For example, what are its deadlines? What is its budget? What other resources (such as administrative support) are available to it? What should be the format of its final report or the nature of its final product? Will it have to give progress reports?

Planning the Team Effort

Once the team assignment is defined, the overall team effort should be planned. Our discussion of team charters in Chapter 2 addresses the issues of how to structure the overall scope and objectives of a team project. In addition, creating a plan for a team's task should include the following steps:

- **Divide the team's overall assignment into parts.** This overcomes psychological hurdles and makes it easier to develop estimates of time and resource needs.
- **Estimate the time and resources needed to complete each part of the assignment and the overall assignment.** At this point, PERT (Project Evaluation and Review Technique) or CPM (Critical Path Method) charts can be very useful. Such charts array activities that must be completed, the completion time for each activity, and the necessary sequencing of activities.
- **Take necessary actions to reduce any gaps between what is needed and what is available.** If there is a deadline and budget for the project, this will help determine if they are appropriate and, if so, how the team can expect to complete its task within those constraints. If it appears that the constraints are infeasible, it is better to voice concerns early rather than after deadlines or budgets have been exceeded. For instance, a case might be made for changing the assignment, getting deadlines extended, adding members to the team, seeking additional resources, or making other adjustments.

Developing the Team

It is critical for leaders to understand how teams may change as they mature, and how different sets of behaviors are needed to manage teams through their various stages of development. In this section, we will consider team expectations about appropriate behaviors for team members in general (norms) and for specific team members (roles) and we will see how these create needs for careful attention to the stages of group development.

Norms

Team norms are the unwritten rules of the team. They are shared expectations about how team members should behave. For example, the team may have norms about how members should dress, how hard they should work, how much members should help one another, or whether team members should keep secrets from others in the organization. Norms may be *prescriptive*—dictating what should be done—or *proscriptive*—dictating what should not be done. Norms were quite evident in the 2003 Tour de France. When Lance Armstrong fell after colliding with a spectator, other lead riders didn't take advantage of the fall to speed ahead and gain precious seconds. Instead, the group—including Armstrong's closest rival Jan Ullrich—waited for Armstrong to remount. This may have seemed remarkable to those not familiar with the sport, but it represented a long-held, cherished tradition in competitive cycling.[3]

Norms are powerful. Because we want to meet the expectations of our team members, norms control our behavior. This is sometimes called **clan control**, and such control may be even stronger than the control imposed by rules and orders. Further, once a team develops norms, those norms tend to persist—often, even after all the original members have eventually left the team and have been replaced by new members.

Team members may import norms when they join the team. For example, members may bring with them the norms of their professions, or they may import the norms of other teams of which they've been members. For instance, if someone has been on a team that valued working extra hours to get a job done, he or she may bring that norm to a new team. Norms may also develop because of some critical event in the life of the team. For example, if a major client stops doing business with a firm because he or she was upset by an employee's rude behavior, norms may develop about the nature of appropriate interaction with clients. Often, though, norms develop gradually in the life of the team.

TEAMS VIDEO: Teamwork Lessons from Geese

This simple animation offers basic but important lessons about the benefits of coordinated team effort. What are key norms of the flock? The video can be accessed on the text website. (Follow this link to view the video: https://www.youtube.com/watch?v=5rOg4WfNDfM.)

Our discussion of norms suggests the following guidelines for team management:

- **Recognize the power of norms.** While unwritten, norms are just as real as, just as powerful as, and perhaps more enduring than written rules and regulations.
- **Identify team norms; reinforce positive norms.**
- **Communicate expectations concerning performance and other goals.**
- **Recognize that norms develop gradually and are resistant to change.**

"Norm" may bring to mind Norm Peterson, the jovial, rotund regular on *Cheers*. *Cheers*, a long-running television program set in a Boston pub, had a cast of characters that exchanged jokes, stories, and insults in the comfort of "a place where everybody knows your name." The characters on *Cheers* did, in fact, share a variety of norms. For example, members shared expectations about where the regulars should sit, how regulars entering the bar should be greeted, what subjects were acceptable for discussion, and how Cheers' patrons should react to challenges from outsiders. An ongoing gag was the "Normisms," Norm's replies to those greeting him when he entered the bar. Go to the text website to view a collection of "Normisms."

Roles

We all wear many hats in life. We may be—at the same time—friends, neighbors, students, siblings, lovers, employees, and much more. Each of these hats carries with it a set of expectations for its wearer. Someone in a parent hat is expected to show concern for his or her children, to provide them with love, guidance, food, and shelter. Someone in a student hat is expected to attend classes, to complete assignments, and to be an active participant in class activities. These various hats are called **roles**.

As shown in Figure 3-2, team members can adopt many roles, not all of them positive. Two sets of roles—task-oriented roles and relations-oriented roles—are vital if the team is to be effective on a continuing basis. **Task-oriented roles** are needed to get the job done. Team members who initiate tasks, gather information for use by the team, offer suggestions, and help motivate others would be performing task-oriented roles. **Relations-oriented roles** are needed to keep the team healthy and its members satisfied. Team members who help keep the group harmonious, assist in helping members resolve disputes, and encourage members as they face barriers are engaging in relations-oriented roles. However, team members may also assume other, self-serving roles. **Self-oriented roles** are roles the member adopts for personal gain. These roles may often hamper team performance and cohesiveness. For instance, some team members gain a sense of power by dominating others or blocking others' attempts to get things done.

Figure 3-2

Team Roles

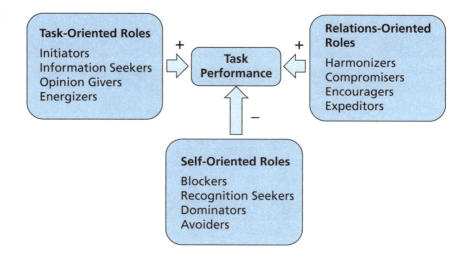

We said that roles carry with them sets of expectations. Sometimes those expectations are unclear, conflicting, or overwhelming in number. Unclear expectations cause **role ambiguity**. Role ambiguity results when team members simply don't know what is expected of them. Conflicting expectations cause **role conflict**.[4] For example, you may experience role conflict if two colleagues tell you to do opposite things, or if your boss tells you to do one thing one day and the opposite the next. You may even feel role conflict if your own values—which carry their own role expectations—conflict with demands of a team or work role. If, for instance, you are told to fire a long-term employee who is near retirement, and this is contrary to your values, role conflict may result. Finally, when role expectations are simply overwhelming—we're expected to do too many things—**role overload** occurs. Role ambiguity, role conflict, and role overload cause **role stress**. Role stress causes dissatisfaction, absenteeism, turnover, poor performance, bullying, a host of physical and mental illnesses, and many other problems.[5]

Especially when roles are in flux, careful attention to minimizing role stress is crucial. For instance, when the State Bank of India was developing ambitious expansion plans, top management recognized that new managerial roles would be a key to success. The bank needed a way to move experienced staff from their traditional hierarchical practices and relationships to new, more flexible and less formal roles. Part of the training process in anticipation of expansion was a series of seminars to discuss role concepts. Subsequently, close attention was paid to matching managers' personalities with the demands of their new roles.[6]

Managers can increase a team's productivity by understanding the different kinds of roles and adhering to the following guidelines.

- **Encourage and reward members who adopt positive roles.**
- **Recognize that both task-oriented and relations-oriented roles are critical to team performance.** A team that focuses only on relations-oriented roles may never get the job done. A team that emphasizes only task-oriented roles is likely to face growing member dissatisfaction, to lose team spirit, and to breed disruptive conflicts.

- **Identify and discourage negative roles.** Team leaders—and other team members—have a responsibility to make it clear that disruptive, self-serving behaviors will not be tolerated.
- **Understand the roles you must play as a team leader—and those you need not play.** Team leaders sometimes feel they must wear all task-oriented and relations-oriented hats. This isn't always necessary, and it may be harmful. While task-oriented and relations-oriented roles are both critical in groups, other team members may fulfill those roles.
- **Do all you can to minimize role ambiguity, role conflict, and role overload.** Make sure that assignments are clear, that messages are consistent and unambiguous, and that responsibilities are not overwhelming.

TEAM SCHOLAR

Deborah Ancona, MIT Sloan School of Management

Dr. Deborah Ancona is Seley Distinguished Professor of Management in the MIT Sloan School of Management.

You've been writing about X-Teams for more than a decade. How would you describe an X-Team? What are its characteristics?

An **X-Team** is an externally active team. While most team models focus on the internal interactions among individual members, like clear goals and roles or conflict management, X-Teams are also active across their boundaries. X-Team members engage in (1) scouting to keep their pulse on what is going on in the external environment; how technologies are changing, markets are shifting, and competitors are striking; (2) ambassadorship to align team activities to strategic priorities and to advocate for team goals; and (3) task coordination to manage the interdependencies between the team and other groups that provide inputs or that will complete team tasks. X-Teams have fluid membership and move through three phases of activity. First, they explore the external environment and create the outside networks needed to connect to stakeholders. Second, they make sense of the information collected in phase one and then decide what one thing they will focus on and how they will get there. In other words they exploit the work from the first phase and iterate to find a real solution. Third, they work to make sure that the product or solution that they produce is exported in a way that spreads the expertise and excitement from the team to others in the organization or the market.

Why and when are X-Teams needed?

X-Teams are needed in dynamic, uncertain contexts where the expertise and information needed to complete the team task exist outside of the team. More and more teams fall into this category as we attempt to solve complex problems in organizations with shifting boundaries and global reach.

Can you give a specific example of an X-Team?

One example of an X-Team was a product development team at Microsoft. The team leader did not believe that the company was focusing enough on software solutions for the Internet generation customer base. The leader pulled other organizational members into her team, got resources from top management, and proceeded to monitor a group of college students to see how this new generation used technology and what they hoped it could do for them going forward. Based on this interaction with potential customers, the team brainstormed ideas for new software and worked with others inside Microsoft to beta test and refine a set of new products that met the needs they had identified. Team members continuously got feedback from customers and monitored competitors. They marketed their ideas to top management until their approach for bringing in the voice of the customer was replicated in other teams. Their products are hitting the marketplace now.

How can organizational structures be designed to support X-Teams?

Organizations can be designed to support X-Teams by encouraging leaders at all levels to bring forward new ideas, by having top management be receptive to these ideas and merge bottom-up and top-down initiatives into a coherent strategy, and by being transparent and communicating the business model and objectives of the firm so that team members can align with these objectives. Organizations also have to reward people for crossing boundaries and challenging the status quo.

What do you see as some of the most important emerging issues regarding teams?

Despite years of research and empirical findings that support "going out before going in," the internal perspective dominates the teams literature, popular press, and team training. This internal model is burnt into our brains. Researchers and practitioners alike would do well to shift their mental models of teams and their team activities to put as much emphasis on planning what they do across their boundaries as what they do inside of them. Teams need to reach out across their boundaries for information, expertise, resources, support, vicarious learning, alignment, coordination and collaboration with others within the firm and outside of the firm. Given the rapidly changing, competitive, networked world that we live in today team members need to learn not to put a wall between themselves and the external world, but rather to reach out to adapt and learn.

Stages of Team Development

There are distinct stages of team development. As shown in Figure 3-3, these stages are called forming, storming, norming, performing, and adjourning.[7] As the names suggest, norms and roles don't become well developed until the team has experienced a lot of jockeying for position, testing of boundaries, and even dealing with conflicts.

In the **forming stage of group development**, team members are getting acquainted and becoming oriented to the task. There is great uncertainty because expectations are unclear. Team members attempt to learn which behaviors are acceptable and which are not. At this stage, leaders can help members become comfortable and feel like part of the team. They can encourage quiet members to build relationships with others and can generally encourage communication and interaction among members.

Figure 3-3

Stages of Group
Development

During the **storming** stage, conflict and disagreement among group members are likely. Members become more assertive in their roles, and their personalities begin to become clearer. The team lacks cohesiveness as there is jockeying for position and forming of subgroups. This stage may be necessary to permit team members to resolve disagreements, uncertainties, and conflicts and to permit agreement and a common vision to develop. However, if the team doesn't get past the storming stage, it cannot become productive. As such, the leader must help the team work through this stage in ways that are ultimately constructive.

By the **norming** stage, conflicts have largely been resolved, and the team becomes more cohesive. Members settle into roles, and team norms, values, and expectations develop. The leader should encourage communication among members at this stage and help team members as they agree on roles, values, and norms.

In the **performing** stage the team is mature. Members have learned the bounds of acceptable behavior, worked through their disagreements, developed norms, and settled in their roles. The focus now is on performance as team members constructively face new challenges, coordinate their activities, and pursue the team's vision. When the team is at this stage, it can largely manage its own affairs. The leader can step back a bit, concentrating on helping the team with its **self-management**.

Finally, in the **adjourning** stage the team dissolves, having accomplished its purposes or breaking up because of internal or external forces.

Again, development of norms and roles takes place over the course of the team development process. It is important to help shape positive norms and roles as early in the life of the team as possible.

Skills Practice 3.1 on the text website gives you an opportunity to analyze a highly successful football team as portrayed in the movie *Remember the*

Titans. Based on a true story, this movie provides an excellent illustration of the stages of group development.

Building Team Spirit

Some teams stick together better than others. There is a real sense of team spirit, and members are proud to be associated with each other and with the team. Teams with high levels of this team spirit—also called **team cohesiveness**—generally are more effective in achieving their goals than teams that lack team spirit.[8] Members of cohesive teams also communicate relatively better with one another, are more satisfied, and feel less tension and anxiety.

For a discussion of the importance of team spirit in the 2008 Ryder Cup, see the Teams in the News feature.

TEAMS IN THE NEWS: Team Cohesiveness in the Ryder Cup

The importance of team cohesiveness was seen in the 2008 Ryder Cup pitting top golfers from the United States against Europe's elite. Despite the fact that the United States had many of the top-ranked golfers in the world, including Tiger Woods, the U.S. team had lost five of the six previous matches. In 2008, with Tiger Woods sidelined with an injury, the U.S. captain, Paul Azinger, faced a real challenge. His response: get the players to think like team players rather than individuals. While a former captain, Jack Nicklaus, joked that his job had been to give a few speeches and make sure the players had "fresh towels, sunscreen, and tees," Azinger knew he had to do more. He said, "Working together for the common good is not normally a function for us out on the PGA tour. We play as individuals."

Azinger called on Ron Braund, his life coach and a corporate team-building specialist, to enhance team spirit as the core of his "secret strategy." Among other innovations, they divided the twelve-man team into three four-man subgroups, called pods. The idea was based on a documentary about the military's Special Forces and their Ryder-Cup-size platoons, which break down into subgroups for some missions. Assistant Coach Olin Browne said, "Each pod was a force unto itself." Pod members played their practice rounds together and were paired with other pod members in the competition. The pods went off sequentially, four by four. Each pod was assigned an assistant captain to tend to players' needs and keep them relaxed and "on message." The U.S. team won easily, 16 ½ to 11 ½. U.S. golfer Boo Weekley said "The whole week has been magical. I think we actually became a family."

Source: J. P. Newport, "Team USA's Management Victory," http://online.wsj.com/articles/SB122246633744980277.

Note that we said that cohesive teams are more effective in achieving *their* goals. Since their goals may not always foster the best interests of the organization, it is important to make sure that team members are aiming for the right sorts of things. If not, increasing team cohesiveness may help attain undesirable goals. So if a team has goals of high performance, creativity, and an honest day's work, greater cohesiveness is probably helpful. If it has goals of leaving work early, pilfering, doing as little as possible on the job, or padding the budget, increased cohesiveness may not be a good thing.

Several things help make teams more cohesive. For example, cohesiveness rises with increases in team status and team goal achievement. Cohesiveness also tends to increase when there is a clear outside threat that requires the team to pull together to meet the challenge. As teams get bigger, cohesiveness declines.

TEAMS IN THE NEWS: "Cleansing from Cubicle to Cubicle"

Companies use a wide variety of team-building exercises to enhance cohesion. Traditionally, these have included things such as office happy hours, trust falls, paintball retreats, team tower-building exercises, and team scavenger hunts.

As discussed in this *New York Times* article, an increasingly popular—though controversial—new team bonding exercise involves group cleanses. With these, teams spend one to five days on all-liquid diets, generally employing vegetable juices. For instance, in 2011 Oprah Winfrey's entire Chicago production staff completed a three-day cleanse. Actress Salma Hayek is a cofounder of Cooler Cleanse company; office cleanses now make up 30% of the firm's business. Employees from Merrill Lynch, the Carlyle Group, Citigroup, and many other companies have participated in the group cleanses. Michael Godshall, a founder of Project Dstllry in Brooklyn, says of his company's office-wide, three-day, 1,200-calorie cleanse, "It was something we could do where we thought, 'We're all in this together.'"

Source: C. Rubin, "Cleansing from Cubicle to Cubicle," *New York Times*, July 11, 2012, p. E1.

Cohesiveness may be especially important at critical points in the life of an organization. For example, when GE Plastics, a division of General Electric Company, acquired rival company Borg-Warner Chemicals, the company faced the formidable task of integrating two very different work cultures. It was decided that some form of team-building experience was needed to make a lasting impression on the participants while serving some larger purpose. A project called Share to Gain was started in which GE Plastics employees from different departments and from the acquired company worked together to renovate five nonprofit facilities in San Diego, CA. The project was credited with building corporate loyalty, enhancing team spirit, and smoothing the pains of integration.[9]

These characteristics suggest the following concrete guidelines for building team cohesiveness.[10]

- **Make it attractive to be a member of the team.** Use logos and team names as appropriate. Emphasize team status. Make team membership an honor.
- **Praise and publicize team accomplishments.** Go for some small wins. That is, make sure the team has some projects and goals that can have clear, short-term consequences. Success on these may build cohesiveness and confidence as the team tackles larger tasks.
- **Keep the team small.** As discussed earlier in the chapter, large teams have coordination problems and lack cohesiveness, and their members may engage in social loafing.
- **Identify outside threats and pressures.** Communicate them to the team, and emphasize how teamwork can counter them.

THAT'S INTERESTING! Hot Groups

Extremely high levels of team spirit, excitement, and energy characterize what have been called **hot groups**.[11] According to Jean Lipman-Blumen and Harold Leavitt, "A hot group is a special state of mind. It's not a name for some new team, task force, or committee. The hot group state of mind is task obsessed and full of passion, coupled with a distinctive way of behaving, a style that is intense, sharply focused, and full-bore. Any group can become a hot group—if it can get into that distinctive state of mind. . . . It is not the name, but that contagious single-mindedness, that all-out dedication to doing something important, that distinguishes a hot group from all others." Hot groups abound in Silicon Valley; the team that created the Macintosh computer is cited as a classic example. To encourage hot groups, according to Lipman-Blumen and Leavitt, it is important to make room for spontaneity, break down barriers, encourage intellectual exchange, select talented people and respect their self-motivation and ability, use information technology to build relationships, and value truth and the speaking of it.

Now, complete Skills Practice 3.2 on the text website to learn how to apply tools to foster a sense of team spirit.

In this chapter we have explored ways to build and develop effective teams. In Chapter 4 we discuss approaches to socializing team members, building trust, motivating, and leading teams.

Summary and Integration

Key takeaways for this chapter include the following:

Team size is very important. In general, teams of 5 or 7 are best.

It is important when forming teams to consider availability of key information, and skills, participation of affected members, selection of a task-oriented leader, and changes in membership across tasks and task stages.

Defining the team's assignment involves specifying the team's purpose, responsibilities, and needs.

Once the team assignment is defined, the overall team effort should be planned. This should include dividing the team's overall assignment into parts, estimating the time and resources needed to complete each part of the assignment and the overall assignment, and taking actions to reduce gaps between what is needed and what is available.

Leaders must understand how teams may change as they mature, and how different sets of leader behaviors are needed to manage teams through stages of development. This requires understanding of team norms and team member roles.

Stages of team development include forming, storming, norming, performing, and adjourning.

Teams with high levels of team spirit—also called team cohesiveness— generally are more effective in achieving their goals.

Notes

1   The classic discussion of this topic was provided by M.S. Granovetter, "The Strength of Weak Ties," *American Journal of Sociology*, 1973, *78(6)*, pp. 1360–1380. For a recent discussion, see P.V. Marsden & K.E. Campbell, "Reflections on Conceptualizing and Measuring Tie Strength," *Social Forces*, 2012, *91(1)*, pp. 17–23.

2   For discussions of action forums at Xerox, see J.O. Whitney & E.K. Warren, "Action Forums: How General Electric and Other Firms Have Learned to Make Better Decisions, Faster," *Journal of World Business*, Winter 1996, pp. 18–27. See also G. Flynn, "Worker Think Tanks Provide Fast Solutions," *Personnel Journal*, January 1996, p. 57.

3   For more on the power of norms in competitive cycling, including those governing the *peleton*—the large group of competitors riding together—see P. Hochman, "Pack Mentality," *Fortune*, June 12, 2006, *153(11)*, pp. 145–152. Unfortunately, recent years have seen evidence of another apparently widespread norm for many top cyclists—doping. See, for instance, A. McLean, A. Tse, & L. Waanamen, "Top Finishers in the Tour de France Tainted by Doping," *New York Times*, October 10, 2012. http://www.nytimes.com/interactive/2012/08/24/sports/top-finishers-of-the-tour-de-france-tainted-by-doping.html?_r=0.

4   For discussions of role conflict and ambiguity, see Y. Fried, H.A. Ben-David, R.B. Tiegs, N. Avital, & U. Yeverechyahu, "The Interactive Effect of Role Conflict and Role Ambiguity on Job Performance," *Journal of Occupational and Organizational Psychology*, 1998, *71(1)*, pp. 19–27; T.C. Tubre & J.M. Collins, "Jackson and Schuler (1985) Revisited: A Meta-Analysis of the Relationships Between Role Ambiguity, Role Conflict, and Job Performance," *Journal of Management*, 2000, *26(1)*, pp. 155–169; and, A.B. Bakker & E. Demerouti, "The Job Demands-Resources Model: State of the Art," *Journal of Managerial Psychology*, 2007, *22(3)*, pp. 309–328.

5   See E.A. Marzabadi & H. Tarkhorani, "Job Stress, Job Satisfaction, and Mental Health," *Journal of Clinical and Diagnostic Research*, 2007, *4*, pp. 224–234; D. Örtqvist & J. Wincent, "Prominent Consequences of Role Stress: A Meta-Analytic Review," *International Journal of Stress Management*, 2006, *13(4)*, pp. 399–422; and, L.J. Hauge, A. Skogstad, & S. Einarsen, "Relationships between Stressful Work Environment and Bullying: Results from a Large Representative Study," *Work & Stress*, 2007, *21(3)*, pp. 220–242.

6   T.K. Das, "Training for Changing Managerial Role Behavior: Experience in a Developing Country," *Journal of Management Development*, 2001, *20(7)*, pp. 579–603. See also A. Akbar & S. Kamili, "Training Delivery and Methodology in Banks: An Empirical Study," *ASBM Journal of Management*, *3(1&2)*, pp. 64–76.

7   These stages were first proposed by B.W. Tuckman, "Developmental Sequence in Small Groups," *Psychological Bulletin*, 1965, *63*, pp. 384–399. For recent discussions, see K. Akrivou, R.E. Boyatzis, & P.L. McLeod, "The Evolving Group: Towards a Theory of Intentional Group Development," *Journal of Management Development*, 2006, *25(7)*, pp. 689–706; J.K. Ito & C.M. Brotheridge, "Do Teams Grow Up One Stage at a Time?: Exploring the Complexity of Group Development Models," *Team Performance Management*, 2008, *14(5/6)*, pp. 214–232; and, D.A. Bonebright, "40 Years of Storming: A Historical Review of Tuckman's Model of Small Group Development," *Human Resource Development Journal*, 2010, *13(1)*, pp. 111–120.

8   For discussions of cohesiveness, see C.W. Langfred, "Is Group Cohesiveness a Double-Edged Sword?" *Small Group Research*, 1998, *29*, pp. 124–143; A.V. Carron & L.R. Brawley, "Cohesion: Conceptual and Measurement Issues," *Small Group Research*, 2000, *31*, pp. 89–106; and, R. Hoigaard, R. Saïfvenbom, & F.E. Tonnessen, "The Relationship between Group Cohesion, Group Norms, and Perceived Social Loafing in Soccer Teams," *Small Group Research*, 2006, *37(3)*, pp. 217–232.

9   D. Bollier, "Building Corporate Loyalty While Rebuilding the Community," *Management Review*, October 1996, pp. 17–22; and, B.W. De La Mater, "Volunteers Converge on Playground," *Berkshire Eagle Online*, October 5, 2008. http://www.berkshireeagle.com/ci_10642123.

10 For more on team building, see J.R. Hackman, "New Rules for Team Building," *Optimize*, July 2002, pp. 50+; E. Yeh, C. Smith, C. Jennings, & N. Castro, "Team Building: A 3-Dimensional Model," *Team Performance Management*, 2006, *12(5/6)*, pp. 192–197; and, M.K. Johnston, "The Influence of Team-Building Exercises on Group Attraction," *Journal of Organizational Culture, Communications and Conflict*, 2007, *11(1)*, pp. 43–52.

11 J. Lipman-Blumen & H.J. Leavitt, *Hot Groups* (New York: Oxford University Press, 1999). See also H.J. Leavitt & J. Lipman-Blumen, "Hot Groups: The Rebirth of Individualism," *Ivey Business Journal,* 2000, *65(1)*, pp. 60–65; and, H.J. Leavitt, "Big Organizations Are Unhealthy for Human Beings," *Academy of Management Learning & Education*, 2007, *62(2)*, pp. 253–263.

Bibliography

Akbar A., & Kamili, S. "Training Delivery and Methodology in Banks: An Empirical Study," *ASBM Journal of Management*, *3(1&2)*, pp. 64–76.

Akrivou, K., Boyatzis, R.E., & McLeod, P.L. "The Evolving Group: Towards a Theory of Intentional Group Development," *Journal of Management Development*, 2006, *25(7)*, pp. 689–706.

Bakker, A.B., & Demerouti, E. "The Job Demands-Resources Model: State of the Art," *Journal of Managerial Psychology*, 2007, *22(3)*, pp. 309–328.

Bollier, D. "Building Corporate Loyalty While Rebuilding the Community," *Management Review*, October 1996, pp. 17–22.

Bonebright, D.A. "40 Years of Storming: A Historical Review of Tuckman's Model of Small Group Development," *Human Resource Development Journal*, 2010, *13(1)*, pp. 111–120.

Carron, A.V., & Brawley, L.R. "Cohesion: Conceptual and Measurement Issues," *Small Group Research*, 2000, *31*, pp. 89–106.

Das, T.K. "Training for Changing Managerial Role Behavior: Experience in a Developing Country," *Journal of Management Development*, 2001, *20(7)*, pp. 579–603.

De La Mater, B.W. "Volunteers Converge on Playground," *The Berkshire Eagle Online*, October 5, 2008. http://www.berkshireeagle.com/ci_10642123

Flynn, G. "Worker Think Tanks Provide Fast Solutions," *Personnel Journal*, January 1996, p. 57.

Fried, Y., Ben-David, H.A., Tiegs, R.B., Avital, N., & Yeverechyahu, U. "The Interactive Effect of Role Conflict and Role Ambiguity on Job Performance," *Journal of Occupational and Organizational Psychology*, 1998, *71(1)*, pp. 19–27.

Granovetter, M.S. "The Strength of Weak Ties," *American Journal of Sociology*, 1973, *78(6)*, pp. 1360–1380.

Hackman, J.R. "New Rules for Team Building," *Optimize*, July 2002, p. 50.

Hauge, L.J., Skogstad, A., & Einarsen, S. "Relationships between Stressful Work Environment and Bullying: Results from a Large Representative Study," *Work & Stress*, 2007, *21(3)*, pp. 220–242.

Hochman, P. "Pack Mentality," *Fortune*, June 12, 2006, *153(11)*, pp. 145–152.

Hoigaard, R., Saïfvenbom, R., & Tonnessen, F.E. "The Relationship between Group Cohesion, Group Norms, and Perceived Social Loafing in Soccer Teams," *Small Group Research*, 2006, *37(3)*, pp. 217–232.

Ito, J.K., & Brotheridge, C.M. "Do Teams Grow Up One Stage at a Time?: Exploring the Complexity of Group Development Models," *Team Performance Management*, 2008, *14(5/6)*, pp. 214–232.

Johnston, M.H. "The Influence of Team-Building Exercises on Group Attraction," *Journal of Organizational Culture, Communications and Conflict*, 2007, *11(1)*, pp. 43–52.

Langfred, C.W. "Is Group Cohesiveness a Double-Edged Sword?" *Small Group Research*, 1998, *29*, pp. 124–143.

Leavitt, H.J. "Big Organizations Are Unhealthy for Human Beings," *Academy of Management Learning & Education*, 2007, *62(2)*, pp. 253–263.

Leavitt, H.J., & Lipman-Blumen, J. "Hot Groups: The Rebirth of Individualism," *Ivey Business Journal*, 2000, *65(1)*, pp. 60–65.

Lipman-Blumen, J., & Leavitt, H.J. *Hot Groups* (New York: Oxford University Press, 1999).

Marsden, P.V., & Campbell, K.E. "Reflections on Conceptualizing and Measuring Tie Strength," *Social Forces*, 2012, *91(1)*, pp. 17–23.

Marzabadi, E.A., & Tarkhorani, H. "Job Stress, Job Satisfaction, and Mental Health," *Journal of Clinical and Diagnostic Research*, 2007, *4*, pp. 224–234.

McLean, A., Tse, A., & Waanamen, L. "Top Finishers in the Tour de France Tainted by Doping," *New York Times*, October 10, 2012. http://www.nytimes.com/interactive/2012/08/24/sports/top-finishers-of-the-tour-de-france-tainted-by-doping.html?_r=0

Miller, G.A. "The Magical Number Seven, Plus or Minus Two: "Some Limits on Our Capacity for Processing Information," *Psychological Review*, 1956, *63(2)*, pp. 81–97.

Örtqvist, D., & Wincent, J. "Prominent Consequences of Role Stress: A Meta-Analytic Review," *International Journal of Stress Management*, 2006, *13(4)*, pp. 399–422.

Rubin, C. "Cleansing from Cubicle to Cubicle," *New York Times*, July 11, 2012, p. E1.

Tubre, T.C., & Collins, J.M. "Jackson and Schuler (1985) Revisited: A Meta-Analysis of the Relationships between Role Ambiguity, Role Conflict, and Job Performance," *Journal of Management*, 2000, *26(1)*, pp. 155–169.

Tuckman, B.W. "Developmental Sequence in Small Groups," *Psychological Bulletin*, 1965, *63*, pp. 384–399.

Walker, J. "Computer Programmers Learn Tough Lesson in Sharing," *Wall Street Journal*, August 27, 2012, p. A1.

Whitney, J.O., & Warren, E.K. "Action Forums: How General Electric and Other Firms Have Learned to Make Better Decisions, Faster," *Journal of World Business,* Winter 1996, pp. 18–27.

Yeh, E., Smith, C., Jennings, C., & Castro, N. "Team Building: A 3-Dimensional Model," *Team Performance Management*, 2006, *12(5/6)*, pp. 192–197.

CHAPTER 4

Socializing, Building Trust, Training, Motivating, and Leading Teams

Learning Objectives

After reading this chapter, you should be able to do the following:

1. Recognize the importance of team socialization and the nature of the socialization process.
2. Understand and employ ways to develop trust in teams.
3. Recognize forms of team training and guidelines for effective team training.
4. Understand approaches to motivating and rewarding team members.
5. Recognize the importance of key traits and behaviors in leading teams.

. . . .

IN THIS CHAPTER WE DISCUSS A VARIETY OF ISSUES that help ensure effective, satisfying teamwork. We first consider the important topic of socializing new team members. We then discuss ways to enhance trust in teams and review evidence on successful team training. Finally, we address guidelines for effective motivation and leadership.

Socializing Team Members

Teams are not static. They evolve over time, and they add and shed members. It is critical that newcomers to the team quickly become full, participative, productive members. In this section we consider the nature of team socialization, phases of the team socialization process, roles in team socialization, the process of identity fusion, and the development of team cognition.

Team Socialization

Just as new members of the organization must learn about its culture, norms, expectations, and, in general, "the ropes to skip and the ropes to know," new team members must meld into the team. **Team socialization** refers to the process by which new members develop into full, participative membership in the team and move from outsiders to insiders. During this process, new members may seek information in order to understand their roles in the team, to develop confidence that they can be successful on the job, and to gain a sense of social acceptance.

Roles in Team Socialization

Clearly, the team leader should do all he or she can to make the new member comfortable in the team, and current team members comfortable with the new entry. The leader may explain, for instance, why this member has been added to the team. For example, what are the new member's qualifications and anticipated roles? The leader must also ensure that other team members become acquainted with the new member, interact, and pass on tacit knowledge (i.e., personal knowledge that is difficult to transfer verbally or in writing). Team members, in turn, should be proactive in their efforts to integrate the new member. They may pass on information about group norms, expectations, and capabilities, and may also provide suggestions and support.

Of course, it's not just newcomers to teams who have to adjust. Rather than being passive recipients of influence, newcomers may themselves serve as influence agents.[1] They may, for instance, upset status relationships in the team. Also, while new team members are often susceptible to current team members' attempts to shape their attitudes and behaviors, they may sometimes actively seek to alter the team's structure, dynamics, or performance. To do so, they must be motivated to introduce new ideas and have the ability to generate such ideas and to convince team members to adopt the ideas. Current members may often reject, and even resent, newcomers' suggestions for change. However, if team performance is presently poor, such inputs may be welcomed.[2]

Identity Fusion[3]

Team members who fully identify with the team experience **identity fusion.** When this happens, they feel fused, or one, with the group. Rather than their properties and the team's properties being distinct, the self-and-other barrier is blurred. The team is seen as equivalent with the personal self. Identity fusion is most common in relational groups, made up of family members or close friends, but it can also occur with teams in organizations. When identity fusion occurs, team members feel a personal responsibility to act on the team's behalf. As a result, they may engage in extreme behavior to support the team.

Team Cognition: Mental Models and Transactive Memory Systems

One important function of the team socialization process is to help develop team mental models and **transactive memory** systems. As described by Steve Kozlowski and Daniel Ilgen, "*Team mental models* and *transactive memory* both refer to cognitive structures or knowledge representations that enable team members to organize and acquire information necessary to anticipate and execute actions. Team mental models refer to knowledge structures or information held in common, whereas transactive memory refers to knowledge of information distribution within a team (i.e., knowledge of who knows what)."[4]

Team mental models are organized knowledge frameworks that allow team members to describe, explain, and predict behavior. **Transactive memory systems (TMS)** are "a form of cognitive architecture that encompasses both the knowledge held by particular group members with a collective awareness of who knows what."[5] Research shows team cognition to be positively related to team performance. When teams have well-developed TMS as well as similar and accurate team mental models, their performance increases.[6]

Developing Trust within the Team

It is almost obvious that trust within a team is critical. Some issues, though, require discussion. For example, what exactly is trust? Why is it important? How is it developed?

What Is Trust?

In an ad for the St. Paul insurance companies, a young girl in the African veld stands steadfast as a huge rhino thunders toward her. The rhino comes to a screeching halt inches from the girl. The girl smiles and kisses the rhino's horn. The ad captures the essence of **trust**—the willingness to put oneself in a position of vulnerability, but with confidence that others will not take advantage of that vulnerability. Figure 4-1 shows some items used to assess trust in teams.[7]

The Importance of Trust in Teams

Trust is important in virtually all interactions in teams, organizations, and life. It is critical for team effectiveness.[8] Research shows that trust serves many roles. For one thing, trust directly influences such desired behaviors as individual performance and engagement in organizational citizenship behaviors. In addition, trust influences how team members respond to actions of their leaders and others. If actors are trusted, their behaviors are interpreted as well motivated and constructive and are likely to yield positive reactions. If actors are not trusted, their behaviors are seen with suspicion, and those behaviors may meet resistance. Further, trust reduces *transaction costs*. That is, interactions don't need to be scripted, and formal agreements are less important. Also, trust fosters **spontaneous sociability**, the willingness of team members to engage in cooperative, altruistic, extrarole behaviors that further attainment of collective goals.

Trust seems more important in some contexts than others. For example, situations may be classified as strong or weak. In a *strong situation* demands of the situation are so compelling that people have little choice but to behave in a certain way. In a *weak situation* people can act on their own volitions. The **strong situation hypothesis** is that factors such as personality and trust are important in weak situations but less so in strong situations.[9]

1. I am able to count on team members for help if I have difficulties on the job.
2. I am confident that my team members will take my interests into account when making work-related decisions.
3. I am confident that my team members will keep me informed about issues that concern my work.
4. I can rely on my team members to keep their word.
5. I trust my team members.

Figure 4-1

Measurement of Trust in Teams

Source: These items are drawn from B.A. de Jong and T. Elfring. "How Does Trust Affect the Performance of Ongoing Teams?: The Mediating Role of Reflexivity, Monitoring, and Effort." *Academy of Management Journal*, 2010, *53(3)*, pp. 535–549.

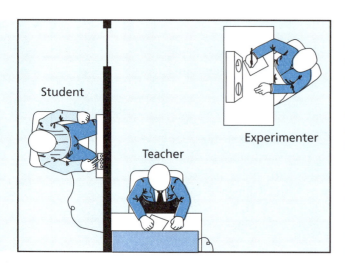

Student

Experimenter

Teacher

In a classic and controversial experiment demonstrating the power of the situation, as shown in the accompanying figure, psychologist Stanley Milgram instructed subjects—labeled "teachers" in the study—in a "learning experiment" to administer increasingly severe shocks to "learners" when learners gave incorrect answers to questions.[10] Subjects thought the learners were also volunteers, but they were actually confederates of the experimenter pretending to receive shocks. The "learners" pleaded to be released or even complained about a heart condition. When "teachers" appeared reluctant to continue, the experimenter gave instructions such as, "The experiment requires that you continue," and "It is absolutely essential that you continue." Surprisingly, in the experimental condition in which "teachers" and "learners" were separated and had no visual contact, 65% of "teachers" obeyed instructions and administered shocks through levels such as "moderate shock," "danger: severe shock," and the two extreme levels of "XXX." Milgram's experiment, which caused many of its subjects long-lasting trauma, led to tightened controls on research conducted at universities and elsewhere.

Bases of Trust[11]

Dispositional Trust

Quite simply, some people are inherently more trusting than others. **Dispositional trust** may result from early trust-related experiences that develop general beliefs about others' trustworthiness that translate to a personality characteristic. For an interesting alternative (or complementary) view, see the following "That's Interesting! The Trust Molecule" feature.

THAT'S INTERESTING! The Trust Molecule

A question that has debated for millennia is why some people are more trusting and caring than others. Some scholars reason, for instance, that early childhood experiences teach us whether people are generally trustworthy. One recent answer is more provocative, surprising, and controversial: there may be a *trust molecule*.[1]

Oxytocin in the blood and brain—often thought of as a female reproductive hormone—seems to be a chemical agent that creates bonds in intimate relationships, business dealings, politics, and society in general. For example, when people's oxytocin levels increase, they are more willing to give money to strangers. When synthetic oxytocin is sprayed into an individual's nasal passages, the person's caring responses surge. Oxytocin levels increase in intimate relationships and even in group activities such as singing, dancing, and praying. Further, behaviors demonstrating trust lead to increased oxytocin in the person being trusted; trust levels rise, leading to a virtuous cycle of reciprocity.

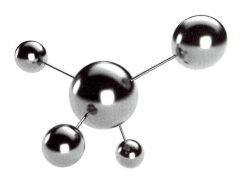

Research shows that even a simple touch can raise the oxytocin level of the person being touched.[2] In fact, Dacher Keltner and his colleagues studied every team and every player in the National Basketball Association. They took notes on many types of touch, such as forms of hugs, head slaps, and fist bumps. Almost without exception, the teams that touched the most had the best records, and vice versa. Perhaps most interesting, early season touching seemed to result in greater cooperation, which then led to better season performance.[3]

Notes

1. P. J. Zak, "The Trust Molecule," *Wall Street Journal*, April 28, 2012, p. C1. This article was based on P. J. Zak, *The Moral Molecule: The Source of Love and Prosperity* (New York: Dutton, 2012). See also M. Shermer, "Kin and Kindness," *Wall Street Journal*, May 25, 2012.
2. M. W. Kraus, C. Huang, & D. Keltner, "Tactile Communication, Cooperation, and Performance: An Ethological Study of the NBA," *Emotion*, 2010, *10(5)*, pp. 745–749.
3. The researchers were aware that players may have touched in some cases *because* there had been a good play. They included a variety of controls and used alternative performance measures, but the findings were robust.

History-Based Trust

As team members or others interact over time, they learn more about one another's dispositions, intentions, and motives. This provides a basis for drawing inferences about trustworthiness. The principle of **social reciprocity** says that you get back what you give to others: what goes around, comes around.[12] It has been said that "the best way to find out if you can trust somebody is to trust them."[13] That is, a show of trust can be used to learn if others are trustworthy. As such, if team leaders and members want others to trust them, care for them, and respect them, they must demonstrate those qualities first.

Third-Party Trust

Third parties in organizations convey trust-related information. For instance, team members may gossip about others' trustworthiness, recounting stories or evidence that allow others to infer whether an individual or subgroup can be trusted. Gossip can, of course, be incomplete or incorrect, but it is sometimes helpful. Correct or not, it is often seen as credible.

Category-Based Trust

We sometimes trust others because we see them as somehow similar to us in terms of social (e.g., gender, age group, race) or organizational (e.g., team membership, level, tenure, functional area) category. We see others who seem similar to us as members of our in-group. We tend to attribute positive characteristics as honesty, cooperativeness, and trustworthiness to in-group members. Even shared gestures, such as a secret handshake, may enhance **category-based trust**.

Role-Based Trust

Consider that we often put our lives in the hands of others—such as airplane pilots or surgeons—whom we may hardly know. This is because we recognize the various hurdles—training, education, certification, and so on—they have surmounted to achieve their positions.

Rule-Based Trust

Rule-based trust is based on shared understandings regarding the system of formal and informal rules governing appropriate behavior. Rule-based trust is sustained within an organization "by socialization into the structure of rules."[14]

Applying the Bases of Trust

These various bases of trust suggest ways that team leaders and members can foster trust. These include the following:

1. **Dispositional.** Seek trustworthy team members. Then, be careful to act in ways to show that members' initial trust is warranted. On the other hand, if some team members are low on dispositional trust, immediate and consistent acts must be taken to show that trust is really deserved.
2. **History-based.** Team leaders can demonstrate trusting behavior by empowering team members, being open to their views, and letting them take some chances. Team members can demonstrate trusting behaviors and reciprocate others' demonstrations of trust.
3. **Third-party based.** Monitor and play the informal communications channel: the grapevine. Foster open communications to avoid misunderstandings. Provide accurate information to squelch unfounded rumors. Try to tune in to the rhythms of the grapevine.
4. **Category-based.** Emphasize similarities. Even things like team names sometimes give a feeling of unity. Also, rites of integration, such as office

parties, foster shared feelings that bring team members together, build their mutual trust, and commit them to the team.

5. **Role-based.** Emphasize team member roles and why members are competent in those roles. Make sure that member qualifications and how they contribute to the team are known.

6. **Rule-based.** Clarify important rules early in the life of a team. For example, early in the life of the team set down guidelines regarding prompt attendance at meetings and the importance of demonstrating mutual respect.

"Swift Trust"[15]

Trust is often developed over time as team members interact and learn about one another. Sometimes, though, **swift trust** is needed. For example, temporary teams, which are formed around a common task with a finite life span, must quickly develop trust. We discuss swift trust in more detail in the context of virtual teams in Chapter 11.

Managing Trust

Kurt Dirks and Donald Ferrin conclude on the basis of their review of trust research that team leaders can take two approaches to managing trust.[16] First, they can try to raise levels of trust among team members using the approaches discussed previously. Second, they can assess situational strength and act accordingly. For example, if levels of trust are low, leaders may want to create a highly structured team environment with little opportunity for trust to play a role. Conversely, if trust among team members is high, leaders may choose to destructure (that is, loosen things up) in order to let trust play a large role.

The Fragility of Trust

Sometimes, as in the case of swift trust, trust is immediate, but it often takes time to build. One thing is very clear, though: trust is fragile. Once we trust someone we may initially reject evidence that such trust is not justified. However, especially if damage from untrustworthiness is great and the untrustworthiness is seen as intentional, trust can vanish almost immediately.[17]

Training Team Members

According to Lisa Delise et al., "Team training is defined as a planned effort designed to improve team performance . . . by assisting individuals in the acquisition of new information, skills, and attitudes essential to effective performance in a team environment. . . ."[18] According to Eduardo Salas et al., team training targets teamwork knowledge, skills, and/or attitudinal competencies (KSAs) as well as team processes and performance for improvement.[19]

Importance of Team Training[20]

While individual training is important to ensure that team members have the knowledge, skills, and abilities needed to execute their parts of team tasks, it is not sufficient. Instead, team members must also learn how to perform mutual tasks and how to work together.

Forms of Team Training

Team training may target taskwork and/or teamwork. **Taskwork-focused team training** targeting taskwork seeks to enhance knowledge, skills, and abilities to develop technical competencies of team members. **Team-focused team training** interventions are designed to improve how team members work together effectively. For example, these interventions might include monitoring one another's performance and offering feedback regarding leadership, management, coordination, and decision making. As shown in Figure 4-2, team training may influence cognitive, affective, process, and performance outcomes. However, the impact of training on those outcomes may depend on moderators such as training content, team membership ability, and team size.

Effectiveness of Team Training

Team training, like most other things in life, can be done well or poorly. As such, it might be surprising to find rather consistent effects of training on personal, team, and organizational outcomes. Nevertheless, there is substantial evidence that team training generally has positive effects. For example, John Hollenbeck et al. wrote that, "a positive relationship between training and performance in team settings is and has been clear for some time."[21] Salas et al., who reviewed the literature on the relationship between team training and team performance, began their concluding comments with, "Team training works!" In their meta-analytic review, they found team training interventions to be successful across a wide variety of settings, tasks, and team types. Their review shows that team training explains 12% to 19% of the variance in a team's performance. Of the various outcomes shown

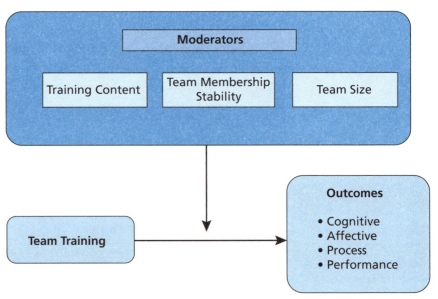

Figure 4-2

Moderators and Consequences of the Impact of Team Training

Source: E. Salas et al., "Does Team Training Improve Team Performance? A Meta-Analysis." *Human Factors: The Journal of the Human Factors and Ergonomics Society*, 2008, *50*, pp. 903–933, p. 907.

in Figure 4-2, team processes (e.g., communication, coordination, decision making) showed the strongest link to team training.

Salas et al. found that the various types of training content—whether team oriented, task oriented, or a mix—had similar outcomes. In general, their review shows that team training is more effective in intact teams, whose members have a shared history, than in ad hoc teams pulled together for a specific task. It also shows that training is more effective in small-sized teams (dyads) and in large teams than in teams with three or four members. In general, as we discuss elsewhere, medium-sized teams may already be performing at relatively high levels. There is also evidence that teams that work together should train together. In this way team members will not only gain skills but also develop trust.

Cross-Training

Top athletes often engage in cross-training. In the context of teams, **cross-training** is "an instructional strategy in which each team member is trained in the duties of his or her teammates."[22] As stated by Marks et al. (2002, p. 4), "The goal of cross-training is to enhance knowledge of interpersonal activities by introducing team members to the roles and responsibilities of their teammates. Cross-training has been touted as contributing to team communication, coordination, and controlled team regulation by encouraging members to understand the activities of those around them."[23]

Gaming

An intriguing development in team training, and in organizations in general, is the increased use of **gaming**, including computer-based gaming.[24] Especially since recent surveys show that 71% of American workers are "not engaged" or "actively disengaged" in their work, firms are seeking ways to apply computer-based gaming mechanics to nongame activities such as recruitment, training, and health and wellness to make them more fun and engaging. The Gartner Group estimates that by 2014, more than 70% of global 2,000 organizations will have at least one "gamified" application.[25] As one example, the Department of Defense, with its Defense Acquisition University, is using games in its core curriculum and in continuous learning programs to train employees in projects that are very expensive, dangerous, or large scale. Other firms using gaming for training and engagement include Google, Microsoft, Deloitte, L'Oreal, and Wells Fargo.[26] Gamification appears to offer many benefits for training—it is an engaging and structured experience with clear goals, specific rules requiring a player to overcome challenges, and instant feedback. Early evidence suggests that it may enhance creativity, learning, participation, and motivation.[27]

Motivating and Rewarding Team Members

Motivation is a key determinant of individual and team performance. Effective team leaders use a variety of tools to motivate their teams. We consider several approaches to motivation, including design of reward systems, in this section.

Basics of Motivation

Motivation comes from the Latin *movere,* "to move." So, motivation is about moving ourselves and others toward some goal. Motivation requires

1. arousal to initiate behavior toward a goal;
2. direction to properly focus that behavior; and
3. persistence to ultimately attain the goal.

Some of the approaches (called **content theories** or **need theories**) help us understand what people want and *why* they want it. Others—called **process theories**—focus on *how* a person becomes motivated as part of an overall process. Think of this set of approaches as a toolkit when working in a team. The questions asked and the corresponding theories we address in this section are these:

- **How can valued outcomes be tied to behaviors in order to reinforce desired behaviors and eliminate undesired behaviors that are related to the achievement of an organization's objectives?** This is the domain of **learning theory.**
- **What do employees want?** That is, what are primary needs? How are they linked? This is addressed by need theories of motivation.
- **How can goals be set to properly motivate behavior and how is the process of attaining goals managed?** This is the question addressed by **goal-setting theory.**
- **What elements must be present in a situation if a person is to be motivated to pursue a desired outcome?** Expectancy theory addresses this issue.
- **What causes a person to see his or her work environment as fair or unfair, and how does this influence motivation?** Equity theory and related theories of fairness examine this question.
- **How can jobs be designed to make them intrinsically motivating?** That is, how can the jobs themselves provide motivation without use of external rewards? **Job characteristics theory** provides one useful approach to the design of jobs that are intrinsically motivating.

Learning Theory

Individuals enter organizations, and situations within organizations, with very different histories of reinforcement. That is, they have learned different things. Some have learned that working hard is the way to get ahead. Others have learned to be stubborn in the face of challenge. Still others have learned to avoid troublesome situations. Thus, many differences in behaviors among employees may be due to the diverse ways their behaviors have been rewarded or punished in the past. They will continue to learn new behaviors and to unlearn past behaviors throughout their work lives. Some of those behaviors may be desirable, and others not.

When people hear about learning theory, they are likely to remember Ivan Pavlov's research on digestion in dogs. In that research, Ivan Pavlov taught a dog to salivate to stimuli, such as a touch on the paw or the sound of a bell. This **classical (or Pavlovian) conditioning** relies on pairing of a stimulus (e.g., food) that leads to some response (e.g., salivation) with another

Figure 4-3
Operant Conditioning

stimulus (e.g., ringing of a bell) that doesn't lead to the response. Through such pairing, the response is transferred to the new stimulus (e.g., ringing the bell results in salivation). Such classical conditioning is difficult to use in organizations and may raise ethical concerns. Importantly, classical conditioning cannot result in learning of a new behavior; it simply transfers a learned behavior from one stimulus to another.

Instead, most learning in organizations relies on the law of effect. The **law of effect** states that behavior that is rewarded will tend to be repeated; behavior that is not rewarded will tend not to be repeated. So if we want someone to continue acting in a certain way, we should see that they are somehow rewarded for acting in that way. If we want them to stop particular undesirable behaviors, we should make sure we are not rewarding them for those behaviors. The sort of conditioning that relies on the law of effect is called **operant conditioning** or, after its best-known researcher and theorist, Skinnerian conditioning.[28] Figure 4-3 illustrates operant conditioning.

Operant conditioning deals with ways to increase desired behaviors and to decrease undesired behaviors. Desired behaviors can be reinforced by rewards (called **positive reinforcement**). It is also sometimes possible to reinforce desired behaviors by removing some noxious consequence. In the case of rats in a maze, properly pressing a lever may cease the administration of a shock (called **escape learning**) or even prevent its onset (called **avoidance learning**). A team leader may reward good performance by a team member by removing some of those member's least desirable tasks.

On the other hand, undesired behaviors may be reduced through punishment, and sometimes there is no other recourse. For several reasons, though, punishment is often ineffective. For example, use of punishment may engender resentment, may lead to revenge and retaliation, and may be constrained by company policies. In addition, punishment leads to adherence only when the person administering the punishment is present or monitoring; additionally, while it may reduce an undesired behavior, it doesn't directly teach a desired behavior. For such reasons, most people are often reluctant to punish.

Sometimes people are engaging in some undesired behavior because it was previously reinforced. For instance, a team members may have learned that if they constantly complained they got what they wanted. If we wish to stop such behavior, we should simply no longer reinforce it. Following this approach is called **nonreinforcement**.

Organizational Behavior Modification

Based on learning theory, **organizational behavior modification** is a rather Orwellian term for the effective application of rewards and punishments in organizations.[29] Here are eight guidelines for effectively using learning techniques in organizations:[30]

1. **Don't give the same reward to all.** Team leaders sometimes want to reward all team members the same. However, it is important to reward

those who exhibit desired behavior (such as high performance or creative ideas) more than those who don't.

2. **Recognize that failure to respond to behavior has reinforcing consequences.** As a team leader or member, you may say, "I'm not going to manipulate my team members by rewarding them when they do well. I respect them too much for that." However, it simply isn't possible to *not* reinforce. Team leaders should ask, "What behavior will I reinforce if I do nothing?"

3. **Tell team members what behavior gets reinforced.** A rather remarkable finding is that people often don't know what their leader wants. Make the contingencies of reinforcement clear to team members. Don't make them guess.

4. **If you punish, make sure team members know what they are doing wrong.** Otherwise, they may assume they're being punished for something else, and the wrong behavior may be changed.

5. **Don't punish team members in front of others.** This causes the individual to lose face and is thus double punishment. Also, team members may not understand or agree with the reason for the punishment.

6. **Make the consequences equal to the behavior.** A slap on the wrist in response to undesirable behaviors may signal to team members that those behaviors are actually acceptable, and perhaps even desired. However, severe penalties may alienate team members, seeming inequitable. Team members may wonder how any infractions they make may be punished. As such, they may become risk averse and unwilling to take anything other than safe courses of action.

7. **Reinforce behaviors as soon as possible.** Immediate reinforcement is powerful.

8. **Make sure that the rewards you provide are actually what team members want.** People want different things, and we're often surprised to know what those things are. As such, use surveys or other means to learn what they really want. Also, consider **cafeteria-style benefit plans**. In these plans, employees can choose from a range of alternative benefits. For instance, employees of differing ages or marital status may desire different benefits. One employee may choose all salary with no other benefits; another may choose the total allowance for pension and insurance contributions. As an example, Du Pont's U.S. employees can choose from a menu of medical, dental, and life insurance options as well as financial planning assistance.[31]

Social Learning

Both classical conditioning and operant conditioning focus on learning from our own experiences. However, much of what we learn comes from the experiences of others. Because others have been burned by a hot stove or have failed in their attempts to start a new company or have found that certain leader behaviors are ineffective, we don't have to get burned ourselves to learn what they learned. Instead, we can benefit from social learning. **Social learning** is learning that occurs through any of a variety of social channels—newspapers, books, television, conversations with family members, friends, teammates, and so on. Social learning accounts for much of our knowledge.

Need Theories of Motivation

All people have needs. A **need** is something that people require. **Satisfaction** is the condition of need fulfillment, such as when a hungry person eats or when a person driven by the desire for success finally achieves that goal. Need theories of motivation see motivation as flowing from unsatisfied needs. That is, motivation is the result of dissatisfaction (and, as such, it is important not to confuse motivation and satisfaction). As seen in Figure 4-4, when a need is not satisfied, we try to find a way to address that need. If those need-satisfying goals are attained, satisfaction results. If not, alternative need-satisfying goals are sought. In the case of repeated frustration, people may seek to reduce their frustration by use of a variety of defense mechanisms.[32] Those **defense mechanisms** are ways in which the person may try to reduce the tensions caused by frustration. These mechanisms might involve physically leaving the source of frustration (e.g., through absenteeism or turnover), mentally leaving (e.g., through apathy or daydreaming), or striking back (e.g., by slowing down on the job or by making negative comments about the company).

Psychologist Abraham Maslow did much of the classic work on motivation theory. He believed that the key to motivating people is understanding that they are motivated by needs, which are arranged in a hierarchy of importance. This hierarchy is known as **Maslow's hierarchy of needs**.[33] Maslow theorized that people seek to satisfy needs at the lowest level of the

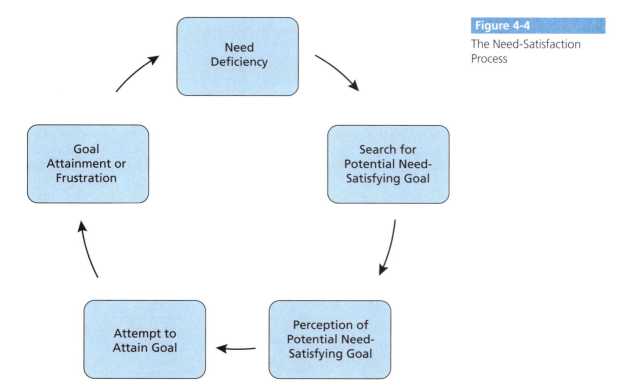

Figure 4-4

The Need-Satisfaction Process

hierarchy before trying to satisfy needs on the next-higher level. What needs motivate a person depends on where that person is on the hierarchy at that time. In particular, Maslow believed that motivation should be examined in terms of five sets of needs:

1. **Physiological.** The need for food, sleep, water, air, and sex
2. **Security.** The need for safety, family stability, and economic security
3. **Social or affiliation.** The need to belong, to interact with others, to have friends, and to love and be loved
4. **Esteem.** The need for respect and recognition from others
5. **Self-actualization.** The need to realize one's potential, to grow, to be creative, and to accomplish

Maslow argued that as we satisfy any one of these five sets of needs, that set becomes less important to us and motivates us less. Eating, for example, satisfies the physiological need of hunger and leaves us less interested in food. In the same way, the need for affiliation and friendship is strongest for someone who feels excluded. Once this person makes friends, the need to belong becomes less important.

Climbing the Hierarchy
Maslow believed that these needs were arranged in a hierarchy from lowest to highest, as shown in Figure 4-5. He suggested that we climb the hierarchy. That is, we first satisfy our basic physiological needs. Only when we have done so are we motivated by the needs at the next-higher level of the hierarchy—the need for safety and security. When this group of needs is met, we move on to the next level, and so on. This move up the hierarchy as needs are satisfied is called **satisfaction progression**.

Lessons from Maslow's Hierarchy
Maslow's view of motivation shows that we work for many reasons besides the paycheck that buys us food and shelter. We work so that we can be with others, gain respect, and realize our potential. Also, Maslow's hierarchy emphasizes that people differ in the needs that are currently most important to them. For example, a worker faced with heavy mortgage payments may focus primarily on security needs. Another, with the mortgage paid off, may

Figure 4-5

Maslow's Hierarchy of Needs

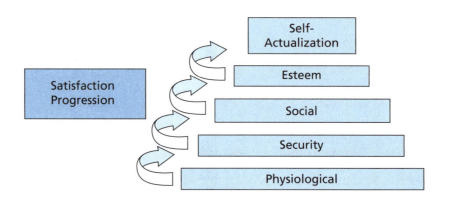

be more concerned about social needs. While the former employee might be strongly motivated by money, the latter may be more motivated by being included in a team. Finally, the hierarchy makes it clear that need importance and need satisfaction are very different things—need importance (which drives motivation) often flows from *dissatisfaction.*

Maslow's need hierarchy provides useful perspectives for understanding motivation, and it has been widely accepted. However, more recent research suggests that it is only partially correct. For instance, satisfying needs at the top of the hierarchy generally does not lead to a decrease in motivation. Instead, people who are able to self-actualize become *more* motivated to take on self-actualizing activities. Also, the climb up the hierarchy is rather unpredictable; once we've satisfied needs at the lowest levels, needs at any of the other levels may become more important to us. Further, if needs at one level of the hierarchy are continually frustrated, individuals may revert their focus to needs lower on the hierarchy. For instance, someone whose social needs are frustrated by not being able to get a date may conclude, "I think I'll get a pizza." This is called **frustration regression.**

Setting Effective Goals[34]

Goals serve many important functions in teams, including these: [35]

- **Goals let team members know what they are expected to do.**
- **Goals relieve boredom.** Consider how boring most video games would be if you didn't keep score and try to reach goals.
- **Reaching goals and receiving positive feedback leads to increased liking for the task and satisfaction with job performance.**
- **Attaining goals leads to recognition by team members, supervisors, and others.**
- **Attaining goals leads to feelings of increased self-confidence, pride in achievement, and willingness to accept future challenges.**

Research on goal setting has yielded some clear and useful findings. Here are some of those findings and guidelines for effective goal setting (see Figure 4-6).[36]

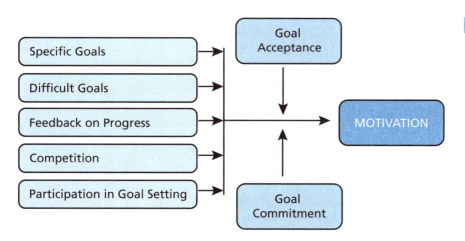

Figure 4-6

Key Goal Characteristics

One famous example of a successful specific goal was President John F. Kennedy's 1961 goal of putting a man on the moon by the end of the decade.

- **Set specific goals.** Quite simply, specific goals lead to higher performance than just "do-your-best" goals. In fact, these kinds of goals have about the same effect as no goals at all. Imagine a runner circling a track, shouting to her coach, "How much farther do I have to go?" A reply from the coach of "Just do your best" won't help much.

  Specific goals are sometimes so powerful they overwhelm other things. If some goals are specific and others are not, the nonspecific goals won't receive much emphasis. Also, there is a danger that a manager may really care about X but, because Y is easier to quantify, will set goals for Y instead.

- **Set difficult goals.** The more difficult the goal, the better the task performance. However, team members must believe the goal is attainable, or they will not accept it. Also, people pursue many goals at the same time. If they believe one is too difficult, they will focus on other, more attainable goals. Interestingly, when people face difficult goals, they engage in more problem analysis and creative behavior than when faced with simple goals. So they work *both* harder and smarter.

- **Give feedback on goal progress.** Feedback keeps behavior on track. Feedback may also stimulate greater effort. A video game without a score would soon be abandoned. And when people get feedback concerning their performance, they tend to set personal or team-improvement goals.

- **Consider the effects of peer competition for goal attainment.** If employees are working toward individual goals, such as salespersons pursuing independent sales goals, competition for goal attainment may be useful. However, competition can hurt if tasks are interdependent, as in teams. In such a case, an employee's attempts to excel may harm the performance of another. Also, if competition focuses on the quantity of output, quality may suffer.

- **Use participation in goal setting.** Participation isn't a panacea. Some people simply don't like to participate, and in some situations (e.g., when under severe time constraints) participation may be inappropriate. In general, though, participation increases understanding and acceptance of the goal. Being involved in goal setting often leads to the setting of more difficult goals, which may in turn lead to higher performance.[37]

- **Encourage goal acceptance. Goal acceptance** is the degree to which individuals or teams accept particular goals as their own. If a goal is not accepted, the other goal attributes don't matter. Goal acceptance is likely to be lacking if goals are seen as unreachable, or no benefit is evident from reaching the goal.
- **Encourage goal commitment. Goal commitment** is the degree to which individuals are dedicated to trying to reach the goals they have adopted. Like goal acceptance, it is a necessary condition for goal-directed effort. Goal commitment is affected by the same factors as goal acceptance. Those factors influence goal acceptance before the goal is set and goal commitment once the individual or team is pursuing the goal.

Team-Based Rewards

As we said earlier in this chapter, it is important that individual contributions to teams be recognized and rewarded. At the same time, a focus only on individual performance may disrupt teamwork.[38] Flattening of organizations, alterations in the organization of work, and changing technology have created interdependencies between jobs that make it difficult to isolate individual contributions.[39] As such, it is also critical that rewards somehow be tied to team performance.

Types of Team-Based Rewards

There are several ways to tie individual compensation to something larger than one's own performance. For example, with **profit sharing** employees receive payments, in addition to their regular salary and bonuses, tied to the company's profitability. However, such rewards are generally seen as largely independent of individual or team performance and thus they do little to motivate team members. Here, we will focus specifically on rewards tied directly to performance of the team.

Potential Benefits of Team-Based Rewards

Team-based rewards may support team goals, reinforce a team-based culture, foster cooperation among team members, and promote team productivity. They may also overcome the problems associated with large-group-level reward plans such as profit sharing.[40] Small-group-level reward systems, such as a team bonus for exceeding a target level of performance, more clearly link performance to rewards and may be more powerful motivators.[41]

Potential Limitations of Team-Based Rewards

While team-based rewards have many potential benefits, they may also introduce problems. For example, some team members may resent having their rewards tied to other team members' contributions. They may feel constrained by slower or less capable team members, and they may fear that team rewards will cause others to free ride, forcing them to do more than their fair share. Team-based rewards may also foster competition between teams, causing team members to focus on their performance at the expense of the other team's performance. For instance, team members may be reluctant to help other teams or to share important information with them. Just as team

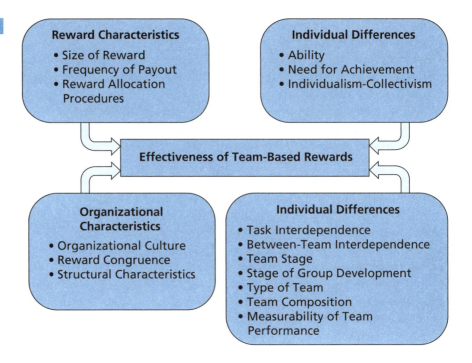

Figure 4-7

Factors Influencing
Effectiveness of Team-
Based Rewards

members must work toward common goals, teams—especially if they are
interdependent—must work toward common organizational goals.

Deciding Whether to Use Team-Based Rewards

After reviewing the literature on team-based rewards, Jacquelyn DeMatteo
et al. concluded that such rewards are more likely to be effective in some
situations than in others. In particular, those authors argued that the effectiveness of team-based rewards is likely to depend on reward characteristics,
individual differences, organizational characteristics, and team characteristics, as shown in Figure 4-7.[42]

For example, team-based rewards are likely to be more effective when
they are substantial, administered frequently, and appear to have been allocated equitably. Further, some individuals, such as those who feel they have
high levels of ability, those with high needs for achievement who want personal control, and those who have individualistic rather than collectivist
orientations (see Chapter 5), may prefer individual rewards. Team-based
rewards are likely to be best received in organizations with a collectivist
culture and resisted in an organization characterized by high **power distance** (with a strong emphasis on the hierarchy and deference to superiors).
Finally, to be effective, team-based rewards must fit with other elements of
organizational strategy.

Using Team-Based Rewards

Here are some guidelines for use of team-based rewards.[43]

- **Involve team members in the design and implementation of the reward
  system.** Members may contribute valuable ideas. In addition, participation enhances acceptance and understanding.

- **Clearly communicate about the reward system.** For example, what is the reason for the reward system? What percentage of rewards are individual and team (and why)? How is the system fair?
- **Reward both individual and team performance.** Some focus on individual contributions is important in order to minimize perceptions of inequity. However, rewards tied to team performance are also needed.
- **Align individual and team performance metrics.** To the degree possible, team and individual performance should have similar metrics. For example, when Home Depot overhauled its performance management system, its first step was to standardize metrics to apply across the board. It scrapped the more than 150 different appraisal forms then being used and developed new metrics in four outcome categories: financial, customer, operational/process, and people. Those same categories apply at the level of the store manager, the team, and the individual.
- **Include peer reviews in evaluations.** Peer assessments provide valuable information and reinforce the degree to which teamwork is seen as important.
- **Clearly articulate the organization's overall goals.** Teams need to understand how they fit into the larger mission of the organization. Show how the team's performance is important in attaining the company's goals.
- **Build relationships.** While team leaders aim to foster strong team performance, they must also recognize individual efforts. When individuals know their inputs are recognized and supported, they are more willing to contribute to the team.

Expectancy Theory

Expectancy theory is an approach to motivation that examines the links in the process from effort to ultimate rewards.[44] At base, expectancy theory says that motivation requires three things:

1. The individual must believe that he or she is able to effectively perform the task (this is called an **expectancy perception**). If not, why try? Expectancy will be low if the individual doesn't feel that he or she has the ability to perform the job well, is constrained by the situation, or doesn't know what is expected.
2. The individual must believe that effective performance will be tied to task outcomes (these links are termed **instrumentalities**), such as increased pay, security, esteem of team members, or approval of the team leader. If not, why does good performance matter?
3. The individual must value those outcomes (the values of outcomes are called **valences**). If not, why try to achieve them?

Expectancy theory provides important implications for team leaders and others. For example:

1. **Recognize that three conditions are necessary to encourage motivation to perform.** These are valued rewards, a perceived link of effort to performance (expectancy), and perceived links of performance to valent

outcomes (instrumentalities). If *any* of those elements is missing, motivation will be low.

2. **Assess perceptions of each of those conditions**. Making such an assessment can provide extremely useful information. For example, you may find that employees don't really value some of the rewards you have been using or that they don't believe their efforts will translate into performance or their performance into rewards. Conversely, you may be surprised to find that employees place great value on rewards that could be easily and inexpensively provided or that employees have surprisingly strong expectancy or instrumentality perceptions.

3. **Identify gaps between employee and management perceptions**. For example, a common response of management upon learning that employees don't believe their rewards are tied to their performance levels is, "They're wrong! We tightly link pay and other rewards to performance." From an expectancy theory perspective, whether or not the employees' perceptions are wrong is irrelevant; perceptions drive behavior. If rewards actually are tied to behaviors in ways that employees don't recognize, management's job is to convince employees of that fact.

4. **Ask what factors may be weakening expectancy perceptions**. Do employees know what they are supposed to do? Have they been properly trained? Are there characteristics of the situation—resource constraints, poor tools, or whatever—that make it difficult for employees to perform well regardless of their efforts?

5. **Ask what factors may be weakening instrumentality perceptions**. Is it true that rewards really aren't tied to performance? Or is management simply not communicating well with employees about the nature of the reward system?

6. **If employees appear to be poorly motivated, work backward**. Try to determine which of the expectancy theory conditions may be lacking.

Equity Theory

It goes without saying that we should treat people fairly. What, though, do we mean by fair? Certainly, fairness has something to do with not cheating others or blatantly playing favorites. But fairness is more complex than that. There are at least two important types of fairness: distributive fairness and procedural fairness. These deal, in turn, with fairness in regard to the sorts of things we get and the processes used to allocate rewards.

Equity theory, which focuses on distributive fairness, is one of a family of theories based on the idea that people want to maintain balance.[45] By focusing on the balance of the inputs, or contributions, people make to the outcomes they receive, equity theory helps us understand how employees determine whether they are being treated fairly. Employee perceptions of fairness influence their level of motivation and the specific behaviors that they are motivated to engage in.

According to equity theorists, people want to maintain distributive fairness. **Distributive fairness** exists when someone thinks people are getting what they deserve—not less, certainly, but *not more either*. According to equity theory, people feel uncomfortable when they get less than they deserve (because they feel cheated) or more than they deserve (because they feel guilty). Research evidence supports this contention.[46] Some people—called *equity sensitives*—are especially focused on equity considerations.[47] There are several reasons why people want to demonstrate distributive fairness:[48]

- **When people experience a situation they feel is not fair, they experience an unpleasant state of tension.** Restoration of distributive fairness reduces that tension.
- **Some people try to be fair because they think others will reward them for being fair.**
- **Behaving fairly may bolster a person's self-esteem.**
- **Most people find it comforting to believe that life is fair. By giving others what we think they deserve, we strengthen that belief.**

Employers may have other, more specific reasons for wanting to treat their employees fairly.[49] They may, for instance, want to conform to business norms, to attract superior workers to the company, to motivate employees to produce, and to develop trust.

Quite simply, equity theory says that when people feel a condition of inequity (again, both overrewarded and underrewarded), they will take actions to restore equity. People determine equity by considering how the ratio of what they receive (outcomes) to their contributions (inputs) relates to that of some comparison other (e.g., a teammate, some average). Outcomes are anything the individual values while inputs are anything the individual feels he or she is contributing. J. Stacy Adams (based on the writings of Aristotle) proposed the following equation for determining equity:[50]

$$\frac{O_p}{I_p} = \frac{O_o}{I_o}$$

Where:

O_p is the person's perception of the outcomes he or she is receiving
I_p is the person's perception of his or her inputs
O_o is the person's perception of the outcomes some comparison person (called a comparison other) is receiving
I_o is the person's perception of the inputs of the comparison other

In the case of underreward inequity, an individual could attempt to restore equity by varying any of the values in the equation (note that these are all perceptions). For example, the individual might try to increase his or her outcomes (perhaps by demanding and getting a raise); the individual might reduce his or her inputs (perhaps by slowing down on the job or by refusing to do unpaid overtime work); the individual might perceptually distort his or her inputs or outcomes (maybe by reasoning that he or she is getting things out of the job that weren't previously considered, or by downgrading the value of inputs). He or she could also, among other things, change the comparison other or leave the frustrating situation. The bottom line, then, is that inequity may lead to dissatisfaction, frustration, and undesirable attitudes or behaviors.

Intrinsic Motivation

There is more to motivation than the carrot and the stick. Use of rewards and punishments to motivate team members is sometimes effective, and perhaps even necessary, for team success. However, motivation through the design of the work may often be more powerful and perhaps even more ethical than such approaches. That is, the job itself can be designed in ways to motivate without use of externally administered rewards and punishments. This is the purpose of **job enrichment**. Such job enrichment would be expected to enhance **intrinsic motivation**, motivation from the job itself. Unlike things such as pay, which are forms of **extrinsic motivation**, intrinsic motivation comes from the job itself—just doing the job is motivating, independent of other rewards.[51]

Job characteristics theory (JCT) attempts to explain how characteristics of their jobs affect people's work behavior and attitudes. It also identifies the conditions under which these effects are likely to be strongest.[52] Figure 4-8 shows the **Job Characteristics Model**. The *core job dimensions*—things that can be directly influenced by team leaders—are characteristics of the job itself that are believed to be key influences on employee intrinsic motivation.

- **Skill variety.** The degree to which the job requires employees to perform a wide range of operations in their work and/or the degree to which employees must use a variety of equipment and procedures in their work.

Figure 4-8

The Job Characteristics Model

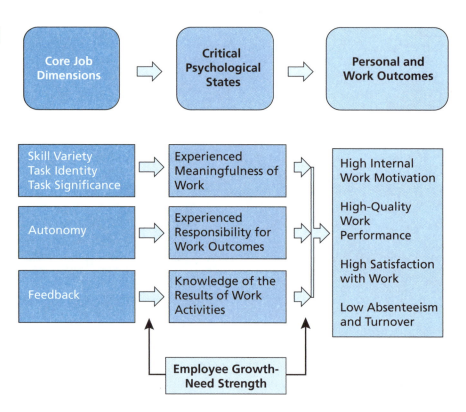

- **Autonomy.** The extent to which employees have a major say in scheduling their work, selecting the equipment they will use, and deciding on procedures they will follow.[53]
- **Task identity.** The extent to which employees do an entire piece of work and can clearly identify the result of their efforts.
- **Task significance.** The extent to which the job has a strong impact on the lives and work of other people.
- **Feedback.** The degree to which employees receive information from the job itself while they are working that reveals how well they are performing on the job.

According to the model, the core task dimensions have an impact on three **critical psychological states:** experienced meaningfulness of work, experienced responsibility for work outcomes, and knowledge of the actual results of work activities. That is, team members need to feel their work is meaningful and that they are in charge of their work outcomes, and they must learn about how they are doing.

The **Job Characteristics Model** provides some clear guidelines for team leaders and others involved in job design. First, of course, it highlights the need to enhance intrinsic motivation by reinforcing team members' beliefs that they are in control of work outcomes (experienced responsibility) and that their jobs are meaningful (experienced meaningfulness of work), and by making sure team members know how well they are doing (knowledge of the results of work). It also suggests that such sources of intrinsic motivation are especially important for members who have a strong need for self-actualization (high growth-need strength).

Group Potency and Collective Efficacy

At the individual level, those who are confident that they can successfully master their tasks at a given level have high self-efficacy. **Self-efficacy** is an individual's appraisal of his or her task-specific capability to achieve a particular level of performance in goal accomplishment. **Team** or **collective efficacy** is self-efficacy at the team level. According to Albert Bandura, who introduced the concept, "**Collective efficacy** is defined as a group's shared belief in its conjoint capabilities to organize and execute the courses of action required to produce given levels of attainment."[54]

Collective efficacy influences a group to initiate action, identifies the amount of effort to expend, and determines how long the group's effort will be sustained. Note that collective efficacy is task specific: it relates to the group's shared belief that it can perform the specific task at a given level. Further, collective efficacy is not an aggregation of team members' self-efficacies. Instead, it is "a shared belief in the team's collective capability to organize and execute courses of action required to produce given levels of goal attainment."[55]

Group potency, unlike collective efficacy, is generalized across tasks.[56] It is assessed by statements such as "No task is too tough for this team."[57] Teams with high group potency are likely to develop high collective efficacy. That is, general feelings or beliefs about team capabilities are likely to transfer to specific tasks. Figure 4-9 shows how group potency, collective efficacy, and group performance are linked.

Figure 4-9

Group Potency, Collective Efficacy, and Group Performance

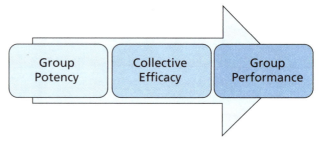

Source: Based on A.D. Stajkovic, D. Lee, and A.J. Nyberg, "Collective Efficacy, Group Potency, and Group Performance," *Journal of Applied Psychology*, 2009, *94(3)*, p. 822.

Many of the things we discuss in this chapter may affect group potency and collective efficacy. For instance, successful socialization, development of high levels of trust, proper training, and effective leadership can all contribute. In general, individual self-efficacy results from successful task performance (called **enactive attainment**), seeing similar others mastering the task (called **vicarious experience**), and getting positive feedback and encouragement (called **verbal persuasion**). Those sources of efficacy should play similar roles at the level of the team.

Leading Teams

Leadership skills are, of course, critical for team leaders. However, all team members will sometimes be assigned leadership roles, and they will often play informal leadership roles. As such, these are extremely important skills for all team members.

Leadership Defined

Leadership is the ability to influence others toward the achievement of goals. Leadership, then, relates to the ability to influence others toward desired outcomes. This suggests that leaders may not always be influencing but can do so when needed. It suggests, too, that leadership is about dealing with others and, as such, that effective leaders need a variety of interpersonal skills. Finally, leadership is related to goal achievement; the leader exerts influence not for its own sake but to yield desired outcomes.

Emerging Perspectives

Recent decades have witnessed major changes in views of leadership. Examples include the following:

- While early leadership approaches emphasized the traits of successful leaders—who successful leaders *are*—newer approaches ask how successful leaders behave—what successful leaders *do.*
- Early approaches to leadership tended to take a universalistic perspective, asking, "What works?" Newer approaches, recognizing that situational factors, such as followers' needs and skills and the various characteristics of the task, must be considered, ask instead, "What works when?"
- Early leadership approaches asked how a leader influences followers. Newer perspectives recognize that, just as leaders are influencing followers, followers are also influencing leaders.

- **While early leadership approaches tended to assume that leaders treat their various followers in similar ways—some leaders are nice, others appear to be bossy, still others are strict, and so on—more recent approaches recognize that leaders may—for good or bad reasons—treat different followers differently.** They may be more considerate with some followers than with others, give some more direction than others, let some participate more in decision making, and so on.
- **While leadership approaches initially focused on the relationship of leaders to their followers, modern views of leadership are more inclusive.** They recognize that those whom leaders influence may include not just subordinates but also many others, including team members and perhaps even hierarchical superiors. Leadership does not have to face downward.
- **Most early approaches to leadership tended to consider how a leader might influence others in a series of transactions.** That is, they viewed leaders and followers as engaging in exchanges in which the leader would offer certain things—rewards, support, protection, or whatever—in return for desired follower behaviors. Newer leadership approaches recognize that, while important, this transactional view is incomplete. Leaders must take actions to transform followers and organizations by communicating values, inspiring, being intellectually stimulating, and showing confidence in the face of crisis. Such transformational leader behaviors may often be critical to the life of an organization.

Leadership and Power

When we think about power we often may focus on use of rewards and threats. However, there are in fact a variety of bases of power in organizations. Successful team leaders develop a power toolbox and draw from it as appropriate. Some bases of interpersonal power include those in this list:[58]

- **Legitimate power** results when one person thinks it is legitimate, or right, for another to give orders or otherwise exert force.
- **Reward power** is based on the perceived ability to reward. It depends on one person's ability to administer desired outcomes to another and to decrease or remove outcomes that are not desired.
- **Coercive power** is based on one person's perceived ability to affect punishment that another receives.
- **Referent power** comes from the feeling of identity, or oneness, that one person has for another, or the desire for such identity. The commercial picturing Michael Jordan and saying, "Be like Mike" was a concise and direct appeal to referent power.
- **Expert power** is based on one person's perception that another has needed relevant knowledge in a given area. For instance, doctors, lawyers, and computer specialists may all have expert power.

Leader Traits

Early approaches to leadership focused on leader traits. They asked, "What is a leader like?" or "What is a successful leader like?" Thousands of studies have tried to answer these questions (and note that they *are* distinct questions). That is, some researchers attempted to determine who *become* leaders while others asked about the traits of a *successful* leader. Those considering the first question—often sociologists—focused on things such as socioeconomic status, age, and physical characteristics. They found, for instance, that taller, more physically attractive individuals from families with higher socioeconomic status were more likely to attain leadership positions. Those examining the traits of a successful leader assessed a broader array of traits. Some of those traits relate to physical factors, some to ability, many to personality, and still others to social characteristics. Of the traits, activity, intelligence, knowledge, dominance, and self-confidence are most often related to leader success, though findings were very inconsistent.

Unfortunately, most reviews of studies relating to leadership traits have concluded that the trait approach has not been fruitful.[59] One early survey of this literature noted that of all traits that showed up in one study or another as related to leadership effectiveness, only five percent were common to four or more studies.[60] In another early study, some high school students emerged as leaders on one type of task, and others emerged as leaders on other tasks.[61] These findings suggest that the traits needed by leaders may depend on the situation.

Despite the generally unsuccessful search for leader traits, the hunt continues. Perhaps the most promising approach is to focus on the roles of the Big Five personality dimensions, discussed in Chapter 5. For example, one statistical review of past research examined relationships of the Big Five dimensions to leader emergence and leader effectiveness.[62] That review concluded that extraversion, openness to experience, agreeableness, and conscientiousness were positively related to leadership while neuroticism was negatively related. Extraversion had the most consistent links to leadership across study settings and leadership criteria.

A basic concern with trait approaches relates to the question of how the findings can be used. Since traits are relatively stable, it is unlikely that leaders can develop them through training. So while information concerning traits of successful leaders might be useful to select leaders and place them in suitable positions, it is otherwise of limited value. In part, this is because trait approaches consider only characteristics of the leader while ignoring the characteristics of followers and situations.

Before moving on, complete Skills Practice 4.1 on the text website to gain some insights into yourself as a leader.

Key Leader Behaviors and Skills

With a few exceptions, then, following trait approaches to leadership hasn't been very fruitful. At one level, this shouldn't be surprising. For example, we might expect different leadership traits to be important in military crisis situations than in leading a team of volunteers for Habitat for Humanity. For another, most of the traits that have been considered are, by definition, difficult to change (traits are fixed while states vary). So, we must try to *behave* like successful leaders. While this may be difficult, it at least holds promise: we can more easily change what we do than who we are. There have been many attempts to find important leader behaviors, and a few promising approaches have received considerable attention.

Autocratic and Democratic Styles

One early approach to leadership considered the degree to which leaders were autocratic or democratic. **Autocratic leaders** make decisions themselves, without inputs from others. **Democratic leaders** let followers participate in making decisions. Thus, as shown in Figure 4-10, autocratic and democratic styles are at opposite ends of a single continuum, differing in degree of delegation of decision-making authority. They differ *only* on this dimension, not necessarily on other variables, such as sensitivity and caring. While there may be a tendency to think of democratic leaders as more caring than autocratic leaders, there are benevolent autocrats who sincerely believe—correctly or not—that they are in the best position to make decisions that will benefit their subordinates and the organization. There are also uncaring democratic leaders who delegate responsibility in an attempt to avoid taking personal accountability for decisions.

Democratic style is consistently linked to higher levels of follower satisfaction. However, the relationship of style to performance is more complex. Democratic style is usually positively, but weakly, related to productivity. There are many factors that determine whether a democratic style is appropriate, including the nature of the task and the personalities of subordinates. When tasks are simple and repetitive, participation has little effect, because "there is little to participate about."[63] When subordinates are intelligent and desire independence, participation is especially important.

Deciding on the appropriate level of participation is extremely important. Participation is empowering and satisfying, and it generates enthusiasm for the decisions that are reached. On the other hand, participation takes time away from other activities. Also, some people don't like to participate, and most people don't want to get involved in decisions they care little about.

Consideration and Initiating Structure

Research makes it clear that effective leaders show concern for *both* the task and the people they lead. Without concern for people, satisfaction, motivation, and team spirit will plummet, and performance will ultimately suffer. Without concern for the task, the job won't get done. Two sets of leader behaviors—consideration and initiating structure—address these concerns.

- **Consideration** is behavior that shows friendship, mutual trust, respect, and warmth. Considerate leaders are friendly and approachable, look out for the personal welfare of team members, back up the members in their actions, and find time to listen to them.
- **Initiating structure** is behavior that helps clarify the task and get the job done. Initiating leaders provide definite standards of performance, set goals, organize work, emphasize meeting deadlines, and coordinate the work of team members.

Autocratic   **Democratic**

Low   **High**

Degree of Participation

Figure 4-10

Autocratic and Democratic Styles

Figure 4-11

Consideration and
Initiating Structure

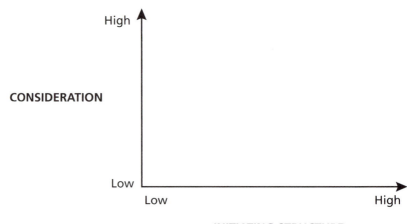

It would be easy—and wrong—to assume that these are somehow conflicting sets of behaviors. That is, it might seem that considerate leaders don't provide a lot of structure or that structuring leaders tend to be inconsiderate. In fact, there is no trade-off between consideration and initiating structure. As shown in Figure 4-11, skillful leaders can exhibit *both* sets of behaviors. *Should* you as a team leader exhibit both? The answer is that you should exhibit them *as needed*. For example, if team members are highly motivated, know their jobs, and have worked well together in the past, initiating structure may not help much. It may, in fact, be resented. The key is that you as a team leader must show *concern* for people and the task, assess the situation, and then draw on your arsenal of behaviors as needed.

In general, research shows that both task and socioemotional leadership are needed for team effectiveness. The task leader focuses on getting the job done while the socioemotional leader (not necessarily the same person) is concerned with maintaining positive relationships in the team, fostering team cohesion, and minimizing dysfunctional intrateam conflict.

When Is Leadership Needed?

Good leaders know when to adopt leadership roles and when to back off. Steve Kerr and John Jermier introduced the concepts of **substitutes for leadership** and **neutralizers of leadership**.[64] Figure 4-12 lists some of these substitutes and neutralizers. The exhibit indicates, for instance, that followers with high levels of ability or tasks that are well structured serve as substitutes for structuring leadership, while follower need for independence neutralizes the effects of such leadership. Similarly, relationship-oriented, supportive, considerate leadership will be neutralized when subordinates have high needs for independence, while tasks that are intrinsically satisfying and cohesive work groups serve as substitutes for such leadership.[65]

Skills Practice 4.2 on the text website will help you develop skill in identifying substitutes for and neutralizers of leadership and matching appropriate leadership behaviors to those situations.

Characteristic	Leadership Type	
	Relationship-Oriented, Considerate Leadership	Task-Oriented, Directive Leadership
Of the Follower		
1. Ability, experience, training, knowledge		*Substitute*
2. Need for Independence	*Neutralizer*	*Neutralizer*
3. "Professional" orientation	*Substitute*	*Substitute*
Of the Task		
1. Unambiguous and routine		*Substitute*
2. Standardized methods		*Substitute*
3. Intrinsically satisfying	*Substitute*	
Of the Organization		
1. Formalization (explicit plans, goals, and areas of responsibility)		*Substitute*
2. Inflexibility (rigid, unbending rules and procedures)		*Neutralizer*
3. Closely knit, cohesive teams	*Substitute*	*Substitute*

Figure 4-12

Some Substitutes for and Neutralizers of Leadership

Source: Based on Kerr & Jermier (1978), p. 378.

TEAMS IN THE NEWS: The Chilean Mine Disaster

The Chilean Mine Disaster offers a dramatic example of the power of team leadership and teamwork under conditions of tremendous time pressure, threat, and stress. On the afternoon of August 5, 2010, more than 700,000 metric tons of rock collapsed, blocking the central passage to the tunnels in the San José copper-gold mine in Chile's Altacama Desert. A second earthquake followed 2 days later. Thirty-three men were trapped deep underground, their location and condition unknown. It was feared that all had died in the collapse or, if alive, that they would surely starve.

Luis Urzua, the shift boss who had been on the job for just 2 months, immediately organized the mine into a society, with discipline and routine. The miners had very limited food and water and only two oxygen tanks. All miners were assigned jobs, however mundane, and were not allowed to just sit and wait. Urzua organized the miners into three shifts, and he took an inventory of tools, equipment, and other resources and determined ways they could be used. The miners engaged in ceremonies and rituals, holding church services, praying, and singing Elvis Presley songs. Small victories—such as the first sighting of the rescue capsule—were causes for celebration. While Urzua was clearly the leader, decision-making processes were democratic, with all members' inputs valued.

The ensuing recovery process took a grueling 69 days, including a 17-day search to locate and contact the miners and a 52-day rescue in which the miners were sustained and pulled up to safety. Following a depressing series of failures in trying to locate the miners, the drilling engineers pulled up a drill bit that had been painted orange by the miners and found there were notes attached. One of the notes read, *"Estamos bien en el refugio, los 33"* ("We are well in the shelter, the 33 of us.)" The nation celebrated. The miners now shared stories about their lives, their bonds tightened, and they developed a common identity, *Los 33*. They vowed to focus on the possibility of rescue and to maintain their dignity, even if the rescue effort failed.

The Chilean mine disaster represented a multiteam system, with one team working on the rescue above the surface, and the trapped miners working below the surface. Each team was well coordinated, efficient, and purposeful. Further, there were high levels of communication and coordination at and between all levels. The rescuers connected miners with experts, communicated with relatives, and sought help from neighboring countries and global partners. National support was clear and total.

Ultimately, as more than a billion people watched in awe worldwide, all team members were rescued, most of them in very good health. Symbolically, after ensuring that all his team members were safe above ground, Urzua, the team leader, was the last to emerge.

Source: This is based in part on F. Rashid, A. C. Edmondson, & H. B. Leonard, "Leadership Lessons from the Chilean Mine Rescue," *Harvard Business Review*, July–August 2013, pp. 113–119; and, T. A. Scandura & M. M. Sharif, "Team Leadership: The Chilean Mine Case," *Management Faculty Articles and Papers*, Paper 13. http://scholarlyrepository.miami.edu/management_articles/13.

Transformational Leadership

The behaviors we have discussed to this point are critical to the effective functioning of teams and organizations. When we think about great leaders, though, we usually picture something more; we expect inspiration, conviction, and vision. These are the essence of transformational leadership.

Transformational leadership is based in the personal values, beliefs, and qualities of the leader. Transformational leaders broaden and elevate the interests of their followers, generate awareness and acceptance of the purposes and mission of the group, and stir followers to look beyond their own interests to the interests of others. Transformational leaders display the following five sets of behaviors.

- **Attributed charisma.** *Charisma* is a Greek word meaning "divinely inspired gift." Max Weber wrote that charismatic leaders reveal a transcendent mission or course of action that may be itself appealing to the potential followers but that is acted upon because the followers believe their leader is extraordinarily gifted. Leaders are seen as being charismatic when they display a sense of power and confidence, remain calm during crisis situations, and provide reassurance that obstacles can be overcome.
- **Idealized influence.** Leaders display idealized influence when they talk about their important values and beliefs; consider the moral and ethical consequences of their decisions; display conviction in their ideals, beliefs, and values; and model values in their actions.
- **Intellectual stimulation.** Intellectually stimulating leaders help followers recognize problems and find ways to solve them. They encourage followers to challenge the status quo. They champion change and foster creative deviance.
- **Inspirational leadership.** Napoleon Bonaparte is reputed to have said that a leader is a dealer in hope. Inspirational leaders give followers hope, energizing them to pursue a vision. They envision exciting new possibilities, talk optimistically about the future, express confidence that goals can be met, and articulate a compelling vision of the future.
- **Individualized consideration.** Transformational leaders do more than just "be nice." They show personal interest and concern in their *individual* followers, and they promote their followers' self-development. They coach their followers, serve as their mentors, and focus them on developing their strengths.

Transformational leadership requires new sets of skills.[66] Transformational leadership has to anticipate changes in the environment, develop skills in visioning and persuasion, be in touch with members' needs, effectively share power with team members, and build members' self-understanding skills and their ability to understand others.

We close here with two important points. First, these ways of behaving have consistently been shown to influence team performance, the satisfaction and motivation of team members, and many other important outcomes.[67] Second, these are all behaviors that a team leader *can* change. The leader can, for example, choose to pay more attention to team members, set inspirational goals, model his or her values, and provide reassurance to the team in the face of obstacles.

Now, assess your own transformational leader behaviors by completing Self-Assessment 4.1 on the text website.

The Language of Leadership

Transformational leaders must be able to inspire; communicate their vision, ideals, and beliefs; provide compelling reassurance; and challenge team members to think in new ways. To do all this, they must be masters of communication—they must speak the language of leadership.

Two aspects of the **language of leadership**—framing and rhetorical crafting—are crucial.[68] **Framing** is presenting the message—defining the purpose in a meaningful way. Two key elements of framing are amplifying values and belief amplification. **Amplifying values** is the process of identifying and elevating certain values as basic to the overall mission. **Belief amplification** is the process of emphasizing factors that support or impede actions taken to achieve desired values.

Rhetorical crafting is using symbolic language to give emotional power to the message. That is, the message provides a sense of direction, and rhetoric heightens its emotional appeal and makes it memorable. Rhetorical techniques of inspirational leaders include using metaphors, analogies, and stories, gearing language to the particular audience, and such speech techniques as alliteration, repetition, and rhythm.

Half a century ago, Martin Luther King, in his famous "I Have a Dream" speech, delivered on the steps of the Lincoln Memorial in 1963, sculpted a masterpiece of language in service of transformational leadership. He spoke of values he held dear—"the inalienable rights of life, liberty, and the pursuit of happiness," "the riches of freedom and the security of justice," the need to "forever conduct our struggle on the high plane of dignity and discipline."

King envisioned exciting new possibilities, speaking with passion of the day when "on the red hills of Georgia the sons of former slaves and the sons of former slave owners will be able to sit down together at a table of brotherhood." He assured his listeners that "with this faith we will be able to hew out of the mountain of despair a stone of hope." He recognized the individual needs and perspectives of his audience members, speaking of the "marvelous new militancy that has engulfed the Negro community" but also of "our white brothers." "We cannot walk alone," he warned. He used words of inclusion, hope, and faith, ending with his vision of the day when "all of God's children . . . will be able to join hands and sing, in the words of the old Negro spiritual, 'Free at last! Free at last! Thank God Almighty, we are free at last!'" He repeated key phrases again and again, and his voice rose in volume and emotion as the speech progressed. The passage of more than 50 years has not dimmed the power of King's message.

Leader Affect and Group Mood

We all have moods. We may have good moods or bad moods, and some of us may regularly have more of one than the other. **Group mood** is the group analogue.

Leaders help set the mood of the team. For one thing, of course, team leaders who are seen as effective and caring help create a positive team mood. Also, the leader's moods may transfer to team members. This **emotional contagion** spreads mood throughout the team.[69] Figure 4-13 presents Sigal Barsade's model of group emotional contagion. Barsade's model shows

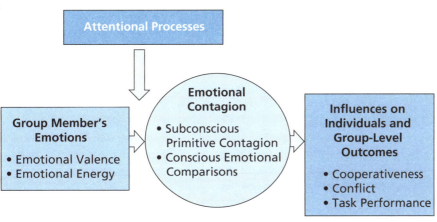

Figure 4-13

A Model of Group
Emotional Contagion

Source: S. G. Barsade. "The Ripple Effect: Emotional Contagion and Its Influence on Group Behavior," *Administrative Science Quarterly*, 2002, *47(4)*, pp. 650.

that strong, positive group emotions lead to both primitive contagion, which is the subconscious, automatic transfer of emotions from person to person, and the conscious focusing on others' emotions and responding in kind. The strengths of those links depend on the degree to which team members are paying attention to others (attentional processes in the model). In turn, positive group mood leads to heightened cooperation, reduced conflict, and increased task performance.[70]

Barsade discusses her research on emotions and other teams topics in the Team Scholar feature.

TEAM SCHOLAR

Sigal Barsade, University of Pennsylvania, Wharton School

Sigal Goland Barsade is the Jack Bernstein Professor of Management at the Wharton School at the University of Pennsylvania. She earned her PhD from the University of California–Berkeley. Her research focuses on the influence of emotions within organizations, including group emotion. She has served on the editorial boards of *Administrative Science Quarterly*, *Academy of Management Review*, *Organizational Behavior and Human Decision Processes*, and *Organization Science*. Her research has been published in journals such as *Administrative Science Quarterly*, *Organizational Behavior and Human Decision Processes*, *Research in Organizational Behavior*, *Journal of Applied Psychology*, *Journal of Personality and Social Psychology*, and *Psychological Science*.

What led to your interest in emotions in work teams?

My interest in work teams first came out of an experience at work with a phenomenon that I later identified to be a classic case of emotional contagion in groups. Prior to beginning my doctoral program, I worked in an organization in which one of my coworkers, Margaret, was very negative. I didn't report to her, but she worked around me. One day Margaret went on vacation, and I literally felt my shoulders lower and noticed that I was more relaxed and happy. The mood of all of the team members around me also became more relaxed and positive. Then Margaret came back, and everything returned to the stressful group environment that it had been prior to her vacation. This led me to become very interested specifically in emotional contagion in groups and how people can be "walking mood inductors" and infect each other with emotions the same way they do with viruses. It also led to a general interest in better understanding of how emotions operate in groups and influence team outcomes.

In general, what do you think are some of the most important roles of emotions in work teams?

Team emotions help to determine how team members will work together. But it is important to recognize the wide breadth and definition of team emotions. It can be the average of the team members' moods, or the range of moods on the team. My research has shown that the configuration of team affective personality or moods influences how teams work together and overall team and company performance. For example, in a study conducted with my colleagues professors Ward and Sonnenfeld, we found that the closer in trait-positive affect the CEO and his or her senior management team were, the more participative the CEO behaved with the team, the less conflict the team experienced—and the companies in which these teams headed were more profitable!

What do you see as some of the most important emerging issues regarding emotions in teams?

Emerging issues that we should be studying within the field of team emotions include gaining a greater understanding of the role of specific discrete emotions in teams; the meaning of emotions in virtual computer-mediated teams; how to take a more dynamic approach to the understanding of emotions as teams transition through different stages; and how to take emotions to the next collective level through the study of emotional culture in teams and organizations.

Summary and Integration

Key takeaways for this chapter include the following:

Maintaining a viable, motivated, productive team requires ongoing socialization of new members. The team leader, current team members, and the newcomer to the team all play important roles in the socialization process.

Trust is critical in teams. Various approaches can be used to enhance forms of trust.

Team training is effective in influencing cognitive, affective, process, and performance outcomes. The impact of training on those outcomes may depend on moderators such as training content, team membership ability, and team size.

Motivation is a key determinant of individual and team performance. Effective team leaders draw on an arsenal of tools to motivate their teams. For proper motivation in teams, some combination of individual and team rewards is needed.

All team members must sometimes adopt leadership roles. Both transactional and transformational leader behaviors are important.

Notes

1 H.-S. Choi & J.M. Levine, "Minority Influence in Work Teams: The Impact of Newcomers," *Journal of Experimental Social Psychology*, 2004, *40*, pp. 273–280.

2 R.C. Ziller & R.D. Behringer, "Assimilation of the Knowledgeable Newcomer under Conditions of Group Success and Failure," *Journal of Abnormal and Social Psychology,* 1960, *60*, pp. 288–291. See also C.J. Gersick & J.R. Hackman, "Habitual Routines in Task-Performing Groups," *Organizational Behavior and Human Decision Processes*, 1990, *47*, pp. 65–97.

3 W.B. Swann, Jr., Á. Gómez, D.C. Seyle, J.F. Morales, & C. Huici, "Identity Fusion: The Interplay of Personal and Social Identities in Extreme Group Behavior," *Journal of Personality and Social Psychology*, 2009, *96(5)*, pp. 995–1011.

4 S.W.J. Kozlowski & D.R. Ilgen, "Enhancing the Effectiveness of Work Groups and Teams," *Psychological Science in the Public Interest*, 2006, *7(3)*, pp. 77–124. The quote is from page 83.

5 L.A. DeChurch & J.R. Mesmer-Magnus, "The Cognitive Underpinnings of Effective Teamwork: A Meta-Analysis," *Journal of Applied Psychology*, 2010, *95(1)*, pp. 32–53. The quote is from page 33.

6 B.-C. Lim & K.J. Klein, "Team Mental Models and Team Performance: A Field Study of the Effects of Mental Model Similarity and Accuracy," *Journal of Organizational Behavior*, 2006, *27*, pp. 403–418.

7 These items are drawn from B.A. de Jong & T. Elfring, "How Does Trust Affect the Performance of Ongoing Teams?: The Mediating Role of Reflexivity, Monitoring, and Effort," *Academy of Management Journal*, 2010, *53(3)*, pp. 535–549.

8 See, for instance, K.T. Dirks & D.L. Ferrin, "The Role of Trust in Organizational Settings," *Organization Science*, *12(4)*, pp. 450–467; and, B.A. de Jong & T. Elfring, "How Does Trust Affect the Performance of Ongoing Teams?: The Mediating Role of Reflexivity, Monitoring, and Effort," *Academy of Management Journal*, 2010, *53(3)*, pp. 535–549.

9 See W.H. Cooper & M.J. Withey, "The Strong Situation Hypothesis," *Personality and Social Psychology Review*, 2009, *13(1,)* pp. 62–72.

10 S. Milgram, "Behavioral Study of Obedience," *Journal of Abnormal and Social Psychology*, 1963, *67(4)*, pp. 371–378; S. Milgram, *Obedience to Authority; An Experimental Review* (New York: Harper & Row, 1974); and, T. Blass, *The Man Who Shocked the World* (New York: Basic Books, 2004).

11 This listing of bases of trust is based primarily on R.M. Kramer, "Trust and Distrust in Organizations: Emerging Perspectives, Enduring Questions," *Annual Review of Psychology*, 1999, *50*, pp. 569–598.

12 For a thorough discussion, see E. Ostrom & J. Walker, *Trust and Reciprocity: Interdisciplinary Lessons from Experimental Research* (New York: Russell Sage Foundation, 2005).

13 Often attributed to Ernest Hemingway, this quotation is actually from *Necessity; A Lovely Day to Die; Root of All Evil* (1984) by Brian Garfield.

14   J.G. March & J.P. Olsen, *Rediscovering Institutions: The Organizational Basis of Politics* (New York: Free Press, 1989), p. 27.

15   D. Meyerson, K.E. Weick, & R.M. Kramer, "Swift Trust and Temporary Groups," in R.M. Kramer & T.R. Tyler (eds.), *Trust in Organizations: Frontiers in Theory and Research* (Thousand Oaks: CA: Sage, 1996), pp. 166–195.

16   K.T. Dirks & D.L. Ferrin, "The Role of Trust in Organizational Settings," *Organization Science*, *12(4)*, pp. 450–467.

17   S.C. Currall & M.J. Epstein, "The Fragility of Organizational Trust: Lessons from the Rise and Fall of Enron," *Organizational Dynamics*, 2003, *32(2)*, pp. 193–206.

18   L.A. Delise, C.A. Gorman, A.M. Brooks, J.R. Rentsch, & D. Steele-Johnson, "The Effects of Team Training on Team Outcomes: A Meta-Analysis," *Performance Improvement Quarterly*, 2010, *22(4)*, pp. 53–80.

19   E. Salas, D. DiazGranados, C. Klein, C.S. Burke, K.C. Stagl, G.F. Goodwin, & S.M. Halpin, "Does Team Training Improve Team Performance? A Meta-Analysis," *Human Factors*, 2008, *50*, pp. 903–933.

20   See, for instance, L.A. Delise, C.A. Gorman, A.M. Brooks, J.R. Rentsch, & D. Steele-Johnson, "The Effects of Team Training on Team Outcomes: A Meta-Analysis," *Performance Improvement Quarterly*, 2010, *22(4)*, pp. 53–80; and, E. Salas, N.J. Cooke, & M.A. Rosen, "On Teams, Teamwork, and Team Performance: Discoveries and Developments," *Human Factors*, 2008, *50(3)*, pp. 540–547.

21   J.R. Hollenbeck, D.S. DeRue, & R. Guzzo, "Bridging the Gap Between I/O Research and HR Practice: Improving Team Composition, Team Training, and Team Task Design," *Human Resource Management*, 2004, *43(4)*, pp. 353–366. The quote is from page 360.

22   C.E. Volpe, J.A. Cannon-Bowers, E. Salas, & P.E. Spector, "The Impact of Cross-Training on Team Effectiveness," *Human Factors*, 1996, *38*, pp. 87–100.

23   See E. Blickensderfer, J.A. Cannon-Bowers, & E. Salas, "Cross-Training and Team Performance," in J.A. Cannon-Bowers & E. Salas (eds.), *Making Decisions under Stress: Implications for Individual and Team Training* (Washington, D.C.: American Psychological Association, 1998), pp. 299–311; M.A. Marks, M.J. Sabella, C.S. Burke, & S.J. Zaccaro, "The Impact of Cross-Training on Team Effectiveness," *Journal of Applied Psychology*, 2002, *87(1)*, pp. 3–13. The quote is from page 4.

24   See J. Meister, "Gamification: Three Ways to Use Gaming for Recruiting, Training, and Health & Wellness," *Forbes*, May 21, 2012.

25   Press release, Gartner Group. http://www.gartner.com/newsroom/id/2251015.

26   See D. Schawbel, "Adam Penenberg: How Gamification is Going to Change the Workplace," *Forbes*, October 7, 2013.

27   For more on gaming applications at work, see R.E. Silverman, "Latest Game Theory: Mixing Work and Play," *Wall Street Journal*, October 10, 2011.

28   B.F. Skinner, *Contingencies of Reinforcement: A Theoretical Analysis* (East Norwalk, CT: Appleton-Century-Crofts, 1969). For an essay marking the 100th anniversary of Skinner's birth, see M. Greengrass, "100 years of B.F. Skinner," *Monitor on Psychology*, 2004, *35(3)*, p.80.

29   See A.D. Stajkovic & F. Luthans, "A Meta-Analysis of the Effects of Organizational Behavior Modification on Task Performance, 1975–95," *Academy of Management Journal*, 1997, *40(5)*, pp. 1122–1149; and, R.G. Miltenberger, *Behavior Modification: Principles and Procedures*, 5th ed. (Belmont, CA: Wadsworth, 2012).

30   W.C. Hamner & E.P. Hamner, "Behavior Modification on the Bottom Line," *Organizational Dynamics*, 1976, *4*, pp. 3–21.

31 See D. Sauey, "Group Life Insurance Is Backbone of Cafeteria Plans," *Credit Union Magazine*, October 2001, p. 60; C. Lee, "Customized Compensation Packages," *Journal of Property Management*, September/October 2001, *66(5)*, pp. 30–38; and, R.R. Sinclair, M.C. Leo, & C. Wright, "Benefit System Effects on Employees' Benefit Knowledge, Use, and Organizational Commitment," *Journal of Business and Psychology*, 2005, *20(1)*, pp. 3–29.

32 C. Argyris, *Integrating the Individual and the Organization* (New York: John Wiley & Sons, 1964).

33 A.H. Maslow, "A Theory of Human Motivation," *Psychological Review*, 1943, *50*, pp. 370–396. For more on Maslow's views, see E. Hoffman, "The Last Interview of Abraham Maslow," *Psychology Today*, January 1992, pp. 68–73; and, K. Dye, A.J. Mills, & T. Weatherbee, "Maslow: Man Interrupted: Reading Management Theory in Context," *Management Decision*, 2005, *43(10)*, pp. 1375–1395. For a recent summary, see K. Dye, "Needs Hierarchy," in E.H. Kessler (ed.), *Encyclopedia of Management Theory*, vol. 2 (Thousand Oaks, CA: Sage, 2013), pp. 503–505.

34 For a recent concise review of goal-setting theory, see E.A. Locke & G.P. Latham, "Goal-Setting Theory," in E.H. Kessler (ed.), *Encyclopedia of Management Theory*, vol. 1 (Thousand Oaks, CA: Sage, 2013), pp. 315–318.

35 This listing is drawn from E.A. Locke & G.P. Latham, *Goal Setting for Individuals, Groups, and Organizations* (Chicago: Science Research Associates, 1984). See also F. Paglieri & C. Castelfranchi, "More Than Control Freaks: Evaluative and Motivational Functions of Goals," *Behavioral and Brain Sciences*, 2008, *31*, pp. 35–36.

36 G.P. Latham & J.J. Baldes, "The 'Practical Significance' of Locke's Theory of Goal Setting," *Journal of Applied Psychology*, 1975, *60*, pp. 122–124. For an application in manufacturing, see T.C. Stansfield & C.O. Longenecker, "The Effects of Goal Setting and Feedback on Manufacturing Productivity: A Field Experiment," *International Journal of Productivity and Performance Management*, 2006, *55(3/4)*, pp. 346–358.

37 See, for instance, G.P. Latham, M. Erez, & E.A. Locke, "Resolving Scientific Disputes by the Joint Design of Crucial Experiments by the Antagonists: Application to the Erez-Latham Dispute Regarding Participation in Goal Setting," *Journal of Applied Psychology*, 1988, *73*, pp. 753–772. See also, G.P. Latham & E.A. Locke, "Enhancing the Benefits and Overcoming the Pitfalls of Goal Setting," *Organizational Dynamics*, 2006, *35(4)*, pp. 332–340.

38 See, for instance, A. Field, "Are You Rewarding Solo Performance at the Team's Expense?" *Harvard Management Update*, Article Reprint No. U0608A.

39 See J.S. DeMatteo, L.T. Eby, & E. Sundstrom, "Team-Based Rewards: Current Empirical Evidence and Directions for Future Research," in L.L. Cummings & B.M. Staw (eds.), *Research in Organizational Behavior* (Greenwich, CT: JAI Press, 1998), pp. 141–183.

40 This is based on J.S. DeMatteo, L.T. Eby, & E. Sundstrom, "Team-Based Rewards: Current Empirical Evidence and Directions for Future Research," in L.L. Cummings & B.M. Staw (eds.), *Research in Organizational Behavior* (Greenwich, CT: JAI Press, 1998), pp. 141–183.

41 T.B. Wilson, "Group Incentives: Are You Ready?" *Journal of Compensation Management*, 1990, *6(3)*, pp. 25–29.

42 This is based on J.S. DeMatteo, L.T. Eby, & E. Sundstrom, "Team-Based Rewards: Current Empirical Evidence and Directions for Future Research," in L.L. Cummings & B.M. Staw (eds.), *Research in Organizational Behavior* (Greenwich, CT: JAI Press, 1998), pp. 141–183.

43 These are largely based on A. Field, "Are You Rewarding Solo Performance at the Team's Expense?" *Harvard Management Update*, Article Reprint No. U0608A.

44 V.H. Vroom, *Work and Motivation* (New York: John Wiley & Sons, 1964). For recent discussions of expectancy theory, see R.G. Isaac, W.J. Zerbe, & D.C. Pitt, "Leadership and Motivation: The Effective Application of Expectancy Theory," *Journal of Managerial Issues*, 2001, *13(2)*, pp. 212–226; and, V.H. Vroom, "Expectancy Theory," in E.H. Kessler (ed.), *Encyclopedia of Management Theory*, vol. 1 (Thousand Oaks, CA: Sage, 2013), pp. 271–276.

45 For a recent discussion of equity theory, see R. Folger, "Equity Theory," in E.H. Kessler (ed.), *Encyclopedia of Management Theory*, vol. 1 (Thousand Oaks, CA: Sage, 2013), pp. 249–253.

46 See E. Walster, G.W. Walster, & E. Berscheid, *Equity: Theory and Research* (Boston: Allyn & Bacon, 1978) for a review of studies on this issue.

47 See G.L. Blakely, M.C. Andrews, & R.H. Moorman, "The Moderating Effects of Equity Sensitivity on the Relationship Between Organizational Justice and Organizational Citizenship Behaviors," *Journal of Business and Psychology*, 2005, *20(2)*, pp. 259–273; and, B.A. Scott & J.A. Colquitt, "Are Organizational Justice Effects Bounded by Individual Differences?: An Examination of Equity Sensitivity, Exchange Ideology, and the Big Five," *Group and Organization Management*, 2007, *32(3)*, pp. 290–325.

48 G.S. Leventhal, "Fairness in Social Relationships," in J. Thibaut, J.T. Spence, & R. Carson (eds.), *Contemporary Topics in Social Psychology*, ed. (Morristown, NJ: General Learning Press, 1976). See also, R.W. Hamilton, "When the Means Justify the Ends: Effects of Observability on the Procedural Fairness and Distributive Fairness of Resource Allocations," *Journal of Behavioral Decision Making*, 2006, *19*, pp. 303–320; and, W.D. Anderson & M.L. Patterson, "Effects of Social Value Orientations on Fairness Judgments," *Journal of Social Psychology*, 2008, *148(2)*, pp. 223–245.

49 This listing is based on G.S. Leventhal, "The Distribution of Rewards and Resources in Groups and Organizations," in L. Berkowitz & E. Walster (eds.), *Advances in Experimental Social Psychology*, vol. 9, (New York: Academic Press, 1976). See also, N.D. Cole & D.H. Flint, "Opportunity Knocks: Perceptions of Fairness in Employee Benefits," *Compensation and Benefits Review*, 2005, *37(2)*, pp. 55–62; and, C.M. Lau & A. Moser, "Behavioral Effects of Nonfinancial Performance Measures: The Role of Procedural Fairness," *Behavioral Research in Accounting*, 2008, *20(2)*, pp. 55–71.

50 J.S. Adams, "Inequity in Social Exchange," in L. Berkowitz (ed.) *Advances in Experimental Social Psychology*, vol. 2 (New York: Academic Press, 1965).

51 See A.P. Brief & R.J. Aldag, "The Intrinsic-Extrinsic Dichotomy: Toward Conceptual Clarity," *Academy of Management Review*, 1977, 2, 496–500; R. Bénabou & J. Tirole, "Intrinsic and Extrinsic Motivation," *Review of Economic Studies*, 2003, *70*, pp. 489–520; and, C.F. Miao, K.R. Evans, & S. Zou, "The Role of Salesperson Motivation in Sales Control Systems: Intrinsic and Extrinsic Motivation Revisited," *Journal of Business Research*, 2007, *60*, pp. 417–425.

52 G.R. Oldham, "Job Characteristics Theory," in E.H. Kessler (ed.), *Encyclopedia of Management Theory*, vol. 1 (Thousand Oaks, CA: Sage, 2013), pp. 407–410.

53 For discussions of the importance of autonomy at work, see G. Wang & R.G. Netemeyer, "The Effects of Job Autonomy, Customer Demandingness, and Trait Competitiveness on Salesperson Learning, Self-Efficacy, and Performance," *Journal of the Academy of Marketing Science*, 2002, *30(3)*, pp. 217–228; and,

S. Hornung & D.M. Rousseau, "Active on the Job—Proactive in Change: How Autonomy at Work Contributes to Employee Support for Organizational Change," *Journal of Applied Behavioral Science*, 2007, *43(4)*, pp. 401–426.

54 A. Bandura, *Self-Efficacy: The Exercise of Control* (New York: Freeman & Company, 1997). See also A. Bandura, "Exercise of Human Agency through Collective Efficacy," *Current Directions in Psychological Science*, 2000, *9*, pp. 75–78.

55 S.W.J. Kozlowski & D.R. Ilgen, "Enhancing the Effectiveness of Work Groups and Teams," *Psychological Science in the Public Interest*, 2006, *7(3)*, p. 90.

56 A.D. Stajkovic, D. Lee, & A.J. Nyberg, "Collective Efficacy, Group Potency, and Group Performance: Meta-Analysis of Their Relationships, and a Test of a Mediation Model," *Journal of Applied Psychology*, 2009, *94(3)*, pp. 824–828.

57 R.A. Guzzo, P.R. Yost, R.J. Campbell, & G.P. Shea, "Potency in Groups: Articulating a Construct," *British Journal of Social Psychology*, 1993, *32*, pp. 87–106.

58 J.R.P. French & B. Raven, "The Bases of Social Power," in D. Cartwright & A.F. Zander (eds.), *Group Dynamics*, 2d ed.(Evanston, IL: Row Peterson, 1960), pp. 259–269.

59 See W.O. Jenkins, "A Review of Leadership Studies with Particular Reference to Military Problems," *Psychological Bulletin*, 1947, *44*, pp. 54–79; R.M. Stogdill, "Personal Factors Associated with Leadership: A Survey of the Literature," *Journal of Psychology*, 1948, *25*, pp. 35–71; and, C.A. Gibb, "Leadership," in G. Lindzey (ed.), *Handbook of Social Psychology* (Reading, MA: Addison-Wesley).

60 C. Bird, *Social Psychology* (New York: Appleton-Century, 1940).

61 L.F. Carter & M. Nixon, "An Investigation of the Relationship between Four Criteria of Leadership Ability for Three Different Tasks," *Journal of Psychology*, 1949, *23*, pp. 245–261.

62 T.A. Judge, J.E. Bono, R. Ilies, & M.W. Gerhardt, "Personality and Leadership: A Qualitative and Quantitative Review," *Journal of Applied Psychology*, 2002, *87(4)*, pp. 765–780. See also T.A. Judge & J.E. Bono, "Five-Factor Model of Personality and Transformational Leadership," *Journal of Applied Psychology*, 2000, *85(5)*, pp. 751–765.

63 A.C. Filley, R.J. House, & S. Kerr, *Managerial Process and Organizational Behavior*, 2nd ed. (Glenview, IL: Scott, Foresman & Company, 1976), p. 226.

64 S. Kerr & J.M. Jermier, "Substitutes for Leadership: Their Meaning and Measurement," *Organizational Behavior and Human Performance*, 1978, 22, pp. 375–403. See also P.M. Podsakoff, S.B. MacKenzie, & W.H. Bonner, "Meta-Analysis of the Relationships between Kerr and Jermier's Substitutes for Leadership and Employee Job Attitudes, Role Perceptions, and Performance," *Journal of Applied Psychology*, 1996, *81*, pp. 380–399; and, T.M. Nielsen, "Substitutes for Leadership," in E.H. Kessler (ed.), *Encyclopedia of Management Theory*, vol. 2 (Thousand Oaks, CA: Sage, 2013), pp. 809–812.

65 For an analysis of substitutes for leadership, see S.D. Dionne, F.Y. Yammarito, L.E. Atwater, & L.R. James, "Neutralizing Substitutes for Leadership Theory: Leadership Effects and Common-Source Bias," *Journal of Applied Psychology*, 2002, *87(3)*, pp. 454–464.

66 R.E. Byrd, "Corporate Leadership Skills: A New Synthesis," *Organizational Dynamics*, 1987, pp. 34–43.

67 For example, see D.E. Elenkov, "Effects of Leadership on Organizational Performance in Russian Companies," *Journal of Business Research*, June 2002, pp. 467+; T. Dvir, D. Eden, B.J. Avolio, & B. Shamir, "Impact of Transformational Leadership on Follower Development and Performance: A Field Experiment," *Academy of Management Journal*, August 2002, *45(4)*, pp. 735+;

and, B.M. Bass, B.J. Avolio, D.I. Jung, & Y. Berson, "Predicting Unit Performance by Assessing Transformational and Transactional Leadership," *Journal of Applied Psychology*, 2003, *88(2)*, pp. 207–218.

68   This is based on J.A. Conger, "Inspiring Others: The Language of Leadership," *Academy of Management Executive*, February 1991, pp. 31–45.

69   S.G. Barsade, "The Ripple Effect: Emotional Contagion and Its Influence on Group Behavior," *Administrative Science Quarterly*, 2002, *47(4)*, pp. 644–675; J.R. Kelly & S.G. Barsade, "Mood and Emotions in Small Groups and Work Teams," *Organizational Behavior and Human Decision Processes*, 2001, *86(1)*, pp. 99–130; and, T. Sy, S. Côté, & R. Saavedra, "The Contagious Leader: Impact of the Leader's Mood on the Mood of Group Members, Group Affective Tone, and Group Processes," *Journal of Applied Psychology*, 90(2), pp. 295–305.

70   S.G. Barsade & D.E. Gibson, "Group Affect: Its Influence on Individual and Group Outcomes," *Current Directions in Psychological Science*, 2012, *21(2)*, pp. 119–123.

Bibliography

Adams, J.S. "Inequity in Social Exchange." In L. Berkowitz (ed.), *Advances in Experimental Social Psychology*, vol. 2 (New York: Academic Press, 1965), pp. 267–299.

Anderson, W.D., & Patterson, M.L. "Effects of Social Value Orientations on Fairness Judgments," *Journal of Social Psychology*, 2008, *148(2)*, pp. 223–245.

Argyris, C. *Integrating the Individual and the Organization* (New York: John Wiley & Sons, 1964).

Bandura, A. "Exercise of Human Agency through Collective Efficacy," *Current Directions in Psychological Science*, 2000, *9*, pp. 75–78.

Bandura, A. *Self-Efficacy: The Exercise of Control* (New York: Freeman & Company, 1997).

Barsade, S.G. "The Ripple Effect: Emotional Contagion and Its Influence on Group Behavior," *Administrative Science Quarterly*, 2002, *47(4)*, pp. 644–675.

Barsade, S.G., & Gibson, D.E. "Group Affect: Its Influence on Individual and Group Outcomes," *Current Directions in Psychological Science*, 2012, *21(2)*, pp. 119–123.

Bass, B.M., Avolio, B.J., Jung, D.I., & Berson, Y. "Predicting Unit Performance by Assessing Transformational and Transactional Leadership," *Journal of Applied Psychology*, 2003, *88(2)*, pp. 207–218.

Bénabou, R., & Tirole, J. "Intrinsic and Extrinsic Motivation," *Review of Economic Studies*, 2003, *70*, pp. 489–520.

Bird, C. *Social Psychology* (New York: Appleton-Century, 1940).

Blakely, G.L., Andrews, M.C., & Moorman, R.H. "The Moderating Effects of Equity Sensitivity on the Relationship between Organizational Justice and Organizational Citizenship Behaviors," *Journal of Business and Psychology*, 2005, *20(2)*, pp. 259–273.

Blass, T. *The Man Who Shocked the World* (New York: Basic Books, 2004).

Blickensderfer, E., Cannon-Bowers, J.A., & Salas, E. "Cross-Training and Team Performance." In J.A. Cannon-Bowers & E. Salas (eds.), *Making Decisions under Stress: Implications for Individual and Team Training* (Washington, D.C.: American Psychological Association, 1998), pp. 299–311.

Brief, A.P., & Aldag, R.J. "The Intrinsic-Extrinsic Dichotomy: Toward Conceptual Clarity," *Academy of Management Review*, 1977, 2, 496–500.

Byrd, R.E., "Corporate Leadership Skills: A New Synthesis," *Organizational Dynamics*, 1987, pp. 34–43.

Carter, L. F., & Nixon, M. "An Investigation of the Relationship between Four Criteria of Leadership Ability for Three Different Tasks," *Journal of Psychology*, 1949, *23*, pp. 245–261.

Choi, H.-S., & Levine, J.M. "Minority Influence in Work Teams: The Impact of Newcomers," *Journal of Experimental Social Psychology*, 2004, *40*, pp. 273–280.

Cole, N.D., & Flint, D.H. "Opportunity Knocks: Perceptions of Fairness in Employee Benefits," *Compensation and Benefits Review*, 2005, *37(2)*, pp. 55–62.

Conger, J.A. "Inspiring Others: The Language of Leadership," *Academy of Management Executive*, February 1991, pp. 31–45.

Cooper, W.H., & Withey, M.J. "The Strong Situation Hypothesis," *Personality and Social Psychology Review*, 2009, *13(1)* pp. 62–72.

Currall, S.C., & Epstein, M.J. "The Fragility of Organizational Trust: Lessons from the Rise and Fall of Enron," *Organizational Dynamics*, 2003, *32(2)*, pp. 193–206.

de Jong, B.A., & Elfring, T. "How Does Trust Affect the Performance of Ongoing Teams?: The Mediating Role of Reflexivity, Monitoring, and Effort," *Academy of Management Journal*, 2010, *53(3)*, pp. 535–549.

DeChurch, L.A., & Mesmer-Magnus, J.R. "The Cognitive Underpinnings of Effective Teamwork: A Meta-Analysis," *Journal of Applied Psychology*, 2010, *95(1)*, pp. 32–53.

Delise, L.A., Gorman, C.A., Brooks, A.M., Rentsch, J.R., & Steele-Johnson, D. "The Effects of Team Training on Team Outcomes: A Meta-Analysis," *Performance Improvement Quarterly*, 2010, *22(4)*, pp. 53–80.

DeMatteo, J.S., Eby, L.T., & Sundstrom, E. "Team-Based Rewards: Current Empirical Evidence and Directions for Future Research." In L.L. Cummings & B.M. Staw (eds.), *Research in Organizational Behavior* (Greenwich, CT: JAI Press, 1998), pp. 141–183.

Dionne, S.C., Yammarito, F. Y, Atwater, L.E., & James, L.R. "Neutralizing Substitutes for Leadership Theory: Leadership Effects and Common-Source Bias," *Journal of Applied Psychology*, 2002, *87(3)*, pp. 454–464.

Dvir, T., Eden, D., Avolio, B.J., & Shamir, B. "Impact of Transformational Leadership on Follower Development and Performance: A Field Experiment," *Academy of Management Journal*, August 2002, *45(4)*, pp. 735+.

Dye, K. "Needs Hierarchy." In E.H. Kessler (ed.), *Encyclopedia of Management Theory*, vol. 2 (Thousand Oaks, CA: Sage, 2013), pp. 503–505.

Dye, K., Mills, A.J., & Weatherbee, T. "Maslow: Man Interrupted: Reading Management Theory in Context," *Management Decision*, 2005, *43(10)*, pp. 1375–1395.

Elenkov, D.E. "Effects of Leadership on Organizational Performance in Russian Companies," *Journal of Business Research*, June 2002, pp. 467+.

Field, A. "Are You Rewarding Solo Performance at the Team's Expense?" *Harvard Management Update*, Article Reprint No. U0608A.

Filley, A.C., House, R.J., & Kerr, S. *Managerial Process and Organizational Behavior.* 2nd ed. (Glenview, IL: Scott, Foresman & Company, 1976).

Folger, R. "Equity Theory." In E.H. Kessler (ed.), *Encyclopedia of Management Theory*, vol. 1 (Thousand Oaks, CA: Sage, 2013), pp. 249–253.

French, J.R.P., & Raven, B. "The Bases of Social Power," In D. Cartwright & A.F. Zander (eds.), *Group Dynamics*, 2d ed.(Evanston, IL: Row Peterson, 1960), pp. 259–269.

Gersick, C.J., & Hackman, J.R. "Habitual Routines in Task-Performing Groups," *Organizational Behavior and Human Decision Processes*, 1990, *47*, pp. 65–97.

Gibb, C.A. "Leadership." In G. Lindzey (ed.), *Handbook of Social Psychology* (Reading, MA: Addison-Wesley), pp. 205–282.

Greengrass, M. "100 years of B.F. Skinner," *Monitor on Psychology*, 2004, *35(3)*, p.80.

Guzzo, R.A., Yost, P.R., Campbell, R.J., & Shea, G.P. "Potency in Groups: Articulating a Construct," *British Journal of Social Psychology*, 1993, *32*, pp. 87–106.

Hamilton, R.W. "When the Means Justify the Ends: Effects of Observability on the Procedural Fairness and Distributive Fairness of Resource Allocations," *Journal of Behavioral Decision Making*, 2006, *19*, pp. 303–320;

Hamner, W.C., & Hamner, E.P. "Behavior Modification on the Bottom Line," *Organizational Dynamics*, 1976, *4*, pp. 3–21.

Hoffman, E. "The Last Interview of Abraham Maslow," *Psychology Today*, January 1992, pp. 68–73.

Hollenbeck, J.R., DeRue, D.S., & Guzzo, R. "Bridging the Gap between I/O Research and HR Practice: Improving Team Composition, Team Training, and Team Task Design," *Human Resource Management*, 2004, *43(4)*, pp. 353–366.

Hornung, S., & Rousseau, D.M. "Active on the Job—Proactive in Change: How Autonomy at Work Contributes to Employee Support for Organizational Change," *Journal of Applied Behavioral Science*, 2007, *43(4)*, pp. 401–426.

Isaac, R.G., Zerbe, W.J., & Pitt, D.C. "Leadership and Motivation: The Effective Application of Expectancy Theory," *Journal of Managerial Issues*, 2001, *13(2)*, pp. 212–226.

Jenkins, W.O. "A Review of Leadership Studies with Particular Reference to Military Problems," *Psychological Bulletin*, 1947, *44*, pp. 54–79.

Judge, T.A., & Bono, J.E. "Five-Factor Model of Personality and Transformational Leadership," *Journal of Applied Psychology*, 2000, *85(5)*, pp. 751–765.

Judge, T.A., Bono, J.E., Ilies, R., & Gerhardt, M.W. "Personality and Leadership: A Qualitative and Quantitative Review," *Journal of Applied Psychology*, 2002, *87(4)*, pp. 765–780.

Kelly, J.R., & Barsade, S.G. "Mood and Emotions in Small Groups and Work Teams," *Organizational Behavior and Human Decision Processes*, 2001, *86(1)*, pp. 99–130.

Kerr, S., & Jermier, J.M. "Substitutes for Leadership: Their Meaning and Measurement," *Organizational Behavior and Human Performance*, 1978, *22*, pp. 375–403.

Kozlowski, S.W.J., & Ilgen, D.R. "Enhancing the Effectiveness of Work Groups and Teams," *Psychological Science in the Public Interest*, 2006, *7(3)*, pp. 77–124.

Kramer, R.M. "Trust and Distrust in Organizations: Emerging Perspectives, Enduring Questions," *Annual Review of Psychology*, 1999, *50*, pp. 569–598.

Kraus, M.W., Huang, C., & Keltner, D. "Tactile Communication, Cooperation, and Performance: An Ethological Study of the NBA," *Emotion*, 2010, *10(5)*, pp. 745–749.

Latham, G.P., & Baldes, J.J. "The 'Practical Significance' of Locke's Theory of Goal Setting," *Journal of Applied Psychology*, 1975, *60*, pp. 122–124.

Latham, G.P., & Locke, E.A. "Enhancing the Benefits and Overcoming the Pitfalls of Goal Setting," *Organizational Dynamics*, 2006, *35(4)*, pp. 332–340.

Latham, G.P., Erez, M., & Locke, E.A. "Resolving Scientific Disputes by the Joint Design of Crucial Experiments by the Antagonists: Application to the Erez-Latham Dispute Regarding Participation in Goal Setting," *Journal of Applied Psychology*, 1988, *73*, pp. 753–772.

Lau, C.M., & Moser, A. "Behavioral Effects of Nonfinancial Performance Measures: The Role of Procedural Fairness," *Behavioral Research in Accounting*, 2008, *20(2)*, pp. 55–71.

Lee, C. "Customized Compensation Packages," *Journal of Property Management*, September/October 2001, *66(5)*, pp. 30–38.

Leventhal, G.S., "Fairness in Social Relationships." In J. Thibaut, J.T. Spence, & R. Carson (eds.), *Contemporary Topics in Social Psychology* (Morristown, NJ: General Learning Press, 1976), pp. 209–239.

Leventhal, G.S. "The Distribution of Rewards and Resources in Groups and Organizations." In L. Berkowitz & E. Walster (eds.), *Advances in Experimental Social Psychology*, vol. 9 (New York: Academic Press, 1976), pp. 91–131.

Lim, B.-C., & Klein, K.J. "Team Mental Models and Team Performance: A Field Study of the Effects of Mental Model Similarity and Accuracy," *Journal of Organizational Behavior*, 2006, *27*, pp. 403–418.

Locke, E.A., & Latham, G.P. "Goal-Setting Theory." In E.H. Kessler (ed.), *Encyclopedia of Management Theory*, vol. 1 (Thousand Oaks, CA: Sage, 2013), pp. 315–318.

Locke, E.A., & Latham, G.P. *Goal Setting for Individuals, Groups, and Organizations* (Chicago: Science Research Associates, 1984).

March, J.G., & Olsen, J.P. *Rediscovering Institutions: The Organizational Basis of Politics* (New York: Free Press, 1989).

Marks, M.A., Sabella, M.J., Burke, C.S., & Zaccaro, S.J. "The Impact of Cross-Training on Team Effectiveness." *Journal of Applied Psychology*, 2002, *87(1)*, pp. 3–13.

Maslow, A.H. "A Theory of Human Motivation," *Psychological Review*, 1943, *50*, pp. 370–396.

Meister, J. "Gamification: Three Ways to Use Gaming for Recruiting, Training, and Health & Wellness," *Forbes,* May 21, 2012. http://www.forbes.com/sites/jeannemeister/2012/05/21/gamification-three-ways-to-use-gaming-for-recruiting-training-and-health-amp-wellness/.

Meyerson, D., Weick, K.E., & Kramer, R.M. "Swift Trust and Temporary Groups." In R.M. Kramer & T.R. Tyler (eds.), *Trust in Organizations: Frontiers in Theory and Research* (Thousand Oaks: CA: Sage, 1996), pp. 166–195.

Miao, C.F., Evans, K.R., & Zou, S. "The Role of Salesperson Motivation in Sales Control Systems: Intrinsic and Extrinsic Motivation Revisited," *Journal of Business Research*, 2007, *60*, pp. 417–425.

Milgram, S. "Behavioral Study of Obedience," *Journal of Abnormal and Social Psychology*, 1963, *67(4)*, pp. 371–378.

Milgram, S. *Obedience to Authority; An Experimental Review* (New York: Harper & Row, 1974).

Miltenberger, R.G. *Behavior Modification: Principles and Procedures*, 5th ed. (Belmont, CA: Wadsworth, 2012).

Nielsen, T.M. "Substitutes for Leadership." In E.H. Kessler (ed.), *Encyclopedia of Management Theory*, vol. 2 (Thousand Oaks, CA: Sage, 2013), pp. 809–812.

Oldham, G.R. "Job Characteristics Theory." In E.H. Kessler (ed.), *Encyclopedia of Management Theory*, vol. 1 (Thousand Oaks, CA: Sage, 2013), pp. 407–410.

Ostrom, E., & Walker, J. *Trust and Reciprocity: Interdisciplinary Lessons from Experimental Research* (New York: Russell Sage Foundation, 2005).

Paglieri, E., & Castelfranchi, C. "More Than Control Freaks: Evaluative and Motivational Functions of Goals," *Behavioral and Brain Sciences*, 2008, *31*, pp. 35–36.

Podsakoff, P.M., MacKenzie, S.B., & Bonner, W.H. "Meta-Analysis of the Relationships between Kerr and Jermier's Substitutes for Leadership and Employee Job Attitudes, Role Perceptions, and Performance," *Journal of Applied Psychology*, 1996, *81*, pp. 380–399.

Rashid, F., Edmondson, A.C., & Leonard, H.B. "Leadership Lessons from the Chilean Mine Rescue," *Harvard Business Review*, July-August 2013, pp. 113–119.

Salas, E., Cooke, N.J., & Rosen, M.A. "On Teams, Teamwork, and Team Performance: Discoveries and Developments," *Human Factors*, 2008, *50(3)*, pp. 540–547.

Salas, E., DiazGranados, D., Klein, C., Burke, C.S., Stagl, K.C., Goodwin, G.F., & Halpin, S.M. "Does Team Training Improve Team Performance? A Meta-Analysis," *Human Factors*, 2008, *50*, pp. 903–933.

Sauey, D. "Group Life Insurance Is Backbone of Cafeteria Plans," *Credit Union Magazine*, October 2001, p. 60.

Scandura, T.A., & Sharif, M.M. "Team Leadership: The Chilean Mine Case," *Management Faculty Articles and Papers*, Paper 13. http://scholarlyrepository.miami.edu/management_articles/13

Schawbel, D. "Adam Penenberg: How Gamification Is Going to Change the Workplace," *Forbes*, October 7, 2013. http://www.forbes.com/sites/danschawbel/2013/10/07/adam-penenberg-how-gamification-is-going-to-change-the-workplace/.

Scott, B.A., & Colquitt, J.A. "Are Organizational Justice Effects Bounded by Individual Differences?: An Examination of Equity Sensitivity, Exchange Ideology, and the Big Five," *Group and Organization Management*, 2007, *32(3)*, pp. 290–325.

Shermer, M. "Kin and Kindness," *Wall Street Journal*, May 25, 2012. http://online.wsj.com/news/articles/SB10001424052702304723304577367920639482882.

Silverman, R.E. "Latest Game Theory: Mixing Work and Play," *Wall Street Journal*, October 10, 2011. http://online.wsj.com/news/articles/SB10001424052970204294504576615371783795248.

Sinclair, R.R., Leo, M.C., & Wright, C. "Benefit System Effects on Employees' Benefit Knowledge, Use, and Organizational Commitment," *Journal of Business and Psychology*, 2005, *20(1)*, pp. 3–29.

Skinner, B.F. *Contingencies of Reinforcement: A Theoretical Analysis* (East Norwalk, CT: Appleton-Century-Crofts, 1969).

Stajkovic, A.D., & Luthans, F. "A Meta-Analysis of the Effects of Organizational Behavior Modification on Task Performance, 1975–95," *Academy of Management Journal*, 1997, *40(5)*, pp. 1122–1149.

Stajkovic, A.D., Lee, D., & Nyberg, A.P. "Collective Efficacy, Group Potency, and Group Performance: Meta-Analysis of Their Relationships, and a Test of a Mediation Model," *Journal of Applied Psychology*, 2009, *94(3)*, pp. 824–828.

Stansfield, T.C., & Longenecker, C.O. "The Effects of Goal Setting and Feedback on Manufacturing Productivity: A Field Experiment," *International Journal of Productivity and Performance Management*, 2006, *55(3/4)*, pp. 346–358.

Stogdill, R.M. "Personal Factors Associated with Leadership: A Survey of the Literature," *Journal of Psychology*, 1948, *25*, pp. 35–71.

Swann, W.B., Jr., Gómez, Á., Seyle, D.C., Morales, J.F., & Huici, C. "Identity Fusion: The Interplay of Personal and Social Identities in Extreme Group Behavior," *Journal of Personality and Social Psychology*, 2009, *96(5)*, pp. 995–1011.

Sy, T., Côté, S., & Saavedra, R. "The Contagious Leader: Impact of the Leader's Mood on the Mood of Group Members, Group Affective Tone, and Group Processes," *Journal of Applied Psychology*, *90(2)*, pp. 295–305.

Volpe, C.E., Cannon-Bowers, J.A., Salas, E., & Spector, P.E. "The Impact of Cross-Training on Team Effectiveness," *Human Factors*, 1996, *38*, pp. 87–100.

Vroom, V.H. "Expectancy Theory." In E.H. Kessler (ed.), *Encyclopedia of Management Theory*, vol. 1 (Thousand Oaks, CA: Sage, 2013), pp. 271–276.

Vroom, V.H. *Work and Motivation* (New York: John Wiley & Sons, 1964).

Walster, E., Walster, G.W., & Berscheid, E. *Equity: Theory and Research* (Boston: Allyn & Bacon, 1978).

Wang, G., & Netemeyer, R.G. "The Effects of Job Autonomy, Customer Demandingness, and Trait Competitiveness on Salesperson Learning, Self-Efficacy, and Performance," *Journal of the Academy of Marketing Science*, 2002, *30(3)*, pp. 217–228.

Wilson, T.B. "Group Incentives: Are You Ready?" *Journal of Compensation Management*, 1990, *6(3)*, pp. 25–29.

Zak, P.J. "The Trust Molecule," *Wall Street Journal*, April 28, 2012, p. C1.

Ziller, R.C., & Behringer, R.D. "Assimilation of the Knowledgeable Newcomer under Conditions of Group Success and Failure," *Journal of Abnormal and Social Psychology*, 1960, *60*, pp. 288–291.

Managing Team Diversity

Learning Objectives

After reading this chapter, you should be able to do the following:

1. Better lead and participate in diverse teams.
2. Recognize important personality dimensions and other individual differences that contribute to diversity and how they influence team processes and outcomes.
3. Understand important elements of diversity arising from cross-cultural differences and how you can develop your cross-cultural skills when working in teams.

· ·

IN THIS CHAPTER WE CONSIDER A VARIETY OF FACTORS that may influence team diversity, including ethnic background, gender, age, racial diversity, personality diversity, and cross-cultural differences.

Insights and Advice

· ·

Sergio Romero, Booz Allen & Hamilton

What kind of work experience do you have leading and working with teams?

As a people and change management consultant, I've led and been a part of many diverse teams. Three years ago, I began my career as an analyst. I was tasked mostly with gathering and distilling data for various project managers. More recently, I've managed client-facing team projects that deal with change management work.

What kinds of team member diversity (e.g., age, gender, nationality, work styles, perspectives) have you experienced on the teams you have been a part of? What kinds of strategies have you used to understand and to manage diversity effectively on these teams?

People and change management is possibly one of the most diverse management consulting areas in the field. Our main function is to transform the systems management practices and the structure of organizations by changing client behavior. Because these clients are quite diverse (i.e., varying in age, gender, nationality, and perspectives), the consulting teams that serve them often reflect this diversity.

Since I'm often switching among a multitude of diverse teams, I've learned to employ my own strategy. First, I aim to understand what motivates and discourages each individual on the team. Then, I try to uncover what it is about each individual's diverse background that serves as an advantage and disadvantage given the context of the task. Finally, I take note of how the group members interact with each other personally and around the task.

What do you feel are the biggest challenges associated with working with diversity issues on teams?

In my experience, diverse teams have the propensity to be either highly effective or highly ineffective. I've noticed that the teams that have been highly effective have taken the time before starting a project to understand the unique strengths and weaknesses of each team member. One of the biggest challenges I've come across is that many teams jump right to the task without taking this time on the front end.

What advice would you give to students in terms of how they can lead and manage diversity issues on teams in the future?

Chances are you're going to be working on diverse teams throughout your career. It's also quite probable that while working on these teams, you'll feel the pressure to quickly turn deliverables around. When this scenario presents itself, take the time before the task begins to understand the unique strengths and weaknesses of each team member. This could take place over coffee or in the break room. Use whatever time is available. Later on, this time will pay dividends as you more accurately allocate work and manage team conflict.

Managing Diversity

The workforce is becoming dramatically more diverse. Diversity refers to the membership mix in organizations in terms of gender, race, ethnic origin, and other characteristics. The Pillsbury Company defines *diversity* as "all the ways in which we differ."[1] Before reading on, complete Self-Assessment 5.1 on the text website.

To get a basic idea of where you are starting in terms of some of the material covered in this section, try working through the "Valuing Individual Differences" Pretest Skills Assessment on the text website. Just do your best. Be as specific as possible in stating your recommendations.

Diversity in teams and organizations has been described as a "two-edged sword."[2] Historically, many companies have focused on just one edge of the sword—the potential problems created by a diverse workforce. According to this perspective, relying heavily on the **similarity-attraction paradigm**, people's perceptions of others that are often inferred on the basis of demographic similarity, leads to attraction among team members. This view may result in the claim that homogeneous teams are likely to be more effective than diverse teams because of the mutual attraction of similar members. On the other hand, more diverse teams are expected to be less productive and cohesive because of misunderstandings and tensions among team members. Further, very real prejudices against members of certain groups, such as blacks and women, can lead to conflict and mistrust. We discuss unique challenges associated with leading and participating in diverse teams later in the chapter.

Increasingly, though, organizations are learning to value diversity. Diversity can provide a powerful competitive advantage.[3] According to **cognitive resource diversity theory,** diversity should enhance performance by bringing more perspectives and a wider range of knowledge to bear on problems, increasing creativity and decision-making effectiveness. In addition, individuals exposed to opposing minority views exert more cognitive effort, think in more divergent ways, and are more likely to identify novel solutions than those who are not.[4]

Kraft Foods spells out its commitment to diversity in metaphors: "A stellar meal requires contrasting and complementing textures and tastes. A winning sports team depends on the different talents of its members. A first-class orchestra needs many varied instruments. And a successful business team requires a variety of thought, energy and insight to attain and maintain a competitive edge. Kraft Foods is comprised of people from different backgrounds, different ethnicities, different work styles, different values and different ways of thinking. We invite these differences. We seek them out. And we know that our business teams and the individuals thrive as a result."[5]

Forms of Diversity

Surface-Level versus Deep-Level Diversity

Surface-level diversity relates to features that are readily apparent, such as gender, race, and age. The workforce has become, and will continue to become, more diverse in each of these features. As one example, there are now four distinct generations in the workforce, including Traditionalists (born before 1945), Baby Boomers (born 1946–1964), Generation Xers (born 1965–1980), and Millennials (born 1981–1999). On the other hand, **deep-level diversity** is based on things such as attitudes, values, beliefs, information, and opinions. We sometimes infer deep-level diversity from surface-level diversity. For example, we may infer that Baby Boomers are optimistic and competitive while Generation Xers are more independent and resourceful.[6] While such inferences may be correct, they may also be in error. As such, true deep-level differences may not be readily evident.

Actual versus Perceived Diversity

Since perceptions of diversity may not be accurate, it is important to consider both actual and perceived diversity. For example, research suggests that when the effects of actual deep-level diversity are controlled for, perceived deep-level diversity is related to higher levels of turnover, lower levels of helping behaviors, and negative job attitudes.[7] Thus, it is important to help team members better understand one another's attitudes, information, and beliefs.

Fostering Diverse Teams

With the increasing diversity of the workplace, a challenge for companies is to formulate and implement policies, practices, and strategies that value everyone.

Companies must do more than accept and tolerate diversity; they must take active steps to successfully foster diversity in the workplace. Some of those steps might include training for tolerance, rewarding diversity efforts, changing employee attitudes toward diversity, and developing personnel policies that support diversity.

Now complete Skills Practice 5.1 on the text website by watching the movie *The Breakfast Club*. This film illustrates some interesting and important issues about the meaning of diversity and learning how to value it.

Training for Tolerance

Firms are adopting many approaches to training for tolerance, sometimes with dramatic results. Nextel Communications conducted an ROI (return on investment) study of the diversity training program it offers to its 13,000 employees, coming up with an ROI of 163%.[8] As another example, at Celanese the top twenty-six officers are each required to join two organizations in which they are a minority. IBM's Systems Storage Division in San Jose, CA (a city where thirty-three languages are spoken), has celebrated an annual diversity day for the last 20 years.[9] Employees dress in various ethnic costumes, perform traditional dances, and prepare authentic dishes for fellow workers. The festival has been so successful in defusing tensions that the plant's diversity council now prepares a monthly bulletin that lists diversity events in the city.

Rewarding Diversity Efforts

Some firms are tying performance appraisal to their efforts to increase diversity. At Celanese, the giant chemical firm discussed earlier, four sets of outcomes are weighted equally in performance appraisals: attainment of workforce diversity goals, financial success, customer satisfaction, and environmental and safety improvements.[10] As a result, managers at Celanese pay attention to diversity, knowing the success of their diversity efforts will be reflected in their salaries and bonuses.

Developing Favorable Attitudes toward Diversity

Research shows that diverse teams with favorable attitudes toward diversity outperform teams that place greater value on similarity.[11] As such, development of favorable attitudes toward diversity is crucial.

Companies are using a variety of innovative approaches to develop more positive employee diversity-related attitudes and skills. For instance, US WEST Dex uses "resource groups," volunteer-driven meetings that address the concerns of particular employees, such as women, blacks, Hispanics, gays, and lesbians.[12] All employees are encouraged to attend, to better understand the feelings and viewpoints of coworkers regarding specific issues they are facing in the company and to offer suggestions. The company also does 6-month follow-ups of programs to determine if employees are applying their new skills to on-the-job situations. In addition, an annual company-wide employee satisfaction survey incorporates questions on the state of diversity at the firm.

TEAMS IN THE NEWS: "Firms Hail New Chiefs (of Diversity)"

This *Wall Street Journal* article discusses how some firms are adding a new executive to their top management teams—chief diversity officer (CDO). CDOs are given the task of creating an environment where women and minorities can flourish. Their responsibilities include recruitment, human resources, marketing, ethics, and legal compliance.

The following link, which can be found on the text website, describes how 60% of Fortune 500 companies have a CDO or other executive role designated for diversity, often reporting directly to the CEO. (Follow this link to view the video: http://online.wsj.com/article/SB10001424052970203899504577129261732884578.html/.)

Confronting the Challenges of Diverse Teams

As we've seen, diverse teams provide many benefits. At the same time, they offer a variety of challenges. This can be especially the case when teams exhibit strong fault lines.

Group Fault Lines

Although we often think of diversity in terms of a single attribute such as race or gender or age, attributes may cluster together. Dora Lau and J. Keith Murnighan have offered a theory of group fault lines.[13] **Fault lines** are hypothetical dividing lines that may split a group into subgroups, generally based on multiple attributes. Lau and Murnighan see group fault lines as analogous to geological fault lines. Faults are fractures in the earth's crust. While they may remain dormant for years without being seen on the surface, earthquakes may result when layers of crust suddenly move along a fault. Similarly, strong group fault lines provide an opportunity for groups to "crack," creating a "teamquake."

Lau and Murnighan give the hypothetical example of a group that included five young, male shipping clerks who had worked for a company for less than 1 year and five middle-aged, female vice presidents who had been with the company for 20 years or more. The authors note that any of a wide array of issues, such as seniority privileges, vacation time for executives, or overtime policy, could result in subgroup conflict, with predictable membership in the subgroups.[14]

Research shows that strong group fault lines have a variety of negative effects on team processes and outcomes. Teams spend time and energy bridging the chasms created by the strong fault lines, so there is less attention to team goals. Team performance, bonuses, learning, creativity, organizational citizenship behaviors, and member satisfaction all suffer. With strong fault lines, intragroup conflict is high.[15] With diverse teams, and especially those with strong fault lines, it is important to take steps to help ensure that team processes are positive. Some ways to do so include managing conflict, providing a bridge across diversity, countering bias, and protecting the views of the minority.

Managing Conflict

Because of the different backgrounds, perspectives, and characteristics of their members, diverse teams may be prone to conflict. This may especially be the case when team members are first working together. For example, one study of homogeneous teams and of diverse teams (each one made up of one African American, one foreign national, one Hispanic American, and one Caucasian American) found the diverse teams initially had trouble agreeing on what was important and clashing about control. Perhaps as a result, the homogeneous teams initially outperformed diverse teams, though over time that gap disappeared.[16] We explore conflict management in more detail in Chapter 9.

Providing a Bridge across Diversity

It is especially important for leaders to provide bridges across differences. Leaders may, for instance, emphasize what is similar among team members rather than what is different. Some studies have found that when a group has a superordinate identity, such as emphasizing being Americans, that bridges across subgroup identities such as African American, Latino, and whites.[17] Leaders can emphasize superordinate goals that all members share, and they can point out common threats. Further, reward systems can influence the salience of diversity. For example, rewarding a diverse team based on team performance decreases the salience of intragroup differences by creating a commonality within the team. Consistent with this, research by Astrid Homan and others showed that teams performed the worst when reward structure converged with diversity (for instance, just one subgroup was rewarded) compared to teams in which the reward structure cut across differences between team members or pointed to a superordinate identity.[18] Homan's views on diversity are presented in the following Team Scholar box.

TEAM SCHOLAR

Astrid C. Homan, University of Amsterdam

Astrid C. Homan is an assistant professor of work and organizational psychology at the University of Amsterdam. Her research interests include team diversity, team processes, team performance, subgroup salience, leadership, and diversity beliefs. She is particularly interested in determining how to harvest the potential value in diversity. Her work is published in outlets such as *Journal of Applied Psychology, Journal of Personality and Social Psychology, Organizational Behavior and Human Decision Processes*, and *Academy of Management Journal*.

What sparked your interest in diversity in work groups?

My first interest related to group processes, as I wondered why some groups are productive and efficient, whereas other groups are not. I quickly found that the composition of the group (on any dimension) was a strong predictor of the processes that occurred within the group. As our societies and organizations get more and more diverse (e.g., more ethnicities, nationalities, women at work), the focus on diversity followed logically from my initial interest.

Can you summarize some key findings about diversity in work groups?

Diversity can instigate both negative and positive group processes. On the one hand, diversity can instigate subgroup formation (e.g., the males versus the females), which can lead to deteriorated group processes such as conflicts, distrust, and bad communication. On the other hand, diversity can positively affect group processes by presenting the group with more available information, ideas, and perspectives, which can in turn by used for more creative and improved team performance. This automatically implies that diversity effects have been found to be inconsistent, that is, diversity is not inherently good or bad for groups. These differential effects are not caused by the type of diversity (that is, visible, demographic differences are not automatically harmful, and invisible, more task-related differences are not always beneficial). Research on diversity has recently taken a successful moderator approach, showing that contextual factors are important in predicting diversity effects. Some factors that seem to positively affect diverse teams are positive diversity climates or beliefs, transformational leadership, and improved team reflexivity.

What are diversity perceptions? Why do you think they are important?

Diversity perceptions pertain to the way the members of a group see or construe their differences. Much research on diversity in teams has measured diversity as actual, objectively existing differences within the group (e.g., proportion of females, variance of age). However, although these differences might objectively be there, they might not be salient or visible to the people within the group. Because we know that people are more influenced by what they perceive than what is actually present, research should include diversity perceptions to understand which differences are actually being seen and how these perceptions influence group behaviors.

What are group fault lines? How does a focus on fault lines improve our understanding of diversity in groups?

Group fault lines are hypothetical dividing lines that split a group up into subgroups. The term *fault line* is used when a group is made up of people who differ from each other on multiple dimensions in such a way that two relatively homogeneous subgroups are present. As an example, think of a team of two older females and two younger males. This group can be split into two subgroups that differ from each other on both gender and age (with people who are highly similar to each other within the subgroups and highly dissimilar to the people in the other subgroup). The negative effects of diversity (subgroup formation) are more likely to occur in groups that have more salient subgroups, that is, when the team has a diversity fault line.

What do you see as some of the most important emerging issues regarding teams?

Teams are still seen as relatively stable entities. The recent work on teams is moving into more complex and changeable settings, in which research teams mirror real-life teams to a larger degree (e.g., acknowledging flex work, virtual teamwork, self-managing teams). Additionally, we know relatively little about how group processes in (diverse) teams feed into actual behavior (e.g., performance). Combining these two emergent issues, a more fine-grained analysis of what actually happens in teams (e.g., by making use of longitudinal research, videotaping groups) should be on the agenda, especially in these times in which teamwork changes not only in terms of team composition but also in terms of how people work together over time and place.

Protecting the Views of the Minority

We've said that diverse groups bring different expertise and perspectives to the table, leading to more unique information. However, a troubling finding is that information exchange among team members focuses on information that is widely known and shared by all members prior to interaction, rather than information that is held uniquely by individuals. As such, views of minority team members may not be shared. This is especially the case for a double minority, who differs from the majority on more than one attribute, and for a solo, the only member of a minority group. Such members may feel especially uncomfortable sharing their information and opinions.

As noted by Elizabeth Mannix and Margaret Neale, "If a team cannot create an environment that is tolerant of diverse perspectives and that reflects cooperative goal interdependence, then the individuals who carry the burden of unique perspectives may be unwilling to pay the social and psychological costs necessary to share their viewpoints."[19] Leader support for minority views and the development of an open, psychologically secure organizational culture are also important.

As we've seen, to successfully foster diversity in the workplace, programs are needed that include training, reward programs, and policies that nurture diversity.[20] Now, try designing a diversity program that includes these elements by completing Skills Practice 5.2 on the text website. This is a very challenging activity. You may be involved in the design and implementation of a diversity program once you get out into the real world, so this sort of practice—however difficult—is important.

Insights and Advice

Wayne Reschke

Wayne Reschke is the vice president for Human Resources at Alliant Energy. Alliant is a $4 billion utility with 1.4 million customers and 4,500 employees across three states. He is responsible for all Human Resource functions as well as strategy, communication, and safety.

Prior to joining Alliant Energy, Wayne spent 25 years as a consultant and in other roles, including the last 12 years as an owner and founding partner of the Center for Organization Effectiveness, a management consulting firm based in Madison, WI, and its assessment division, *surveysbydesign*. He also served as a lecturer in the Wisconsin School of Business and the Fluno Center for Executive Education at the University of Wisconsin–Madison. He has a bachelor's degree in history from Northwestern University and master's degree in counseling/organizational behavior; he completed post-master's work in human resources management at the University of Wisconsin–Madison Industrial Relations Research Institute. He is very heavily involved in community activities, including as chair of Heartwalk.

Do you have any general advice for team leaders and/or members?

In building team cohesiveness, trust, and effectiveness, there is no substitute for getting results. When the team experiences success, even early small wins or achievements, it builds trust among team members and confidence in both the team and the team leader. Other efforts at team development (i.e., traditional team-building training/experiences) are helpful but not sufficient. Such efforts are often the first things that leaders try when things aren't going well, instead of focusing on getting some accomplishments that would naturally generate team cohesion.

One opportunity for achievement is in team meetings. Meetings are often experienced as ineffectual, dysfunctional, and a waste of time. Since meetings are a principal arena for team interactions and task accomplishment, if they are seen as not accomplishing much, then the sense of optimism, confidence, and trust erodes—if we can't make progress together in a meeting, how can we hope to get the project done? So, attention to successful meeting facilitation and concrete outcomes goes a long way to creating a high performing team.

When do you think teams should be used? When should they be avoided?

I think that we use teams too often and/or in the wrong ways. There are certainly times when a team is the best approach—when multiple skill sets, perspectives, and appropriate staffing are essential to getting good results. But we tend to go to that strategy automatically without thinking

TEAM MANAGEMENT COACH

it through and then structure the team work the same even when the tasks are quite different. For example, a project may require getting input from multiple stakeholders. We often simply put all those stakeholders on the team for the duration of the project. Instead, it may be best to have a small team of two or three individuals for the whole project, and then bring in those stakeholders at appropriate times for review and input.

Avoid using a team when you can't identify clear reasons why the team would produce a better result than an individual.

Do you think it is best to put together a diverse team, to pick the best team members available regardless of diversity, or some combination?

In selecting team members, I think it is wise to attend to *both* the value of diversity and the "best" members based on other considerations/qualifications. You need the right skill sets, knowledge, and organizational representation as the starting point, which will often yield diversity of thought, though not necessarily gender or racial diversity. Yet such diversity can be valuable, for it brings different perspectives that will often lead to better outcomes. I've often said, if we have people on the team who either don't have a different perspective or don't speak up, we don't need them on the team. If their voice isn't different then what is already represented, then they're redundant. In short then, shoot for the right skills *and* a diverse team.

Understanding Personality

While we tend to think of diversity in terms of things such as race, gender, and ethnic origin, as we've just discussed, the variety of personalities in the workplace is also critical. Personality determines how people respond to new situations, how they interact with others, whether they can work on their own, and much else. Personality also influences whether people behave ethically or unethically, are helpful or self-serving, are conscientious or try just to get by, and feel in control of their situations or at the mercy of fate. For all of these reasons and many others, we must understand and be sensitive to personality differences in the workplace.

Personality is the organized and distinctive pattern of behavior that characterizes an individual's adaptation to a situation and endures over time.[21] The distinctive character of personality allows us to tell people apart—try to think of two people with identical personalities. The enduring character of personality permits us to recognize people and to anticipate their behaviors. Try to imagine a situation in which people had no enduring qualities. For instance, suppose your boss acted like a different person from day to day. While this could be interesting for a while, it would soon lead to chaos.

As we'll discuss, there are many reasons why personality is important in teams. For instance, members with certain personality characteristics may enhance such team processes and outcomes as conflict, satisfaction, motivation, and effectiveness, while members with other personality characteristics may detract from the quality of team processes and outcomes. Further, some mixes of team members' personality characteristics may enhance team processes and outcomes, while others may detract from them. Thus, when considering personality in teams, it is important to consider not just individual personality characteristics but also how team member characteristics fit together.

In this section, we first consider emotional intelligence, a skill that includes the abilities to understand what motivates other people, how they work, and how to work cooperatively with them as well as to understand ourselves and to be able to use that understanding in our lives. We then address specific personality dimensions that are important in teams.

Emotional Intelligence

In *The Nicomachean Ethics,* Aristotle wrote, "Anyone can become angry—that is easy. But to be angry with the right person, to the right degree, at the right time, for the right purpose, and in the right way—this is not easy."[22] Aristotle called on us to manage our emotional lives with intelligence. Our passions, when properly managed, can help us to act, prosper, and survive. Mismanaged, they can create havoc. The challenge, then, is to bring intelligence to our emotions.[23]

Most experts now agree that IQ scores are heavily influenced by a relatively narrow range of language and math skills. So IQ taps only a small part of the full human intellect. Further, the skills assessed by IQ tests may be relevant to classroom performance, but IQ scores do little to predict performance in the real world. This suggests the benefits of a broader view of intelligence. In one compelling demonstration of the need for this expanded view, children at age 4 were given an IQ test and the Marshmallow Test—in that test the child is given a marshmallow and told that if he or she can put off eating it until later, he or she can have two. Twelve to 14 years later, this measure of impulse control was twice as strong a predictor as IQ of how children did on the Scholastic Aptitude Test (SAT). It also predicted adjustment, popularity, confidence, and dependability.

When people—whether experts or not—are asked to describe an intelligent person, they use phrases such as "solves problems well," "displays interest in the world at large," "accepts others for what they are," "admits mistakes," "is goal oriented," and "converses well." Such phrases suggest that people focus on the worldly side of intelligence, as opposed to just academic intelligence.

Howard Gardner, in *Frames of Mind*, discusses several forms of intelligence, including logical-mathematical, linguistic, bodily-kinesthetic, visual-spatial, musical, interpersonal, and intrapersonal intelligence.[24] Gardner argues that these intelligences are intrinsically equal in value and that the degree to which people possess them helps explain how they learn and fare in the workplace. He further argues that it is possible to hone these intelligences and that they wither with lack of use.

Only the first two of these intelligences fit into traditional conceptions of IQ. Gardner's personal intelligences—interpersonal and intrapersonal—are defined as follows:

- **Interpersonal intelligence.**—The ability to understand other people: what motivates them, how they work, and how to work cooperatively with them.
- **Intrapersonal intelligence.**—The capacity to form an accurate model of oneself and to be able to use that model to operate effectively in life.

Together, interpersonal intelligence and intrapersonal intelligence comprise emotional intelligence.

Goleman, author of *Emotional Intelligence* and *Working with Emotional Intelligence*, describes **emotional intelligence** (EQ) as a different way of being smart. Emotional intelligence is not IQ; it is how someone does in life, manages feelings, gets along with others, and is empathetic and motivated.[25]

While the sorts of intelligence gauged by IQ tests reside in the **neocortex**, or rational brain, EQ resides in the **amygdala**, in the deep recesses of the brain's limbic system. The amygdala's chemical surges produce everything from blind rage to fear to avoidance of pain to euphoria. As noted by Aristotle, our passions play important roles. They motivate us and may help with our success and even survival. However, the emotional brain may highjack the rational brain. As a result, fear, rage, and jealousy may prevent teams from rationally addressing problems. The ability to effectively deal with emotions is, thus, critical in teams.

Emotional intelligence involves a rich set of abilities. These include self-awareness (recognizing an emotion as it engulfs us), self-regulation (controlling reactions to emotion-laden events so that our response fits the situation), motivation (directing emotions in the service of a desirable goal), empathy (recognizing emotions in others), and social skill (managing the emotions in others). A more complete summary of the dimensions of emotional intelligence is shown in Figure 5-1.[26]

As suggested previously, EQ is critical in organizations, and in life in general. For example, EQ is needed to effectively manage diversity, to work in teams, and to adapt to new situations. In organizations, EQ has been shown to relate to leadership ability, group performance, individual performance, quality of interpersonal exchange, change-management skills, and the ability to conduct effective performance appraisals.[27] It has also been found to relate to team performance.[28] Emotional intelligence of team members—especially awareness of one's own emotions and management of others' emotions—is related to team cohesiveness.[29] EQ has also been shown to be associated with learning in teams.[30]

Strategies for Enhancing Emotional Intelligence

Some practical strategies can be implemented to develop your emotional intelligence:[31]

- **Manage emotions instead of suppressing them.** Allowing people's emotions to be expressed in the context of the discussion of business issues may not seem natural or comfortable to many people who have been conditioned to think that so-called objective information is the only information that is valid. In reality, allowing workers to express how they feel about specific issues or changes being implemented in a company can be very valuable to understanding and managing their commitment to a goal or strategy and their motivation to perform. In short, remember to ask others not only what they think or believe about an issue, but also how they feel about it.

- **Recognize your hot buttons.** A hot button is simply something that happens that elicits a strong emotional reaction from you. Everyone has hot

Component	Definition	Hallmarks
Self-Awareness	Knowing one's emotions, strengths, weaknesses, drives, values, and goals—and their impact on others	• Self-confidence • Realistic self-assessment • Self-deprecating sense of humor • Thirst for constructive criticism
Self-Regulation	Controlling or redirecting disruptive emotions and impulses	• Trustworthiness • Integrity • Comfort with ambiguity and change
Motivation	Being driven to achieve for the sake of achievement	• A passion for the work itself and for new challenges • Unflagging energy to improve • Optimism in the face of failure
Empathy	Considering others' feelings, especially when making decisions	• Expertise in attracting and retaining talent • Ability to develop others • Sensitivity to cross-cultural differences
Social Skill	Managing relationships to move people in desired directions	• Effectiveness in leading change • Persuasiveness • Extensive networking • Expertise in building and leading teams

Figure 5-1

Dimensions of Emotional Intelligence

Source: Based in part on D. Goleman, "What Makes a Leader?" *Harvard Business Review*, January 1, 2004, p. 88.

buttons: it might happen when your direct reports are late to meetings or don't complete their projects by the deadlines you give them. To deal effectively with your own emotional reactions, it is important to identify what your hot buttons are and to develop a sense of how you will control your reactions if and when they are pushed.

• **If you are not an optimist, become one.** Being pessimistic can generate negative energy around an issue and foster conflict, stress, and dysfunctional work culture. These can then undermine your ability to achieve desired objectives associated with your team or work unit. The key here is to try to maintain an overall positive attitude and approach to dealing with any issue. This is not saying that you should not address difficult issues because they are negative, but rather that you want to be careful to frame the discussion of negative issues or problems within an overall constructive approach that attempts to be as positive as possible.

• **Read the emotions of others.** This involves the use of empathy (i.e., trying to see the situation from the perspective of another person) to develop a sense of what others' emotions are around the discussion of an issue. Through the use of empathy, you as a team leader or member will be able to understand where others are coming from, which will help you to identify appropriate things that you can say or do to handle a situation in the most effective manner possible.

- **Use your emotional intelligence to help others boost theirs.** The team members and others you interact with possess varying levels of emotional intelligence. Remember that although the people you work with may all be very intelligent and hard working in general, they may not necessarily possess high levels of EQ. So, you may need to act as a coach for others to help them better understand and develop their own emotional intelligences.

Now, assess your emotional intelligence along six dimensions by using the scale in Self-Assessment 5.2 on the text website.

Important Personality Dimensions

It is especially important to understand how people with particular personalities may behave in team and other settings. In this section we review some personality characteristics related to behavior or performance. Before we consider these characteristics, complete Self-Assessment 5.3 on the text website.

Risk-Taking Propensity

People—even those in the same position in the same organization—differ markedly in their **risk-taking propensity**.[32] Some are risk averse. They like to play it safe, choosing alternatives that are likely to give a relatively low but certain return. Others—risk seekers—like to gamble. They prefer alternatives that may turn out very well or very poorly to those with little variance in outcomes. Risk takers tend to make fast decisions based on relatively little information. People with different degrees of risk-taking propensity will make very different decisions in the same situation.[33]

It is important to note that groups are subject to what is termed polarization.[34] **Polarization** is the tendency of group attitudes and decisions to be more extreme than those of the individual members before interaction. So, a team made up of members who are moderately risk taking is likely to be even more risk tasking, and a team whose members oppose a political candidate is likely to show even greater opposition after interaction.

Proactive Personality

Proactivity is the extent to which people take actions to influence their environments. Proactive individuals look for opportunities, show initiative, take action, and persevere until they are able to bring about change. People with proactive personalities engage in high levels of entrepreneurial activities and have relatively high levels of job performance.[35] This is consistent with the idea that the modern workplace rewards take-charge, self-motivated individuals. As a result, having a proactive personality is a highly valued trait for team members.

Authoritarianism

Authoritarian individuals believe that power and status should be clearly defined and that there should be a hierarchy of authority.[36] They feel that authority should be concentrated in the hands of a few leaders and that this authority should be obeyed. Authoritarian leaders expect unquestioning obedience to their commands; authoritarian submissive subordinates willingly give it. If a team leader is authoritarian and his or her team members are not, frustration or conflict may result. Authoritarian individuals are likely to be most comfortable in organizations that emphasize rules and following the chain of command. They may be uncomfortable if asked to give their opinions to team leaders or members, especially if they see them as being of higher status. They may also have difficulty taking responsibility or participating in self-managed teams.

Dogmatism

Dogmatic individuals are closed minded. They have rigid belief systems and doggedly stick to their opinions, refusing to revise them in the face of conflicting evidence. Dogmatic individuals make decisions quickly, based on relatively little information, and are confident in those decisions. They like to follow the rules and are unlikely to consider novel alternatives. They may perform acceptably in well-defined, routine situations, especially if there are time constraints. In other cases, especially those demanding creativity, they do poorly. In a team setting it may be important to ensure that dogmatic members do not force the team to premature, inadequately reasoned decisions. It may also be necessary to take steps to prevent dogmatic team members from blocking new ideas.

Locus of Control

Locus of control refers to the degree to which individuals believe that the things that happen to them are the result of their own actions. Those who believe that such things are within their own control have an *internal locus of control*. Others have an *external locus of control*; they see their lives as being controlled by fate, circumstance, or chance. Externals are unlikely to believe that they can do better if they try harder or that the rewards and punishments they receive depend upon how well they do. For each of these reasons, internals may be more highly motivated than externals. Internals have also been shown to be likely to respond in more positive ways to stress than externals, to behave in more ethical ways, to feel more empowered, and to be more entrepreneurial.[37]

As such, internals are likely to be more productive team members. However, if team members have external loci of control, it may be especially important to support them and to help assure them that they can do well.

Tolerance for Ambiguity

Individuals with a high **tolerance for ambiguity** welcome uncertainty and change. Those with low tolerance for ambiguity see such situations as threatening and uncomfortable. Since teams are increasingly facing dynamic, unstructured situations, high tolerance for ambiguity is clearly an important characteristic of team members.

Machiavellianism

Individuals with **Machiavellian** personalities think any behavior is acceptable if it achieves their goals. Machiavellians try to manipulate others. They are unemotional and detached. They look out for Number One and aren't likely to be good team players. Not surprisingly, they also are relatively likely to be unethical.[38] As such, it is important to recognize Machiavellians, to bring their unethical activities to light, and to foster a climate in which such behaviors are not tolerated.

Self-Monitoring

Self-monitoring is the extent to which people vary their behavior to match the situation and make the best possible impression on others.[39] High self-monitors pay close attention to their audience and tailor their behaviors accordingly. For instance, a high self-monitor may act humble and respectful when dealing with the boss but be boastful and ill mannered with subordinates. Similarly, a high self-monitor may present very different opinions to different audiences. High self-monitors are chameleon-like, able to change their behaviors to fit the audience. Low self-monitors, on the other hand, react to situations without looking to others for behavioral cues; they present the same face in different situations.

While the high self-monitor's chameleon-like behavior may seem somehow devious, it can also be seen as sensitive to the demands of the situation. Evidence seems clear that high self-monitors tend to do better. For example, a study that tracked business graduates showed that high self-monitors got more promotions, either cross-company or within their original firm, than low self-monitors.[40] High self-monitors receive better performance ratings and more promotions than low self-monitors and are more likely to emerge as leaders.[41]

Type A and Type B Behavior Patterns

The **Type A behavior pattern** is characterized by feelings of great time pressure and impatience. Type A's work aggressively, speak explosively, are very competitive, and find themselves constantly struggling. The opposite pattern, called the **Type B behavior pattern**, is characterized by low stress, patience, and steady pacing at work. Type B's are relaxed, cooperative, and easygoing. Individuals with Type A behavior patterns are much more likely than others to experience high stress levels and to show a variety of symptoms of stress, including coronary heart disease. Type A's have trouble delegating responsibility to others, don't work well in groups, and are impatient with tasks requiring prolonged problem solving. Because of these limitations and the health risks of being a Type A, relatively few Type A's rise to high levels in organizations. In teams, Type A's can bring energy, but they can also be disruptive.

The Myers-Briggs Type Indicator

The **Myers-Briggs Type Indicator (MBTI)** is a popular tool for assessing personalities and forming teams.[42] The MBTI gauges personality along 4 dimensions, yielding 16 ($2 \times 2 \times 2 \times 2$) "types." Note that the MBTI gauges preferences. The dimensions are these:

- **Extraversion (E) versus Introversion (I).** Extraverts are outgoing, are energized by people and things, and don't like to be isolated from others. Introverts prefer to spend time alone and are energized by concepts and ideas.

- **Sensing (S) versus Intuition (N).** Sensing types prefer to be precise and concrete. They like specific, detailed information and prefer to develop a single idea in depth. Intuitive types like to see the big picture. They are imaginative, like to explore what is new, and look to the future.
- **Thinking (T) versus Feeling (F).** Thinking types prefer to be rational and systematic; they prefer to use careful analysis, logic, and hard facts to reach conclusions. Feeling types prefer to rely on their feelings and to go with their gut.
- **Perception (P) versus Judgment (J).** Perception types enjoy a variety of frequent changes, learn by exploring what engages curiosity, and are casual and easy-going. Judgment types prefer schedules, routines, and systems, like to plan in advance, and are orderly and systematic.

Within each of the dimensions, opposite types may have trouble understanding and empathizing with each other. However, these opposites are generally complementary in teams. For example, extraverts open lines of communication among team members, while introverts provide internal reflection on team discussions. Sensing types bring up pertinent facts and keep track of detail while intuitive types recognize possibilities and see the big picture. Thinking types analyze, organize, and weigh the evidence while feeling types arouse enthusiasm, persuade, and conciliate. Judging types help keep a team on schedule while perceiving types help the team explore and be open to new possibilities.

Now, complete Skills Practice 5.3 on the text website to gain a greater understanding of your own and your team members' personalities and work styles.

The Big Five Personality Dimensions

Hundreds of personality characteristics have been identified, of which we have considered several of the most important. Evidence is accumulating that virtually all personality measures can be categorized into five consistent sets, now called the **Big Five**: extraversion, agreeableness, conscientiousness, emotional stability, and openness to experience. The Big Five dimensions, summarized in Figure 5-2, hold up remarkably well across national cultures and over time.[43]

- **Extraversion.** Extraverts tend to be outgoing and gregarious, dominant and ambitious, and adventuresome. Extraverts tend to have positive emotions, to have a large number of close friends, and to take on leadership roles.
- **Agreeableness.** Agreeable persons are trusting, caring, good-natured, cheerful, and gentle. Agreeableness is especially significant in careers where teamwork or customer service is important.
- **Conscientiousness.** Conscientious individuals are hardworking and persistent, responsible and careful, and well organized. Conscientious individuals have higher levels of job performance, engage in fewer counterproductive work behaviors, are more satisfied, are absent less often, and are less likely to leave the firm than those who are less conscientious.[44]

Figure 5-2

The Big Five Personality
Dimensions

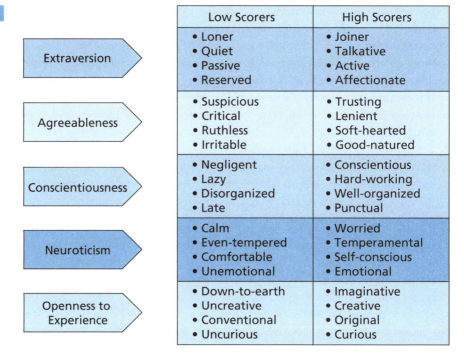

	Low Scorers	High Scorers
Extraversion	• Loner • Quiet • Passive • Reserved	• Joiner • Talkative • Active • Affectionate
Agreeableness	• Suspicious • Critical • Ruthless • Irritable	• Trusting • Lenient • Soft-hearted • Good-natured
Conscientiousness	• Negligent • Lazy • Disorganized • Late	• Conscientious • Hard-working • Well-organized • Punctual
Neuroticism	• Calm • Even-tempered • Comfortable • Unemotional	• Worried • Temperamental • Self-conscious • Emotional
Openness to Experience	• Down-to-earth • Uncreative • Conventional • Uncurious	• Imaginative • Creative • Original • Curious

- **Emotional stability.** Emotional stability is best recognized by its absence: anxiety, hostility, depression, self-consciousness, vulnerability, and impulsiveness. Emotional stability is positively related to job performance.[45]
- **Openness to experience.** Individuals who are open to experience tend to be intelligent, imaginative, and unconventional. They do better than their opposites in learning new skills.

This suggests that agreeableness, conscientiousness, and emotional stability are likely to be helpful in teams. Openness to experience is especially important for teams with creative tasks. As noted earlier, extraverts help facilitate team interactions but may benefit from introverts' reflection.

Take a few minutes now to rate yourself on these dimensions by completing Self-Assessment 5.4 on the text website.

Our discussion of personality should not be taken to suggest that people have no control over their actions. Instead, personality characteristics suggest tendencies to behave in certain ways. People's conscious decisions may help them overcome troublesome behavior patterns. For instance, employees may be able to take actions to alter Type A behavior patterns, to ensure that they consider more information before making a decision, and to modify their risk preferences.

Still, throughout your career you will be working with people who react very differently from one another with respect to risk, uncertainty, new ideas, rules and regulations, and much else. Some of your team members and others are likely to be more manipulative, self-serving, and unethical than others. Some will be self-starters, and some will need a push. Some will be driven, and some will be laid back. These diverse personalities will provide opportunities and challenges as you build teams, try out new practices, and simply get through the workday. By recognizing this variety and its implications, you will have made a good start toward successfully understanding, predicting, and influencing others on your team and in the workplace.

Now, complete Skills Practice 5.4 on the text website. This exercise gives you the opportunity to administer some of the self-assessment measures of personality presented earlier in this chapter to a small sample of working individuals (managers or individual contributors) to develop a personality profile for each of these individuals and to draw some conclusions about their work styles.

Recognizing Cross-Cultural Differences

With *globalization*, the world's peoples are becoming more interconnected with respect to the cultural, political, technological, and environmental aspects of their lives. What does this mean for you?

- **You are likely to be on teams made up of members from other cultures.** With virtual teams you may be videoconferencing or otherwise interacting with team members in other countries.
- **You are likely to spend at least part of your career in other countries**—in fact, some companies now require international experience for their top managers.
- **According to Andrew Grove, Chairman of Intel, with globalization "every employee will compete with every person in the world who is capable of doing the same job.** There are a lot of them, and many of them are very hungry."[46]
- **You may suddenly find yourself working for a foreign firm.** Increasingly, you may be working for a firm headquartered in Germany, Sweden, Japan, or almost anywhere else in the world.
- **You will be managing a culturally diverse workforce even if you never leave the United States.** Consider the following: the Census Bureau estimates that by the year 2050, Asian Americans, Hispanics, African Americans, and other nonwhite groups will comprise 47% of the U.S. population.

So whether you are living in Lima, Ohio, or Lima, Peru, you will be managing a culturally diverse workforce, dealing with global competitors, or even working for a foreign firm.

Cultural Intelligence

Earlier in this chapter we discussed emotional intelligence, the ability to understand and to manage your own emotions and those of others in the workplace. **Cultural intelligence** focuses on the ability to understand and manage culture and cultural differences in the workplace.

David Thomas and Kerr Inkson developed a process model that specifies five stages that an individual can go through in developing cultural intelligence:[47]

- **Stage 1: Reactivity to external stimuli.** This stage reflects the lowest level of cultural intelligence. Individuals in this stage typically do not even recognize that cultural differences exist. As a result, they possess very little interest in learning about cultures. Often, these individuals are also rather ethnocentric in that they assume that the beliefs, values, and customs of their own culture are the best or that people from other cultures should adapt to their way of thinking and doing things.

- **Stage 2: Recognition of other cultural norms and motivation to learn about them.** In this stage, people start to recognize that cultural differences exist, and they may become motivated to begin to learn about other cultures. People at this stage focus on finding quick and easy ways to understand and to manage cultural differences. At this point, people are still not capable of substantial adaptation to cultural differences.
- **Stage 3: Accommodation of other cultural norms and rules in one's own mind.** At this stage people can begin to link a deeper understanding of different cultural norms to actual behavior in dealing with people from other cultures. Individuals in this stage are often still not very skilled in how they exhibit various behaviors for adapting to cultural differences.
- **Stage 4: Assimilation of diverse cultural norms into alternative behaviors.** Individuals in this stage of cultural development have become highly skilled in understanding and adapting to cultural differences. They can move seamlessly from one culture to another in an almost effortless manner. People from other cultures see those at this stage as possessing a deep understanding of their culture's norms and customs.
- **Stage 5: Proactivity in cultural behavior based on recognition of cultural cues that others do not perceive.** At this stage an individual is so skilled in understanding cultural differences that he or she can actually identify changes in a cultural context and anticipate how to behave even before people who are from that culture are able to do so.

A variety of strategies can be used to develop your cultural intelligence while you are still in school, including the following:

- **Study abroad, especially in a country that is culturally much different from your home country.**
- **Complete an international internship.**
- **Travel abroad as a tourist as much as possible.**
- **Find a business mentor from another country—such as an alumna or alumnus from your college or university.**
- **Get a job teaching English abroad.**
- **Complete a foreign mission/humanitarian service experience (e.g., Peace Corps).**
- **Take classes on international business (e.g., study trip courses to other countries) and foreign languages you are interested in.**
- **Attend lectures and movies on your campus that deal with international issues.**
- **Read international news sections of major newspapers or magazines, such as the *Economist*, which focus on international issues.**
- **Join a student organization that focuses on international issues.**

What might we expect as we deal with people from other national cultures? Geert **Hofstede**, a Dutch researcher who worked as a psychologist for

IBM, studied 116,000 people working in sixty-four countries and identified five important dimensions along which national cultures differ:[48]

- **Individualism versus collectivism**. In *individualistic cultures*, such as the United States and Australia, the cultural belief is that the individual comes first—social frameworks are loosely knit, and people are chiefly expected to look after their own interests and those of their immediate family. There is an emphasis on individual achievement. Society offers individuals a great amount of freedom, and people are used to making independent decisions and taking independent action. In *collectivist cultures*, such as Colombia and Pakistan, there are tight social frameworks; people expect the groups of which they are members to look after them and protect them in times of trouble. In exchange for security, loyalty is expected. A saying that reflects the collectivist view is this: "The nail that sticks out will be pounded down."
- **Power distance**. This is the degree to which a society accepts the fact that power in institutions and organizations is distributed unequally. A high power distance society, such as the Philippines, Mexico, or India, accepts wide differences in power in organizations. Employees show great respect for authority, titles, status, and rank. Titles are important in bargaining. A low power distance society, such as Denmark, Israel, or Ireland, plays down inequalities as much as possible.
- **Uncertainty avoidance**. This term refers to the way societies deal with risk and uncertainty. In low uncertainty avoidance countries, such as Switzerland and Denmark, people are relatively comfortable with risks and tolerate behaviors and opinions that differ from their own. In high uncertainty avoidance countries, such as Japan and Greece, there is a high level of anxiety among the people. Formal rules and other mechanisms are used to provide security and reduce risk. There is less tolerance for deviant ideas and behaviors, and people strive to believe in absolute truths.
- **Quality versus quantity of life**. Some cultures, such as Japan and Austria, emphasize the *quantity of life* and value assertiveness and the acquisition of money and material things. Other cultures, such as the Scandinavian countries, emphasize the *quality of life* and the importance of relationships, and they show sensitivity and concern for the welfare of others. In quality of life cultures, people stop to smell the roses. In quantity of life cultures, people try to get as many roses as possible.
- **Time orientation**. Citizens of some countries, such as Japan and Hong Kong, have a *long-term orientation*, derived from values that include thrift (saving) and persistence in achieving goals. Those from other countries, such as France and Indonesia, have a *short-term orientation*, derived from values that express a concern for maintaining personal stability or happiness and living for the present.

These dimensions have important implications for teams:

- **Team rewards may be more acceptable to members from collectivist cultures than to those from individualistic cultures.**

- **Team members from cultures differing in uncertainty avoidance may disagree on how risky decisions should be.** Members from cultures higher on uncertainty avoidance may also have trouble accepting novel ideas and may want considerable structure in meetings.
- **Autocratic leadership styles may be accepted by members of high power distance cultures but may be resented by members from low power distance cultures.**
- **Team members from cultures emphasizing quality of life may place more value on team relationships and processes, while members from cultures emphasizing quantity of life may focus more on team outcomes.**
- **Members from cultures differing in time orientation may disagree on the importance of long-term and short-term goals.**

Another key factor is whether cultures are high or low **context**. In a **high-context culture**, such as most Asian, Hispanic, African, and Arab countries, the context in which a communication occurs is just as important as the words that are actually spoken, and cultural clues are important in understanding what is being communicated. The context includes the social setting, use of phrasing, gestures, tone of voice, and the person's history and status. In a **low-context culture**, such as Germany or the United States, the words used by the speaker explicitly convey the speaker's message to the listener.

Figure 5-3 summarizes how various factors in teams are likely to be influenced by national culture.

Nonverbal communications, discussed in Chapter 6, while important in all settings, are especially critical in high-context cultures. Most immigrants to the United States are now coming from high-context cultures. Nonverbal communications have dramatically different meanings across cultures.[49] For

Figure 5-3

Some Roles of National Culture in Teams

Factor	Example of How Culture Matters
Team Rewards	More acceptable in collectivist cultures than in individualistic cultures
Risk Taking	More risk taking in low uncertainty avoidance cultures
Leadership Style	Autocratic style more acceptable in high power distance cultures; democratic style more acceptable in low power distance cultures
Team Relationships and Processes	Relatively more important in cultures emphasizing quality of life
Team Outcomes	Relatively more important in cultures emphasizing quantity of life
Goal Orientation	Greater emphasis on long-term goals in long-term orientation cultures
Communications	Meaning of message heavily influenced by context in high-context cultures; meaning of message conveyed primarily by words in low-context cultures

instance, nodding your head means "Yes" in most countries but "No" in Bulgaria and Greece. The classic "OK" sign of thumb and forefinger forming a circle can imply "money" in Japan, means "worthless" in France, and is considered an obscene gesture in Brazil, Germany, and Russia. In Saudi Arabia, to cross your legs in such a way that you display the sole of your foot to your host is a grievous affront. While North Americans often wave to signal "Hello" or "Goodbye," this action signals "No!" in much of Europe.

There are also cultural differences in the meaning of eye contact. While Americans generally expect eye contact in a conversation, many Asians and Hispanics consider eye contact, especially with a superior, to be utterly disrespectful. In countries such as Libya, looking a woman in the eye for more than a short time is considered a form of assault.

Now, go to Skills Practice 5.5 on the text website to further develop an understanding of international business etiquette, manners, and culture.

Summary and Integration

Here are key takeaways for this chapter:

> Diversity in teams can enhance the creativity and quality of the output of work teams. Team leaders need to build diversity into the composition of a team based on all types of differences, not just gender and racial or ethnic background. In addition, team leaders need to leverage the power of diversity by fostering a culture and work process that uses the knowledge and skills of all team members.

> Team leaders and members need to understand the ways in which other members of a team are different from one another in terms of how they think, make decisions, communicate, and more. This knowledge enables team leaders and members to better understand and adapt to others and to work more effectively with them.

> Team leaders and members need technical skills, but they must also develop critical soft skills, such as emotional intelligence, that enhance their ability to understand and to manage others' reactions to the work a team is doing and to resolve issues that arise during a project or process.

Notes

1   P. Digh, "Coming to Terms with Diversity," *HRMagazine*, November 1998, pp. 117–120. For a discussion of other definitions of diversity, see Q. M. Roberson, "Disentangling the Meanings of Diversity and Inclusion in Organizations," *Group and Organization Management*, 2006, *31(2)*, pp. 212–236.

2   D.A. Kravitz, "Diversity in Teams: A Two-Edged Sword Requires Careful Handling," *Psychological Science in the Public Interest*, 2005, *6(2)*, pp. i–ii.

3   For instance, see T.H. Cox, "Managing Cultural Diversity: Implications for Organizational Competitiveness," *Academy of Management Executive*, 1991, *5(3)*, pp. 45–56; K.E. Joyce, "Lessons for Employers from *Fortune*'s '100 Best,'" *Business Horizons*, March/April 2003, *46(2)*, pp. 77–84; and, D. van Knippenberg & M.C. Schippers, "Work Group Diversity," *Annual Review of Psychology*, 2007, *58*, pp. 515–541.

4   C.J. Nemeth & J.L. Kwan, "Minority Influence, Divergent Thinking and Detection of Correct Solutions," *Journal of Applied Social Psychology*, 1987, *17*, pp. 788–799.

5   P. Digh, "Coming to Terms with Diversity," *HRMagazine*, November 1998, p. 120. Betsy Holden, CEO of Kraft Foods, was chosen as one of *Working Woman*'s Champions of Diversity award recipients; see A. Finnegan, "Champions 2001," *Working Woman*, April 2001, *26(4)*, p. 50.

6   L.C. Lancaster and D. Stillman, *When Generations Collide* (New York: Collins Business, 2005).

7   M. Zellmer-Bruhn, M. Maloney, A. Bhappu, & R. Salvador, "When and How Do Differences Matter?: An Exploration of Perceived Similarity in Teams," *Organizational Behavior and Human Decision Processes*, 2008, *107(1)*, pp. 41–59.

8   D. Kirkpatrick, J.J. Phillips, & P.P. Phillips, "Getting Results from Diversity Training—In Dollars and Cents," *HR Focus*, October 2003, p. 3; and, J.J. Phillips & P.P. Phillips, "Show Me the Money: The Use of ROI in Performance Improvement, Part 1," *Performance Improvement*, 2007, *46(9)*, pp. 8–22.

9   F. Rice, "How To Make Diversity Pay," *Fortune*, August 8, 1994, p. 84; and, S. Lakshminarayan, "A Social Marketing Based Strategy for Planning Diversity Events," *Journal of Diversity Management*, 2006, *1(1)*, pp. 39–48. For discussions of diversity issues at Denny's, see S.T. Brathwaite, "Denny's: A Diversity Success Story," *Franchising World*, July/August 2002, pp. 28–29; and, C. Riesch & B.H. Kleiner, "Discrimination towards Customers in the Restaurant Industry," *Equal Opportunities International*, 2005, *24(7/8)*, pp. 29–37.

10   F. Rice, "How to Make Diversity Pay," *Fortune*, August 8, 1994, pp. 78–86. See also, C.A. Swody & G.N. Powell, "Determinants of Employee Participation in Organizations' Family-Friendly Programs: A Multi-Level Approach," *Journal of Business and Psychology*, 2007, *22*, pp. 111–122.

11   A. Homan, D. van Klippenberg, G. Van Kleef, & C. De Dreu, "Bridging Faultlines by Valuing Diversity: Diversity Beliefs, Information Elaboration, and Performance in Diverse Work Groups," *Journal of Applied Psychology*, 2007, *92(5)*, pp. 1189–1199.

12   "The Diversity Initiative at US WEST Dex," *Successful Meetings*, March 1998, pp. 55–57.

13   D. Lau & J.K. Murnighan, "Demographic Similarity and Faultlines: The Compositional Dynamics of Organizational Groups," *Academy of Management Review*, 1998, *23*, pp. 325–340.

14   For more on group fault lines, see S.M.B. Thatcher & P.C. Patel, "Group Faultlines: A Review, Integration, and Guide to Future Research," *Journal of Management*, 2012, *38*, pp. 969–1009; D. van Knippenberg & M. Schippers, "Work Group Diversity," *Annual Review of Psychology*, *58*, pp. 515–541; and, A.M. Carton & J.N. Cummings, "A Theory of Subgroups in Teams," *Academy of Management Review*, *37(3)*, pp. 441–470.

15   For a good review, see S.M.B. Thatcher & P.C. Patel, "Group Faultlines: A Review, Integration, and Guide to Future Research," *Journal of Management*, 2012, *38*, 969–1009.

16   W.E. Watson, K. Kumar, & L.K. Michaelsen, "Cultural Diversity's Influence on Interaction Process and Performance: Comparing Homogeneous and Diverse Task Groups," *Academy of Management Journal*, 1993, *36(3)*, pp. 590–602.

17   Y. Huo, "Procedural Justice and Social Regulation across Group Boundaries: Does Subgroup Identification Undermine Relationship-Based Governance?" *Personality and Social Psychology Bulletin*, 2003, *29*, pp. 336–348; and, Y. Huo, H. Smith, T. Tyler, & A. Lind, "Superordinate Identification, Subgroup

Identification, and Justice Concerns: Is Separatism the Problem; Is Assimilation the Answer?" *Psychological Science*, 1996, 7, pp. 40–45.

18   A.C. Homan, J.R. Hollenbeck, S. Humphrey, D. van Klippenberg, D.R. Ilgen, & G.A. van Kleef, "Facing Differences with an Open Mind: Openness to Experience, Salience of Intragroup Differences, and Performance of Diverse Work Groups," *Academy of Management Journal*, 2008, *51*, pp. 1204–1222.

19   E. Mannix & M.A. Neale, "What Differences Make a Difference? The Promise and Reality of Diverse Teams in Organizations," *Psychological Science in the Public Interest*, 2005, *6(2)*, p. 46.

20   For discussions of company programs to enhance diversity, see "Driving Diversity," *Hispanic*, May 2003, *16(5)*, p. 46; W.J. Mott, Jr., "Developing a Culturally Competent Workforce: A Diversity Program in Progress," *Journal of Healthcare Management*, September/October 2003, *48(5)*, pp. 337+; K. Gray, "Enterprise Rent-A-Car: Recruiting Program is a Driving Force Behind Enterprise's Success," *NACE Journal*, Spring 2003, *63(3)*, p. 19; and L.F. Pendry, D.M. Driscoll, & S.C.T. Field, "Diversity Training: Putting Theory into Practice," *Journal of Occupational and Organizational Psychology*, 2007, *80(1)*, pp. 27–50. For a critical perspective on the business case for diversity, see F. Hansen, "Diversity's Business Case Doesn't Add Up," *Workforce*, April 2003, *82(4)*, pp. 28–32.

21   For evidence on the stability of personality, see B.J. Small, C. Hertzog, D.F. Hultsch, and R.A. Dixon, "Stability and Change in Adult Personality Over 6 Years: Findings from the Victoria Longitudinal Study," *Journals of Gerontology: Series B*, May 2003, *58B(3)*, pp. P166-P170; and, J. Rantanen, R.-L. Metsäpelto, T. Feldt, L. Pulkkinen, & K. Kokko, "Long-Term Stability in the Big Five Personality Traits in Adulthood," *Scandinavian Journal of Psychology*, 2007, *48*, pp. 511–518.

22   Aristotle, *The Nichomachean Ethics of Aristotle*, trans. F.H. Peters, 5th ed. (London: Kegan Paul, Trench, Truebner & Co., 1893).

For more on the relevance of Aristotle's views to behavior in organizations, see T. Morris, *If Aristotle Ran General Motors: The New Soul of Business* (New York: Henry Holt, 1997); R. Duska & J. DesJardins, "Aristotelian Leadership and Business," *Business & Professional Ethics Journal*, Fall 2001, *20(3/4)*, pp. 19–38; and, M. Alzola, "Character and Environment: The Status of Virtue in Organizations," *Journal of Business Ethics*, 2008, *78*, pp. 343–357.

23   D. Goleman, *Emotional Intelligence* (New York: Bantam Books, 1995). For a review incorporating this concept, see Q.N. Huy, "Emotional Capability, Emotional Intelligence, and Radical Change," *Academy of Management Review*, 1999, *24*, pp. 325–345. See also D. Goleman, *Working with Emotional Intelligence* (New York: Bantam Books, 1998); H.A. Elfenbein & N. Ambady, "Predicting Workplace Outcomes from the Ability to Eavesdrop on Feelings," *Journal of Applied Psychology*, October 2002, *87(5)*, pp. 963–971; and, J.D. Mayer, R.D. Roberts, & S.G. Barsade, "Human Abilities: Emotional Intelligence," *Annual Review of Psychology*, 2008, *59*, pp. 507–536.

24   H. Gardner, *Frames of Mind* (New York: Basic Books, 1993). Also, see J.L. Nolen, "Multiple Intelligences in the Classroom," *Education*, Fall 2003, *124(1)*, pp. 115–119; and, R. Akbari & K. Hosseini, "Multiple Intelligences and Language Learning Strategies: Investigating Possible Relations," *System*, 2008, *36*, pp. 141–155.

25   See D. Goleman, *Emotional Intelligence* (New York: Bantam Books, 1995); and, D. Goleman, *Working with Emotional Intelligence* (New York: Bantam Books, 1998).

26 Goleman, D. "What Makes a Leader?" *Harvard Business Review*, January 1, 2004, pp. 82–91.

27 See D. Goleman, *Working with Emotional Intelligence* (New York: Bantam Books, 1998); and, P.J. Jordan & A.C. Troth, "Managing Emotions during Team Problem Solving: Emotional Intelligence and Conflict Resolution," *Human Performance*, 2004, *17(2)*, pp. 195–218.

28 Z. Naseer, S. Chisti, F. Rahman, & N.B. Jumani, "Impact of Emotional Intelligence on Team Performance in Higher Education Institutes," *International Online Journal of Educational Sciences*, 2011, *3(1)*, pp. 30–46; E.S. Koman, & S.B. Wolff, "Emotional Intelligence Competencies in the Team and Team Leader: A Multi-Level Examination of the Impact of Emotional Intelligence on Team Performance," *Journal of Management Development*, 2008, *27(1)*, pp. 55–75; and, C.I. . Farh, M.-G. Seo, & P.E. Tesluk, "Emotional Intelligence, Teamwork Effectiveness, and Job Performance: The Moderating Role of Job Content," *Journal of Applied Psychology*, 2012, *97(4)*, pp. 890–900.

29 A. Moore & K. Mamiseishvili, "Examining the Relationship between Emotional Intelligence and Group Cohesion," *Journal of Education for Business*, 2012, *87(5)*, pp. 296–302.

30 R. Ghosh, B. Shuck, & J. Petrosko, "Emotional Intelligence and Organizational Learning in Work Teams," *Journal of Management Development*, 2012, *31(6)*, pp. 603–619.

31 D. Stauffer. "Boosting Your Emotional Intelligence," *Harvard Business Review*, October 1997, p. 1–4. See also, J. Welch & S. Welch, "Emotional Mismanagement," *Business Week*, July 28, 2008, p. 84.

32 See Z. Shapira, *Risk Taking: A Managerial Perspective* (New York: Russell Sage Foundation, 1995). For a cross-cultural comparison of risk taking, see H. Lobler & J. Bode, "Risk Taking under Transition: An Empirical Comparison between Chinese, Western-, and Eastern-German Managers," *Thunderbird International Business Review*, January/February 1999, pp. 69–81; and, M. Kloep, N. Güney, F. Çok, & Ö.F. Simsek, "Motives for Risk-Taking in Adolescence: A Cross-Cultural Study," *Journal of Adolescence*, 2009, *32*, pp. 135–151.

33 See, for instance, L.V. Ryan and A.K. Buchholtz, "Trust, Risk, and Shareholder Decision Making: An Investor Perspective on Corporate Governance," *Business Ethics Quarterly*, January 2001, *11(1)*, pp. 177–194; and, P.R. Das & B. Talreja, "Risk Taking and Decision Making of Working and Non-Working Subjects," *Journal of the Psychological Researches*, 2006, *50(2)*, pp. 95–100.

34 See, for instance, C.R. Sunstein, "Deliberative Troubles?: Why Groups Go to Extremes," *Yale Law Journal*, 2000, *110(1)*, 71–119.

35 D.J. Campbell, "The Proactive Employee: Managing Workplace Initiative," *Academy of Management Executive*, August 2000, *14(3)*, pp. 52–66; C.J.L. Cunningham & G.M. De La Rosa, "The Interactive Effects of Proactive Personality and Work-Family Interference on Well-Being," *Journal of Occupational Health Psychology*, 2008, *13(3)*, pp. 271–282.

36 See, for instance, M. Kemmelmeier, E. Burnstein, K. Krumov, & P. Genkova, "Individualism, Collectivism, and Authoritarianism in Seven Societies," *Journal of Cross-Cultural Psychology*, May 2003, *34(3)*, pp. 304–322; and, A. Wolfe, "The Authoritarian Personality Revisited," *Chronicle of Higher Education*, 2005, *52(7)*, pp. B12–B13.

37 For instance, see R.A. Bernardi, "The Relationships among Locus of Control, Perceptions of Stress, and Performance," *Journal of Applied Business Research*, 1997, *13*, pp. 1–8; O.C. Hansemark, "Need for Achievement, Locus of Control and the Prediction of Business Start-Ups: A Longitudinal Study," *Journal of*

Economic Psychology, June 2003, *24(3)*, pp. 301–320; and, T.W.H. Ng, K.L. Sorensen, & L.T. Eby, "Locus of Control at Work: A Meta-Analysis," *Journal of Organizational Behavior*, 2006, 27, pp. 1057–1087.

38 For more on Machiavellianism, see K. Bass, T. Barnett, & G. Brown, "Individual Difference Variables, Ethical Judgments, and Ethical Behavioral Intentions," *Business Ethics Quarterly*, 1999, 9, 183–205; and, J. Marta, A. Singhapakdi, & K. Kraft, "Personal Characteristics Underlying Ethical Decisions in Marketing Situations: A Survey of Small Business Managers," *Journal of Small Business Management*, 2008, *46(4)*, pp. 589–606.

39 For examinations of self-monitoring, see W.S. Long, E.J. Long, & G.H. Dobbins, "Correlates of Satisfaction with a Peer Evaluation System: Investigation of Performance Levels and Individual Differences," *Journal of Business and Psychology*, 1998, *12*, pp. 299–312; and, D.B. Turban & T.W. Dougherty, "Role of Protégé Personality in Receipt of Mentoring and Career Success," *Academy of Management Journal*, 1994, 37, pp. 688–702.

40 M. Kilduff & D.V. Day, "Do Chameleons Get Ahead?: The Effects of Self-Monitoring on Managerial Careers," *Academy of Management Journal*, 1994, 37, pp. 1047–1060.

41 D.V. Day, D.J. Schleicher, A.L. Unckless, & N.J. Hiller, "Self-Monitoring Personality at Work: A Meta-Analytic Investigation of Construct Validity," *Journal of Applied Psychology*, April 2002, *87(2)*, pp. 390–401. See also, P.F. Hewlin, "And the Award for Best Actor Goes to . . .: Facades of Conformity in Organizational Settings," *Academy of Management Review*, October 2003, *28(4)*, pp. 633–642.

42 For discussions of the MBTI see R.M. Capraro & M.M. Capraro, "Myers-Briggs Type Indicator Score Reliability across Studies: A Meta-Analytic Reliability Generalization Study," *Educational and Psychological Measurement*, 2002, *62(4)*, pp. 590–602; P. Berry, C. Wood, & B. Thornton, "The Myers-Briggs Type Indicator as a Tool to Facilitate Learning Outcomes for Team Building in the Classroom," *College Teaching & Styles Journal*, 2007, *3(4)*, pp. 13–20; B.S. Kulpers, M.J. Higgs, N.V. Tolkacheva, & M.C. de Witte, "The Influence of Myers-Briggs Type Indicator Profiles on Team Development Processes," *Small Group Research*, 2009, *40(4)*, pp. 436–464; J.B. Lloyds, "The Myers-Briggs Type Indicator and Mainstream Psychology: Analysis and Evaluation of an Unresolved Hostility," *Journal of Beliefs and Values*, 2012, *33(1)*, pp. 23–34.

43 See, for instance, T.A. Judge, C.A. Higgins, & C.J. Thoresen, "The Big Five Personality Traits, General Mental Ability, and Career Success across the Life Span," *Personnel Psychology*, 1999, 52, pp. 621–652; F. De Fruyt & I. Mervielde, "RIASEC Types and Big Five Traits as Predictors of Employment Status and Nature of Employment," *Personnel Psychology*, 1999, 52, pp. 701–727; and F. Lievens, F. De Fruyt, & K. Van Dam, "Assessors' Use of Personality Traits in Descriptions of Assessment Centre Candidates: A Five-Factor Model Perspective," *Journal of Occupational and Organizational Psychology*, December 2001, *74(5)*, 623–635.

44 T.A. Judge & R. Ilies, "Relationship of Personality to Performance Motivation: A Meta-Analytic Review," *Journal of Applied Psychology*, August 2002, *87(4)*, pp. 797–807; J.F. Salgado, "Predicting Job Performance Using FFM and Non-FFM Personality Measures," *Journal of Occupational and Organizational Psychology*, September 2003, *76(3)*, pp. 323–346; and T.A. Judge, D. Heller, & M.K. Mount, "Five-Factor Model of Personality and Job Satisfaction: A Meta-Analysis," *Journal of Applied Psychology*, June 2002, *87(3)*, pp. 530–541.

45 Ibid.

46   A.S. Grove, "A High-Tech CEO Updates His Views on Managing and Careers," *Fortune*, September 18, 1995, p. 229.

47   D.C. Thomas & K. Inkson, *Cultural Intelligence: People Skills for Global Intelligence* (San Francisco, CA: Berrett-Koehler).

48   See G. Hofstede, *Culture's Consequences: International Differences in Work-Related Values* (Beverly Hills, CA: Sage, 1980). For studies using the framework, see D.N. Ross, "Culture as a Context for Multinational Business: A Framework for Assessing the Strategy-Culture 'Fit'," *Multinational Business Review*, 1999, 7, pp. 13–19; and M. Kemmelmeier, E. Burnstein, K. Krumov, & P. Genkova, "Individualism, Collectivism, and Authoritarianism in Seven Societies," *Journal of Cross-Cultural Psychology*, May 2003, *34(3)*, pp. 304–322.

49   The following examples are based on R.E. Axtell, *Gestures* (New York: John Wiley & Sons, Inc., 1991) and, R.E. Axtell, *Do's and Taboos around the World*, 3rd ed. (New York: John Wiley & Sons, Inc., 1993).

Bibliography

Akbari, R., & Hosseini, K. "Multiple Intelligences and Language Learning Strategies: Investigating Possible Relations," *System*, 2008, *36*, pp. 141–155.

Alzola, M. "Character and Environment: The Status of Virtue in Organizations," *Journal of Business Ethics*, 2008, *78*, pp. 343–357.

Aristotle. *The Nichomachean Ethics of Aristotle*, trans. F.H. Peters, 5th ed. (London: Kegan Paul, Trench, Truebner & Co., 1893).

Axtell, R.E. *Do's and Taboos around the World*, 3rd ed. (New York: John Wiley & Sons, Inc., 1993).

Axtell, R.E. *Gestures* (New York: John Wiley & Sons, Inc., 1991).

Bass, K., Barnett, T., & Brown, G. "Individual Difference Variables, Ethical Judgments, and Ethical Behavioral Intentions," *Business Ethics Quarterly*, 1999, *9*, 183–205.

Bernardi, R.A. "The Relationships among Locus of Control, Perceptions of Stress, and Performance," *Journal of Applied Business Research*, 1997, *13*, pp. 1–8.

Berry, P., Wood, C., & Thornton, B. "The Myers-Briggs Type Indicator as a Tool to Facilitate Learning Outcomes for Team Building in the Classroom," *College Teaching & Styles Journal*, 2007, *3(4)*, pp. 13–20.

Brathwaite, S.T. "Denny's: A Diversity Success Story," *Franchising World*, July/August 2002, pp. 28–29.

Campbell, D.J. "The Proactive Employee: Managing Workplace Initiative," *Academy of Management Executive*, August 2000, *14(3)*, pp. 52–66.

Capraro, R.M., & Capraro, M.M. "Myers-Briggs Type Indicator Score Reliability across Studies: A Meta-Analytic Reliability Generalization Study," *Educational and Psychological Measurement*, 2002, *62(4)*, pp. 590–602.

Carton, A.M., & Cummings, J.N. "A Theory of Subgroups in Teams," *Academy of Management Review*, *37(3)*, pp. 441–470.

Cox, T.H. "Managing Cultural Diversity: Implications for Organizational Competitiveness," *Academy of Management Executive*, 1991, *5(3)*, pp. 45–56.

Cunningham, C.J.L., & De La Rosa, G.M. "The Interactive Effects of Proactive Personality and Work-Family Interference on Well-Being," *Journal of Occupational Health Psychology*, 2008, *13(3)*, pp. 271–282.

Das, P.R., & Talreja, B. "Risk Taking and Decision Making of Working and Non-Working Subjects," *Journal of the Psychological Researches*, 2006, *50(2)*, pp. 95–100.

Day, D.V., Schleicher, D.J., Unckless, A.L., & Hiller, N.J. "Self-Monitoring Personality at Work: A Meta-Analytic Investigation of Construct Validity," *Journal of Applied Psychology*, April 2002, *87(2)*, pp. 390–401.

De Fruyt, F. & Mervielde, I. "RIASEC Types and Big Five Traits as Predictors of Employment Status and Nature of Employment," *Personnel Psychology*, 1999, *52*, pp. 701–727.

Digh, P. "Coming to Terms with Diversity," *HRMagazine*, November 1998, pp. 117–120.

"The Diversity Initiative at US WEST Dex," *Successful Meetings*, March 1998, pp. 55–57

"Driving Diversity," *Hispanic*, May 2003, *16(5)*, p. 46.

Duska, R., & DesJardins, J. "Aristotelian Leadership and Business," *Business & Professional Ethics Journal*, Fall 2001, *20(3/4)*, pp. 19–38.

Elfenbein, H.A., & Ambady, N. "Predicting Workplace Outcomes from the Ability to Eavesdrop on Feelings," *Journal of Applied Psychology*, October 2002, *87(5)*, pp. 963–971.

Farh, C.I.C., Seo, M.-G., & Tesluk, P.E. "Emotional Intelligence, Teamwork Effectiveness, and Job Performance: The Moderating Role of Job Content," *Journal of Applied Psychology*, 2012, *97(4)*, pp. 890–900.

Finnegan, A. "Champions 2001," *Working Woman*, April 2001, *26(4)*, p. 50.

Gardner, H. *Frames of Mind* (New York: Basic Books, 1993).

Ghosh, R., Shuck, B., & Petrosko, J. "Emotional Intelligence and Organizational Learning in Work Teams," *Journal of Management Development*, 2012, *31(6)*, pp. 603–619.

Goleman, D. *Emotional Intelligence* (New York: Bantam Books, 1995).

Goleman, D. "What Makes a Leader?" *Harvard Business Review*, January 1, 2004, pp. 82–91.

Goleman, D. *Working with Emotional Intelligence* (New York: Bantam Books, 1998).

Gray, K. "Enterprise Rent-A-Car: Recruiting Program Is a Driving Force Behind Enterprise's Success," *NACE Journal*, Spring 2003, *63(3)*, p. 19.

Grove, A.S. "A High-Tech CEO Updates His Views on Managing and Careers," *Fortune*, September 18, 1995, p. 229.

Hansemark, O.C. "Need for Achievement, Locus of Control and the Prediction of Business Start-Ups: A Longitudinal Study," *Journal of Economic Psychology*, June 2003, *24(3)*, pp. 301–320.

Hansen, F. "Diversity's Business Case Doesn't Add Up," *Workforce*, April 2003, *82(4)*, pp. 28–32.

Hewlin, P.F. "And the Award for Best Actor Goes to . . .: Facades of Conformity in Organizational Settings," *Academy of Management Review*, October 2003, *28(4)*, pp. 633–642.

Hofstede, G. *Culture's Consequences: International Differences in Work-Related Values* (Beverly Hills, CA: Sage, 1980).

Homan, A.C., Hollenbeck, J.R., Humphrey, S., van Klippenberg, D., Ilgen, D.R., & van Kleef, G.A. "Facing Differences with an Open Mind: Openness to Experience, Salience of Intragroup Differences, and Performance of Diverse Work Groups," *Academy of Management Journal*, 2008, *51*, pp. 1204–1222.

Homan, A., van Klippenberg, D., Van Kleef, G., & De Dreu, C. "Bridging Faultlines by Valuing Diversity: Diversity Beliefs, Information Elaboration, and Performance in Diverse Work Groups," *Journal of Applied Psychology*, 2007, *92(5)*, pp. 1189–1199.

Huo, Y. "Procedural Justice and Social Regulation across Group Boundaries: Does Subgroup Identification Undermine Relationship-Based Governance?" *Personality and Social Psychology Bulletin*, 2003, *29*, pp. 336–348.

Huy, Q.N. "Emotional Capability, Emotional Intelligence, and Radical Change," *Academy of Management Review*, 1999, *24*, pp. 325–345.

Huo, Y., Smith, H., Tyler, T., & Lind, A. "Superordinate Identification, Subgroup Identification, and Justice Concerns: Is Separatism the Problem; Is Assimilation the Answer?" *Psychological Science*, 1996, 7, pp. 40–45.

Jordan, P.J., & Troth, A.C. "Managing Emotions during Team Problem Solving: Emotional Intelligence and Conflict Resolution," *Human Performance*, 2004, *17(2)*, pp. 195–218.

Joyce, K.E. "Lessons for Employers from *Fortune*'s '100 Best,'" *Business Horizons*, March/April 2003, *46(2)*, pp. 77–84.

Judge, T.A., & Ilies, R. "Relationship of Personality to Performance Motivation: A Meta-Analytic Review," *Journal of Applied Psychology*, August 2002, *87(4)*, pp. 797–807.

Judge, T.A., Heller, D., & Mount, M.K. "Five-Factor Model of Personality and Job Satisfaction: A Meta-Analysis," *Journal of Applied Psychology*, June 2002, *87(3)*, pp. 530–541.

Judge, T.A., Higgins, C.A., & Thoresen, C.J. "The Big Five Personality Traits, General Mental Ability, and Career Success across the Life Span," *Personnel Psychology*, 1999, *52*, pp. 621–652.

Kemmelmeier, M., Burnstein, E., Krumov, K., & Genkova, P. "Individualism, Collectivism, and Authoritarianism in Seven Societies," *Journal of Cross-Cultural Psychology*, May 2003, *34(3)*, pp. 304–322.

Kilduff, M., & Day, D.V. "Do Chameleons Get Ahead?: The Effects of Self-Monitoring on Managerial Careers," *Academy of Management Journal*, 1994, *37*, pp. 1047–1060.

Kirkpatrick, D., Phillips, J.J., & Phillips, P.P. "Getting Results from Diversity Training—In Dollars and Cents," *HR Focus*, October 2003, p. 3.

Kloep, M., Güney, N., Çok, F., & Simsek, Ö.F. "Motives for Risk-Taking in Adolescence: A Cross-Cultural Study," *Journal of Adolescence*, 2009, *32*, pp. 135–151.

Koman, E.S., & Wolff, S.B. "Emotional Intelligence Competencies in the Team and Team Leader: A Multi-Level Examination of the Impact of Emotional Intelligence on Team Performance," *Journal of Management Development*, 2008, *27(1)*, pp. 55–75.

Kravitz, D.A. "Diversity in Teams: A Two-Edged Sword Requires Careful Handling," *Psychological Science in the Public Interest*, 2005, *6(2)*, pp. i–ii.

Kulpers, B.S., Higgs, M.J., Tolkacheva, N.V., & de Witte, M.C. "The Influence of Myers-Briggs Type Indicator Profiles on Team Development Processes," *Small Group Research*, 2009, *40(4)*, pp. 436–464.

Kwoh, L. "Firms Hail New Chiefs (of Diversity)," *Wall Street Journal*, January 5, 2012. http://online.wsj.com/article/SB1000142405297020389950457712926173 2884578.html

Lakshminarayan, S. "A Social Marketing Based Strategy for Planning Diversity Events," *Journal of Diversity Management*, 2006, *1(1)*, pp. 39–48.

Lancaster, L.C., & Stillman, D. *When Generations Collide* (New York: Collins Business, 2005).

Lau, D., & Murnighan, J.K. "Demographic Similarity and Faultlines: The Compositional Dynamics of Organizational Groups," *Academy of Management Review*, 1998, *23*, pp. 325–340.

Lievens, F., De Fruyt, F., & Van Dam, K. "Assessors' Use of Personality Traits in Descriptions of Assessment Centre Candidates: A Five-Factor Model Perspective," *Journal of Occupational and Organizational Psychology*, December 2001, *74(5)*, pp. 623–635.

Lloyds, J.B. "The Myers-Briggs Type Indicator and Mainstream Psychology: Analysis and Evaluation of an Unresolved Hostility," *Journal of Beliefs and Values*, 2012, *33(1)*, pp. 23–34.

Lobler, H., & Bode, J. "Risk Taking Under Transition: An Empirical Comparison between Chinese, Western-, and Eastern-German Managers," *Thunderbird International Business Review*, January/February 1999, pp. 69–81.

Long, W.S., Long, E.J., & Dobbins, G.H. "Correlates of Satisfaction with a Peer Evaluation System: Investigation of Performance Levels and Individual Differences," *Journal of Business and Psychology*, 1998, *12*, pp. 299–312.

Mannix, E., & Neale, M.A. "What Differences Make a Difference? The Promise and Reality of Diverse Teams in Organizations," *Psychological Science in the Public Interest*, 2005, *6(2)*, pp. 31–55.

Marta, J., Singhapakdi, A., & Kraft, K. "Personal Characteristics Underlying Ethical Decisions in Marketing Situations: A Survey of Small Business Managers," *Journal of Small Business Management*, 2008, *46(4)*, pp. 589–606.

Mayer, J.D., Roberts, R.D., & Barsade, S.G. "Human Abilities: Emotional Intelligence," *Annual Review of Psychology*, 2008, *59*, pp. 507–536.

Moore, A., & Mamiseishvili, K. "Examining the Relationship between Emotional Intelligence and Group Cohesion," *Journal of Education for Business*, 2012, *87(5)*, pp. 296–302.

Morris, T. *If Aristotle Ran General Motors: The New Soul of Business* (New York: Henry Holt, 1997).

Mott, W.J., Jr. "Developing a Culturally Competent Workforce: A Diversity Program in Progress," *Journal of Healthcare Management*, September/October 2003, *48(5)*, pp. 337+.

Naseer, Z., Chisti, S., Rahman, F., & Jumani, N.B. "Impact of Emotional Intelligence on Team Performance in Higher Education Institutes," *International Online Journal of Educational Sciences*, 2011, *3(1)*, pp. 30–46.

Nemeth, C.J., & Kwan, J.L. "Minority Influence, Divergent Thinking and Detection of Correct Solutions," *Journal of Applied Social Psychology*, 1987, *17*, pp. 788–799.

Ng, T.W.H., Sorensen, K.L., & Eby, L.T. "Locus of Control at Work: A Meta-Analysis," *Journal of Organizational Behavior*, 2006, *27*, pp. 1057–1087.

Nolen, J.L. "Multiple Intelligences in the Classroom," *Education*, Fall 2003, *124(1)*, pp. 115–119.

Pendry, L.F., Driscoll, D.M., & Field, S.C.T. "Diversity Training: Putting Theory into Practice," *Journal of Occupational and Organizational Psychology*, 2007, *80(1)*, pp. 27–50.

Phillips, J.J., & Phillips, P.P. "Show Me the Money: The Use of ROI in Performance Improvement, Part 1," *Performance Improvement*, 2007, *46(9)*, pp. 8–22.

Rantanen, J., Metsäpelto, R.-L., Feldt, T., Pulkkinen, L., & Kokko, K. "Long-Term Stability in the Big Five Personality Traits in Adulthood," *Scandinavian Journal of Psychology*, 2007, *48*, pp. 511–518.

Rice, F. "How to Make Diversity Pay," *Fortune*, August 8, 1994, pp. 78–86.

Riesch, C., & Kleiner, B.H. "Discrimination towards Customers in the Restaurant Industry," *Equal Opportunities International*, 2005, *24(7/8)*, pp. 29–37.

Roberson, Q.M. "Disentangling the Meanings of Diversity and Inclusion in Organizations," *Group and Organization Management*, 2006, *31(2)*, pp. 212–236.

Ross, D.N. "Culture as a Context for Multinational Business: A Framework for Assessing the Strategy-Culture 'Fit,'" *Multinational Business Review*, 1999, 7, pp. 13–19.

Ryan, L.V., & Buchholtz, A.K. "Trust, Risk, and Shareholder Decision Making: An Investor Perspective on Corporate Governance," *Business Ethics Quarterly*, January 2001, *11(1)*, pp. 177–194.

Salgado, J.F. "Predicting Job Performance Using FFM and Non-FFM Personality Measures," *Journal of Occupational and Organizational Psychology*, September 2003, *76(3)*, pp. 323–346.

Shapira, Z. *Risk Taking: A Managerial Perspective* (New York: Russell Sage Foundation, 1995).

Small, B.J., Hertzog, C., Hultsch, D.F., & Dixon, R.A. "Stability and Change in Adult Personality Over 6 Years: Findings from the Victoria Longitudinal Study," *Journals of Gerontology: Series B*, May 2003, *58B(3)*, pp. P166–P170.

Stauffer, D. "Boosting Your Emotional Intelligence," *Harvard Business Review*, October 1997, pp. 1–4.

Sunstein, C.R. "Deliberative Troubles?: Why Groups Go to Extremes," *Yale Law Journal*, 2000, *110(1)*, 71–119.

Swody, C.A., & Powell, G.N. "Determinants of Employee Participation in Organizations' Family-Friendly Programs: A Multi-Level Approach," *Journal of Business and Psychology*, 2007, *22*, pp. 111–122.

Thatcher, S.M.B., & Patel, P.C. "Group Faultlines: A Review, Integration, and Guide to Future Research," *Journal of Management*, 2012, *38*, pp. 969–1009.

Thomas, D.C., & Inkson, K. *Cultural Intelligence: People Skills for Global Intelligence* (San Francisco, CA: Berrett-Koehler, 2004).

Turban, D.B., & Dougherty, T.W. "Role of Protégé Personality in Receipt of Mentoring and Career Success," *Academy of Management Journal*, 1994, *37*, pp. 688–702.

van Knippenberg, D., & Schippers, M.C. "Work Group Diversity," *Annual Review of Psychology*, 2007, *58*, pp. 515–541.

Watson, W.E., Kumar, K., & Michaelsen, L.K. "Cultural Diversity's Influence on Interaction Process and Performance: Comparing Homogeneous and Diverse Task Groups," *Academy of Management Journal*, 1993, *36(3)*, pp. 590–602.

Welch, J., & Welch, S. "Emotional Mismanagement," *Business Week*, July 28, 2008, p. 84.

Wolfe, A. "The Authoritarian Personality Revisited," *Chronicle of Higher Education*, 2005, *52(7)*, pp. B12–B13.

Zellmer-Bruhn, M., Maloney, M., Bhappu, A., & Salvador, R. "When and How Do Differences Matter?: An Exploration of Perceived Similarity in Teams," *Organizational Behavior and Human Decision Processes*, 2008, *107(1)*, pp. 41–59.

CHAPTER 6

Fostering Effective Communication in Teams

Learning Objectives

After reading this chapter, you should be able to do the following:

1. Recognize the importance of communication in organizations.
2. Understand the primary functions of communication.
3. Identify barriers to communication.
4. Review approaches to overcoming barriers to communication.
5. Employ guidelines for effective speaking.
6. Develop skills for active listening.
7. Understand guidelines for effective coaching.
8. Understand the importance, forms, and uses of nonverbal communication.
9. In general, communicate more effectively with team members and other stakeholders in order to enhance team effectiveness.

TOM PETERS AND ROBERT WATERMAN SOUGHT IN THEIR BOOK *In Search of Excellence: Lessons from America's Best-Run Companies* to discover the secrets of America's truly excellent companies.[1] Their findings led them to argue that the amount, nature, and uses of communication in the excellent companies were remarkably different from those of their nonexcellent peers. Peters and Waterman found that the excellent companies they examined used a variety of philosophies, practices, and structures to encourage communication. At IBM and Delta Airlines, open-door policies were pervasive. At Hewlett-Packard and United Airlines, managers practiced management by wandering about: they got out of their offices and communicated informally. Corning Glass installed escalators rather than elevators in its new engineering building to increase the chance of face-to-face contact. At Citibank, the desks of operations officers and lending officers were moved to the same floor and intermingled to encourage communication. Intel's new buildings in Silicon Valley were designed to have an excess of small conference rooms, filled with blackboards to facilitate communication, where people could eat lunch or solve problems. What these examples have in common, according to Peters and Waterman, is "lots of communication."

This emphasis on communication is not surprising. Communication affects virtually every area of work. Communication with employees about plant closings, performance appraisals, organizational goals, probable salary increases and job changes, and even the date of the company picnic is essential to the proper functioning of the firm. If communication is inaccurate or inadequate, uncertainty, apprehension, errors, and dissatisfaction may ensue.

As evidence of the importance of communication in teams, consider the case of surgical errors. A recent study estimated that there are now more than 200,000 preventable deaths from avoidable medical error in the United States each year, twice the number as a decade earlier and more than the number of deaths caused by car crashes.[2] Remarkably, up to 60% of those deaths may result from communication failures.[3] Among surgical teams, communication failures include distraction, failure to get information from key team members, unwillingness of team members to comment when they see a surgeon making a mistake, failure to communicate because of stress, and many others. One study of forty-eight surgical procedures found 129 communication failures among team members, with almost 40% of those errors resulting in visible negative effects, including team tension, delay, procedural error, patient inconvenience, inefficiency, and conflict.[4] Partly as a result, training surgical teams to communicate more effectively is now a major endeavor in hospitals and other health care facilities.

TEAMS VIDEO: The Power of Communication in Teams

Alex "Sandy" Pentland is the director of MIT's Human Dynamics Laboratory and the chair of Sociometric Solutions. He and his colleagues at the Human Dynamics Laboratory have attempted to identify the group dynamics that characterize high performing teams. Their initial observations suggested that the key to high performance might lie in the way the team was communicating.

They subsequently studied a diverse set of industries to find workplaces that had similar teams with varying performance. The members of those teams were equipped with electronic badges (often called *sociometers*) that collected data on their communication behaviors, such as tone of voice, body language, whom they talked to and how much, and other factors. Dr. Pentland and his colleagues found patterns of communication to be the best predictor of a team's success. In fact, those patterns were as significant as all other factors—including individual intelligence, personality, skill, and the content of discussions—combined.

Go to the text website to read more about this research and to see Dr. Pentland discuss it.

Source: A. Pentland, "The New Science of Building Great Teams," *Harvard Business Review,* 2012, *90(4)*, pp. 60–69.

In this chapter we consider functions of communication, identify barriers to effective communication and ways to overcome them, provide guidelines for effective speaking, offer suggestions for active listening, provide suggestions for effective coaching and counseling, and discuss the importance and forms of nonverbal communication.

Before continuing, complete Self-Assessment 6.1 on the text website to assess your communication style and interpret your results.

Functions of Communication

Communication is the transfer of information from one person to another. It may serve several important functions.[5]

- **Information function.** Communication provides information to be used for decision making.
- **Motivational function.** Communication encourages commitment to organizational objectives, thus enhancing motivation.
- **Control function.** Communication clarifies duties, authority, and responsibilities, thereby permitting control.
- **Emotive function.** Communication permits the expression of feelings and the satisfaction of social needs; it may also help vent frustrations.

As Self-Assessment 6.1 demonstrated, people tend to use different styles when communicating. For instance, some are careful to explain their views, while others are not. Some are more assertive than others. Some are very concerned about the other person's feelings, while others say we should keep emotions out of our discussions. Some rely more on nonverbal communications than others, and so on.

Understanding Communication Barriers

Unfortunately, many things can interfere with effective communication, often with disastrous consequences. Some of the more common barriers to effective communication include semantics, distraction, misrepresentation, information retention, and perceptual factors.

Semantics
Semantics, or *code noise*, occurs when the meaning of a message to the sender differs from its meaning to the recipient. Too often, this may be the result of jargon, involving pretentious terminology or language specific to a particular profession or group. Here is a sampling of jargon relating to computers and the modern workplace:

- *Salmon day:* Fighting uphill; swimming against the current.
- *Blamestorming:* Discussing a project failure with coworkers.
- *PEBCAK:* "Problem exists between chair and keyboard." That is, an operator error.[6]
- *Easter eggs:* Undocumented bits of code hidden in computer applications and operating systems that, once accessed, provide a bit of information or entertainment, such as a game, a joke, or the names of people who developed the program.[7]
- *Sticky eyeballs:* People who spend a lot of time at a website.
- *Cube farm:* Rows of cubicles instead of private offices.
- *RTM:* Read the manual.

Although team members may often share backgrounds, training, and associated terminology, it is important to make sure that jargon is not interfering with team understandings. This is especially the case when team members are from different specialties or different cultures.

Deloitte Consulting, an arm of the accounting firm Deloitte Touche Tohmatsu, developed a software program, Bullfighter, which identifies jargon in documents. Its goal was to make it easier for investors to decipher what companies are trying to say. The program can also be used in firms to help ensure that messages are jargon free.[8] A link to a free download of the program is provided on the text website.

Distraction

Distraction, or *psychological noise*, occurs when a recipient does not understand the sender's message because he or she is simply thinking about something else. For instance, the recipient may be distracted by financial worries or upcoming deadlines. Often, of course, recipients don't understand senders' messages because they are thinking about their own replies rather than concentrating on the message to which they are going to reply. Therefore, it is important to minimize distraction by providing an appropriate setting for teams and encouraging active listening, to be discussed later in the chapter.

Misrepresentation

Misrepresentation may also cause a failure of communication and may take various forms. Deliberate lies are an extreme example. People may lie on their résumés (sometimes called *padding*), in their advertising messages (sometimes called *puffery*), and in their campaign promises (sometimes called *politics*). More often, information may be subtly distorted to the sender's benefit. A memo that focuses on sales increases but downplays drops in profit, an annual report that tries to hide changes in accounting format, and a brochure from a drug manufacturer that ignores hazardous side effects would be examples of this kind of misrepresentation. Some team members, such as Machiavellians, may be especially prone to misrepresentation. Team leaders should try to develop a culture that discourages misrepresentation, be alert for misrepresentation when it occurs, and take immediate action to demonstrate that it will not be tolerated.

Information Retention

Information is a valuable resource. Those who control it are in positions of power. Some employees may retain specific sorts of information, such as a formula or a filing system, and thereby make themselves more necessary. Others are in positions that give them the ability to channel—or not to channel—information to various individuals inside and outside the organization. Still others are in positions in which they process information but send only some of it along. Each of these sorts of individuals has the potential to create barriers to proper communication.[9]

In teams, it is critical that members share important information. Team member information sharing is related to team performance, cohesion, satisfaction with decisions, and knowledge.[10] Unfortunately, as we've discussed, some types of people may be reluctant to share information.

In the following Team Scholar feature, Dr. Stefan Schulz-Hardt discusses the need for open information search and sharing in teams, especially in the case of information that is known only to some team members. He also addresses the importance of communication in facilitating productive team conflict, an issue we explore further in Chapter 9.

TEAM SCHOLAR

Dr. Stefan Schulz-Hardt

Stefan Schulz-Hardt is professor of industrial, economic, and social psychology at the University of Goettingen in Germany and a principal investigator at the Courant Research Centre on the evolution of social behavior. His primary research interests are group decision making and group performance, social information search and processing, escalating commitment, and stress at the workplace. He has authored or coauthored numerous articles in top journals in the field of social psychology as well as industrial and organizational psychology. Currently, he is associate editor of the *Journal of Economic Psychology*.

You have used hidden profile tasks in some of your research. What are hidden profile tasks? Why are they important in understanding team processes and outcomes?

Hidden profiles are group decision making tasks where the superiority of the best decision alternative is hidden from the individual group members. That is, one of the alternatives is better than the others, but none of the group members can detect this superiority based on his or her individual information. To identify this best alternative, the group members have to combine and integrate their unique information.

These tasks constitute the prototype of situations where interacting in a group to make a collective decision can pay off with regard to decision quality. Obviously, if most or all group members can already find the best solution when considering only their individual information (we call this a manifest profile), performance gains can hardly be obtained by having groups discuss and decide the issue. However, if the additional knowledge that is available at the group level alters the decisional implication of the group members' individual knowledge, then such performance gains are possible. Unfortunately, they occur very seldom—groups frequently fail to solve hidden profiles.

Some of your related work has examined information search and sharing in team decision making. What are major lessons from that research?

In my view, there are—at least—two lessons to be learned from these studies: the first one is that information search and information exchange in groups are systematically biased. Group members predominantly search for and discuss information that supports rather than contradicts their initially formed decision preferences, and they also talk more about information that everybody already knew prior to discussion (so-called shared information) than about group members' unique (unshared) information. Such biases make it difficult to solve hidden profiles, because detecting the best alternative in a hidden profile requires group members to integrate information that is new to them and that challenges their initial opinions.

The second lesson might seem less remarkable or less sexy at first glance, but I realize more and more that it might be the even more important one: in groups, information search and information exchange often simply are quantitatively insufficient to make a good decision. If groups do not discuss long enough or fail to exchange enough information, they often cannot come up with the best decision. And the same seems to be true for the processing of the discussed information: although the processing of information is also often biased (by the same asymmetries that I have outlined for the discussion of information), a very fundamental barrier for high decision quality seems to be the fact that group members often are too superficial in their elaboration of the discussed information and, hence, fail to realize its implications.

What are key findings of your research on productive conflict in work teams?

With regard to the processes outlined in my previous point, we have shown that group discussions are less biased and more intensive (i.e., more information is exchanged and discussed) if group members have dissent in their individual prediscussion preferences and if this dissent is expressed in the group. As a consequence of these effects, prediscussion dissent raises decision quality in hidden profile situations (please note that, by definition, it cannot increase decision quality in manifest profile situations). Although some of these effects can be mimicked by means of artificial dissent (i.e., by using a dialectical decision technique such as, for example, devil's advocacy), authentic dissent seems to have more impact than contrived dissent has.

What can be done to enhance productive conflict in work teams?

This is something that we have not addressed in our own studies so far, but from the work of several other researchers we know that certain moderators are crucial for the facilitation or suppression of productive conflict in groups. For example, participative leadership (as compared to directive leadership) makes it more likely that dissent will be expressed and will enhance the quality of group processes and outcomes. Similarly, establishing decision structures that make sure that everybody gets heard can help to prevent the suppression or silence of dissenters. Finally, group norms are also relevant: if open debate and a self-critical attitude are an integral part of the group's procedural norms, dissent will be more likely to be expressed and, if expressed, will be more helpful as if preserving harmony is what the group values most.

What do you see as some of the most important emerging issues regarding teams?

An issue that I find to be particularly important is addressing the temporal dynamics of group processes. At least in social psychological lab research, which is my home court, the usual strategy is to compose ad hoc groups of strangers and investigate them at one or two task trials. However, having groups perform a particular task is an investment that might take some time to pay off. Hence, the widespread neglect of a longer time perspective might be one of the reasons why social psychological group research has a wealth of findings on group failures but only occasionally finds synergy and performance gains in groups. It makes an already effortful and time-consuming type of research even more effortful and time consuming, but I think that extending the temporal perspective of (laboratory) group research is inevitable and indispensable if we want to gain a realistic understanding of the benefits and drawbacks of working in groups.

Perceptual Factors

Most perceptual errors are directly relevant to communication. Stereotyping may cause us to ignore or distort the messages of people we have classified in certain ways. We may as a result, for instance, misinterpret or look skeptically on conciliatory gestures. Selective perception may cause us to ignore communication which conflicts with our beliefs and expectations. Halo error (the tendency to base our evaluations of various things, such as task performance, on a general impression rather than on actual levels of those things) may lead us to bias our evaluation of a message because of some unrelated characteristic of the message sender, such as physical appearance. Projection (the tendency to project our own feelings onto others) may lead us to infer information in a message we receive based upon our own feelings. If we are angry, for instance, we may see anger in the message.

Overcoming Communication Barriers

There are many approaches to overcoming the causes of communication failures. For instance, feedback, repetition of the messages, use of multiple channels of communication, and simplified language may reduce problems due to semantics, selective perception, and distraction. Simplified language includes use of simple words and phrases; short and familiar words; personal pronouns (such as *you* and *them*); short sentences and paragraphs; active verbs; and illustrations, examples, and charts.

Also, in this age of Facebook, Twitter, and texting, information overload may be increasingly problematic. In Korea and Japan, some companies are taking a novel approach to reducing communication overload. They specify one hour in the morning when no one—including the chief executive—is to be interrupted by phone calls, coworkers, or meetings. Some corporations, including Samsung and Hyundai, say the system has enhanced creativity and produced major administrative productivity gains.[11] Information overload may also be alleviated by the **exception principle**. This principle states that only exceptions should be reported—there is no need for messages stating that the production line didn't break down or that absenteeism or competitive conditions are unchanged.

Now, complete Skills Practice 6.1 on the text website. This exercise requires you to get out into the real world to interview a manager about communication issues.

TEAMS IN THE NEWS: "Doodling for Dollars"

To facilitate communication in meetings, companies are encouraging their employees to doodle their ideas and draw diagrams to help explain complicated concepts.

As discussed in this article, companies such as Facebook are incorporating whiteboards, chalkboards, and writable glass on surfaces to foster creativity. Fans of doodling say it can help generate ideas, fuel collaboration, simplify communication, and retain information. It can be especially useful for global colleagues who don't share a first language.

Other companies, such as Zappos, are hiring graphic recorders who sketch, cartoon-style, what is discussed at meetings to help keep employees engaged. Read more about doodling and how various organizations are using it by accessing the links on the text website. www.routledge.com/cw/aldag

Source: R. E. Silverman, "Doodling for Dollars," *New York Times*, April 25, 2012, p. B1.

Guidelines for Effective Speaking

As a team leader or member, you will often need to speak, whether in a formal presentation or simply to persuasively make a point. Effective speakers communicate logically, clearly, and confidently.[12] Effective speaking requires thorough preparation.

Knowing your purpose and your audience is critical; 2,800 years ago Aristotle said that outstanding communicators must first understand their audiences and gear their language and persuasive appeals to them. Physical delivery, including presence, voice control, eye contact, and other nonverbal cues, to be discussed in the next section, may make the difference between success and failure. The way you speak reflects your intelligence, ability to think, and ability to organize. These abilities are highly valued in business and in society in general and can be crucial in social relationships and job opportunities.

We now present guidelines for effective speaking. As either a team leader or as a team member the quality of your arguments and presentations will influence team outcomes and, quite likely, the success of your career:

- **Determine the purpose of your communication.** Is it to explain ideas to others? To recognize outstanding efforts? To entertain? To induce an emotion? To instill a belief? Your speech should be tailored to facilitate the desired purpose of your communication.

- **Consider issues of time and space.** Determine the best time and location for delivering your message. Consider how much time you will have and how your message might relate to other messages delivered before and after it. Think about what recent events might be in the minds of your listeners and whether you should refer to those events.

- **Adapt to your listeners.** Consider the size of the audience as well as factors such as audience age, gender, interests, level of knowledge about the subject, and values. You'll need to prepare very differently for a one-to-one talk, a small-group presentation, or a lecture to a large audience. Also consider audience expectations. For example, is the audience expecting an entertaining after-dinner talk, a stirring inspirational message, or how-to tips? Consider as well if there may be hearing-impaired audience members or an international audience that cannot speak fluent English.

- **Use appropriate vocabulary.** Speak at the proper level for the particular audience. Seek clarity. Avoid use of words that may have different meanings to various members of the audience and avoid unnecessary jargon.

- **Practice voice control**. Consider proper speech volume, pitch, and speaking rate. Avoid mumbling and awkward pauses. It is helpful to listen to yourself on audiotape and to observe your mannerisms on videotape. Ask others to critique your presentations.

- **Use appropriate gestures.** Properly used, gestures can make a presentation more engaging, and they may help disguise anxiety. Avoid short, jerky movements that may appear as nervousness and use a variety of gestures so you don't seem to be in a rut. Use gestures to reinforce spoken points or even as substitutes.

- **Organize your presentation.** Any oral presentation can be divided into three parts: gaining attention, presenting the information, and closing effectively. The amount of time devoted to gaining attention will depend on the audience members' familiarity with, and interest in, the subject. A personal greeting, a stunning statement or opinion, a suspenseful question, or humor may help gain attention. To effectively share information, consider how you can give the subject high priority in the minds of listeners, how you can bring the subject more clearly into focus, and how you can develop it in a form that satisfies your listeners. Finally, pay attention to an effective closing to provide a sense of completion and reinforce key points.

Skills Practice 6.2 on the text website will increase your skill in tailoring your business presentations to characteristics of your audience. This is a critical skill in teams.

Mastering Active Listening

Obviously, face-to-face verbal communication involves speaking. More than that though, it also requires listening.[13] Unfortunately, most people would rather talk than listen. According to an old joke, the opposite of talking isn't listening; it's waiting to talk.[14] Before reading on, complete Skills Practice 6.3 on the text website.

Listening can take many forms. Casual or marginal listening, such as when colleagues chat about sports over lunch, requires only a passive effort, since there is little pressure to learn or remember the message. With attentive listening, as when a manager is delivering a performance appraisal, the listener is motivated to hear, understand, and remember. With **active listening**, such as in counseling situations and conflict interviews, it is important to listen to more than just the content of the message. Attention to nonverbal cues will also be important. Active listening requires that you convey to the speaker a sense of trust, identify with his or her feelings and thoughts, and encourage him or her to be as specific as possible about feelings and concerns.

Here are some guidelines for active listening.[15]

- **Control the physical environment.** Try to minimize noise and other distractions, such as an uncomfortable room temperature or improper lighting. Don't sit near doorways or under air-conditioning vents. If the location is noisy or uncomfortable, move to a quieter setting. Take steps to minimize unnecessary distractions.
- **Be alert.** Give your full attention and allot the necessary time to listen.
- **Be mentally prepared.** Do your homework in advance of the conversation. Anticipate the encounter by learning new terminology and background information about the persons, organization, or issues.
- **Be emotionally prepared.** Keep an open mind about what is being said, even if it is unpleasant. Give the speaker the opportunity to complete his or her message before raising questions.
- **Be attentive.** Continually review the speaker's message and tie the various ideas or segments of the message together. Think of each idea as a link in a chain. Take notes if necessary but record only main points. Develop an effective system of note taking.
- **Read nonverbal cues.** Pay attention to the speaker's tone of voice, expressions, gestures, and other nonverbal cues.
- **Distinguish among facts, inferences, and value judgments.** Try to sort out whether what is being said is a fact that can be verified, an inference (that is, a conclusion reached after consideration of a set of facts), or a personal judgment based on the speaker's value system. These may all be important, but you should do your best to determine which is which.
- **Offer and solicit feedback.** The best form of feedback in a listening situation is to paraphrase the speaker's message. This allows the speaker to

verify the accuracy and completeness of what was transmitted and to make necessary changes or additions.

Active listening is a critical skill for managers but is often done poorly. Skills Practice 6.3 on the text website focuses on helping you to develop the ability to listen to others more effectively.

Coaching and Counseling

One key function of communication is that of coaching team members and others to improve their performance and career development. Here are some guidelines for effective coaching.[16]

- **Create a situation where you are prepared to coach and the employee is open to coaching.** Develop a climate of trust and mutual respect where employees feel open to share their views, needs, and concerns and to try new ideas.
- **Use reflective listening—focus both on words and their emotional content.** Facilitate self-discovery by letting employees think for themselves and present their opinions. Ask, "What do you think?"
- **Talk to your employees, not at them.** Avoid phrases such as "You should . . . " and "I want . . . "; instead, ask questions such as "What can we do about this?" and "How can we get this done?"
- **Value different perspectives.** Try to understand the differing motivations, work values, goals, and capabilities of individual employees. Learn what tasks interest them, what they find difficult, and what they aspire to do or achieve.
- **Mutually identify goals.** Focus on behaviors rather than attitudes; behaviors can be changed, while attitudes tend to be inflexible. If you feel an employee has a "bad attitude," give feedback on behaviors that might be changed rather than criticizing the attitude.

Forms of Nonverbal Communication

Even though verbal communication is clearly important, we can often learn about the attitudes and beliefs of teammates and others by attending to their nonverbal cues. Nonverbal communication can take many forms, as shown in Figure 6-1, including paralanguage, hand movements, facial expressions, eye contact, posture, touch, dress, and proxemics.[17] It is critical to remember, as discussed in Chapter 5, that the meaning of nonverbal cues can vary dramatically across cultures. It is always wise to learn about what gestures, eye contact, touch, and other forms of nonverbal communication mean when dealing with people from other cultures.

Paralanguage concerns *how* something is said rather than what is said. It includes all vocal aspects of speech other than words.[18] For example, voice qualities—such as pitch, rhythm, tempo, and volume—influence interpretation of a verbal message. A soft, low-pitched voice and a slow rate indicate liking, while a high-pitched voice indicates anger. Moderate rate, pitch, and volume indicate boredom.[19] Similarly, **vocal characterizers**, such as coughing, yawning, clearing the throat, and grunting, may be important. While

Figure 6-1

Forms of Nonverbal
Communications

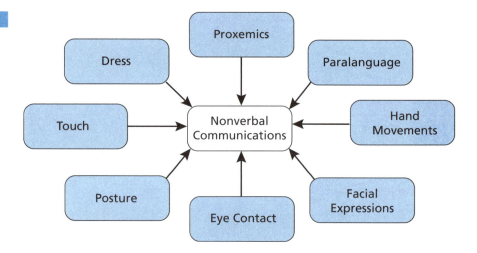

they can sometimes be used effectively, they generally are distracting and annoying and should be avoided. **Verbal qualifiers** are variations in tone or intensity of speech. For example, increases in rate or volume may indicate impatience or anger, respectively. The power of verbal qualifiers can be seen by repeating the sentence "I didn't say he stole your car" seven times, stressing a different word each time. Finally, vocal segregates are pauses between utterances, and may include "ahs" and "ums." Prolonged pauses suggest a lack of confidence and organization.[20]

There are several types of hand movements. Some have a specific meaning that is understood in a particular culture or occupation, such as a thumbs-up gesture. Others, such as touching oneself or others, may be associated with anxiety, guilt, hostility, or suspicion. For example, interviewers are sometimes taught that a hand-to-face movement is a sign of deception.[21]

By one estimate, the human face can make 250,000 different expressions.[22] The Roman scholar Pliny the Elder wrote more than 2,000 years ago that "the face of man is the index to joy and mirth, to severity and sadness." Facial expressions are generally understood to have a particular meaning. For example, facial expressions communicating six emotions—happiness, sadness, anger, fear, surprise, and disgust—are recognized worldwide. Even when people try to suppress facial expressions, they may make very short expressions lasting a fraction of a second that will reveal true meaning.

Eye contact is a major regulator of conversation. Generally, eye contact suggests understanding and interest.[23] Seeking eye contact connotes the desire to open a conversation. Conversely, someone hoping to avoid communication—such as an unprepared student in class—will avoid eye contact. People tend to associate poor eye contact with deception.[24]

Posture is the way people position their bodies with respect to others. For example, if a customer's arms are relaxed and open, and he or she leans forward to talk to a salesperson, the customer's posture reflects approval and acceptance of the salesperson's message. If the customer leans back with arms tightly crossed, the posture suggests rejection or disagreement.[25]

Touch can convey warmth, understanding, and intimacy. Touch may also enhance positive feelings about the touching person and the situation. For example, studies show that when a store assistant, server in a restaurant, or product demonstrator lightly touched a customer on the arm, the customer saw the touching person more positively, had a more positive attitude toward the situation, and was more likely to comply with the toucher's suggestions.[26] Note, though, that this research involved casual touching of the arm. In contrast, many other forms of touching may be resented, and unwanted touching can be a form of sexual harassment.[27] Research shows that observers can identify anger, fear, disgust, love, and sympathy by watching someone being touched on the arm.[28]

When we encounter others, one of the first things we notice is the way they are dressed. Dress can convey characteristics such as image, mood, identity, power, wealth, and authority.[29] People who are dressed formally are better able to command respect. For instance, research has shown that pedestrians are more likely to cross against traffic lights when led by a well-dressed person than when led by a poorly dressed individual.[30] People in positions of authority, such as doctors and police officers, often wear distinctive uniforms to reinforce their status.[31] In addition, we all wear our own uniforms, that is, the particular way we choose to dress to communicate something about ourselves to others.

Proxemics is the use of interpersonal space (that is, proximity) to convey status or degree of intimacy. Sitting at the head of a table conveys status, standing close to another conveys intimacy, and sitting behind a desk (as opposed to alongside it) indicates a superior-subordinate relationship. Two elements of proxemics—personal space and seating arrangements—are especially relevant in organizational settings. We discuss proxemics in more detail in Chapter 7.

Again, nonverbal communications can have different—and even opposite—meanings across cultures. If used improperly they can offend, upset, and even anger members of other cultures.

In this chapter we have discussed how communication is critical for bridging differences and, in general, for improving team attitudes, cohesiveness, performance, and other processes and outcomes. In Chapter 7 we offer approaches to facilitating team processes, including advice on running team meetings, coaching and performance management, and making effective team decisions.

Summary and Integration

Team leaders and members need to recognize that effective communication is the foundation of a great team and that managing communications well requires an ongoing investment of time and effort to ensure that everyone is kept on the same page and in the loop.

Effective communication in teams requires understanding of, and development of, skills to properly anticipate and respond to barriers to communication.

It is important to recognize that communication does more than just transfer information in teams. It also serves to motivate; clarify duties, authority, and responsibilities; and permit the expression of feelings.

Among critical roles for team leaders and members are effective speaking, active listening, and proficient coaching and counseling. Fortunately, team leaders and members can develop skills in each of these roles.

Nonverbal communications, in forms such as proxemics, paralanguage, facial expressions, posture, dress, and eye contact, are critical to sensitive and effective communication. It is key to understand how nonverbal communications vary dramatically in nature and importance across cultures.

Notes

1   T.R. Peters & R.H. Waterman, *In Search of Excellence: Lessons from America's Best-Run Companies* (New York: Harper and Row, 1982).

2   K. Harmon, "Deaths from Avoidable Medical Error More Than Double in Past Decade, Investigation Shows," *Scientific American*, August 10, 2009. http://www.scientificamerican.com/blog/post/deaths-from-avoidable-medical-error-2009-08-10/?id=deaths-from-avoidable-medical-error-2009-08-10.

3   L. Lingard, S. Espin, S. Whyte, G. Regehr, G.R. Baker, R. Reznick, J. Bohnen, B. Orser, D. Doran, & E. Grober, "Communication Failures in the Operating Room: An Observational Classification of Recurrent Types and Effects," *Quality and Safety in Health Care*, 2004, *13*, pp. 330–334.

4   Ibid. See also, K.M. Sutcliffe, E. Lewton, & M.M. Rosenthal, "Communication Failures: An Insidious Contributor to Medical Mishaps," *Academic Medicine*, 2004, *79(2)*, pp. 186–194.

5   W.G. Scott and T.R. Mitchell, *Organization Theory: A Structural and Behavioral Analysis* (Homewood, IL: Richard D. Irwin, 1976). See also C. Mast & M. Huck, "Internal Communication and Leadership," in A. Zerfass, B. van Ruler, & K. Sriramesh (eds.), *Public Relations Research: European and International Perspectives and Innovations* (Berlin: VS Verlag für Sozialwissenschaften, 2008), pp. 147–162.

6   M. Master, "Could You Be a BDU?" *Across the Board*, May 1999, p. 71.

7   M. Rowh, "Cy*ber*speak (si ber spek) n. Language or Terms Related to Computers or Digital Technology," *Office Systems*, April 1999, p. 8. For more information on wireless jargon, see H. Fountain, "802.11 What?: A Guide to Wireless Jargon," *New York Times*, May 4, 2004, p. G9.

8   J.D. Glater, "Holy Change Agent!: Consultants Edit out Jargon," *Wall Street Journal*, June 14, 2003, p. C.1.

9   For a discussion of information retention and other barriers to knowledge sharing in virtual teams, see B. Rosen, S. Furst, & R. Blackburn, "Overcoming Barriers to Knowledge Sharing in Virtual Teams," *Organizational Dynamics*, 2007, *36(3)*, pp. 259–273.

10 J.R. Mesmer-Magnus & L.A. DeChurch, "Information Sharing and Team Performance: A Meta-Analysis," *Journal of Applied Psychology*, 2009, *94(2)*, 535–546.

11 *Wirtschaftswoche* (Germany), as reported in *ManpowerArgus*, July 1997, No. 346, p. 11.

12 This section, including the listing of guidelines for effective speaking, is based primarily on W.P. Galle, Jr., B.H. Nelson, D.W. Luse, & M.F. Villere, *Business Communication: A Technology-Based Approach* (Chicago: Irwin, 1996), pp. 447–458. For a set of guidelines for effective speaking, go to the text website.

13 For discussions of listening, see S. Caudron, "Listen Up!" *Workforce*, August 1999, pp. 25–27; R.C. Boyle, "A Manager's Guide to Effective Listening," *Manage*, July 1999, pp. 6–7; R.A. Prince & K.M. File, "Listen Then Talk: The Difference between Top Financial Advisors and the Rest Is That the Top Advisers Really, Really Listen," *Financial Planning*, November 1, 1998, pp. 167–168; and, B. Brooks, "The Power of Active Listening," *American Salesman*, 2006, *51(6)*, pp. 12–14.

14 See C. Crossen, "The Crucial Question for These Noisy Times May Just Be: 'Huh?'" *Wall Street Journal*, July 19, 1997, pp. A1 & A6. For a discussion of the importance of listening in organizations, see C. Jacobs & D. Coghlan, "Sound from Silence: On Listening in Organizational Learning," *Human Relations*, 2005, *58(1)*, pp. 115–138.

15 This section is based on W.P. Galle, Jr., B.H. Nelson, D.W. Luse, & M.F. Villere, *Business Communication: A Technology-Based Approach* (Chicago: Irwin, 1996), pp. 444–447. See also B. Brooks, "The Power of Active Listening," *American Salesman*, 2006, *51(6)*, pp. 12–14; and, M.J. McMains & K. Shannon, "Active Listening Revisited," *Journal of Police Crisis Negotiations*, 2007, *6(2)*, pp. 111–115.

16 These guidelines are based in part on P.M. Buhler, "A New Role for Managers: The Move from Directing to Coaching," *Supervision*, August 1998, pp. 17–19; S.A. Mobley, "Judge Not: How Coaches Create Healthy Organizations," *Journal for Quality and Participation*, July/August 1999, pp. 57–60; W.J. Rinke, "Be a Coach, Not a Cop," *Executive Excellence*, June 1998, p. 17; B. Rosner, "How Do You Coach the Best From Your Employees?" *Workforce*, November 1998, pp. 24–25; and, P. Simonsen & L. Davidson, "Do Your Managers Have the Right Stuff?" *Workforce*, August 1999, pp. 47–52.

17 This discussion of types of nonverbal communication is based in part on G.B. Davis & M.H. Olson, *Management Information Systems: Conceptual Foundations, Structure, and Development*, 2nd ed. (New York: McGraw-Hill Book Company, 1985). See also W.W. Kurkul, "Nonverbal Communication in One-On-One Music Performance Instruction," *Psychology of Music*, 2007, *35(2)*, pp. 327–362.

18 This discussion of paralanguage is based on W.P. Galle, Jr., B.H. Nelson, D.W. Luse, & M.F. Villere, *Business Communication: A Technology-Based Approach* (Chicago: Irwin, 1996), pp. 534–535. See also L.H. Chaney & C.G. Green, "Presenter Behaviors: Actions often Speak Louder Than Words," *American Salesman*, April 2002, *47(4)*, pp. 22–27; and, K.A. Gorgos, "Lost in Translation: Why the Video Record Is Actually Verbatim," *Buffalo Law Review*, July 2009 *(56)*, pp. 1057–1128.

19 J.R. Davitz & L. Davitz, "Nonverbal Vocal Communication of Feeling," *Journal of Communication*, 1961, *11*, pp. 81–86. See also A. Esposito, "The Amount of Information on Emotional States Conveyed by the Verbal and Nonverbal Channels: Some Perceptual Data," in Y. Stylianou, M.F. Zanuy, A. Esposito, & C. Action (eds.), *Progress in Nonlinear Speech Processing* (Berlin/Heidelberg: Springer, 2007), pp. 249–268.

20 See J. Sterrett, "Body Language and Job Interviews," *Journal of Business Education*, 1977, *53*, pp. 122–123; and, H. Peeters & F. Lievens, "Verbal and Nonverbal Impression Management Tactics in Behavior Description and Situational Interviews," *International Journal of Selection and Management*, 2006, *14(3)*, pp. 206–222.

21 See J.L. Waltman and S.P. Golen, "Detecting Deception During Interviews," *Internal Auditor*, August 1993, pp. 61–63; L. Koller, "To Catch a Liar," *Internal Auditor*, October 2002, pp. 42–47; and M. Hartig, P.A. Granhag, & O. Kronkvist, "Strategic Use of Evidence During Police Interviews: When Training to Detect Deception Works," *Law and Human Behavior*, 2006, *30*, pp. 603–619.

22 R.L. Birdwhistell, *Kinesics in Context: Essays on Body Motion Communications* (Philadelphia: University of Pennsylvania Press, 1970). See also A.S. Adejimola, "Language, Communication and Information Flow in Entrepreneurship," *African Journal of Business Management*, 2008, *2(x)*, pp. 201–208.

23 For discussions of the importance of eye contact, see M. Brody, "Delivering Your Speech Right between Their Eyes," *Supervision*, June 1994, p. 18; and, J. Hall, E. Coats, & L. LeBeau, "Nonverbal Behavior and the Vertical Dimension of Social Relations: A Meta-Analysis" *Psychological Bulletin*, 2005, *131(6)*, pp. 898–924.

24 E. Bekkering & J.P. Shim, "i2i Trust in Videoconferencing," *Communications of the ACM*, pp. 103–107; and, R.M. Henig, "Looking for the Lie," *New York Times Magazine*, February 5, 2006. http://www.nytimes.com

25 See, for instance, D. Booher, "Executive Presence," *Executive Excellence*, May 2003, *20(5)*, p. 19; and, A.M. Smith, "A Cross-Cultural Perspective on the Role of Emotion in Negative Service Encounters," *Service Industries Journal*, 2006, *26(7)*, pp. 709–726.

26 J. Hornik, "Tactile Stimulation and Consumer Response," *Journal of Consumer Response*, December 1992, pp. 449–458. See also N. Guéguen & C. Jacob, "The Effect of Touch on Tipping: An Evaluation in a French Bar," *Hospitality Management*, 2005, *24*, pp. 295–299; J. Peck & T.L. Childers, "If I Touch It I Have to Have It: Individual and Environmental Influences on Impulse Purchasing," *Journal of Business Research*, 2006, *59*, pp. 765–769; and, N. Guéguen, C. Jacob, & G. Boulbry, "The Effect of Touch on Compliance with a Restaurant's Employee Suggestion," *Hospitality Management*, 2007, *26*, pp. 1019–1023.

27 For instance, see F. Dobbin & E.L. Kelly, "How to Stop Harassment: Professional Construction of Legal Compliance in Organizations," *American Journal of Sociology, 2007, 112(4)*, pp. 1203–1243; and, T.J. Elkins & S. Velez-Castrillon, "Victims' and Observers' Perceptions of Sexual Harassment: Implications for Employers' Legal Risk in North America," *The International Journal of Human Resource Management*, 2008, *19(8)*, pp. 1435–1454.

28 M.J. Hertenstein, D. Keltner, B. App, B.A. Bulleit, & A.R. Jaskolka, "Touch Communicates Distinct Emotions," *Emotion*, 2006, *6(3)*, pp. 528–533.

29 See W.P. Galle, Jr., B.H. Nelson, D.W. Luse, & M.F. Villere, *Business Communication: A Technology-Based Approach* (Chicago: Irwin, 1996), pp. 444–447. The quote is from p. 532. See also A. Griswold, "How to Dress the Part: Work Wardrobes Convey Department and Rank," *Adweek*, May 19, 2003, *44(20)*, p. 37; and, K.K.P. Johnson, J.-J. Yoo, M. Kim, & S.J. Lennon, "Dress and Human Behavior: A Review and Critique," *Clothing and Textiles Research Journal*, 2008, *26(1)*, pp. 3–22.

30 M. Lefkowitz, R. Blake, & J. Mouton, "Status of Actors in Pedestrian Violations of Traffic Signals," *Journal of Abnormal and Social Psychology*, 1955, *51*, pp. 704–706. See also J. A. Hall, "Nonverbal Behavior, Status, and Gender:

How Do We Understand Their Relations?" *Psychology of Women Quarterly*, 2006, *30(4)*, pp. 384–391.

31 As an interesting example, see "Britain's Judges May Flip Wigs over Makeover," *Wall Street Journal*, May 14, 2003, p. B.5.C.

Bibliography

Adejimola, A.S. "Language, Communication and Information Flow in Entrepreneurship," *African Journal of Business Management*, 2008, *2(x)*, pp. 201–208.

Bekkering, E., & Shim, J.P. "i2i Trust in Videoconferencing," *Communications of the ACM*, pp. 103–107.

Birdwhistell, R.L. *Kinesics in Context: Essays on Body Motion Communications* (Philadelphia: University of Pennsylvania Press, 1970).

Booher, D. "Executive Presence," *Executive Excellence*, May 2003, *20(5)*, p. 19.

Boyle, R.C. "A Manager's Guide to Effective Listening," *Manage*, July 1999, pp. 6–7.

"Britain's Judges May Flip Wigs over Makeover," *Wall Street Journal*, May 14, 2003, p. B.5.C.

Brody, M. "Delivering Your Speech Right between Their Eyes," *Supervision*, June 1994, p. 18.

Brooks, B. "The Power of Active Listening," *American Salesman*, 2006, *51(6)*, pp. 12–14.

Buhler, P.M. "A New Role for Managers: The Move from Directing to Coaching," *Supervision*, August 1998, pp. 17–19.

Caudron, S. "Listen Up!" *Workforce*, August 1999, pp. 25–27.

Chaney, L.H., & Green, C.G. "Presenter Behaviors: Actions often Speak Louder Than Words," *American Salesman*, April 2002, *47(4)*, pp. 22–27.

Crossen, C. "The Crucial Question for These Noisy Times May Just Be: 'Huh?'" *Wall Street Journal*, July 19, 1997, pp. A1 & A6.

Davis, G.B., & Olson, M.H. *Management Information Systems: Conceptual Foundations, Structure, and Development*, 2nd ed. (New York: McGraw-Hill Book Company, 1985).

Davitz, J.R., & Davitz, L. "Nonverbal Vocal Communication of Feeling," *Journal of Communication*, 1961, *11*, pp. 81–86.

Dobbin, F., & Kelly, E.L. "How to Stop Harassment: Professional Construction of Legal Compliance in Organizations," *American Journal of Sociology, 2007, 112(4)*, pp. 1203–1243.

Elkins, T.J., & Velez-Castrillon, S. "Victims' and Observers' Perceptions of Sexual Harassment: Implications for Employers' Legal Risk in North America," *International Journal of Human Resource Management*, 2008, *19(8)*, pp. 1435–1454.

Esposito, A. "The Amount of Information on Emotional States Conveyed by the Verbal and Nonverbal Channels: Some Perceptual Data." In Y. Stylianou, M.F. Zanuy, A. Esposito, & C. Action (eds.), *Progress in Nonlinear Speech Processing* (Berlin/Heidelberg: Springer, 2007), pp. 249–268.

Fountain, H. "802.11 What?: A Guide to Wireless Jargon," *New York Times*, May 4, 2004, p. G9.

Galle, W.P., Jr., Nelson, B.H., Luse, D.W., & Villere, M.F. *Business Communication: A Technology-Based Approach* (Chicago: Irwin, 1996), pp. 444–447.

Glater, J.D. "Holy Change Agent!: Consultants Edit out Jargon," *Wall Street Journal*, June 14, 2003, p. C.1.

Gorgos, K.A. "Lost in Translation: Why the Video Record Is Actually Verbatim," *Buffalo Law Review*, July 2009 *(56)*, pp. 1057–1128.

Griswold, A. "How to Dress the Part: Work Wardrobes Convey Department and Rank," *Adweek*, May 19, 2003, *44(20)*, p. 37.

Guéguen N., & Jacob, C. "The Effect of Touch on Tipping: An Evaluation in a French Bar," *Hospitality Management*, 2005, *24*, pp. 295–299.

Guéguen, N., Jacob, C. & Boulbry, G. "The Effect of Touch on Compliance with a Restaurant's Employee Suggestion," *Hospitality Management*, 2007, *26*, pp. 1019–1023.

Hall, J.A. "Nonverbal Behavior, Status, and Gender: How Do We Understand Their Relations?" *Psychology of Women Quarterly*, 2006, *30(4)*, pp. 384–391.

Hall, J., Coats, E., & LeBeau, L. "Nonverbal Behavior and the Vertical Dimension of Social Relations: A Meta-Analysis," *Psychological Bulletin*, 2005, *131 (6)*, pp. 898–924.

Harmon, K. "Deaths from Avoidable Medical Error More Than Double in Past Decade, Investigation Shows," *Scientific American*, August 10, 2009. http://www.scientificamerican.com/blog/post/deaths-from-avoidable-medical-error-2009-08-10/?id=deaths-from-avoidable-medical-error-2009-08-10.

Hartig, M., Granhag, P.A., & Kronkvist, O. "Strategic Use of Evidence During Police Interviews: When Training to Detect Deception Works," *Law and Human Behavior*, 2006, *30*, pp. 603–619.

Henig, R.M. "Looking for the Lie," *New York Times Magazine*. February 5, 2006. http://www.nytimes.com

Hertenstein, M.J., Keltner, D., App, B., Bulleit, B.A., & Jaskolka, A.R. "Touch Communicates Distinct Emotions," *Emotion*, 2006, *6(3)*, pp. 528–533.

Hornik, J. "Tactile Stimulation and Consumer Response," *Journal of Consumer Response*, December 1992, pp. 449–458.

Jacobs, C., & Coghlan, D. "Sound from Silence: On Listening in Organizational Learning," *Human Relations*, 2005, *58(1)*, pp. 115–138.

Johnson, K.K.P., Yoo, J.-J., Kim, M., & Lennon, S.J. "Dress and Human Behavior: A Review and Critique," *Clothing and Textiles Research Journal*, 2008, *26(1)*, pp. 3–22.

Koller, L. "To Catch a Liar," *Internal Auditor*, October 2002, pp. 42–47.

Kurkul, W.W. "Nonverbal Communication in One-On-One Music Performance Instruction," *Psychology of Music*, 2007, *35(2)*, pp. 327–362.

Lefkowitz, M., Blake, R., & Mouton, J. "Status of Actors in Pedestrian Violations of Traffic Signals," *Journal of Abnormal and Social Psychology*, 1955, *51*, pp. 704–706.

Lingard, L., Espin, S., Whyte, S., Regehr, G., Baker, G.R., Reznick, R., Bohnen, J., Orser, B., Doran, D., & Grober, E. "Communication Failures in the Operating Room: An Observational Classification of Recurrent Types and Effects," *Quality and Safety in Health Care*, 2004, *13*, pp. 330–334.

Mast, C., & Huck, M. "Internal Communication and Leadership." In A. Zerfass, B. van Ruler, & K. Sriramesh (eds.), *Public Relations Research: European and International Perspectives and Innovations* (Berlin: VS Verlag für Sozialwissenschaften, 2008), pp. 147–162.

Master, M. "Could You Be a BDU?" *Across the Board*, May 1999, p. 71.

McMains, M.J., & Shannon, K. "Active Listening Revisited," *Journal of Police Crisis Negotiations*, 2007, *6(2)*, pp. 111–115.

Mesmer-Magnus, J.R., & DeChurch, L.A. "Information Sharing and Team Performance: A Meta-Analysis," *Journal of Applied Psychology*, 2009, *94(2)*, 535–546.

Mobley, S.A. "Judge Not: How Coaches Create Healthy Organizations," *Journal for Quality and Participation*, July/August 1999, pp. 57–60.

Peck, J., & Childers, T.L. "If I Touch It I Have to Have It: Individual and Environmental Influences on Impulse Purchasing," *Journal of Business Research*, 2006, *59*, pp. 765–769.

Peeters, H., & Lievens, F. "Verbal and Nonverbal Impression Management Tactics in Behavior Description and Situational Interviews," *International Journal of Selection and Management*, 2006, *14(3)*, pp. 206–222.

Pentland, A. "The New Science of Building Great Teams," *Harvard Business Review*, 2012, *90(4)*, pp. 60–69.

Peters, T.R., & Waterman, R.H. *In Search of Excellence: Lessons from America's Best-Run Companies* (New York: Harper and Row, 1982).

Prince, R.A., & File, K.M. "Listen Then Talk: The Difference between Top Financial Advisors and the Rest Is That the Top Advisers Really, Really Listen," *Financial Planning*, November 1, 1998, pp. 167–168.

Rinke, W.J. "Be a Coach, Not a Cop," *Executive Excellence*, June 1998, p. 17.

Rosen, B.S., Furst, S., & Blackburn, R. "Overcoming Barriers to Knowledge Sharing in Virtual Teams," *Organizational Dynamics*, 2007, *36(3)*, pp. 259–273.

Rosner, B. "How Do You Coach the Best from Your Employees?" *Workforce*, November 1998, pp. 24–25.

Rowh, M. "Cy*ber*speak (si ber spek) n. Language or Terms Related to Computers or Digital Technology," *Office Systems*, April 1999, p. 8.

Scott, W.G., & Mitchell, T.R. *Organization Theory: A Structural and Behavioral Analysis* (Homewood, IL: Richard D. Irwin, 1976).

Silverman, R.E. "Doodling for Dollars," *New York Times*, April 25, 2012, p. B1.

Simonsen, P., & Davidson, L. "Do Your Managers Have the Right Stuff?" *Workforce*, August 1999, pp. 47–52.

Smith, A.M. "A Cross-Cultural Perspective on the Role of Emotion in Negative Service Encounters," *The Service Industries Journal*, 2006, *26(7)*, pp. 709–726.

Sterrett, J. "Body Language and Job Interviews," *Journal of Business Education*, 1977, *53*, pp. 122–123.

Sutcliffe, K.M., Lewton, E., & Rosenthal, M.M. "Communication Failures: An Insidious Contributor to Medical Mishaps," *Academic Medicine*, 2004, *79(2)*, pp. 186–194.

Waltman, J.L., & Golen, G.P. "Detecting Deception During Interviews," *Internal Auditor*, August 1993, pp. 61–63.

Wirtschaftswoche (Germany), as reported in *ManpowerArgus*, July 1997, No. 346, p. 11.

Facilitating Team Processes

CHAPTER 7

Learning Objectives

In this chapter, we focus on the Facilitating the Team component of our High Performance Teams Model. After reading this chapter, you should be able to do the following

1. Design and conduct effective team meetings.
2. Understand how to use facilitation strategies to enhance the effectiveness of a team process.
3. Better master the stages of the problem-solving process.
4. Use special-purpose team decision-making techniques, including the devil's advocate, brainstorming, the affinity technique, and the nominal group technique, to enhance team decision making.

Designing and Conducting Team Meetings

Meetings are a big part of the workday. For example, the Executive Time Use Project, an ongoing study conducted by a team of researchers from the London School of Economics and Harvard Business School, found that company CEOs spend more than 18 hours a week in meetings.[1] Unless properly managed, meetings can be frustrating, boring, and generally a waste of time. Alternatively, well-run meetings can reap the tremendous potential benefits of teams. The ability to run a meeting well is a valuable skill. In this section, we provide guidelines for helping team members become acquainted, providing a facilitating setting, considering spatial arrangements, and giving structure to meetings.

Helping Team Members Become Acquainted

It's very important for team members to know and be comfortable with one another. If they aren't, meetings will be tense.[2]

- **Before the first meeting, distribute members' biographical sketches, along with the team's assignment and other relevant materials.**
- **Before each meeting, give members a chance to socialize.**
- **At the first meeting, introduce each member or have the members introduce themselves.**
- **Use appropriate icebreaker exercises.[3]** Doing so might involve stories, exercises, or even jokes. Icebreakers can help overcome initial discomfort in teams. Until team members know whom they are dealing with, they may be uncomfortable and perhaps suspicious. However, icebreakers themselves can make team members nervous and uncomfortable if they

aren't handled well.[4] Skills Practice 7.1 on the text website gives you a chance to develop skill in using icebreaker and energizer activities for a team meeting.

- **During long meetings, provide breaks.**

Providing a Facilitative Setting

Make sure the team can work in a comfortable space without distractions. Use a room that is large enough to accommodate the number of participants, but not so large as to make them feel lost. Provide flipcharts, whiteboards, and other writing surfaces. Avoid long, narrow tables, since they restrict eye contact and communication—a "U"-shaped seating arrangement works well. Try to have a comfortable lighting level. Offer flexibility in how team members can arrange themselves and their work.[5]

Considering Spatial Arrangements

Sometimes the little things can make a big difference in teams. For example, when people come into a conference room for a meeting, they usually sit wherever they want. The team leader may—or may not—consciously choose a seat at the head of a conference table or in front of the group, but everything else is often left to chance. In fact, though, the way team members are arranged can make a big difference in how interaction takes place and how well the team performs.

At least three aspects of spatial arrangements are important in teams: (1) how far apart team members are; (2) who are sitting in high-status positions; and (3) how team members are arranged relative to one another. Let's look at these aspects in turn. As discussed in Chapter 5 and noted later in this section, these aspects—especially interpersonal distance—may vary substantially across cultures.

Interpersonal Distance

Suppose you meet a friend in the hallway and stop to chat. How close would you likely stand to your friend? Chances are you'd stand just far enough away that you could reach out and put your thumb in your friend's ear (a so-called rule of thumb). The point is that we have certain comfortable distances for particular types of interactions, often called bubbles. When people are too close to us or too far away, we tend to feel uneasy. Put another way, we have a sense of **personal space**, an area around us that we treat as an extension of ourselves, and we want people to be in specific parts—or zones—of that personal space for particular activities. There are four **zones of personal space**, as shown in Figure 7-1.[6]

For those raised in the United States, the *intimate zone* is typically a bubble extending to about 19 inches from the skin. As the name suggests, we let others enter this zone only for the very best of reasons, such as lovemaking, protecting, and comforting. When other circumstances—such as a crowded elevator—force us to allow people into the intimate zone, we tend to treat them as objects rather than as persons.

The *personal zone* ranges from about 1.5 feet to 4 feet from the person. It is used for comfortable interaction with others and connotes closeness and friendship.

Figure 7-1

Zones of Personal Space
for Those Raised in the
United States

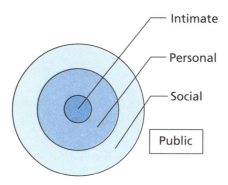

Intimate

Personal

Social

Public

The *social zone*, from 4 to 12 feet, is used for most impersonal business. People working together use the inner part of the zone. The outer part is used for more formal interactions.

Finally, the *public zone*, more than 12 feet from the body, is beyond the range of comfortable interaction.

Again, interpersonal distances corresponding to the zones of personal space vary dramatically across cultures. For instance, in northern Europe, the bubbles tend to be quite large, and people keep their distance. In southern France, Italy, Greece, and Spain, the bubbles are smaller. A distance seen as intimate in northern Europe overlaps normal conversational distance in southern Europe. As a result, Mediterranean Europeans get too close for the comfort of Germans, Scandinavians, English persons, and those of northern European ancestry.[7] For an example of the importance of personal space on joint U.S.-Russian space flights, see the following Teams in the News box.

TEAMS IN THE NEWS: Personal Space on the International Space Station

For an interesting example of how cross-cultural differences in personal space and other matters may lead to conflict, consider the International Space Station (ISS). While the American and Russian/Soviet space programs each discovered a variety of psychosocial risks associated with long-duration space missions, when the two countries began working together on the ISS there were concerns about how cultural differences would present additional risk factors. Even though there are differences across cultures in the degree of focus on the individual or group, gender norms, personal hygiene norms, emotional expressivity, and many other dimensions, personal space differences were one particular concern. Russians, relative to Americans, are more accustomed to living in small spaces, having few personal belongings, and living and working in close proximity to others. In fact, there is no word for "privacy" in Russian, and little concept of it. The closest Russian terms back-translate as "seclusion," "keeping secret," and "loneliness." When U.S. citizens express wishes for private time, Russians are likely to see this as indicating the speakers are ill, unfriendly, or offended. Research will be ongoing to see whether these national cultural differences will in fact cause major problems among the select population of space program personnel.

Source: J. B. Ritsher, "Cultural Factors and the International Space Station," *Aviation, Space, and Environmental Medicine*, 2005, *76(6)*, pp. B135–B144.

Businesspersons entering other cultures must be especially careful to learn appropriate zones for various interactions. Typically, people experience discomfort when their personal space is inappropriately entered. They may protest or leave the situation rather than accept it.[8]

Eye Contact

When leaders enter a room, where do they go? Often, they choose a position at the front of the room, or an elevated position, or a position at the head of a conference table. These positions have one thing in common: they each give the leader the chance to make direct eye contact with as many others as possible. In general, leaders tend to position themselves in a way that gives them a lot of potential eye contact with others. In turn, people who are in such positions (again, at the head of a conference table, in a central position in a room, or in an elevated position) are more likely to be seen as leaders. They are perceived (other things equal) to have more status and to be more leader-like, and they have more communication directed toward them than might occur if they were in less visible positions.

Seating Arrangements

Suppose you and another individual were about to sit down at a conference table. Where would the two of you sit? Across from each other? Side by side? Corner to corner? Far apart? Your response probably depends on how the two of you would expect to be interacting, if at all. As shown in Figure 7-2, this is just what happens. If people expect to cooperate, they tend to sit side by side. If they expect to be in conflict, as in many bargaining situations, they tend to sit face to face. If they plan to engage in casual conversation, they sit corner to corner. If they don't plan to interact at all (for

Figure 7-2

Seating Arrangements for
Different Activities

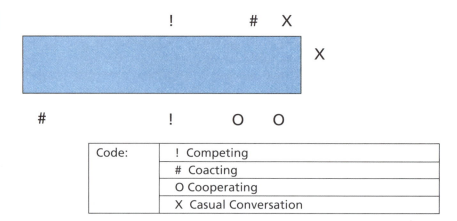

Code:	! Competing
	# Coaching
	O Cooperating
	X Casual Conversation

example, if they are each going to be working on their own homework) they tend to sit distant opposite.

Here's the more interesting finding: if people are *randomly* seated in these relative positions, they are more likely to interact in these ways than if seated differently. For example, people seated across from each other are more likely to get into an argument than if seated next to each other or corner to corner.

TEAMS IN THE NEWS: More Meetings Are Stand-Up Jobs

Increasingly, many meetings have *no* seating arrangements. Instead, especially in the high-tech world, stand-up meetings are in vogue. Atomic Object, a Michigan software development firm, holds these meetings early in the morning.

The idea of stand-up meetings is to eliminate long-winded discussions in which participants talk endlessly, play games on their cellphones, or simply tune out.[1]

The stand-up meeting boom is due in part to growing use of Agile. *Agile* calls for compressing development projects into short pieces. Agile also involves stand-up meetings in which team members quickly update their team members with three things: what they have done since yesterday's meeting; what they are doing today; and what obstacles may hinder getting work done.

To learn more about Agile project development methodology, go to the text website.

Note

1. R.E. Silverman, "No More Angling for the Best Seat; More Meetings Are Stand-Up Jobs," *Wall Street Journal*, February 2, 2012.

Giving Structure to Meetings: Before, During, and After

Team leaders are sometimes reluctant to provide structure. They don't want to be seen as bossy, and they believe (or hope) that things will somehow work themselves out. This is unfortunate since meetings need—and team members welcome—structure. The key point here is that providing appropriate structure does not mean dominating the process. Instead, it gives team members clear bounds within which to operate.

Before the Meeting

- **Define the purpose of the meeting and ensure that there is actually a need for the meeting.** It may be hard to believe, but many team meetings in organizations are organized because the leader feels the team should be having meetings because this is what teams do. However, these leaders fail to consider what the objective would be or whether a meeting needs to be called to accomplish it. For example, many students are all too familiar with the General Member Meetings that student organizations hold throughout a term. Unfortunately, many of these meetings are filled with a long list of announcements about and updates on upcoming events and opportunities that could easily have been e-mailed to the members. So, when is a team meeting a good idea? A meeting is needed when there are issues that need to be discussed, evaluated, and decided on, and when you need the input of people with different perspectives and expertise on the issues. A meeting is also needed when it is important to get the team members who will be involved with a task or project to understand and to buy in to it.
- **Solicit input from team members regarding issues to be discussed at the meeting.** This can be done through a simple e-mail sent to all team members a few days before the meeting to capture their concerns. Team leaders will need to make decisions about which issues can or should be addressed at the upcoming meeting versus those that there may not be time to discuss. It would be a good idea to contact team members whose issues cannot be addressed before the meeting and explain why their concerns will not be on the agenda.
- **Create a formal meeting agenda and send it to all team members.** Diane Bryant, CIO of Intel, says, "Every meeting needs an agenda emailed out beforehand, even if it's just someone one on one. And we hold each other responsible. If someone doesn't prepare and comes in with a half-baked idea, the meeting is often adjourned, and you come back when you're

ready."[9] The agenda should list basic information such as the date, time, location of the meeting, and the meeting's duration. The agenda should also list the issues to be discussed and decided on at the meeting, how much time will be allocated for each issue, and who will be responsible for leading the discussion of the issue or reporting out an update on the current status of an issue. Skills Practice 7.2 on the text website gives you the chance to develop a meeting agenda.

During the Meeting

- **Conduct a check-in.** This is a simple activity in which each team member shares how he or she is doing or anything that is new. A check-in is usually done in a round-robin fashion, going around the table. When a person does a check-in, he or she may say positive things such as "I'm doing great today. I'm really looking forward to the weekend." Others may be less positive and say things like, "I am really overwhelmed right now with multiple project deadlines, and my daughter is sick at home, so I'm trying to juggle a lot of stuff right now." The value of doing a check-in is to for the team leader and members to take each other's pulse. If you know that a team member is distracted with a lot of things going on, it may be helpful to remember this if that team member is not fully engaged in the team meeting or if he or she failed to prepare properly for the meeting.

- **At the beginning of the meeting, review progress to date and establish the task of the meeting.** This may involve approving the minutes or summary (a documentation of what was done and decided at a previous meeting) from the team's last meeting as well as re-stating the desired takeaway for this meeting, such as making a key decision about a plan of action, assigning responsibilities to team members for a new project, or other action.

- **Conduct a brief icebreaker or energizer activity to enhance team members' engagement in the meeting.** Use of an icebreaker can be especially important if team members do not know each other well or if the team leader feels that the level of energy and motivation on the team is low on that particular day. Again, Skills Practice 7.1 relates to the development of such activities.

- **Assign the roles of timekeeper and scribe to team members.** The timekeeper has the basic responsibility of tracking how much time is being spent on each agenda time relative to the time allotted for discussing that issue. The timekeeper typically notifies the team when time has almost run out for discussing an issue and when it has expired completely. This individual also warns the team leader when the stated end time for the meeting is approaching. The scribe is responsible for documenting what is discussed and decided on at the meeting. These are referred to as *the minutes of the meeting*. After the meeting is over, the scribe typically gives the notes to the team leader to e-mail out to the team. The scribe's work is critical to ensure that a team's meetings and work processes are documented.

- **Early in the meeting, use the meeting agenda you created to get a report from each team member with a preassigned task.** This ensures that team members who have accomplished their tasks are recognized for their work. It also makes it clear that members with tasks will be called on to report on them.

- **Manage the discussion to ensure fair participation.** Peggy Klaus, executive coach and president of Klaus and Associates, says, ". . . set some rules of participation. Lay down the law at the beginning of the meeting. Even if it takes five minutes, it saves time if people know that if someone goes off topic, the moderator can interrupt."[10] The team leader—and other team members—must make sure that all members have the opportunity to participate. If one or a few members dominate the process, the benefits of using a team will quickly evaporate. Here are some tips for encouraging fair participation:[11]

  - Establish norms for fair participation, sometimes called **ground rules**. For example, state early in the meeting, "Let's make sure we all have a chance to make our views known. I hope we'll all feel free to speak up, but also that we'll let others have their say."

  - Provide guiding comments. If someone has been dominating the process, say something to the effect of "Janet, I think you've done a good job of stating your position. Let's see if someone else has any comments." If someone hasn't been contributing, say something like "Donna, is there anything you'd like to add?" People are often anxious to make a point but are reluctant to say anything unless they're directly asked to participate.

  - Use a **round-robin process**, asking members to give their comments in turn. For example, the leader may simply say, "Let's go around the table and see what each of us has to say." Sometimes, as when team members have made up lists of ideas, the round-robin technique may be used to have each member in turn give his or her first idea, then in turn give his or her second idea, and so on.

  - Ask members to write down their ideas. This will result in more unique, clearly stated ideas.

- **Use team facilitation strategies to enhance the effectiveness of the team meeting.**[12] An effective team leader must be adept at constantly monitoring, evaluating, and adapting to the interpersonal dynamics among members of the team. This requires a proactive and systematic approach to managing meetings. Figure 7-3 presents a summary of diagnostic questions that team leaders and team members should be asking during a meeting and some potential interventions for facilitating a meeting process.

- **At the end of the meeting, summarize what was accomplished, where the team is on its schedule, and what will be the team's task at the next meeting.** The team can attempt to schedule its next meeting at this point or the team leader can follow up on this after the meeting. These activities give the team a sense of movement and accomplishment.

Figure 7-3

Summary of Team
Facilitation Diagnostic
Questions and Potential
Interventions

Team Process Dimension	Diagnostic Questions to Ask	Potential Interventions
Participation	• Who are the high participators? Why? • Who are the low participators? Why? • How are the silent people treated? • Who talks to whom? Who responds to whom?	• Clarify points made earlier that were not considered • Reinforce a prior point to elaborate on it • Query—Ask a team member for his/her ideas
Influence	• Which members are listened to when they speak? Why? What are their ideas? • Which members are ignored when they speak? Why? What are their ideas? • Are there any shifts in influence? If so, whose influence is shifting? Why? • Is there any rivalry within the team? Are there struggles among individuals or subgroups for leadership? • Who interrupts whom? Does this reflect relative power within the group? • Are minority views consistently ignored regardless of possible merit?	• Support or reinforce the views or positions of people whose positions are not being heard • State the opinions of certain individuals who are dominating the discussion • Broaden the discussion of a given topic or issue
Conflict	• Does the team tend to consider only a few alternatives when problem solving? Are areas of agreement overemphasized while leaving areas of disagreement unexplored? • What criteria are used to establish agreement (majority vote, consensus, no opposition viewed as agreement)? • Do team members advocate more than they inquire? • How do team members feel about their participation in the team? How do they react in team meetings (e.g., frustrated, defensive, enthusiastic)? • Are team members overly competitive with each other? Are team members overly nice or polite to each other? Are only positive feelings expressed? Do members agree with each other too easily? What happens when members disagree?	• Be clear about appropriate behaviors for team members • Reinforce and support desirable behaviors • Raise the issue of inappropriate behavior directly • Ground discussions of issues in current data to minimize the personal nature of the discussion • Generate several meaningful alternatives for the team to consider • Create a sense of fairness by empowering or sharing power across team members • Make sure that team goals are commonly held by the team

Source: Based on L. A. Hill and M. T. Farkas. "A Note on Team Process," Harvard Business School Background Note 402-032, Harvard Business School, October 4, 2001.

- **Make public and clear each member's assignment for the next meeting.** This creates a sense of responsibility. It also makes sure people know what they're expected to do and that tasks don't get duplicated by more than one team member or fall through the cracks, being ignored by all members. This information can be used to develop the agenda for the next meeting.
- **Conduct a check-out.** The purpose of this activity is to go around the table in a round-robin fashion and ask each team member to comment on their thoughts about the meeting, what was accomplished, and how they feel about the meeting and the overall direction of the team. For example, someone who is feeling very positive may say something like "This was a great meeting. We accomplished a lot and I am excited to move forward with our plans." Someone who is less positive might say, "I think we made some progress today, but I am concerned that we are falling behind schedule relative to our timeline. I hope that we can increase our sense of urgency in moving forward." The check-out is a very useful activity to provide a sense of closure to the meeting and to take the pulse of the team members again.

After the Meeting

- **Review the meeting minutes and send them out to all team members.** This will help ensure that all team members maintain a common understanding of what happened at the meeting. Ideally, this should be done within a couple days after the meeting took place.
- **Follow up with team members or others based on decisions made in the meeting.** Doing so may involve holding additional meetings with individual team members or subgroups of the overall team to discuss and work on issues. In some cases, meetings may be needed to address performance issues or concerns of individual team members.
- **Schedule the next meeting.** After the team leader has determined that another meeting is needed, he or she can send out a formal meeting request. If the size of the team is large and individual team members' schedules are busy, then a Web-based meeting-scheduling program can be used. Two of the most commonly used applications (both are free) are Meeting Wizard and Doodle. Links to both can be found on the text website. These applications make it easy to coordinate the scheduling of team meetings. In order to set up a meeting, a team leader simply selects potential dates/times for meetings and e-mails them to team members. The system summarizes responses from team members regarding their availability, after which the team leader can formally confirm a meeting date/time when everyone is available. Meeting Wizard can even send out meeting reminders to team members.
- **Develop the agenda for the next meeting.** Based on the team leader's assessment of the team's progress and a review of previous meeting minutes, he or she should draft the agenda for the next team meeting and send it out to team members.

TEAMS IN THE NEWS: Random Meetings and a Robot at Evernote

In an interview with the *New York Times*, Phil Libin, chief executive of Evernote, a provider of note-taking and archiving technology, discusses the unique culture at his firm.[1] To keep in touch with his employees when he's out of the office, Libin uses a 6-foot two-wheeled Anybots robot with a video conferencing system and built-in laser pointer. Libin sees through its eyes and ears, and it has a screen so employees can see him. The robot rolls around so Libin can have casual conversations at employees' desks. To ensure that employees at the headquarters in Mountain View, California, and those at a studio in Austin, Texas, don't feel separated, he has set up giant 70-inch TVs with built-in high-end video cameras set up in high-traffic areas at both sites. The TVs essentially serve as windows between the sites.

In addition, the company has recently implemented Evernote Officer Training involving random meetings. Libin got the idea from a friend who served on a Trident nuclear submarine. The friend said that to be an officer on the subs, you have to know how to do everyone else's job. If employees sign up for the voluntary program, they are randomly assigned to a meeting in a totally different department in order to observe and absorb. They can act as full members in the meetings, talking and asking questions.

To read more of the interview and learn more about Evernote's policies and practices, including its unlimited vacations, check the links on the text website.

Note

1. A. Bryant, "Here's $1,000. Now, Please Take Your Vacation," *New York Times*, April 8, 2012, p. BU2.

Making Team Decisions

In this age of empowerment, self-managing teams, and job enrichment, teams are increasingly being called on to make decisions. In this section, we discuss the problem-solving process, note some biases that may interfere with team decision making, offer guidelines to avoid overreliance on concurrence seeking, and discuss four special-purpose team decision-making techniques.

The Problem-Solving Process

Successful problem solvers recognize making a good decision is more than just choosing one option over another. Instead, they follow the five steps in the **problem-solving process** shown in Figure 7-4.

Define the Problem

Careful problem definition is crucial. Unless proper time and care are taken at this stage, teams may solve the wrong problem. A problem occurs when there is a gap between the desired and the actual situation. Declining profits, high scrap rates, or inability to increase market share are all possible problems. Too often, the problem is defined in terms of symptoms. For instance, management may define the problem as employee apathy instead of seeing that apathy as a symptom of a deeper problem, such as an inadequate pay structure. Or the problem may be defined in terms of a preferred solution. A problem statement such as "Gloria is a poor manager" focuses on proposed solutions relating to Gloria. It doesn't directly address the criterion of interest, such as declining performance in Gloria's department.[13] Here are some guidelines for writing a good problem statement:

- **State the problem explicitly.** We have a tendency to assume the problem is too obvious to require an explicit statement. However, even so-called obvious problems are seen differently by different people or not seen at all.
- **Specify the standard(s) violated.** There are many different types of standards that may be violated. These could be personal (such as violation of privacy or trust), group (such as violation of equal treatment or lack of opportunity to participate), organizational (such as poor quality or high scrap rates), or even societal (such as socially irresponsible behavior).
- **State the problem in specific behavioral terms.** Don't use broad generalizations such as lack of communications, personality conflicts, or the like. What specific behavioral standards are being violated? What specific

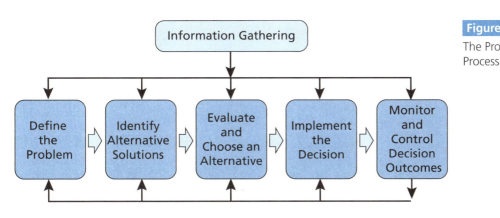

Figure 7-4
The Problem-Solving Process

behavioral change is desired? What behavior would constitute a solution to the problem?

- **Specify whose problem it is.** This helps identify who must be involved in problem resolution. That is, who owns the problem? The problem statement should make clear the perspective being taken. For instance, is the problem statement from the perspective of a particular manager? Of a team?

- **Avoid stating the problem merely as an implied solution.** For instance, suppose productivity has declined. A problem statement such as "The plant manager must find ways to motivate employees to improve productivity" implies a solution—motivating employees. In fact, though, the problem may lie in equipment problems, management decisions, or much else. Prematurely focusing on employee motivation inappropriately narrows the scope of inquiry.

- **Avoid stating the problem as a dilemma.** People sometimes state a problem as an unsolvable predicament. They may say, "The problem is that we will lose no matter which action we take" or "We've been handed a hopeless situation." This may come from a desire for sympathy or attention or to gain vengeance or avoid effort, but it does nothing to solve the problem.

Identify Alternative Solutions

Alternatives are the various approaches that may be taken to solve the problem. Good solutions require good alternatives. Unfortunately, in the rush to judgment the alternative-generation stage is often slighted. For example, team members may come up with two or three ideas, begin evaluating them, and then fail to generate more alternatives. At this stage **divergent thinking** is needed.[14]

That is, problem solvers must stretch their minds, seeking new possibilities. Creativity is especially important at the alternative-generation stage. We discuss two creativity enhancement techniques—brainstorming and the affinity technique—later in the chapter. In the business world, divergent thinking is sometimes called thinking outside the box, where the box is the conventional approach to thinking and acting.

Evaluate and Choose an Alternative

Once alternatives are thoroughly generated, they can be evaluated and a choice can be made. This stage requires **convergent thinking**, a narrowing in on a solution. There are two general approaches to evaluation and choice. With **screening approaches**, each alternative is identified as satisfactory or unsatisfactory. Unsatisfactory alternatives are screened out, leaving only those that can clear all hurdles. **Scoring approaches** assign a total score to each alternative. Then the alternative with the best score can be chosen. Later in this chapter we discuss a variety of ways to improve evaluation and choice.

Implement the Decision

Together, the first three stages of the problem-solving process are called **decision making**. The problem-solving process isn't over once these stages have been completed, however. Unfortunately, decisions do not implement themselves. Necessary resources must be available for implementation. Also, those who will be involved in implementation must fully understand and accept the solution. For that reason, implementers are often encouraged to participate in the earlier stages of the process.

A fundamental question at this stage is how long to persist in trying to implement the decision successfully. It is easy to err in either direction. The many difficulties that typically arise when trying to implement a major decision can lead to frustration, discontent, and the temptation to throw in the towel. As noted by Rosabeth Moss Kanter, "Everything looks like a failure in the middle."[15]

At the same time, decision makers are also prone to **escalation of commitment**. This is the tendency to "throw good money after bad," continuing to pour more time and resources into a failing project. Some powerful forces lead to escalation of commitment.[16] For instance, we find it hard to ignore sunk costs, the resources that have already been expended. Also, as long as more resources are being put into a project, no one has to admit failure. Further, there are many social rewards for persistence; people tend to praise managers who stick to their guns in the face of opposition and bleak odds. For these and other reasons, escalation of commitment is a tempting, and dangerous, tendency. Decision makers in organizations, like other gamblers, have got to know when to fold'em. Here are some guidelines for minimizing the dangers of inappropriate escalation of commitment:[17]

- **Create stopping rules prior to launching a project.** These stopping rules specify the conditions under which the project should be abandoned.[18]
- **Specify objective criteria for evaluating the status of a project.**
- **Actively gather information on project performance—and accept warning signals when they occur.**
- **Make it clear that pulling the plug is a viable option and don't be afraid to follow through when needed.**
- **Be wary of penalizing managers if their projects fail.** If managers feel their careers will be damaged by failure, they may escalate commitment rather than admit failure.
- **Seek objective views on project status, such as from external auditors.**

Now, complete Skills Practice 7.3 on the text website in which you will analyze the movie *Thirteen Days*, starring Kevin Costner. This movie tells the story of the Cuban Missile Crisis in the early 1960s where escalation of commitment brought the United States and the Soviet Union dangerously close to war.

Monitor and Control Decision Outcomes

The final step in the problem-solving process is to monitor decision outcomes and take necessary corrective action. If decision control is to be effective, steps must be taken to ensure that necessary information is gathered. Contingency plans must be developed to permit changes if the decision does not turn out well. **Contingency planning** is the process of developing alternative courses of action that can be followed if a decision, perhaps because of unexpected events, does not work out as planned. Contingency plans ensure that backups are available, and they help remove the panic element in unforeseen situations. The book and movie *The Perfect Storm* describe a situation in which a series of freakish weather conditions came together in the worst possible way to create a horrendous storm. Contingency plans are sometimes developed to deal with a worst-case scenario, the situation in which events fall together in the worst possible way to create the organizational equivalent of a perfect storm. Thus, contingency planning requires preparing for the worst even while hoping for the best.

Now that we have examined each of the steps in the general problem-solving process, complete Skills Practice 7.4 on the text website to develop skill in applying the problem-solving process to business problems.

PDCA: A Team Problem-Solving Process

One tool that is especially useful for team problem solving is the Plan-Do-Check-Act or PDCA Model that was developed by W. Edwards Deming, the late quality management guru. PDCA says that teams need to implement each of the four steps in the process as shown in Figure 7-5.

- **Plan.** In this phase a team selects a problem that it wants to solve. For example, the problem could be a product development process that is too inefficient. Or it could be a service process that is failing to meet the expectations of its end users or customers. The team then analyzes the problem by observing it, evaluating it through data collection and other means in order to understand the problem and its underlying cause(s). Based on this analysis, the team develops a plan that the team feels is a potential solution to the problem.
- **Do.** In this phase a team implements the solution it identified in the Plan phase.
- **Check.** The team now collects empirical data in order to assess the degree to which the implemented solution helped to solve the problem.

Figure 7-5

The PDCA Model

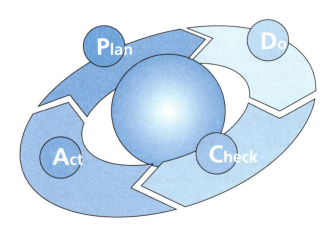

- **Act.** Based on the results of the evaluation of the solution, the team determines what to act on next. The focus is more on implementing steps to standardize the work process with the change or improvement as part of it and maximizing the ability of the team to sustain the improvement associated with the change.

After one complete iteration of the **PDCA cycle,** the team starts the process again by planning to identify another solution that will further enhance the effectiveness or efficiency of a process. Use of the PDCA Model becomes the basis for a team's ongoing efforts to support continuous improvement in the implementation of its key work processes.

Biases

Teams, like individuals, are subject to a variety of biases. The team leader, and team members, should be aware of these biases and take steps to prevent them. Some important decision biases include the following:

- **Conservatism in information processing.** When we get new information, we tend to underrevise our past estimates. For instance, if we initially believe the probability of an event is .5 and receive new information that should increase (according to Bayes Theorem, which calculates how much a prior probability should be revised in the face of new diagnostic information) the probability to .8, we are more likely to revise our estimate to only .6 or .7. Conservatism leads to inadequate response to changing situations.
- **Framing effects.** The way information is framed can influence choices. For example, suppose a gas station charges 5 cents a gallon more for a credit card purchase than for a cash payment. That difference will be viewed differently if it is presented as a cash discount than if it is called a credit card surcharge. Further, theory and research show that we tend to evaluate alternatives in terms of changes from the status quo rather than as absolute values.[19] So, for example, we may behave differently if we think we have gained 20 pounds and will have difficulty losing them than if we start anew and think in terms of gaining or losing pounds from our current weight. Be careful not to automatically accept the way an issue is initially framed. Instead, try framing issues in different ways.
- **Hindsight bias.** Hindsight bias (or Monday morning quarterbacking) is the phenomenon of I knew it all along: the tendency for people who learn of the outcome of an event to believe falsely that they would have predicted the reported outcome. Hindsight bias results in distorted views of the accuracy of past decisions and thus causes us to underestimate the degree to which our decisions could be improved. Unfortunately, hindsight bias is extremely difficult to overcome.
- **Confirmation bias.** This type of bias is our tendency to seek, interpret, and recall information in ways that confirm our preconceptions.[20] Especially when emotionally significant issues and established beliefs are involved, we prefer information sources that favor our preconceptions and avoid disconfirming sources. Further, we interpret ambiguous situations to favor our views and are more likely to remember confirming than disconfirming

information. As such, team leaders and members should be open to—and even seek—information that may refute their positions. They should also try to examine all information, confirming or disconfirming, with equal rigor. Team leaders should make it clear that it is better for the team to identify potential flaws than to have those flaws surfaced by customers, competitors, and others. The leader may even want to devote an entire meeting to finding potential flaws in a favored alternative.

- **Overconfidence bias.** Hindsight bias, confirmation bias, and other factors result in overconfidence and occurs when people's subjective confidence in their judgments is greater than their objective accuracy.[21] For instance, in some quizzes people who report they are 99% sure their answer is correct are wrong 40% of the time. As stated by cowboy-philosopher Will Rogers, "It's not what we don't know that gives us trouble. It's what we know that ain't so."

- **Illusory correlation.** This type of bias is the tendency to see relationships between variables that do not in fact exist, perhaps because of our stereotypes or expectations.[22] For instance, if we believe Friday the 13th is unlucky, we are likely to be especially aware of bad events that occur on that date. As a check on our thinking, we should be careful to also consider the good events that occur on Friday the 13th and the bad events that occur on other dates.

Guidelines to Avoid Overreliance on Concurrence Seeking

In his groupthink model, discussed in Chapter 9, Irving Janis focused on the dangers of having too many yes men willing to agree with a dominant view (perhaps the team leader's) without critical evaluation. While the validity of the full groupthink model is controversial, guidelines that Janis provided to avoid overreliance on concurrence seeking are definitely useful.[23] In particular, Janis suggested the following:

- The team leader should encourage all team members to air their doubts and objections.
- Early in deliberations, leaders should adopt an impartial stance rather than stating their preferences.
- Before the team reaches a final decision, the leader should encourage members to discuss the team's deliberations with trusted associates and then report back to the team.
- The team should invite outside experts to meetings and encourage them to challenge members' views.
- When the issue being dealt with involves a competitor, time should be devoted to assessing warning signals from the competitor and alternative scenarios of the competitor's intentions.
- When the team is considering alternatives, it should from time to time split into subgroups to meet separately, under different leaders, and then get together to resolve differences.
- After a preliminary consensus concerning the preferred alternatives is reached, the team should hold a second-chance meeting when members can express remaining doubts and rethink the entire issue before making a final choice.

Insights and Advice

. . . .

Heather Hilleren, founder and CEO, Hevva Corp.

Heather Hilleren is the founder and CEO of Hevva Corp., best known for LocalDirt.com (the online platform for buying and selling local food) and the mobile app Locavore. Prior to starting Hevva, she spent nearly 10 years at Whole Foods Market where she received the Regional All Star award in 2001 for her work as leader of both front end systems and customer service teams. As team leader she was responsible for all hiring, training, managing, and firing for a team of 30–35 employees. She received an MBA in entrepreneurship from the University of Madison–Wisconsin in 2005.

Do you have any general advice for team leaders and/or members?

1. You are always looking for (and training) your replacement.
2. When solving a crisis, your first words to the team member should be, "What happened?"
3. If there are two sides to the story, get both before acting.
4. Good employees always work better when reaching for a goal or solving a problem or crisis. If you don't give them this, they will create their own, and it may not be the crisis you want. (Think of the movie *Groundhog Day* and what happens when you have to live the same day over and over again.) For some people, the only time a routine day is okay is when they have big crises in their personal lives.
5. If you have already made up your mind, never ask, "What do you think?

When do you think teams should be used?

Whenever the workload requires it, or when different perspectives are needed.

When do you think use of teams should be avoided?

When the team leader is only going to micromanage the project and re-do the work. And, when the additional hours for team members to update each other and coordinate takes more time than they save.

Are there any special techniques you like to use when working with team members in meetings or other settings?

Engage them. Give them tasks or roles, however small. At best, your role is to keep them on task, giving them enough room to make their own discoveries and conclusions.

Can you tell us about a time when you were involved in a team that was especially successful? Why do you think it was so successful?

My team had the highest productivity and morale of any store in the region. It was because we (the entire team) had learned how to communicate, encourage, and support each other. New employees felt a great deal of pressure to do the same. One person in the team said, "It's like we are a big family."

What sorts of behaviors do you think are helpful in teams?

1. Following up
2. Giving responsibility
3. Allowing team members to try and fail (don't intervene unless it's really big)
4. Giving trust (and letting them know it)
5. Pointing out team members' success and telling others about it
6. Supporting team members' projects and professional growth
7. Encouraging team members to think about what comes next in their career, and helping them achieve it, even if it isn't working for you

Using Special-Purpose Team Techniques

When we think of bringing people together to deal with problems, we probably envision a committee meeting, with people arranged—notebooks open and pens poised—around a conference table. In fact, though, there are more entrees on the group menu than just the committee *du jour*. Here, we will present four specific alternatives to traditional interacting groups: the devil's advocate, brainstorming, the affinity technique, and the nominal group technique. Each of these techniques is easy and effective to use, can be completed in a single session, and serves a specific purpose. Your mastery of these techniques can add valuable skills to your team management arsenal.

To Encourage Healthy Dissent: The Devil's Advocate

Beginning in the twelfth century, the Roman Catholic Church instituted strict procedures to determine who was, or wasn't, worthy of sainthood. One barrier on the road to sainthood was the devil's advocate. The devil's advocate—a position that wasn't abolished until 1983—was a church officer whose role was to spot flaws in the arguments on behalf of a candidate for sainthood. Now the **devil's advocate** refers to an individual or group given the responsibility for challenging a proposal.[24] The idea is to find flaws while they may still be remedied, or to recognize that they are fatal before competitors, customers, or others become aware of them.

The devil's advocate's role is to make sure that the team takes a hard second look at its preferred alternative. Designating a devil's advocate makes it clear that dissent is legitimate. It brings out criticisms that might not otherwise be aired, and it highlights underlying assumptions.

However, devil's advocates must be used with caution. If they are employed too often or if they are overly severe in their criticisms, they may cause problems. Some team members may become demoralized if their views are constantly criticized. As a result, they may come up with safe solutions, not especially risky or creative but able to stand up to criticism. Also, if the devil's advocate is successful in finding fatal problems with a plan or alternative, there may be no new plan or alternative to take its place. That is, the devil's advocate approach focuses on what is wrong without pointing out what is right.

TEAMS IN THE NEWS: "Every Team Should Have a Devil's Advocate"

In an interview with the *New York Times*, Ori Hadomi, CEO of Mazor Robotics, a medical technology company based in Israel, talks about the importance of fostering a culture of openness in trust in which employees are willing and able to learn from mistakes.[1] Hadomi says one common mistake he sees at Mazor Robotics is that team members are often overly optimistic. As a result, one of the members of the company's executive committee was appointed as a devil's advocate. That devil's advocate thinks critically but constructively and says,

"Let's be more humble with our assumptions." Read the interview on the text website.

Note

1. A. Bryant, "Every Team Should Have a Devil's Advocate," *New York Times*, December 24, 2011, p. BU2.

To Generate Creative Ideas: Group Brainstorming

People sometimes use the term *brainstorming* any time they sit around and try to come up with ideas. In fact, though, brainstorming is a specific technique with a set of rules. **Group brainstorming** seeks to create the right atmosphere for relaxed, spontaneous thinking. A small group of employees is brought together, presented with the problem, and told to follow four rules:

- **Don't criticize any ideas.** This creates a climate of psychological safety, reducing inhibitions.
- **Freewheel.** Any idea, no matter how wild, is fine.
- **Try to come up with as many ideas as possible.** The more ideas, the better.
- **Try to combine and improve.** Hitchhiking on others' ideas may create a chain of inspiration.

Many companies are using brainstorming to develop new product ideas, marketing approaches, and creative advertising strategies. For example, Adaptec, a California semiconductor firm, believes it is difficult to build real consensus on important corporate decisions without an empathetic business organization. Employees at all levels of the organization attend interdepartmental brainstorming sessions. These sessions usually produce ideas that reflect the company's overall competencies better than ideas arising from any single department. Adaptec also engages in interdepartmental communications programs so that each department is exposed to the elementary concepts used in other departments. For example, finance people attend sessions in marketing and operations. Employees at all levels appreciate seeing the whole picture and feeling involved.[25]

Diverse brainstorming teams, or teams that include members who hold minority views, typically produce not only more ideas but also higher-quality ideas than homogeneous teams.[26]

Some companies are now using idea centers to employ brainstorming and associated tools for enhancing group creativity.[27] United Technologies Automotive, a subsidiary of Lear Corporation, added an Idea Center to its Dearborn, Michigan, headquarters. The center is a focal point for brainstorming and systems development, incorporating the latest technology and designed to stimulate the free flow of ideas. The center allows

> **TEAM WORDS OF WISDOM**
>
> "New ideas pass through three periods:
> 1) It can't be done.
> 2) It probably can be done, but it's not worth doing.
> 3) I knew it was a good idea all along!"
>
> ARTHUR C. CLARKE

members from various product teams to meet in a supportive setting and is aimed at reducing costs, improving quality, and speeding up product development time.[28]

New electronic tools promise to make brainstorming even more effective. At IBM, meeting rooms are equipped with personal computers for each participant, and a large color monitor is located where everyone can see it. Participants type in their ideas, comments, or reactions on their keyboards. Their input, which is anonymous, appears simultaneously on the monitor as well as on each computer screen. Everyone gets a chance to contribute, and no one can dominate the process. IBM has since 2001 held Web-based Innovation Jams, electronically bringing together more than 100,000 IBM employees, suppliers, family members, and others to brainstorm ideas for emerging business opportunities. IBM stressed that the output of the jams would be public goods. Although IBM planned to develop its own proprietary projects from outputs of the jams, it also invited others to do the same. One 72-hour jam yielded more than 100,000 individual postings, resulting in thirty-one follow-up projects in various parts of IBM.[29]

TEAMS VIDEO: Innovation Jam

Follow this link to see videos on the IBM Innovation Jam Channel: http://ibminnovationjam.magnify.net/.

We discuss one popular and effective electronic tool for facilitating brainstorming and other team decision processes, ThinkTank, in Chapter 11. ThinkTank is also described at: http://www.groupsystems.com/.[30] IBM's electronic brainstorming teams, described earlier, use a version of ThinkTank.

As befits a technique meant to enhance creativity, there are some creative variants of brainstorming. With *stop-and-go brainstorming*, short periods of brainstorming (10 minutes or so) are interspersed with short periods of evaluation. *Reverse brainstorming* brings fresh approaches by turning the problem around. How could we stifle creativity? How could we decrease morale? How could we lower productivity? With large groups, the *Phillips 66 technique* can be used. After the problem is explained and clearly understood, small groups of six members brainstorm for 6 minutes. Then a member of each group presents the best ideas or all ideas to the larger group.

To Generate Creative Ideas: The Affinity Technique

Brainstorming is a simple and useful tool for generating creative ideas. Another good creativity-enhancement tool is the **affinity technique**,[31] which a team can use to enhance the effectiveness of its decision making. The technique can be used whenever a team is attempting to identify

creative solutions to a problem. For example, the affinity technique can be used to identify ideas for improving customer service, product quality, or productivity. The affinity technique achieves its purpose by requiring a team to systematically generate potential solutions to a problem, cluster them in terms of their similarities, name the clusters, and then use a voting procedure to identify which ideas should be given the highest priority. The outcome of using the affinity technique is a set of key ideas that the team feels are potentially good solutions to a problem. These can be ordered based on the number of votes each idea received. The team would focus on implementing the solution that received the largest number of votes from the team members.

Now use Skills Practice 7.5 on the text website to work in a group to apply the affinity technique for group decision making. Again, this is an excellent tool for addressing problems that require creative solutions.

To Generate a Team Solution: The Nominal Group Technique

In Chapter 1 we pointed out benefits and drawbacks associated with using teams. Here's an important thing to recognize in looking at those lists: the benefits generally result simply from the many perspectives, skills, and resources brought to a team by its members, while the drawbacks usually result from the interaction of team members. For example, interaction may permit some people to dominate others, to block others' ideas, or to bully. Of course, interaction is often needed—we want the chance to air our views and to get others' ideas and reactions, and we often simply like to be able to talk with our colleagues. Still, there may be times when interaction really isn't needed and when, therefore, we might want to restrict it.

A **nominal group** (a group in name only) is another name for a coacting (that is, noninteracting) group. For instance, if you and your teammates

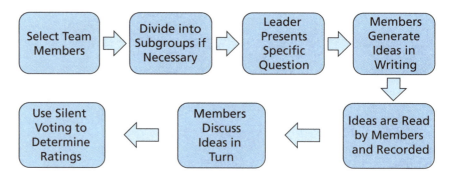

Figure 7-6

Steps in the Nominal Group Technique

were all sitting around a table and writing down ideas on how to cut down on your raw material costs, without discussing your ideas or interacting in other ways, you would be members of a coacting group. With a coacting group, members are working together on the same task, but they aren't talking with one another or communicating in other ways.

The **nominal group technique** uses a blend of coacting and interacting stages in order to capture the benefits of groups while minimizing potential problems.[32] It seeks to

- encourage all members to make inputs,
- prevent dominant members from controlling the process,
- ensure that all ideas get a fair hearing, and
- allow members to evaluate alternatives without fear of retribution.

To do all this, the nominal group technique uses the steps shown in Figure 7-6.

Each of the steps shown in Figure 7-6 is important, but one of them—the silent generation of ideas in writing without interaction—deserves further comment. By taking just 15 minutes or so to complete this step, you can achieve the following benefits:

- Ideas are generated without being evaluated.
- Members focus their time directly on the search for ideas.
- Nobody can dominate the process.
- Everyone makes inputs.
- Ideas are put in writing.

An interview with the codeveloper of the nominal group technique, André Delbecq, is included in the Team Scholar feature.

TEAM SCHOLAR

André L. Delbecq, University of Santa Clara

André L. Delbecq holds the J. Thomas and Kathleen L. McCarthy University Chair at Santa Clara University. His scholarship focuses on executive decision making, organizational design, managing innovation, and leadership spirituality. He

was eighth dean of fellows of the Academy of Management, past president of the Midwest and Western Academies of Management, and former executive director of the Organization Behavior Teaching Society.

The nominal group technique (NGT) has gained remarkable success worldwide, and research on NGT is very positive. What led you to develop the NGT?

My doctoral studies focused on creative group problem solving in the early 1960s. The group dynamics movement sought to more fully harness the intellectual gifts of subordinates moving away from leader-dominated bureaucracy. However, while creative group techniques worked in small-group laboratories, position power, personality attributes, vested interests, and a lack of common background and vocabulary often led to a regression toward leader dominance in actual organizational settings.

In the early 1970s I was involved with local community action groups that were part of President Lyndon Johnson's War on Poverty. Here racial, cultural, and educational differences amplified the tendency for leader dominance. The elements of NGT were assembled experientially through trial and error as I tested different protocols to achieve effective citizen participation when defining community problems, selecting solution elements, and establishing priorities.

What do you see as some key factors in the widespread appeal, acceptance, and application of the NGT?

The most important explanation of NGT's success is that it works. NGT is simple, robust, self-validating, and leads to high participant satisfaction. It is easy to facilitate even if you have no prior experience. Beginning with my research in partnership with Andrew Van de Ven, years of empirical evidence have validated NGT outcomes. However, it was not so much empirical studies but user friendliness that accelerated NGT's adaptation.

There were also historical factors at play. The technique was promulgated in the 1970s when educated participants (often supported by the GI Bill) flooded older bureaucracies. Leaders lacked the interpersonal and team skills we now take for granted as the result of maturing organizational behavior training.

Are there variants of NGT you think may be useful?

Computers now make it possible to record and display participant inputs without the nuisance and slowness of flip pads. Voting can be accomplished with electronic aids. So NGT is easily technologically enhanced. But if the fundamentals remain in place, results consistent with the earlier research pertain.

What are some noteworthy applications of the NGT?

NGT has been used for citizen input by the U.S. Corps of Engineers around major infrastructure projects. It is frequently adopted in redesign efforts for health care delivery and to maintain a continuous quality improvement context in private-sector business. NGT remains a valued tool for pooling judgments by senior executives and boards when establishing priorities.

Gaining Acceptance of New Techniques

Each of the tools we've just discussed works well and is widely used in modern organizations. Still, it sometimes seems difficult to try something different; people know what to expect in committees, and they're comfortable with them even as they lament the time they're wasting in one meeting after another. Here are some tips for gaining acceptance of new team processes.

- **Just do it.** Take charge and announce that you're going to handle the meeting differently today. Your assurance in presenting and using these tools will go a long way toward ensuring their acceptance and enthusiastic use. A leader who is forceful and assured is seen as charismatic and is likely to have enthusiastic followers.
- **Explain why you're doing something different.** Point out that the tool you're going to use is the best available for the task you're about to undertake—coming up with good ideas, making sure concerns are aired, or coming up with a creative solution.
- **Point out that these are widely used, effective techniques.** Give specific examples of how they're used in companies such as IBM, American Express, Xerox, and Adaptec.
- **Treat this as a skill-building experience both for yourself and for your colleagues.** Point out to team members that they will all be team leaders, formal or informal, and that learning these techniques may be of great value to them.
- **Point out that mastering more group tools adds to the team's resources.** The tools don't have to be used all the time, but they're available when needed.

In this chapter we have considered a variety of approaches to facilitating team processes. In Chapter 8 we turn our attention to the increasingly critical issue of managing change in teams, including how to anticipate and minimize potentially harmful consequences.

Summary and Integration

Here are the key takeaways from this chapter:

Too much time, money, and resources in teams and organizations are wasted due to unproductive and inefficient meetings. The foundation for an effective team meeting is the basic agenda that provides structure for the team meeting.

Team meetings must be viewed as a process that consists of premeeting, in-meeting and postmeeting activities. Team facilitation strategies provide valuable diagnostic questions for evaluating team meeting dynamics and interventions for handling issues that may arise in terms of participation, influence, and conflict.

Team decision making requires the use of tools such as the affinity technique and the nominal group technique in order to ensure that the team's decision making process is systematic and based on the balanced participation of all members.

Notes

1   E.A. Silverman, "Where's the Boss?: Trapped in a Meeting," *Wall Street Journal*, February 14, 2012.

2   See J. Sansing, "Tips for Building Rapport at That Crucial First Meeting," *American Agent & Broker*, May 2003, pp. 20 & 22; and, J. Lynn, "Life Styles: First Impressions, You Can't Do Them Over," *Commercial Law Bulletin*, July/August 2001, *16(4)*, pp. 32–33.

3   See, for instance, V. Johnson, "Icebreakers: Thawing out Frosty Communication," *Successful Meetings*, July 1992, and L.D. DeSilets & P.S. Dickerson, "Using Icebreakers to Open Communication," *Journal of Continuing Education in Nursing*, 2008, *39(7)*, pp. 292–293.

4   See B. Dahmer, "Kinder, Gentler Icebreakers," *Training & Development*, August 1992; M.M. Kennedy, "A Cold Shoulder to Icebreakers," *Across the Board*, April 1995, *32(4)*, p. 13; and, D. McGrath & A. Higgins, "Implementing and Evaluating Reflective Practice Group Sessions," *Nurse Education in Practice*, 2006, 6, pp. 175–181.

5   For a variety of guidelines on running meetings, including layout, see K. Tyler, "The Gang's All Here," *HRMagazine*, 2000, *45(5)*, pp. 104–113; K. Lalli, "Creating Team Spaces That Work," *Facilities Design and Management*, Spring 1998, pp. 22–24; L.R. Hudak, "Space Odyssey," *Successful Meetings*, September 2002, pp. 31–32 & 42–43; and J.L. Yang, "What's the Secret to Running Great Meetings?," *Fortune*, October 27, 2008, p. 26.

6   These zones were first presented by E.T. Hall in *The Hidden Dimension* (Garden City, NY: Doubleday, 1968). For a recent consideration of interpersonal distance in shopping malls across cultures, see A. Ozdemir, "Shopping Malls: Measuring Interpersonal Distance under Changing Conditions and across Cultures," *Field Methods*, 2008, *20(3)*, pp. 226–248.

7   See E.T. Hall & M.R. Hall, *Understanding Cultural Differences* (Yarmouth, ME: Intercultural Press, 1990); and, B.J. Hurn, "The Influence of Culture on International Business Negotiations," *Industrial and Commercial Training*, 2007, *39(7)*, pp. 354–360.

8   See M. Skinner, "Avoid a Culture Clash Overseas," *Successful Meetings*, May 2001, p. 38. See also, D.R. May, G.R. Oldham, & C. Rathert, "Employee Affective and Behavioral Reactions to the Spatial Density of Physical Work Environments," *Human Resource Management*, 2005, *44(1)*, pp. 21–33.

9   J.L. Yang, "What's the Secret to Running Great Meetings?" *Fortune*, October 27, 2008, p. 26.

10   Ibid.

11   For more on approaches to encouraging participation, see R.Y. Arterberrie, S.W. Eubanks, D.R. Kay, S.E. Prahst, & D.P. Wenner, "Team Collaboration: Lessons Learned Report," NASA/TM: 2005–213210, January 2005; and, J. Koh, Y.-G. Kim, B. Butler, & G.W. Bock, "Encouraging Participation in Virtual Communities," *Communications of the ACM*, 2007, *50(2)*, pp. 69–73.

12   M.T. Farkas. "A Note on Team Process," Harvard Business School Background Note 402-032, October 4, 2001.

13   For more on problem definition, see G.H. Wedberg, "But First, Understand the Problem," *Journal of Systems Management*, June 1990, pp. 20–28; S. Tomas,

"Creative Problem-Solving: An Approach to Generating Ideas," *Hospital Materiel Management Quarterly*, May 1999, *20(4)*, pp. 33–45; and, T.L. Saaty & M.P. Niemira, "A Framework for Making a Better Decision," *Research Review*, 2006, *13(1)*, pp. 1–4.

14   See, for instance, M. Kilgour, "Improving the Creative Process: Analysis of the Effects of Divergent Thinking Techniques and Domain Specific Knowledge on Creativity," *International Journal of Business and Society*, 2006, *7(2)*, pp. 79–107; and, T.B. Ward, "Creative Cognition as a Window on Creativity," *Methods*, 2007, *42*, pp. 28–37.

15   B.A. Stein & R.M. Kanter, "Leadership for Change: The Rest of the Story," *Frontiers of Health Services Management*, Winter 1993, p. 29.

16   This listing is based on B.M. Staw & J. Ross, "Understanding Behavior in Escalation Situations," *Science*, October 1986, pp. 216–220. See also K.F.E. Wong & J.Y.Y. Kwong, "The Role of Anticipated Regret in Escalation of Commitment," *Journal of Applied Psychology*, 2007, *92(2)*, pp. 545–554.

17   See M. Keil & R. Montealegre, "Cutting Your Losses: Extricating Your Organization When a Big Project Goes Awry," *Sloan Management Review*, Spring 2000, pp. 55–68; and, E. Biyalogorsky, W. Boulding, & R. Staelin, "Stuck in the Past: Why Managers Persist with New Product Failures," *Journal of Marketing*, 2006, *70*, pp. 108–121.

18   For instance, see J. Zaslow, "Moving On—You've Got to Know When to Fold 'Em: The Science of a Well-Timed Exit," *Wall Street Journal*, January 2, 2003, p. D.1.

19   A. Tversky & D. Kahneman, "Prospect Theory: An Analysis of Decision under Risk," *Econometrica*, *47(2)*, pp. 263–292.

20   R.S. Nickerson, "Confirmation Bias: A Ubiquitous Phenomenon in Many Guises," *Review of General Psychology*, 1998, 2, 175–220.

21   D.A. Moore & P.J. Healy, "The Trouble with Overconfidence," *Psychological Review*, 2008, *115*, pp. 502–517.

22   A. Tversky & D. Kahneman, "Judgment under Uncertainty: Heuristics and Biases," *Science*, 1974, *185*, pp. 1124–1131.

23   See I.L. Janis, *Victims of Groupthink* (Boston, MA: Houghton Mifflin, 1972). For a critical review of the validity of groupthink, see R.J. Aldag & S.R. Fuller, "Beyond Fiasco: A Reappraisal of the Groupthink Phenomenon and a New Model of Group Decision Processes," *Psychological Bulletin*, 1993, *113(3)*, pp. 533–552.

24   See, for instance, R.T. Watson & C. Saunders, "Managing Insight Velocity: The Design of Problem Solving Meetings," *Business Horizons*, 2005, *48*, pp. 285–295.

25   See P.G. Hansen, "Getting Your Team on the Same Side," *Financial Executive*, March/April 1994, pp. 43–49; and, A. Romano, G. Passiante, & V. Elia, "New Sources of Clustering in the Digital Economy," *Journal of Small Business and Enterprise Development*, 2001, *8(1)*, pp. 19–27.

26   For recent studies providing reviews of evidence regarding group brainstorming, see J. Wegge & S.A. Haslam, "Improving Work Motivation and Performance in Brainstorming Groups: The Effects of Three Group Goal-Setting Strategies," *European Journal of Work and Organizational Psychology*, 2005, *14(4)*, pp. 400–430; and, E.F. Rietzschel, B.A. Nijstad, & W. Stroebe, "Productivity Is Not Enough: A Comparison of Interactive and Nominal Brainstorming Groups on Idea Generation and Selection," *Journal of Experimental Social Psychology*, 2006, *42*, pp. 244–251.

27 See J. Sorcher, "New Gains," *Home Textiles Today*, February 2000, pp. 38–41; and, A.M. Moss, "Idea Center Inspires Laminate Design," *FDM, Furniture Design & Manufacturing*, 2000, *72(2)*, pp. 62–65.

28 See D. Jewett, "Supplier Builds Itself an Incubator for Ideas," *Automotive News*, December 16, 1996, p. 20.

29 J. Birkinshaw, J. Bessant, & R. Delbridge, "Finding, Forming, and Performing: Creating Networks for Discontinuous Innovation, p. 23. http://cosmic.rrz.uni-hamburg.de/webcat/hwwa/edok07/f10844g/SIM48.pdf

30 See W.H. Cooper, R.B. Gallupe, & S. Pollard, "Some Liberating Effects of Anonymous Electronic Brainstorming," *Small Group Research*, 1998, *29*, pp. 147–178; and, D.M. DeRosa, C.L. Smith, & D.A. Hantula, "The Medium Matters: Mining the Long-Promised Merit of Group Interaction in Creative Idea Generation Tasks in a Meta-Analysis of the Electronic Group Brainstorming Literature," *Computers in Human Behavior*, 2007, *23*, pp. 1549–1581.

31 See, for instance, E.W. Duggan, "Generating Systems Requirements with Facilitated Group Techniques," *Human-Computer Interaction*, 2003, *18(4)*, pp. 373–394; and, C. Tennant & P. Roberts, "The creation and application of a self-assessment process for new product introduction," *International Journal of Project Management*, 2003, *21(2)*, pp. 77–87.

32 For applications and discussions of the nominal group technique, see C.L. Asmus & K. James, "Nominal Group Technique, Social Loafing, and Group Creative Project Quality," *Creativity Research Journal*, 2005, *17(4)*, pp. 349–354; R. Kristofco, R. Shewchuk, L. Casebeer, B. Bellande, & N. Bennett, "Attributes of an Ideal Continuing Medical Education Institution through Nominal Group Technique," *Journal of Continuing Education in the Health Professions*, 2005, *25(3)*, pp. 221–228; and, P.P. Lago, M.G. Beruvides, J.Y. Jian, M. Canto, A. Sandoval, & R. Taraban, "Structuring Group Decision Making in a Web-Based Environment By Using the Nominal Group Technique," *Computers & Industrial Engineering*, 2007, *52(2)*, pp. 277–295.

Bibliography

Aldag, R.J., & Fuller, S.R. "Beyond Fiasco: A Reappraisal of the Groupthink Phenomenon and a New Model of Group Decision Processes," *Psychological Bulletin*, 1993, *113(3)*, pp. 533–552.

Arterberrie, R.Y., Eubanks, S.W., Kay, D.R., Prahst, S.E., & Wenner, D.P. "Team Collaboration: Lessons Learned Report," NASA/TM: 2005–213210, January 2005.

Asmus, C.L., & James, K. "Nominal Group Technique, Social Loafing, and Group Creative Project Quality," *Creativity Research Journal*, 2005, *17(4)*, pp. 349–354.

Birkinshaw, J., Bessant, J., & Delbridge, R. "Finding, Forming, and Performing: Creating Networks for Discontinuous Innovation, p. 23. http://www.london.edu/facultyandresearch/research/docs/sim48.pdf.

Biyalogorsky, E., Boulding, W., & Staelin, R. "Stuck in the Past: Why Managers Persist with New Product Failures," *Journal of Marketing*, 2006, 70, pp. 108–121.

Bryant, A. "Every Team Should Have a Devil's Advocate," *New York Times*, December 24, 2011, p. BU2.

Bryant, A. "Here's $1,000. Now, Please Take Your Vacation," *New York Times*, April 8, 2012, p. BU2.

Cooper, W.H., Gallupe, R.B., & Pollard, S. "Some Liberating Effects of Anonymous Electronic Brainstorming," *Small Group Research*, 1998, 29, pp. 147–178.

Dahmer, B. "Kinder, Gentler Icebreakers," *Training & Development*, August 1992, *46(8)*, p. 46..

DeRosa, D.M., Smith, C.L., & Hantula, D.A. "The Medium Matters: Mining the Long-Promised Merit of Group Interaction in Creative Idea Generation Tasks in a Meta-Analysis of the Electronic Group Brainstorming Literature," *Computers in Human Behavior*, 2007, *23*, pp. 1549–1581.

DeSilets, L.D., & Dickerson, P.S. "Using Icebreakers to Open Communication," *Journal of Continuing Education in Nursing*, 2008, *39(7)*, pp. 292–293.

Duggan, E.W. "Generating Systems Requirements with Facilitated Group Techniques," *Human-Computer Interaction*, 2003, *18(4)*, pp. 373–394.

Farkas, M.T. "A Note on Team Process," HBS Background Note 402-032, October 4, 2001.

Hall, E.T., *The Hidden Dimension* (Garden City, NY: Doubleday, 1968).

Hall, E.T., & Hall, M.R. *Understanding Cultural Differences* (Yarmouth, ME: Intercultural Press, 1990).

Hansen, P.G. "Getting Your Team on the Same Side," *Financial Executive*, March/April 1994, pp. 43–49.

Hudak, L.R. "Space Odyssey," *Successful Meetings*, September 2002, pp. 31–32 & 42–43.

Hurn, B.J. "The Influence of Culture on International Business Negotiations," *Industrial and Commercial Training*, 2007, *39(7)*, pp. 354–360.

Janis, I.L. *Victims of Groupthink* (Boston, MA: Houghton Mifflin, 1972).

Jewett, D. "Supplier Builds Itself an Incubator for Ideas," *Automotive News*, December 16, 1996, p. 20.

Johnson, V. "Icebreakers: Thawing out Frosty Communication," *Successful Meetings*, July 1992.

Keil, M., & Montealegre, R. "Cutting Your Losses: Extricating Your Organization When a Big Project Goes Awry," *Sloan Management Review*, Spring 2000, pp. 55–68.

Kennedy, M.M. "A Cold Shoulder to Icebreakers," *Across the Board*, April 1995, *32(4)*, p. 13.

Kilgour, M. "Improving the Creative Process: Analysis of the Effects of Divergent Thinking Techniques and Domain Specific Knowledge on Creativity," *International Journal of Business and Society*, 2006, *7(2)*, pp. 79–107.

Koh, J., Kim, Y.-G., Butler, B., & Bock, G.W. "Encouraging Participation in Virtual Communities," *Communications of the ACM*, 2007, *50(2)*, pp. 69–73.

Kristofco, R., Shewchuk, R., Casebeer, L., Bellande, B., & Bennett, N. "Attributes of an Ideal Continuing Medical Education Institution through Nominal Group Technique," *Journal of Continuing Education in the Health Professions*, 2005, *25(3)*, pp. 221–228.

Lago, P.P., Beruvides, M.G., Jian, J.Y., Canto, M., Sandoval, A., & Taraban, R. "Structuring Group Decision Making in a Web-Based Environment by Using the Nominal Group Technique," *Computers & Industrial Engineering*, 2007, *52(2)*, pp. 277–295.

Lalli, K. "Creating Team Spaces That Work," *Facilities Design and Management*, Spring 1998, pp. 22–24.

Lynn, J. "Life Styles: First Impressions, You Can't Do Them Over," *Commercial Law Bulletin*, July/August 2001, *16(4)*, pp. 32–33.

May, D.R., Oldham, G.R., & Rathert, C. "Employee Affective and Behavioral Reactions to the Spatial Density of Physical Work Environments," *Human Resource Management*, 2005, *44(1)*, pp. 21–33.

McGrath, D., & Higgins, A. "Implementing and Evaluating Reflective Practice Group Sessions," *Nurse Education in Practice*, 2006, 6, pp. 175–181.

Moore, D.A., & Healy, P.J. "The Trouble with Overconfidence," *Psychological Review*, 2008, *115*, pp. 502–517.

Moss, A.M. "Idea Center Inspires Laminate Design," *FDM*, *Furniture Design & Manufacturing*, 2000, *72(2)*, pp. 62–65.

Nickerson, R.S. "Confirmation Bias: A Ubiquitous Phenomenon in Many Guises," *Review of General Psychology*, 1998, 2, 175–220.

Ozdemir, A. "Shopping Malls: Measuring Interpersonal Distance under Changing Conditions and across Cultures," *Field Methods*, 2008, *20(3)*, pp. 226–248.

Rietzschel, E.F., Nijstad, B.A., & Stroebe, W. "Productivity Is Not Enough: A Comparison of Interactive and Nominal Brainstorming Groups on Idea Generation and Selection," *Journal of Experimental Social Psychology*, 2006, 42, pp. 244–251.

Ritsher, J.B. "Cultural Factors and the International Space Station," *Aviation, Space, and Environmental Medicine*, 2005, *76(6)*, pp. B135–B144.

Romano, A., Passiante, G., & Elia, V. "New Sources of Clustering in the Digital Economy," *Journal of Small Business and Enterprise Development*, 2001, *8(1)*, pp. 19–27.

Saaty, T.L., & Niemira, M.P. "A Framework for Making a Better Decision," *Research Review*, 2006, *13(1)*, pp. 1–4.

Sansing, J. "Tips for Building Rapport at That Crucial First Meeting," *American Agent & Broker*, May 2003, pp. 20 & 22.

Silverman, E.A. "Where's the Boss?: Trapped in a Meeting," *Wall Street Journal*, February 14, 2012. http://online.wsj.com/news/articles/SB10001424052970204 642604577215013504567548.

Silverman, R.E. "No More Angling for the Best Seat; More Meetings Are Stand-Up Jobs," *Wall Street Journal*, February 2, 2012.

Skinner, M. "Avoid a Culture Clash Overseas," *Successful Meetings*, May 2001, p. 38.

Sorcher, J. "New Gains," *Home Textiles Today*, February 2000, pp. 38–41.

Staw, B.M., & Ross, J. "Understanding Behavior in Escalation Situations," *Science*, October 1986, pp. 216–220.

Stein, B.A., & Kanter, R.M. "Leadership for Change: The Rest of the Story," *Frontiers of Health Services Management*, Winter 1993, p. 29.

Tennant, C., & Roberts, P. "The Creation and Application of a Self-Assessment Process for New Product Introduction," *International Journal of Project Management*, 2003, *21(2)*, pp. 77–87.

Tomas, S. "Creative Problem-Solving: An Approach to Generating Ideas," *Hospital Materiel Management Quarterly*, May 1999, *20(4)*, pp. 33–45.

Tversky, A., & Kahneman, D. "Judgment under Uncertainty: Heuristics and Biases," *Science*, 1974, *185*, pp. 1124–1131.

Tversky, A., & Kahneman, D., "Prospect Theory: An Analysis of Decision under Risk," *Econometrica*, *47(2)*, pp. 263–292.

Tyler, K. "The Gang's All Here," *HRMagazine*, 2000, *45(5)*, pp. 104–113.

Ward, T.B. "Creative Cognition as a Window on Creativity," *Methods*, 2007, 42, pp. 28–37.

Watson, R.T., & Saunders, C. "Managing Insight Velocity: The Design of Problem Solving Meetings," *Business Horizons*, 2005, *48*, pp. 285–295.

Wedberg, G.H. "But First, Understand the Problem," *Journal of Systems Management*, June 1990, pp. 20–28.

Wegge, J., & Haslam, S.A. "Improving Work Motivation and Performance in Brainstorming Groups: The Effects of Three Group Goal-Setting Strategies," *European Journal of Work and Organizational Psychology*, 2005, *14(4)*, pp. 400–430.

Wong, K.F.E., & Kwong, J.Y.Y. "The Role of Anticipated Regret in Escalation of Commitment," *Journal of Applied Psychology*, 2007, *92(2)*, pp. 545–554.

Yang, J.L. "What's the Secret to Running Great Meetings?" *Fortune*, October 27, 2008, p. 26.

Zaslow, J. "Moving On—You've Got to Know When to Fold 'Em: The Science of a Well-Timed Exit," *Wall Street Journal*, January 2, 2003, p. D.1.

CHAPTER 8

Managing Change in Teams

Learning Objectives

After reading this chapter, you should be able to do the following:

1. Identify and discuss key stages in the change process.
2. Recognize the need to identify and manage potential forces for and against change.
3. Understand key sources of resistance to change.
4. Recognize approaches to overcoming resistance to change.
5. Identify when each approach to overcoming resistance to change is most appropriate.
6. Understand the steps necessary for successful team-based insurrections.
7. Better manage difficult transitions.

. . . .

IN EXAMINING TEAM ISSUES THROUGHOUT THE TEXT, WE MAKE it clear that change has been pervasive in the environment of teams as well as in teams themselves. We devote Chapter 11 to new developments in teams, including new team forms and features. There, we will discuss in detail various forces demanding change in teams. These include, among others, globalization, increased rates of turnover, growing computer literacy, the explosion of information technology, new office forms, reduced focus on hierarchy, and robotics.

In this chapter we examine ways to successfully facilitate change in its many forms. We discuss the change process, consider the process of identifying and managing forces for and against change, and address key sources of resistance to change. Then, we consider approaches to overcoming resistance to change, including when each is likely to be most effective. Finally, we address team-based insurrections and provide guidelines for dealing with difficult transitions.

Before proceeding, complete Self-Assessment 8.1 on the text website. It gauges your general attitudes toward change. Then, complete Skills Practice 8.1 on the website to better understand how practicing managers deal with change.

The Change Process

Change may be planned or reactive. **Planned change** occurs when team leaders or others develop and install programs or other activities to alter activities in a timely and orderly way. **Reactive change** occurs when team leaders or others simply respond to pressures for change when it comes to their

The Lewin Change Model

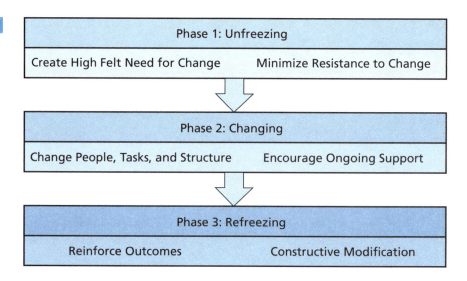

attention. Planned change is often seen as superior to reactive change, especially when change is extensive and lengthy. However, both forms of change are important. Although it is clear that firms must take actions to anticipate and prepare for change, they must also have the flexibility and resources to recognize and respond to emerging demands and environmental shocks.

Whether change is planned or reactive, understanding and implementing the steps in the change process will increase the chances for success. Kurt **Lewin's Change Model** includes three general stages, shown in Figure 8-1.[1]

Figure 8-1 shows that successful change requires first creating a situation in which change is seen as necessary and desirable (**unfreezing**), then taking steps to bring about the change (**changing**), and finally ensuring that conditions are appropriate to reinforce the change (**refreezing**). We address these steps throughout the remainder of the chapter.

Skills Practice 8.2 on the text website will help you to develop skill in applying Lewin's change process model to a realistic organizational situation. Be sure to address all three phases of the model.

Balancing Forces for and against Change

As we'll see, there are many sources of resistance to change. Of course, however, change does occur. This suggests that the forces in support of change sometimes overcome sources of resistance.

Lewin, whose model of the stages of change is shown in Figure 8-1, also introduced the idea of **force field analysis**.[2] As shown in Figure 8-2, this perspective sees the success of change attempts as depending on whether forces in support of change are greater than those opposing change. Many factors, varying in strength and duration, oppose and support change. In order to develop a successful change effort, it is important to anticipate and manage potential sources of resistance to the change as well as potential forces favoring the change. In the following section we discuss sources of resistance to change. We then consider approaches to minimize resistance and develop support for change.

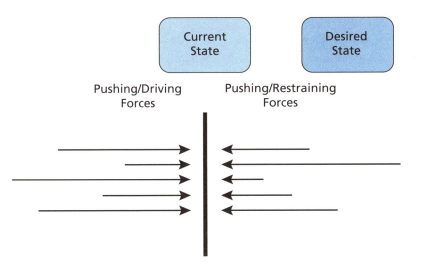

Figure 8-2

Force Field Analysis

Sources of Resistance to Change

Niccolo Machiavelli wrote, "There is nothing so difficult as to implement change, since those in favor of the change will be small in number and those opposing the change will be numerous and enthusiastic in their resistance to change."[3] Therefore, it is important to recognize that resistance to change is likely and to prepare to deal with it.

It is often tempting to dismiss resistance to change as irrational or petty. In fact, though, people often have many reasons to resist a particular change, some of them very reasonable. Sources of resistance to change are shown in Figure 8-3.

Self-Interest

It is natural for team members to have interests in benefiting themselves directly. Theories of motivation are based on the idea that we seek positive outcomes and try to avoid negative outcomes. Resistance is likely to occur if a proposed change threatens those interests. Being assigned to manage a new product may increase one's prestige while lessening the prestige of those who did not receive the assignment. Changes may threaten—among other things—skills, power, relationships with others, social status, and self-esteem.

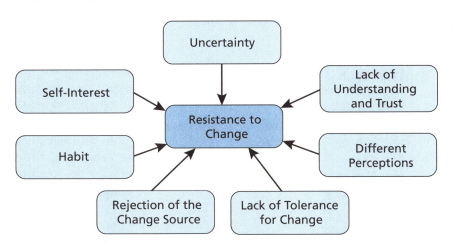

Figure 8-3

Sources of Resistance to Change

Uncertainty

Change brings uncertainty. Team members may resist a change because they cannot see how the change will affect their work and lives. Often, they expect the worst. And they know that any change may predict future change. As such, even those who expect to emerge unscathed from a major change (e.g., a reorganization, merger, or implementation of new technology) may wonder about what further changes the initial change may precipitate, and how their work and personal lives will be affected. This concern can lead to a dogged resistance and a preference for the status quo.

Lack of Understanding and Trust

Often, proposed changes are not adequately explained to those who will be affected by them. For example, Ciba Geigy employees learned as they drove to work one day that their company was merging with Sandoz to form Novartis and that the combined company would probably employ at least 10% fewer workers.[4] Failure to understand the change increases the chances that members or departments will resist the change. Unfortunately, in one study only 28% of surveyed workers reported that their managers do a good job of explaining decisions to them, and only 27% reported that they're involved in decisions that affect them.[5]

Lack of trust, discussed in Chapter 4, can also support resistance to change. Prior experiences with those supporting or initiating change may have involved misrepresentations or deceit. In this case, resistance may be based simply on who supports the proposed change.

Differing Perceptions

Differences of opinion about the need for change and what the change will accomplish can be a cause of resistance. People tend to see situations and events differently because of prior experiences and training. An engineer is likely to view a change in the production process differently than an accountant. The engineer may perceive the change in terms of increasing efficiency in the production of a good. The accountant may perceive the change in terms of the cost increase that will be reflected in the price of the product. Thus, resistance may result from legitimate disagreements over the potential outcomes of change based on differing perceptions.

Lack of Tolerance for Change

Some people feel comfortable with change while others feel uncomfortable. Even when team members are shown that the change will not threaten their self-interest, that the results are certain, that full understanding and trust exist, and that perceptions agree, team members may still resist change. For example, some people prefer to drive the same route to work even when they agree that a different route is quicker, safer, and less crowded. They are unwilling to change because they like the comfortable familiarity of the old route. Alan Watts (see the Team Words of Wisdom) took the opposite view.

TEAM WORDS OF WISDOM

"The only way to make sense out of change is to plunge into it, move with it, and join the dance."

ALAN WATTS, BRITISH PHILOSOPHER, WRITER, AND SPEAKER

In Figure 8-4 we indicate some reasons why individual team members may differ in their attitudes toward change.

Now, complete Self-Assessment 8.2 on the text website to assess your own readiness for change.

		Figure 8-4
• General Attitudes toward Change	• As suggested earlier, some people are generally more or less tolerant of, and welcoming of, change than others.	Individual Differences in Attitudes toward Change
• Tolerance for Ambiguity	• Change and anticipation of change generate uncertainty and ambiguity. Some people are more or less comfortable with such uncertainty than others.[1]	
• Change Self-Efficacy	• Team members are likely to be more comfortable with change if they feel they are capable of successfully dealing with it. Some members will have higher change self-efficacy than others.[2]	
• Resilience	• Some people bounce back from change and adversity better than others; they are resilient.[3] Resilience is likely to make team members more willing to accept and embrace change since they feel they'll be able to bounce back if the change does not go well.	
• Cynicism	• Team members may differ in their general levels of cynicism. That is, some may generally distrust others, including initiators of change, more than others.[4]	
• Learning Orientation	• Learning orientation is the degree to which team members have a strong desire to improve and master their skills and abilities and view new situations as opportunities to improve their competence.[5] Those with strong learning orientations are likely to be more comfortable with change.	
• Coping Style	• When dealing with challenging, uncertain developments, individuals differ in their coping styles. Some cope with change by withdrawing, rebelling, or resorting to drugs, alcohol, or other means. Others approach the situations with a problem-focused orientation. The latter orientation generally leads to more productive and satisfying outcomes.[6]	

[1] See K. K. Katsaros & C. S. Nicolaidis. "Personal Traits, Emotions, and Attitudes in the Workplace: Their Effects on Managers' Tolerance for Ambiguity." *The Psychologist-Manager Journal*, 2012, *15(1)*, pp. 37–55.
[2] L. T. Eby, D. M. Adams, J. E. A. Russell, & S. H. Gaby, "Perceptions of Organizational Readiness for Change: Factors Related to Employees' Reactions to the Implementation of Team-Based Selling," *Human Relations*, 2000, *53(3)*, pp. 419–442.
[3] For example, see J. Shin, M. S. Taylor, & M.-G. Seo. "Resources for Change: The Relationships of Organizational Inducements and Psychological Resilience to Employees' Attitudes and Behaviors toward Organizational Change." *Academy of Management Journal*, 2012, *55(3)*, pp. 727–748.
[4] A. E. Reichers, J. P. Wanous, & J. T. Austin. "Understanding and Managing Cynicism about Organizational Change." *Academy of Management Executive*, 1997, *11(1)*, pp. 48–59; J. P. Wanous, A. E. Reichers, & J. T. Austin. "Cynicism about Organizational Change: An Attribution Process Perspective." *Psychological Reports*, 2004, *94(3)*, pp. 1421–1434; and J. Richards & K. Kosmala, "'In the End, You Can Only Slag People Off for So Long': Employee Cynicism through Work Blogging." *New Technology, Work and Employment*, 2013, *28(1)*, pp. 66–77.
[5] For discussions of the role of learning orientation in reactions to change, see K. J. Klein & A. P. Knight. "Innovation Implementation: Overcoming the Challenge." *Current Directions in Psychological Science*, 2005, *14(5)*, pp. 243–246; and, C.O.L.H. Porter, J. W. Webb, & C. I. Gogus. "When Goal Orientations Collide: Effects of Learning and Performance Orientation on Team Adaptability in Response to Workload Imbalance." *Journal of Applied Psychology*, 2010, *95(5)*, pp. 935–943.
[6] See, for instance, R. S. Lazarus & S. Folkman. *Stress, Appraisal, and Coping*. New York: Springer, 1984; and, M. Beasley, T. Thompson, and J. Davidson, "Resilience in Response to Life Stress: The Effects of Coping Style and Cognitive Hardiness," *Personality and Individual Differences*, 2003, *34*, pp. 77–95.

Approaches to Overcoming Resistance to Change

What can team leaders do to reduce human inertia and encourage participation, cooperation, or at least compliance? Some primary approaches to dealing with resistance to change are summarized in Figure 8-5.[6]

Aristotle argued that all attempts to encourage others to change their minds, feelings, and behavior can be summarized in terms of the **rhetorical triangle**, shown in Figure 8-6. It is useful to consider the change approaches in the context of the rhetorical triangle.[7]

Here, *logos* refers to convincing another person to accept a change through reason, logic, and data; *ethos* through the strength of your moral character and the trust that followers have in you; and *pathos* through appeals to your target audience's emotional and psychological needs.

Logos

When people are told about a change at work that will affect them, they normally react by first asking "Why?" When you initiate change, be prepared

Figure 8-5

Change Approaches

Tactic	Characteristics
Education and Communication	Explaining the need for or logic of the change
Participation and Involvement	Having members participate in the planning and implementation of the change
Facilitation and Support	Gradual introduction of the change process and provision of support to people affected by the change
Negotiation and Agreement	Negotiating and bargaining to win acceptance or reduce resistance to change
Manipulation and Co-optation	Covertly steering individuals or groups away from resistance to change through selective use of information, or assigning potential resisters to a desired position in the change process
Coercion	Demanding that members support the change or be threatened with the loss of rewards and resources

Source: Based on J.P. Kotter and L.A. Schlesinger. "Choosing Strategies for Change." *Harvard Business Review*, 1979, *57(2)*, pp. 106–114.

Figure 8-6

The Rhetorical Triangle

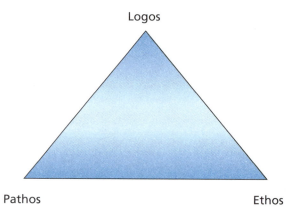

Logos

Pathos   Ethos

to provide a clear rationale in a direct, well-supported manner, using education and communication as your persuasive method. Here are key steps for accomplishing this objective:

- **Do your homework.** Gather relevant facts that prove a real problem exists. Identify potential causes and pinpoint probable causes. Thoroughly describe the problem or opportunity, its causes, the need to do something about it, alternative solutions, and the cost and benefits of each. Communicate clearly the advantages and disadvantages of the change.
- **Identify sources of support**. Who could help you sell the change? Idea champions (individuals who have the passion and energy to advocate for acceptance of the change), venture teams (teams assembled to manage a new venture or initiative), and innovation departments may all prove useful, as may external change agents.[8]
- **Anticipate questions and objections.** Think about the change from others' points of view. Identify the questions that you would have and the objections that you would raise if you were the target of this change.
- **Sell the benefits of the change in terms of the perspective of those who will have to go through it.** How will the change help to make things better and avoid or reduce bad consequences? It is easiest to sell the need for change when there is a **burning platform**, a dramatic, vivid demonstration that the current situation is unacceptable. Plummeting profits, competitive threats, irate customers, or lawsuits may all serve as burning platforms. For example, when the patent on Prozac, Eli Lilly's major product, was due to expire in 2004, Sidney Taurel, the chair and CEO, labeled 2004 as Year X, and talked about it as a "burning platform."[9] In another example, General Dennis Reimer, the U.S. Army's chief of staff, spoke of the Army's attempts at change. He explained that with the end of the Cold War and the fall of the Berlin Wall, the Army was in a different world and that it has to be able to change to serve the nation's needs. However, General Reimer noted that the Army is a conservative organization and that it believes in the "first rule of wingwalking: You don't let go of what you've got in your hands until you've got something else in your hands."[10] As such, change can best be sold when the present situation is unacceptable and there is something else to hold on to—some promising new beginning.
- **Use catalytic mechanisms to reinforce the change.**[11] **Catalytic mechanisms** help to translate objectives into performance by making stretch goals reachable. These mechanisms generally involve a dramatic policy shift that turns normal corporate practice on its head, requiring people to act in new ways that further the overarching corporate goal. For example, at the minerals supplier Granite Rock, employees were galvanized by the introduction of a catalytic mechanism—a new policy called short pay. At the bottom of each Granite Rock invoice are the words, "If you are not satisfied for any reason, don't pay us for it. Simply scratch out the line item, write a brief note about the problem, and return a copy of this invoice along with your check for the balance." This led employees to quickly identify and correct quality problems throughout the company.[12] The company subsequently won the Malcolm Baldrige Quality Award.

- **Listen in depth to concerns, questions, and fears.** Recall that guidelines for effective listening were presented in Chapter 6.
- **Create an implementation plan that answers the key questions most people have when faced with change: who, what, where, when, why, and how?**

Ethos

People cooperate with a leader who has high credibility, a combination of competence and trustworthiness. We tend to believe someone who demonstrates expertise and authoritativeness; has the requisite qualifications; and comes across as experienced, informed, skilled, and intelligent. When faced with a persuasive argument, the audience asks, "Does this person *know* the truth?" The other dimension is trustworthiness: one's character, moral fiber, and personal integrity. When faced with a persuasive argument, the audience asks, "Does this person *tell* the truth?"

Pathos

You may have a rational idea for change, one that has a great cost-benefit ratio. You also may be seen as a trusted person of strong moral character and technical competence. However, it is important to also attend to your target audience's emotional and psychological needs.

If the change that you are initiating threatens people's emotional safety and security—if it lowers their self-confidence or self-esteem—you may get begrudging compliance or none at all. One effective way to satisfy people's emotional needs and to stimulate high motivation is to get them actively involved in the change itself. When people feel that they have had a voice in shaping the change and its implementation, they tend to adopt ownership of it. Such participation and involvement can be sought at stages in the process or throughout.

Using participation in planning and implementing changes simultaneously enriches people's work, raises self-esteem and self-confidence, and hones their problem-solving skills. In this way, you may turn what at first looks like win-lose into a win-win proposition for all.

Other Approaches to Change

As a team leader, and sometimes as a team member, you can use other forms of persuasion, such as manipulation and coercion. These forms involve managing people through misinformation and even lies; demanding change in a forceful, dictatorial manner; or threatening people with punishments if they fail to comply. Do these tactics work? Sometimes, but usually at high costs to morale, positive working relationships, willing cooperation, and your trustworthiness as a leader.

Figure 8-7 provides a summary of situations in which the various change approaches are likely to be selected.[13]

Skills Practice 8.3 on the text website will help you develop skill to effectively manage and overcome employee resistance to change.

Tactic	Best Used When
Education and Communication	Resistance to change is due to lack of information or inaccurate information and analysis.
Participation and Involvement	The initiators of change don't have all the information they need to design the change, and others have considerable power to resist.
Facilitation and Support	People are resisting change because of fear or adjustment problems.
Negotiation and Agreement	Someone or some group will clearly lose out in the change and that party has considerable power to resist.
Manipulation and Co-optation	Other tactics won't work or are too expensive.
Coercion	The initiator of change has power, and change must occur quickly.

Figure 8-7

Deciding When to Use the Change Approaches

Team-Based Change: Team Insurrections

Even though we have primarily focused on teams as targets of change, they may also serve as important change agents. One example is what has been called a **team insurrection**, a change that is driven through a grassroots, bottom-up effort led by a work team. The concept of the team insurrection was developed based on an incident at IBM in which a team called "Get Connected" identified a huge opportunity for IBM—to assume a leadership position in delivering Web-based services in the future—and how it rallied others in the company to pursue the same focus. This team insurrection enabled IBM to achieve a competitive advantage for itself over rivals such as Sun Microsystems.[14]

Here are steps for fostering a team insurrection:

- **Step 1: establish a point of view.** The team uses clear and persuasive data to develop a compelling perspective for an idea that possesses strong emotional appeal to others in an organization and connects the idea to its bottom-line results. Thus, Step 1 involves coupling pathos with logos.
- **Step 2: write a manifesto.** The team uses its point of view to create a brief report that articulates the idea in a compelling manner. This manifesto is shared with others throughout the organization to raise awareness and to stimulate interest in the idea.
- **Step 3: create a coalition.** The manifesto generates interest and buzz about the idea in the organization. Informal meetings and interaction among interested parties create a critical mass of supporters and parties revolving around the idea.
- **Step 4: pick the target.** At this point, the insurrection possesses considerable support among lower-ranking employees. It then needs support from top management. The team focuses on identifying a senior manager who is willing to serve as the champion of the idea.

- **Step 5: co-opt and neutralize.** Successful insurrections focus on converting adversaries and nonbelievers into supporters by demonstrating how they could benefit from the idea as well. The goal is to achieve as many win-win outcomes as possible.
- **Step 6: find a translator.** One individual may serve as the liaison between the insurrection and members of top management. This person maintains lines of open communication with upper management and works to build and sustain support for the idea.
- **Step 7: win small, win early, and win often.** Small wins build a sustainable momentum for the idea for the long-term. According to Karl Weick, small wins are compact, motivating, noncontroversial, and less likely to draw the attention of opponents.[15] As small wins are achieved, the insurrection is rewarded by senior management in the form of the allocation of more people and financial resources to continue to build on the implementation of the idea.

Managing Difficult Transitions

Changes, even if apparently successful, often have difficult and painful outcomes. Something like a major layoff is a painful transition, but so is a major technological change, reorganization of a team, or simply the voluntary departure of a friend and colleague. In each case valued skills are lost, status relationships may change, uncertainty is introduced, and social relationships change. It is critical to think about transitions before they occur, both in order to carry out the transition and to think through the full consequences of the transition, and thus to see if it is really desirable.

In cases where transitions involve some people leaving, as in some reorganizations, it is important to take actions not only for the people who are leaving, but also for those who are staying, including those who are affected and those who are just watching. The latter might include others elsewhere in the organization, friends, or users of services. It is especially important to think about losses that may result from the transition, and how they will be dealt with. It is comforting to say that cutting back jobs or reshuffling teams or introducing a new technology will save money. It is uncomfortable to think about potential losses; that is dissonance inducing. So, we tend not to do it.

The following is a list of things to keep in mind during transitions. Especially when dealing with major, emotional issues, it may be important to seek employee participation in managing the change and perhaps to form teams to help manage the transition.

1. Clearly Explain the Reasons for the Transition: Show How Endings Ensure Continuity

As we've seen, the process of unfreezing is critical. It is necessary to sell the problem before selling the solution—and then explain how the change will improve the situation. It is important to show how the change assures continuity, how it is not just uncertainty inducing but is also protective and maintaining. Making these points may include appeals to organizational culture (see Chapter 9): how is the change consistent with important values that firm members hold? How would past heroes in the organization have felt about the change?

2. Explain Why the Transition Is Occurring
in the Way It Is Occurring

It's not enough to say the competitive situation demands changes. Why *these* changes? Why me? Procedural fairness is critical. If a change is presented as a way to deal with a problem or opportunity, but there is no evidence that other alternatives, perhaps less painful, have been considered, those hurt by the change will understandably be suspicious and angry. Maintaining procedural fairness is also important strategically: if we haven't considered alternatives, we may be presenting a poor solution. In the U.S. Congressional debates regarding the credit crisis of 2008, many weren't convinced by the argument that a so-called bailout bill should be passed simply because the economy was in crisis. They asked why they should vote for the *specific* bill presented to them.

3. Minimize Uncertainty: Define What Is Over and What Is Not

Give people information—and do it again and again. There are many rationalizations for not communicating. Some common ones include the following:

- **They don't need to know it yet.** We'll tell them when the time comes. It will just upset them now.
- **They already know it.** We announced it.
- **I told the supervisors.** It's their job to tell the rank and file.
- **We don't know all the details ourselves, so there's no point in saying anything until everything has been decided.**

Of course, sometimes laws or competitive situations may preclude passing on some information. But most of the time information is withheld simply because team leaders and others are afraid to give it. When lacking such information, though, team members expect the worst and behave accordingly.

4. Identify Who Is Losing What

In the case of a layoff or a major restructuring affecting teams, it sometimes seems obvious that those laid off, those faced with an increased workload, or those forced into a less desirable working situation are losing a lot. But beyond that, their colleagues and peers may also be losers; they may, for instance, lose social support networks and feel survivor guilt. And perhaps *all* employees are losing something: a culture of certainty, an implicit guarantee of permanent employment. So, who are the obvious losers? Who are the secondary losers? What does the firm lose? What does everyone—team members and the firm—lose?

5. Acknowledge Losses Openly and Sympathetically

It is important to acknowledge losses and show your concern for the affected people. Honest and open display of concern may help enhance feelings of equitable treatment.

6. Expect and Accept Signs of Grieving

When endings take place, people get angry, sad, frightened, depressed, and confused.[16] These emotions are sometimes taken as signs of poor morale, but they may be signs of grieving. It is important to expect these signs and to be ready to deal with them. Remember that those immediately affected by change may not be the only grievers. It is estimated that hidden grief costs U.S. companies up to $75.1 billion annually.[17]

7. Provide Fair Compensation for Losses

Carefully consider the nature of losses. For instance, is there loss of status, team membership, recognition, or pleasant working conditions? Sometimes compensation can be concrete, such as a severance package in the case of layoffs. Often, though, symbolic actions are important to show respect. These might include, for instance, words of support and encouragement, celebrations of accomplishments, enhanced flexibility and autonomy in job responsibilities, or new, more impressive sounding titles.

8. Facilitate the Coping of Those with Losses

Firms must consider what they can do to reduce employee stress or to reduce its negative effects. In the case of layoffs, this would involve doing everything possible to ease the stress of termination and facilitate movement to a new position. For instance, provide counseling and allow for gradual transition to the new situation.

9. Mark the Endings

There is a sense of incompleteness and emptiness when endings are not marked. This is one reason we have funerals and wakes. But we also have going-away parties or a ceremony to retire an athlete's number. These are ceremonies that recognize loss, but they also reaffirm the value of what is lost. These ceremonies are symbols of worth.

10. Treat the Past with Respect

Sometimes managers, in trying to make the future appear promising, ridicule or demean the old ways of doing things. Managers may engage in what are known as rites of degradation: finding scapegoats for blame and implying that by banishing the scapegoat, things will be better.[18] Doing so often enhances resistance to change because many people identify with the good old days and feel their self-worth is at stake when the past is attacked. One can point out the positive features of the new situation in ways that are not judgmental. Unless there is a compelling and concrete reason to criticize the past, don't.

11. Plan for New Beginnings

It is critical that those who survive change can look forward to new beginnings, that there is not just a sense of loss but also a sense of promise. Beginnings are typically wonderful and awful. An Italian writer, Cesare Pavese, wrote that "the only joy in the world is to begin," but Walter Bagehot, an English political scientist, wrote that, "one of the greatest pains of human nature is the pain of a new idea." Beginnings are exciting and scary. But without planning for new beginnings, there is only a sense of ending.

In this chapter we have considered stages of the change process, addressed the balancing of forces for and against change, considered sources of resistance to change and ways they may be minimized, explored stages in team insurrections, and suggested ways to help deal with difficult transitions. In Chapter 9 we turn our attention to potential problems in teams and what can be done to prevent or overcome them.

Summary and Integration

Key takeaways from this chapter include the following:

There are three primary stages to the change process—unfreezing, changing, and refreezing—and each is critical.

Successful change demands understanding and balancing the forces for and against change. Doing so requires identifying and managing potential sources of resistance to change as well as potential sources of support.

When change is introduced to a team, it is likely that at least some members will be hesitant to support the change. Team leaders and others must seek to recognize and understand these sources of resistance.

Team leaders can use strategies for overcoming resistance to change such as education, communication, participation, and involvement to obtain member buy-in for changes. The most appropriate approach will depend on the source of resistance, power of the initiator, cost, availability of relevant information, and other factors.

Change in organizations is sometimes initiated not by top management or team leaders but by the team itself. Team-based insurrections involve several steps and require buy-in from many others in the organization.

Even if attempts at implementing change are successful, they may carry social, career, emotional, financial, and other costs for team members and others. Because transitions are often difficult, care should be taken to help members understand the need for change, recognize losses, and cope with those losses.

Notes

1 See B. Burnes & B. Cooke, "Kurt Lewin's Field Theory: A Review and Re-Evaluation," *International Journal of Management Reviews*, 2013, *15(4)*, pp. 408–425; and, M. van den Heuvel, E. Demerouti, A.B. Bakker, & W.B. Schaufeli, "Adapting to Change: The Value of Change Information and Meaning-Making," *Journal of Vocational Behavior*, 2013, *83*, pp. 11–21.

2 For further discussion and applications of force field analysis, see G.L. Duffy, J. Bauer, & J.W. Moran, "Solve Problems with Open Communication," *Quality Progress*, 2001, *34(7)*, p. 160; A.W. Kruglanski, J.J. Bélanger, X. Chen, C. Köpetz, A. Pierro, & L. Mannetti, "The Energetics of Motivated Cognition: A Force-Field Analysis," *Psychological Review*, 2012, *119(1)*, pp. 1–20; and,

D.J. Swanson & A.S. Creed, "Sharpening the Focus of Force Field Analysis," *Journal of Change Management*, 2013, pp. 28–47.

3   For a discussion of Machiavelli's views on change, see D. McGuire & K. Hutchings, "A Machiavellian Analysis of Organisational Change," *Journal of Organizational Change Management*, 2006, *19(2)*, pp. 192–209.

4   For some steps taken to lessen the impacts of those layoffs, see P.A. Gloor & S.M. Cooper, "The New Principles of a Swarm Business," *MIT Sloan Management Review*, 2007, *48(3)*, pp. 80–84.

5   M. Boles & B.P. Sunoo, "Three Barriers to Managing Change," *Workforce*, January 1998, p. 25. For more on the role of trust in change, see D.A. Garvin & M.A. Roberto, "Change through Persuasion," *Harvard Business Review*, 2005, *83(2)*, pp. 104–112.

6   For a discussion of helping employees accept and adapt to change, see J.P. Kotter & L.A. Schlesinger, "Choosing Strategies for Change," *Harvard Business Review*, 1979, *57(2)*, pp. 106–114; J.L. Bennett, "Change Happens," *HR Magazine*, September 2001, pp. 149–156; and, S. Simmerman, "Square Wheels," *Executive Excellence*, June 2003, *20(6)*, pp. 15–16. For research on sources of resistance to change, see M. Pardo del Val & C.M. Fuentes, "Resistance to Change: A Literature Review and Empirical Study," *Management Decision*, 2003, *41(2)*, pp. 148–155; and, J.R. Schultz, "Eight Steps to Sustain Change," *Quality Progress*, 2007, *40(11)*, pp. 25–31.

7   For a good discussion of use of logos, ethos, and pathos for persuasive communication, see L.D. Rosenberg, "Aristotle's Methods for Outstanding Oral Arguments," Litigation, 2007, *33(4)*, pp. 33–39. See also, A.D. Brown, S. Ainsworth, & D. Grant, "The Rhetoric of Institutional Change," *Organization Studies*, 2012, *33(3)*, pp. 297–321.

8   To learn more about idea champions, see M.E. Mullins, S.W.J. Kozlowski, N. Schmitt, & A.W. Howell, "The Role of the Idea Champion in Innovation: The Case of the Internet in the Mid-1990s," *Computers in Human Behavior*, 2008, *24(2)*, pp. 451–467. For more on venture teams, see G.N. Chandler & D.L. Lyon, "Involvement in Knowledge-Acquisition Activities by Venture Team Members and Venture Performance," *Entrepreneurship Theory and Practice*, 2009, *33(3)*, pp. 571–592.

9   I.D. Colville & A.J. Murphy, "Leadership as the Enabler of Strategizing and Organizing," *Long Range Planning*, 2006, *39*, pp. 663–677; the quote is from page 649. See also S. Kelman, "Downsizing, Competition, and Organizational Change in Government: Is Necessity the Mother of Invention?" *Journal of Policy Analysis and Management*, 2006, *25(4)*, pp. 875–895.

10 A.J. Vogl, "The Army after Next," *Across the Board*, June 1999, p. 44.

11 See J. Collins, "Turning Goals into Results: The Power of Catalytic Mechanisms," *Harvard Business Review*, July/August 1999, pp. 70–82.

12 See also "Discipline and Desire," *Harvard Business Review*, July/August 1999, p. 10. This is the editors' introduction to an issue of *HBR* dealing with the need to balance discipline and desire. The editors write, "Management, like all human pursuits, is subject to two very different and often contradictory forces: the heart's desire and the mind's discipline."

13 Based in part on J.P. Kotter & L.A. Schlesinger, "Choosing Strategies for Change," *Harvard Business Review*, March/April 1979, pp. 106–114. See also D.R. Self & M. Schaeder, "Enhancing the Success of Organizational Change: Matching Readiness Strategies with Sources of Resistance," *Leadership & Organization Development Journal*, 2009, *30(2)*, pp. 167–182.

14 See G. Hamel, "Waking up IBM: How a Group of Unlikely Rebels Transformed Big Blue," *Harvard Business Review*, July-August 2000, pp. 137–146.

15 For a good discussion of the nature and benefits of small wins, see K.E. Weick, "Small Wins: Redefining the Scale of Social Problems," *American Psychologist*, 1984, *39*, pp. 57–64. See also T.M. Amabile & S.J. Kramer, "The Power of Small Wins," *Harvard Business Review*, 2011, *89(5)*, pp. 70–80; T.A. Amabile & S.J. Kramer, *The Progress Principle: Using Small Wins to Ignite Joy, Engagement, and Creativity at Work* (Boston, MA: Harvard Business Press Books, 2011); and, G. Nebojša, L. Vladana, & D. Gordana, "The Importance of Small Wins," *International Journal of Economics and Law,* 2013, *3(7)*, pp. 39–46.

16 For discussions of organizational change processes as resembling death and dying, see D. Zell, "Organizational Change as a Process of Death, Dying, and Rebirth," *Journal of Applied Behavioral Science*, March 2003, pp. 73–96; and, G. Blau, "Exploring Antecedents of Individual Grieving Stages During an Anticipated Workplace Closure," *Journal of Occupational and Organizational Psychology*, 2008, *81(3)*, pp. 529–550.

17 For a good discussion of grief at work, see M.A. Hazen, "Grief and the Workplace," *Academy of Management Perspectives*, 2008, *22(3)*, pp. 78–86.

18 For discussions of rites of degradation, see H.M. Trice & J.M. Beyer, "Studying Organizational Culture through Rites and Ceremonials," *Academy of Management Review*, 1984, *9(4)*, pp. 653–669; and, L. Huey & T. Kemple, "'Let the Streets Take Care of Themselves': Making Sociological and Common Sense of 'Skid Row,'" *Urban Studies*, 2007, *44(12)*, pp. 2305–2319.

Bibliography

Amabile T. M. & Kramer, S. J. "The Power of Small Wins," *Harvard Business Review*, 2011, *89(5)*, pp. 70–80.

Amabile, T. A, & Kramer, S. J. *The Progress Principle: Using Small Wins to Ignite Joy, Engagement, and Creativity at Work* (Boston, MA: Harvard Business Press Books, 2011).

Bennett, J.L., "Change Happens," *HR Magazine*, September 2001, pp. 149–156.

Blau, B. "Exploring Antecedents of Individual Grieving Stages during an Anticipated Workplace Closure," *Journal of Occupational and Organizational Psychology*, 2008, *81(3)*, pp. 529–550.

Boles, M., & Sunoo, B.P. "Three Barriers to Managing Change," *Workforce*, January 1998, p. 25.

Brown, A.D., Ainsworth, S., & Grant, D. "The Rhetoric of Institutional Change," *Organization Studies*, 2012, *33(3)*, pp. 297–321.

Burnes, B., & Cooke, B. "Kurt Lewin's Field Theory: A Review and Re-Evaluation," *International Journal of Management Reviews*, 2013, *15(4)*, pp. 408–425.

Chandler, G.N., & Lyon, D.L. "Involvement in Knowledge-Acquisition Activities by Venture Team Members and Venture Performance," *Entrepreneurship Theory and Practice*, 2009, *33(3)*, pp. 571–592.

Collins, J. "Turning Goals into Results: The Power of Catalytic Mechanisms," *Harvard Business Review*, July/August 1999, pp. 70–82.

Colville, I.D., & Murphy, A.J. "Leadership as the Enabler of Strategizing and Organizing," *Long Range Planning*, 2006, *39*, pp. 663–677.

"Discipline and Desire," *Harvard Business Review*, July/August 1999, p. 10.

Duffy, G.L., Bauer, J., & Moran, J.W. "Solve Problems with Open Communication," *Quality Progress*, 2001, *34(7)*, p. 160.

Eby, L.T., Adams, D.M., Russell, J.E.A., & Gaby, S.H. "Perceptions of Organizational Readiness for Change: Factors Related to Employees' Reactions to the Implementation of Team-Based Selling," *Human Relations*, 2000, *53(3)*, pp. 419–442.

Garvin, D.A., & Roberto, M.A. "Change through Persuasion," *Harvard Business Review*, 2005, *83(2)*, pp. 104–112.

Gloor, P.A., & Cooper, S.M. "The New Principles of a Swarm Business," *MIT Sloan Management Review*, 2007, *48(3)*, pp. 80–84.

Hamel, G. "Waking up IBM: How a Group of Unlikely Rebels Transformed Big Blue," *Harvard Business Review*, July-August 2000, pp. 137–146.

Hazen, A.M. "Grief and the Workplace," *Academy of Management Perspectives*, 2008, *22(3)*, pp. 78–86.

Huey, L., & Kemple, T. "'Let the Streets Take Care of Themselves': Making Sociological and Common Sense of 'Skid Row,'" *Urban Studies*, 2007, *44(12)*, pp. 2305–2319.

Katsaros, K.K., & Nicolaidis, C.S. "Personal Traits, Emotions, and Attitudes in the Workplace: Their Effects on Managers' Tolerance for Ambiguity," *Psychologist-Manager Journal*, 2012, *15(1)*, pp. 37–55.

Kelman, S. "Downsizing, Competition, and Organizational Change in Government: Is Necessity the Mother of Invention?" *Journal of Policy Analysis and Management*, 2006, *25(4)*, pp. 875–895.

Klein, K.L., & Knight, A.P. "Innovation Implementation: Overcoming the Challenge," *Current Directions in Psychological Science*, 2005, *14(5)*, pp. 243–246.

Kotter, J.P., & Schlesinger, L.A. "Choosing Strategies for Change," *Harvard Business Review*, 1979, *57(2)*, pp. 106–114.

Kruglanski, A.W., Bélanger, J.J., Chen, X., Köpetz, C., Pierro, A., & Mannetti, L. "The Energetics of Motivated Cognition: A Force-Field Analysis," *Psychological Review*, 2012, *119(1)*, pp. 1–20.

Lazarus, R.S., & Folkman, S. *Stress, Appraisal, and Coping* (New York: Springer, 1984); and, M. Beasley, T. Thompson, & J. Davidson, "Resilience in Response to Life Stress: The Effects of Coping Style and Cognitive Hardiness," *Personality and Individual Differences*, 2003, *34*, pp. 77–95.

McGuire, D., & Hutchings, K. "A Machiavellian Analysis of Organisational Change," *Journal of Organizational Change Management*, 2006, *19(2)*, pp. 192–209.

Mullins, M.E., Kozlowski, S.W.J., Schmitt, N., & Howell, A.W. "The Role of the Idea Champion in Innovation: The Case of the Internet in the Mid-1990s," *Computers in Human Behavior*, 2008, *24(2)*, pp. 451–467.

Nebojša, G., Vladana, L., & Gordana, D. "The Importance of Small Wins," *International Journal of Economics and Law,* 2013, *3(7)*, pp. 39–46.

Pardo del Val, M., & Fuentes, C.M. "Resistance to Change: A Literature Review and Empirical Study," *Management Decision*, 2003, *41(2)*, pp. 148–155.

Porter, C.O.L.H., Webb, J.W., & Gogus, C.J. "When Goal Orientations Collide: Effects of Learning and Performance Orientation on Team Adaptability in Response to Workload Imbalance," *Journal of Applied Psychology*, 2010, *95(5)*, pp. 935–943.

Reichers, A.E., Wanous, J.P., & Austin, J.T. "Understanding and Managing Cynicism about Organizational Change," *Academy of Management Executive*, 1997, *11(1)*, pp. 48–59.

Richards, J., & Kosmala, K. "'In the End, You Can Only Slag People Off for So Long': Employee Cynicism through Work Blogging," *New Technology, Work and Employment*, 2013, *28(1)*, pp. 66–77.

Rosenberg, L.D. "Aristotle's Methods for Outstanding Oral Arguments," *Litigation*, 2007, *33(4)*, pp. 33–39.

Schultz, J.R. "Eight Steps to Sustain Change," *Quality Progress*, 2007, *40(11)*, pp. 25–31.

Self, D.R., & Schaeder, M. "Enhancing the Success of Organizational Change: Matching Readiness Strategies with Sources of Resistance," *Leadership & Organization Development Journal*, 2009, *30(2)*, pp. 167–182.

Shin, J., Taylor, M.S., & Seo, M.-G. "Resources for Change: The Relationships of Organizational Inducements and Psychological Resilience to Employees' Attitudes and Behaviors toward Organizational Change," *Academy of Management Journal*, 2012, *55(3)*, pp. 727–748.

Simmerman, S. "Square Wheels," *Executive Excellence*, June 2003, *20(6)*, pp. 15–16.

Swanson, D.J., & Creed, A.S. "Sharpening the Focus of Force Field Analysis," *Journal of Change Management*, 2013, pp. 28–47.

Trice, H.M., & Beyer, J.M. "Studying Organizational Culture through Rites and Ceremonials," *Academy of Management Review*, 1984, *9(4)*, pp. 653–669.

van den Heuvel, M., Demerouti, E., Bakker, A.B., & Schaufeli, W.B. "Adapting to Change: The Value of Change Information and Meaning-Making," *Journal of Vocational Behavior*, 2013, *83*, pp. 11–21.

Vogl, A.J. "The Army after Next," *Across the Board*, June 1999, pp. 43–47.

Wanous, J.P., Reichers, A.E., & Austin, J.T. "Cynicism about Organizational Change: An Attribution Process Perspective," *Psychological Reports*, 2004, *94(3)*, pp. 1421–1434.

Weick, K.E. "Small Wins: Redefining the Scale of Social Problems," *American Psychologist*, 1984, *39*, pp. 57–64.

Zell, D. "Organizational Change as a Process of Death, Dying, and Rebirth," *Journal of Applied Behavioral Science*, March 2003, pp. 73–96.

Dealing with Team Problems

Learning Objectives

After reading this chapter, you should be able to do the following:
1. Diagnose team problems.
2. Recognize and deal with problem behaviors by team members.
3. Better understand key group dysfunctions and recognize ways to avoid them.
4. Manage conflict within and between teams.
5. Take steps to turn around failing teams.

MANY STUDENTS AND PRACTITIONERS COMMENT THAT THEY "HATE WORKING IN TEAMS!" Some of the most common reasons for this sentiment are the frustrations of having to do more than one's fair share of the work to compensate for those who are not committed to the team process, dealing with personality clashes and work style differences, taking the extra time required to plan and coordinate the activities of multiple team members, and finding times and places where everyone can meet. The good news is that many of these team problems can be reduced or eliminated through an understanding of some fundamental strategies and tools for managing teams.

In this chapter we discuss key factors in dealing with special problems in teams. We begin by examining the critical issue of diagnosing team problems—what, if any, are the actual problems, and what if we don't recognize actual problems? We then consider common problem behaviors in teams and suggest approaches to their amelioration. Next, we discuss what is probably the most universally accepted and cited model of group dysfunctions, the groupthink model. We then examine conflict within and between teams, including conflict styles, consider when each is appropriate, and provide guidelines for conflict management. Finally, we offer suggestions for turning around failing teams, including team crisis management and team culture change.

Diagnosing Team Problems

We said in Chapter 7 that properly defining the problem is the crucial first step in the problem-solving process. Failure to do so can cause teams to solve the wrong problem.

It is often tempting when considering problems in teams to try to find an obvious suspect: a troublesome team member, a severe time constraint, a history of conflict, or whatever. Again, there is a strong tendency to define the problem—a gap between the current and desired situation—in terms of its symptoms and/or preferred solutions.

Some biases are important to consider when defining a problem (see discussion of other biases in Chapter 7). For one, we are subject to **fundamental attribution error**. This is the tendency to attribute praise and blame to people rather than to situations. For example, we tend to overpraise and overblame leaders when things go well or poorly. This is perhaps because we find it difficult to change situations, but easier to replace or punish people. For example, when a football team goes into a slump, the coach is often replaced, even though many other things—perhaps a lucky bounce of the ball, a tough schedule, or an unfortunate gust of wind—may have contributed to losses. In fact, the evidence is that football coaches are often scapegoats. A study of 26 teams in the National Football League over almost 20 years found that teams that replaced their coaches did no better than those with similar records that did not dismiss their coaches.[1]

Similarly, we may be tempted to blame or praise a team member when failure or success is in fact largely due to the situation. For example, a team member may be late for an important meeting or miss a key deadline on a project. Our tendency is to attribute the cause of their behavior to our perception that these team members are irresponsible or lazy. In fact, that team member may have been late due to a car accident or a death in the family. Building a strong system and culture of open communication on a team can help to foster the type of relationships between team members that can reduce the frequency of fundamental attribution errors.

Also, our expectations may influence our definition of the problem as well as our diagnosis of the problem's cause. If, for instance, we are told that Bob is a lazy worker, we may look for signs that he is lazy. As a result, if Bob doesn't complete work by a deadline, we may assume it is due to his laziness, when in fact it might be the result of others' interference or of work overload. This can result in a **self-fulfilling prophecy** (also known as Pygmalion Effect), in which our expectations shape reality.[2] That is, our expectations cause us to see others in ways consistent with those expectations, to behave accordingly, and to cause others to then behave according to our expectations. So, if we continually treat Bob as if he is lazy, he may become lazy. The self-fulfilling prophecy can have a powerful effect on our attitudes toward working on teams and the quality of our team experiences. Specifically, if we enter a new team project or assignment with a negative attitude about what working on that team will be like, we will likely end up behaving accordingly and maintaining a negative attitude toward that team. Team leaders can address this issue by shaping positive expectations about the team from the early stages of the team's existence. They can educate team members about the positive aspects of the team's assignment and the benefits members will derive from their experiences on the team.

As pointed out in Chapter 7, a team's problem is often defined in terms of symptoms, limiting appropriate exploration of deeper causes. Here we summarize the guidelines for writing a good problem statement that were presented in that chapter.

- **State the problem explicitly.**
- **Specify the standard(s) violated.**
- **State the problem in specific behavioral terms.**
- **Specify whose problem it is.**
- **Avoid stating the problem merely as an implied solution.**
- **Avoid stating the problem as a dilemma.**

Types of Problem Team Behaviors

In Chapter 3 we discussed roles in teams, including self-oriented roles. Those self-oriented roles often interfere with attempts to attain task and socioemotional goals and lead to many types of problem behaviors by team members. Here we will consider four types of team members with problem behaviors: freeloaders, complainers, bullies, and martyrs.[4]

- **Freeloaders (social loafers).** Some team members simply don't carry their fair share of the team's workload; they engage in social loafing.[5] Such freeloaders detract directly from team performance by their lack of contribution. In addition, they may provoke conflict in the team as other members refuse to carry an unproductive member. To minimize social loafing, it may help to finds ways to identify individual members' outputs; freeloading is especially likely when members' contributions are anonymous or cannot be separately evaluated. Encouraging interdependence among team members so members can identify and respond to social loafers is also useful.[6]
- **Complainers (whiners).** These members constantly complain about the team's scheduling, activities, progress, or other matters. They see the project as a waste of time, feel they aren't being treated well, or simply hate to work in teams. A Gallup poll of 31,265 employees concluded that 18% are "actively disengaged," negative, and complain about their employers.[7]

  Complainers damage team morale, and other members often spend an inordinate amount of time and energy trying to placate them. A whiner's steady stream of negativity can be draining on others, causing distraction and loss of productivity.[8] Further, whiners' negative emotions may carry over to others through emotional contagion: when people are in a certain mood, whether elated or depressed, that mood is often communicated to others.[9] So, a whiner can dispirit the entire team.

To deal with a whiner's complaints about a coworker or boss, it may be helpful to deflect them by saying something like, "It sounds like you and he have something to talk about."[10] When PaceButler CEO Tom Pace became concerned by employees' constant grousing, he offered cash awards to any of his seventy employees who did not complain or gossip for 7 days. At PaceButler, team members monitor themselves and each other. Workers going a week without complaints are eligible to enter a monthly $500 drawing. The program made everyone think before they talked and seemed to make the workplace more positive and productive.[11]

- **Bullies (dominators).** Some members actively disrupt the team by pushing their opinions on others. Bullies seem to revel in making others feel inadequate or unintelligent. They may feel they are better prepared or more knowledgeable than others and are anxious to display their expertise, or they may use bullying to cover up their inadequacies. In either case, their insistence on controlling the team process leads to ill will and lack of team coordination.[12]
- **Martyrs.** These are members who feel (whether correctly or not) that they are carrying the load for the team. They see themselves as being forced to cover for incompetent team members, as having all the worst assignments, and as doing far more than their fair share. Unlike complainers, they really don't want anything to change; they just want others to feel guilty and to acknowledge their burden. This often creates conflict as other team members chafe at the martyr's claims, attributions, and attitudes.

Practical Guidelines for Dealing with Problem Behaviors

Many of these problem behaviors can be avoided or alleviated through proper planning and team management.

- **Choose team members carefully.** Take team membership seriously. Think about whether potential members are likely to get along rather than only whether they possess necessary technical knowledge and skills. Pick members who have a genuine interest in the task outcome. Make clear to each member why he or she is needed on the team.[13] A structured interviewing process based on an analysis of the job requirements of team members can be very beneficial. In addition, using current team members to conduct peer interviews with prospective team members can be helpful in assessing their potential compatibility.
- **Offer training.** Give members guidance on how to deal with problem behaviors. Members can, for instance, be shown videos of teams successfully dealing with problem members in a number of specific work situations. Such videos may describe forms of potential problem behaviors, show team members' disappointment with such behaviors, make

role expectations clear, and suggest specific ways to address problem behaviors.[14] An important consideration when implementing any kind of training program is to take action as the team leader to ensure that what is learned about how to handle problem team members transfers to the performance of team members on a day-to-day basis. Team leaders can do this by reinforcing and rewarding team members for behaving in ways that are consistent with what they learned about handling team members from the training program.

- **Provide clear goals.** Make sure the team knows what it is expected to do and why its task is important. Emphasize clear, well-defined goals and the consequences of the team's decisions. Direction provided at the first team meeting is crucial and will establish lasting precedents for the team. Team leaders must view their role as maintaining the team's focus on its goals by discussing the importance of the goals and the actions needed to achieve them at team meetings and through written and electronic communications.

- **Clearly define member responsibilities.** Many problems in teams occur because members' responsibilities are unclear. Early agreement on a clear and equitable division of responsibilities will work wonders in preventing future conflict. Tools such as the role responsibilities matrix discussed in Chapter 2 are useful in helping a team to clarify and to differentiate the respective roles of team members.

- **Use peer evaluations.** Team members and leaders must be willing and able to provide—and accept—honest feedback about their individual behaviors and the final outcome of the team's work.[15] Members are more willing to do their fair share and to curtail other problem behaviors if they know their contributions will be evaluated. Using 360-degree feedback (with which the employee receives feedback from four sources: the supervisor, subordinates, peers or coworkers, and self ratings) and other approaches that employ peer evaluations are helpful in this regard.[16]

- **Reward superior performance.** Team members who excel should somehow be rewarded for their contributions. This can take the form of positive peer evaluations, praise, or celebrations of accomplishments. While this may seem like a commonsense strategy, linking rewards to performance is often difficult in practice since various team members may value different rewards.

- **Don't let social considerations overwhelm concern with the task.** Many teams develop norms of peaceful coexistence—members are reluctant to openly confront others and to generate hurt feelings. As a result, social loafing and complaining is never challenged. Members must be willing to appeal to norms of fair participation and to openly deal with problem team members. Team leaders can address this issue by using team-building activities to facilitate breaking the ice and building trust among team members (e.g., ropes courses, self-disclosure activities that require sharing some personal information with each other) as well as promoting informal interaction and open communication on a daily basis.

- **Appeal to the shadow of the future.** Remind team members that they are likely to be working together on future tasks and that inappropriate behavior on this task won't be forgotten.[17]
- **Remove problem team members.** As a last resort, it may be necessary to remove an intransigent member from the team. While this is unpleasant, problem behaviors that sap team morale and performance cannot be allowed to continue unabated.

While problem behaviors can endanger team processes and outcomes, team leaders and members should resist the temptation to react to them with anger and abuse. The following "Teams in the News" feature reinforces this point.

TEAMS IN THE NEWS: When the Boss Is a Screamer

We've all heard about bad bosses. In fact, there are many bad boss contests. An exemplar of a bad boss is one who screams, intimidates subordinates, uses nonverbal communications to send subtle criticisms, and rules by fear. A 2012 *Wall Street Journal* article discusses the drawbacks of such behavior. Employees of abusive bosses may do one or more of the following:

- Quit their jobs at higher rates.
- Avoid dealing with conflicts, allowing them to escalate.
- Bring less creativity to their jobs.
- Become less competent in performing their jobs.
- Be less able to store and manage information in short-term memory.

So, while abusive styles by leaders or team members may sometimes seem to lead to short-term results, they are likely to result in resentment, dissatisfaction, turnover, and poor performance. (Follow this link to view the video: http://online.wsj.com/article/SB10000872396390444772404577589302193682244.html?KEYWORDS=when+the+boss+is+a+screamer#articleTabs%3Dinteractive%26project%3DWORKFAM0815/. The video is also available on the text website.)

Source: For more on destructive leadership, see D. V. Krasikova, S. G. Green, & J. M. LeBreton, "Destructive Leadership: A Theoretical Review, Integration, and Future Research Agenda," *Journal of Management*, 2013, *39(5)*, pp. 1308–1338.

Groupthink

Any discussion of problems in teams inevitably leads to mentions of groupthink. According to Irving Janis, **groupthink** is "the mode of thinking that persons engage in when concurrence-seeking becomes so dominant in a cohesive in-group that it tends to over-ride realistic appraisals of alternative courses of action." Janis states, "Groupthink refers to a deterioration of mental efficiency, reality testing, and moral judgment that results from in-group pressures."[18]

Example of Fiascoes
often Attributed to
Groupthink: The British
Petroleum Oil Spill

As shown in Figure 9-1, Janis felt that groupthink resulted from antecedents including group cohesiveness, structural faults of the organization, and
a provocative situational context. These were seen as leading to an excessive tendency toward concurrence seeking. Identified groupthink symptoms
included these:

- **An illusion of invulnerability.** The sense that the group is beyond harm
  creates excessive optimism that encourages taking extreme risks.
- **Belief in the inherent morality of the group.** Members believe in the
  rightness of their cause and therefore ignore the ethical and moral consequences of their decisions.
- **Collective rationalization.** Members discount warnings and do not reconsider their assumptions.
- **Stereotypes of outsiders.** Negative views of the enemy as weak and
  incompetent make effective responses to conflict seem unnecessary.
- **Self-censorship.** Doubts and deviations from the perceived group consensus are not exposed.
- **An illusion of unanimity.** The majority view and judgments are assumed
  to be unanimous.
- **Direct pressure on dissenters.** Members do not express their doubts and
  deviations from the perceived group consensus because of pressure from
  other group members.
- **Self-appointed mindguards (analogous to bodyguards).** Members take it
  upon themselves to shield the group and the leader from information that
  is problematic or contradictory to the group's cohesiveness, view, and/or
  decisions.

Figure 9-1

Groupthink Model

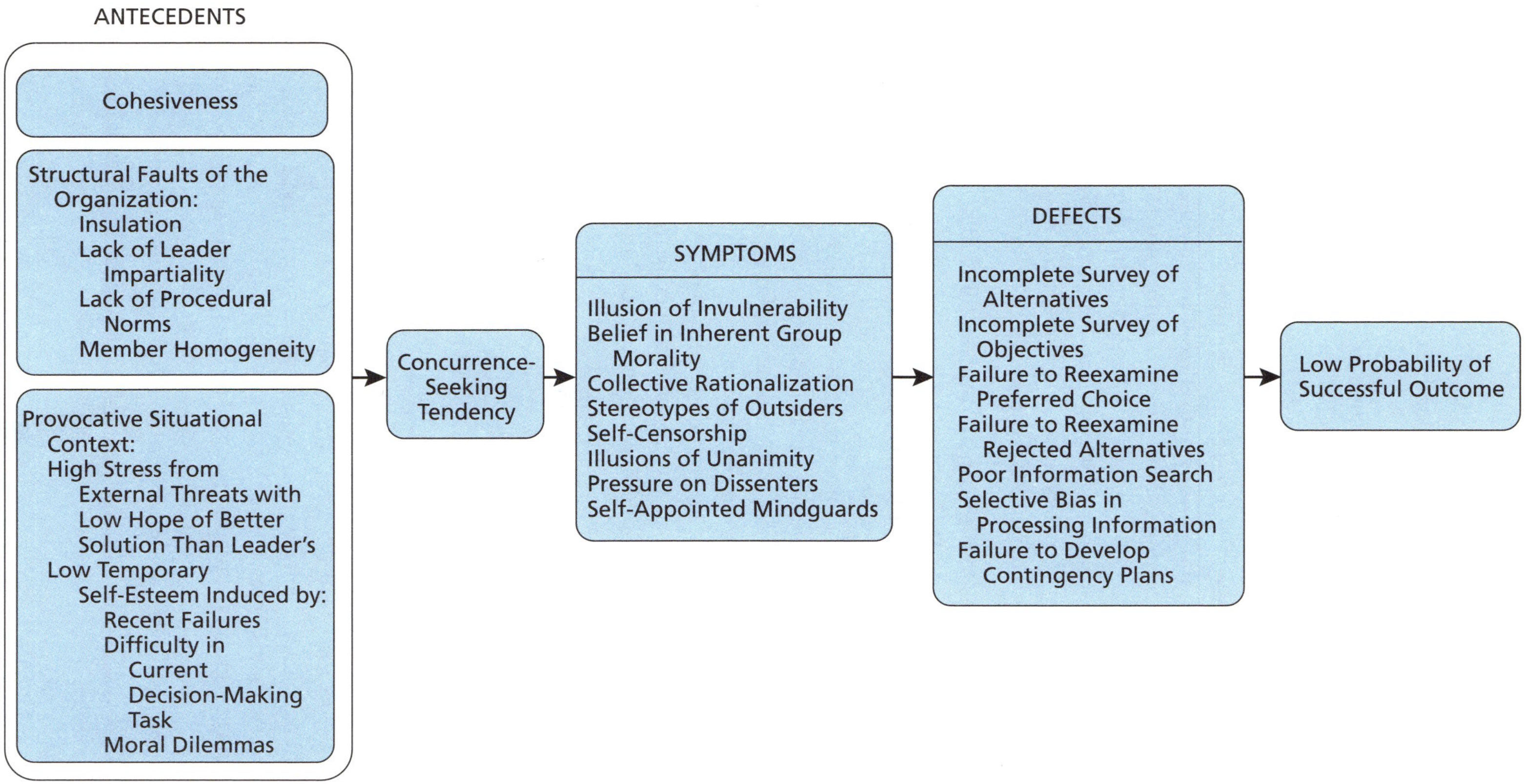

ANTECEDENTS

Cohesiveness

Structural Faults of the Organization:
Insulation
Lack of Leader Impartiality
Lack of Procedural Norms
Member Homogeneity

Provocative Situational Context:
High Stress from External Threats with Low Hope of Better Solution Than Leader's
Low Temporary Self-Esteem Induced by:
Recent Failures
Difficulty in Current Decision-Making Task
Moral Dilemmas

Concurrence-Seeking Tendency

SYMPTOMS

Illusion of Invulnerability
Belief in Inherent Group Morality
Collective Rationalization
Stereotypes of Outsiders
Self-Censorship
Illusions of Unanimity
Pressure on Dissenters
Self-Appointed Mindguards

DEFECTS

Incomplete Survey of Alternatives
Incomplete Survey of Objectives
Failure to Reexamine Preferred Choice
Failure to Reexamine Rejected Alternatives
Poor Information Search
Selective Bias in Processing Information
Failure to Develop Contingency Plans

Low Probability of Successful Outcome

Source: Adapted from I.L. Janis and L. Mann. *Decision Making: A Psychological Analysis of Conflict, Choice, and Commitment.* New York, Free Press, 1977, p. 132. Adaption printed in R.J. Aldag and S. Riggs Fuller. "Beyond Fiasco: A Reappraisal of the Groupthink Phenomenon and a New Model of Group Decision Processes." *Psychological Bulletin*, 1993, *113(3)*, pp. 533–552. Copyright 1993 by the American Psychological Association, reprinted with permission.

Janis saw these symptoms as leading to various defects, including the following:

- **Incomplete survey of alternatives.** Members focus on just a few alternatives, failing to consider others.
- **Failure to reexamine the preferred choice.** The alternative preferred by most members is not critically examined for nonobvious risks.
- **Failure to reexamine rejected alternatives.** Alternatives initially judged to be unsatisfactory are not reexamined to find ways to make them acceptable.
- **Poor information search.** Search for information is selective and biased, with little attempt to obtain information from unbiased experts.
- **Selective bias in processing information.** Members process information selectively, favoring facts and opinion that support their initial preference.
- **Failure to develop contingency plans.** Since members do not expect or discuss resistance to, setbacks from, or difficulties with the preferred alternative, they see no need to come up with backup plans.

Janis saw these defects as resulting in a low probability of achieving successful decision outcomes.

The Janis groupthink model provided some valuable information about group processes and outcomes. For example, the listing of symptoms offers a useful set of factors that may interfere with effective group processes. Similarly, the array of defects subsumes many common team failures to properly gather, evaluate, and use information. And, again, Janis offered a very useful set of guidelines to prevent group dysfunctions.

We should note that other research does not support the full groupthink model.[19] Janis wrote that ". . . it does not suffice merely to see if a few of the eight telltale symptoms of groupthink can be detected. Rather, it is necessary to see if practically all the symptoms were manifested and the expected immediate consequences—the symptoms of defective decision making—are also present."[20] However, other research that has reported any evidence of groupthink has found only a few symptoms or instances of defective decision making. In most research there has been lack of support for the model, or even findings contrary to the model.[21] For example, it has become clear that cohesiveness is *not* a precursor of groupthink. On the contrary, members of cohesive teams feel *more* comfortable in expressing their opinions and raising concerns. This has led various scholars to call for dropping cohesiveness as a critical antecedent of groupthink. Such a change would, though, undermine Janis's key premise.

Nevertheless, Janis's presentation of the groupthink model has raised awareness of common group dysfunctions, and Janis has offered a very useful set of recommendations—discussed in Chapter 7—for preventing and/or ameliorating these potential dysfunctions. Even though the groupthink model may be an inadequate oversimplification of group decision processes, it had spawned interest in, and emphasis on, means of preventing group dysfunction.[22]

Managing Conflict

All organizations experience conflict. Teams may experience both conflict within teams—**intrateam conflict**—and conflict between teams—**interteam**

conflict. There are many costs, but also many potential benefits, to conflict. The way in which conflict is handled determines whether it is beneficial or destructive. As such, the challenge is not to eliminate conflict but to ensure that is effectively managed.

Skills Practice 9.1 on the text website gives you the opportunity to learn more about conflict and conflict handling from a practicing manager.

A Conflict Model

A model presented by Lou Pondy offers important insights regarding the conflict process.[23] The model, shown in Figure 9-2, illustrates that there are several steps in the conflict process and that a variety of things may determine whether conflict ever becomes overt or manifest.

Latent Conflict

Latent conflict is essentially conflict waiting to happen; it occurs when conditions are right for open conflict to develop. Latent conflict is influenced by the aftermath of preceding conflict situations and by environmental effects. The latter include scarcity of resources, ambiguous jurisdictions, incompatible goals, task interdependence, competitive reward systems, and differentiation.

Felt Conflict

Felt conflict is experienced as discomfort and tension. The party experiencing felt conflict is motivated to reduce those negative feelings. Felt conflict may be heightened by other tensions inside or outside the organization. For example, if a person is also experiencing pressures at home or is worried about losing his or her job, that person may already be sore. As such, he or she may feel even greater tension from further irritants.

Perceived Conflict

Perceived conflict is the awareness that we are in a conflict situation. For example, when we learn that there will be budget cuts, we may realize that a struggle over scarce resources is likely. Perceived conflict depends in part on

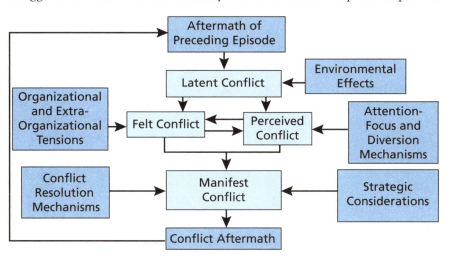

Figure 9-2

A Conflict Model

mechanisms that may exist to direct attention to or away from the conflict. For example, a sudden crisis may shift our attention from the current conflict situation. Conversely, if we know that others are watching to see how we will do, we may be more conscious of the conflict. Note that felt conflict and perceived conflict are mutually reinforcing. When we perceive conflict, we are likely to experience tension, and when we feel conflict, we are likely to think about it.

Manifest Conflict

After conflict is perceived and felt, it may or may not become open, or manifest. As was seen in Figure 9-2, whether conflict becomes manifest depends on whether mechanisms are in place to resolve conflict as well as whether engaging in open conflict seems wise. Conflict-resolution mechanisms might include such things as a focus on larger goals, use of mediators, separation of parties, or use of negotiating techniques (discussed later in this chapter). Strategic considerations might include, for instance, a decision that the conflict just isn't worth it. While we may want a bigger share of the budget, we may decide that fighting for it would lead to more costs than benefits.

Conflict Aftermath

Conflict is likely to breed more conflict and, when it does, that conflict is likely to take on a life of its own. Witness, for instance, long-standing feuds for which the original insult, misdeed, or misunderstanding has been long forgotten but for which bitterness and even hatred are unabated. Failure to address the situation after a conflict has been theoretically resolved may result in damaged or destroyed working relationships between team members or between teams. This could lead to a cold war phenomenon in which communication breaks down between team members, team morale plummets, and a culture of mistrust emerges. Failure to manage the **conflict aftermath** could result in a win the battle but lose the war scenario in which a conflict has apparently been resolved but the working relationships between team members are no longer functional.

Conflict Types

Karen "Etty" Jehn (interviewed in the Team Scholar feature) proposed three types of conflict: relationship, task, and process.[24] **Relationship conflict** (sometimes called emotional conflict or affective conflict) results from things such as personality clashes; anger; tension; annoyance; and conflict about personal taste, values, and interpersonal styles. **Task conflict** (also called cognitive conflict) refers to disagreements over ideas and opinions pertaining to the team's task. **Process conflict** is conflict regarding things such as how a project should be addressed and who should do what.

Recently, Jehn and her colleagues proposed on the basis of their research that the team conflict types can be collapsed into task and interpersonal conflict, each with three dimensions.[25] These types and examples are shown in Figure 9-3.

Figure 9-3

Team Conflict Types and Examples

Task Conflict	
Dimension	**Examples**
Divergent Task	Conflicts in opinions and different perspectives. Differences in opinions concerning the analysis of the case. Conflict only over ideas.
Convergent Task	Disagreements on the main issues and on recommendations. Differing opinions about how to address issues, define issues, solutions, and so on. Different views on answers.
Logistical Coordination	Conflict on when to schedule meetings. Conflict on length of time to spend on projects. Conflict regarding hours to be worked and how late to work in the evenings.

Interpersonal Conflict	
Dimension	**Examples**
Status Conflict	I felt my opinion was not valued. Ego clashes, arrogance. One person always having to be right. This person seemed oppressive.
Compatibility Conflict	Sometimes personalities conflicted. Cultural differences were evident. Conflict on communication style.
Commitment Conflict	Not everyone felt that everyone was always mentally there. Amount of information put in by certain member. Commitments were made initially but were not followed up or backed up with the required efforts.

Source: Adapted from C. Bendarsky, K. Behfar, L. Weingart, G. Todorave, J. Bear, & K. Jehn. "Revisiting the Dimensions of Intra-Group Conflict: Theoretical and Psychometric Construct Refinement." Paper presented at the 23rd Annual International Association of Conflict Management Conference, Boston, MA, June 24–27, 2010.

Figures 9-2 and 9-3 show that intrateam conflict can occur for many reasons. Some of those reasons, such as ego clashes and arrogance, are almost certain to be dysfunctional. Others, such as different perspectives, may enhance creativity.

Potential Benefits of Conflict

We've said that conflict in teams is not always bad. In fact, as Figure 9-2 suggested, conflict has a variety of potential benefits:

- **Diagnostic functions.** Conflict may help bring to the surface underlying tensions and concerns. In many cases, getting these issues on to the table will enable the team to better understand and resolve them.
- **Motivational functions.** In the absence of conflict, there may be a tendency to resort in what Janis and Mann have called **unconflicted adherence.**[26]

That is, the team may continue to engage in past practices even though they are no longer appropriate. Because there is no manifest conflict, the team lacks vigilance and becomes apathetic.[27]

- **Expressive functions.** Conflict may provide an opportunity for people to recognize and value differences of opinion, open up their world views, expand their perspectives, and solve problems. Lacking conflict, team members may simply assume that others share their views and may see no need to reexamine their views or to seek others' views.
- **Learning functions.** Conflict may give the parties the opportunity to learn, to improve, to practice tolerance, and to achieve satisfactory resolution of emotional tension that often hampers their creativity, productivity, trust, and communications both on and off the job.[28]
- **Surgical functions.** Conflict may, in extremes, help identify elements of the team or organization that are so troublesome that they should be removed.

Nevertheless, conflict can sometimes cause (and/or reflect) serious problems. As suggested earlier, the consequences of conflict in teams depend in part on the nature of the conflict. Interpersonal conflict is generally dysfunctional. Task conflict, since it may foster creativity and encourage consideration of minority opinions, can often be helpful. Further, as we've discussed, conflict management may be especially necessary in diverse teams, with members varying in cultures, backgrounds, personalities, perspectives, and so on.

TEAM SCHOLAR

Dr. Karen "Etty" Jehn, Professor of Management, University of Melbourne, Melbourne, Australia

Karen A. "Etty" Jehn is professor of organizational behavior at Melbourne Business School. She earned her PhD from Northwestern University. Her research focuses on intragroup conflict, group composition and performance, and lying in organizations. Her two most recent research interests are asymmetry of perceptions and member entitlement in work groups. To learn more about Professor Jehn and her research on teams, visit her website at http://www.mbs.edu/go/person/karen-jehn

Previous research identified two forms of intragroup conflict: relationship and task. To those you added process conflict. What is process conflict and why is it important?

I think of the types of conflict in the following way. Task conflict is about the *what*—what will the team be doing and arguments about that. Relationship conflict is the *who*—are you arguing with certain people over personal (nontask) issues such as commuting, politics, fashion, and so on. Process conflict is the *how*—how will you get the task done, how will you divide resources and tasks? Talking about process conflict is important because while this type seems to be task related, it acts more like relationship conflict (negative for satisfaction and performance) because people take criticisms of their skills personally, as well as not getting a fair share of resources.

You've recently written an article titled "The Paradox of Intragroup Conflict: A Meta-Analysis." What is that paradox? What do your findings suggest about that paradox?

The main paradox researchers seem to be trying to figure out is when task conflict might be beneficial. There are certain circumstances under which this is so (e.g., nonroutine tasks, open conflict norms), but our most recent discovery is about whether people perceive the task conflict as a challenge (they have the ability to overcome it) versus as a threat (they do not have the resources to handle the conflict). Whether people feel they have the ability to overcome the challenge determines whether they perceive and deal with the conflict in a constructive way for the group.

You've been examining the importance of team member value congruence. Why is value congruence important?

The idea of being validated leads to members being better and happier team members. There is less misidentification and miscommunication, thus improving group processes.

What do you see as some of the most important emerging issues regarding teams?

My most recent issues that I think are important to teams are asymmetry and entitlement of members. Asymmetry refers to the idea that members may perceive the same reality in different ways. For instance, I might think we are having a huge relationship conflict, and you may think everything is fine. The difference in perception causes great distress for the person not validated and leads to a meta-conflict, or conflict about conflict. How can you resolve a conflict if you don't even agree that it exists? Secondly, I've begun to do research on entitled group members— those who feel they deserve to be leaders or get benefits without putting in any effort (yes, they do exist! Moreso in the higher levels of organizations, unfortunately). These members are not team players and often are the ones who wreak havoc in their teams by being manipulative and self-focused.

Conflict Styles

Parties to a conflict situation tend to adopt one of five conflict strategies or styles, each with its own objectives, behaviors, rationales, and probable outcomes. These strategies reflect differing levels of emphasis on assertiveness (attempting to satisfy one's own interests) and cooperativeness (attempting to satisfy the other party's concerns) as shown in Figure 9-4.[29]

Competing

With a competing (or forcing) style, the party is assertive and uncooperative, attempting to satisfy his or her own needs at the expense of those of the other party. If the party is successful, this results in a form of win-lose outcome, with a clear winner and loser.

Figure 9-4

Conflict Styles

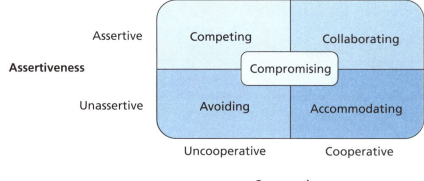

Examples of Actions Associated with the Use of a Competing Style[30]

- Pursue your own goals with determination, regardless of the other person's concerns.
- Make the first move in the conflict to gain control of the situation and maximize chances of obtaining your demands.
- Prolong the discussion of the issues until the other person tires and gives in to your approach for handling the problem.

Avoiding

A party adopting an avoiding strategy is neither assertive nor cooperative, neglecting the interests of both parties by trying to sidestep the conflict or put off making a decision. Regular use of this strategy may lead to frustration, uncertainties, and stalemates, yielding a lose-lose outcome, with neither party's needs being satisfied.

Examples of Actions Associated with the Use of an Avoiding Style

- Downplay the seriousness of the problem and suggest the two of you not waste time with the matter.
- Tell the other person that the problem does not concern you.
- Explain that there is no point in trying to resolve a conflict between two people with such basically different personalities.

Compromising

A compromising party shows moderate levels of both assertiveness and cooperation. The compromise doesn't fully satisfy the needs of either party, but the pain is shared.

Examples of Actions Associated with the Use of a Compromising Style

- Point out to the other person that if you both will make a few concessions, the conflict can be resolved quickly.

- Point out that if the agreement is to be resolved, some sacrifices must be made by both of you.

Accommodating

Some parties are cooperative without being assertive, thus satisfying the other party's needs while neglecting their own. The accommodating party may thus become a sucker, being taken advantage of and losing stature and self-esteem. This creates another win-lose situation, with the accommodating party being the loser.

Examples of Actions Associated with the Use of an Accommodating Style

- Offer to handle the problem any way the other person wants.
- Go along with whatever the other person requests, rather than get into the difficulties of direct confrontation.

Collaborating

A negotiator adopting the collaborating style is both cooperative and assertive, focusing on satisfying the needs of both parties. This style—sometimes called a problem-solving style—has the potential for yielding win-win outcomes.

Examples of Actions Associated with the Use of a Collaborating Style

- Try to sort out where each of you stands and identify options available to meet both parties' needs.
- Suggest that you take your ideas and the other person's ideas and put them together to make an even more workable idea.
- Express your concern about the differences between you and let the other person know you want a resolution that satisfies both of you.

Skills Practice 9.2 on the text website allows you to analyze the conflict-handling styles of a group of individuals working together on a complex task in the movie *Twelve Angry Men*.

Contingency Factors for Handling Conflict

Now that we have established that there are five basic conflict-handling styles, you might be thinking, "Which conflict style is the best one to use?" Many students believe that collaborating or compromising are always the best conflict styles to use, and that competing and accommodating would always be the least effective strategies. As it turns out, there is no single conflict-handling style that is the best approach to use for all situations! The key is to understand the characteristics of the particular situation (the task, goals, and so on) and then to match the most appropriate conflict strategy to this situation.

Here, we consider when each style may be most appropriate.[31]

- **Competing.** The competing, or forcing, conflict style generally leads to antagonism and festering resentment. It may be necessary when time is of the essence, and we are sure we are correct or when the other party would take advantage of a more collaborative approach. In each of these cases, though, we should be sure to question our assumptions before resorting to competition. That is, is there really a time constraint? How can we be sure we are correct? What evidence do we have that the other party cannot be trusted?

- **Avoiding.** The avoiding style is generally unproductive, but it may be appropriate when conflicts are trivial. It may also be useful as a temporary tactic to let parties cool down during heated disputes.
- **Accommodating.** The accommodating style may be acceptable when the other party has great power, or the issue isn't really important to us. However, appeasement may be seen as a sign of weakness and may lead to even greater demands rather than to peace in our times. In the long term, it may generate rather than resolve conflict.
- **Compromising.** Compromising involves an attempt to find a satisfactory middle ground (i.e., to split the difference by reaching an agreement that, while not ideal for either party, seems equitable). Compromise may be necessary when there is little chance of agreement, both parties have equal power, and there are time constraints. Even when such conditions exist (and again, we should be sure to question whether they really do), compromising is unlikely to yield more than an equally unsatisfactory outcome.
- **Collaborating.** This problem-solving style is mutually beneficial when a win-win solution is sought that fully satisfies the interests of both parties. This style requires trust, open sharing of information, and creativity. This is often seen as the ideal style and should be sought unless the parties to conflict have perfectly opposing interests.[32] Even in the latter case, though, we should be sure to examine whether those interests are truly opposing or whether in fact the apparent incompatibility is due to misperceptions or failure to see the big picture.

As we've just discussed, some of these approaches generally work better than do others, but each may be appropriate in certain situations. The situations in which each style may be appropriate are summarized in Figure 9-5[33].

Figure 9-5	Conflict Style	Appropriate Situation
Fitting Conflict Style to the Situation	Competing	• When quick, decisive action is vital. • On important issues when unpopular actions need implementing (e.g., cost-cutting, enforcing unpopular rules, discipline). • On issues vital to company welfare when you know you are right. • Against people who take advantage of noncompetitive behavior.
	Collaborating	• To find an integrative solution when both sets of concerns are too important to be compromised. • When your objective is to learn. • To merge insights from people with different perspectives. • To gain commitment by incorporating concerns into a consensus. • To work through feelings that have interfered with a relationship.

Compromising	• When goals are important, but not worth the effort or potential disruption of more assertive modes. • When opponents with equal power are committed to mutually exclusive goals. • To achieve temporary settlements to complex issues. • To arrive at expedient solutions under time pressure. • As a backup when collaboration or competition is unsuccessful.
Avoiding	• When an issue is trivial, or more important issues are pressing. • When you perceive no chance of satisfying your concerns. • When potential disruption outweighs the benefit of resolution. • To let people cool down and regain perspective. • When gathering information supersedes the need for an immediate decision. • When others can resolve the conflict more effectively. • When issues seem tangential or symptomatic of other issues.
Accommodating	• When you find you are wrong—to allow a better position to be heard, to learn, and to show your reasonableness. • When issues are more important to others than to yourself—to satisfy others and maintain cooperation. • To build social credits for later issues. • To minimize loss when you are outmatched and losing. • When harmony and stability are especially important. • To allow subordinates to develop by learning from mistakes.

Figure 9-5
(continued)

Intervention Type	Characteristics
Conflict Process Coaching	Direct intervention in a team to improve the quality of conflict the team is having. Examples include how resources are allocated to the team, changes in group structure, goal definition, team rewards and norms, and team membership.
Changing the Individuals	Training individuals to enhance their tolerance, emotional intelligence, and conflict-management skills.
Team (re)Design	Changes in things such as the amount of team member interdependence, goal definition, and team membership.
Task Process Coaching	Interventions to improve the quality of team conflict, including trust-building exercises, and of group processes such as the nominal group technique, devil's advocate, and brainstorming.

Figure 9-6
Conflict-Intervention Approaches

Source: Based on R. Wageman and A. Donnenfeld, "Intervening in Intra-Team Conflict." In K. M. Behfar and L. L. Thompson (eds.), *Conflict in Organizational Groups: New Directions in Theory and Practice*. Evanston, IL, Northwestern University Press, pp. 261–280.

Conflict-Intervention Approaches

Ruth Wageman and Ashley Donnenfeld have presented a useful typology of conflict-intervention approaches, shown in Figure 9-6.[34]

Negotiating Good Outcomes

Among the styles we've discussed, the competing style is a win-lose (distributive) approach while the collaborative style is a win-win (integrative) approach. Although a **distributive approach** to negotiation focuses on getting as much as possible from the other party (taking the biggest possible slice of the pie), an **integrative** approach seeks to get as big a total as possible (enlarging the pie).

In fact, most negotiations have elements of both approaches. That is, it is desirable to first find ways to move toward an integrative solution, and then to try to assure an adequate slice of the pie for oneself. As such, integrative and distributive approaches are not mutually exclusive. Parties to negotiation can use integrative approaches to enlarge the pie as well as distributive approaches to bargain for a good slice.

Managing Interteam Relations and Conflict

As illustrated in the "Teams in the News" feature, teams often need to work effectively with other teams as partners or collaborators. Relationships between teams are sometimes harmonious but are often conflict laden. For example, teams may have different goals, be competing for resources, or have incompatible working practices with their codependent teams.

TEAMS IN THE NEWS: Law Enforcement Agencies and the Boston Marathon Bombings

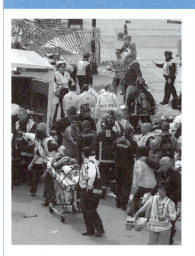

On April 15, 2013, at 2:50 p.m. Eastern Standard Time, two bombs exploded near the finish line of the Boston Marathon in a terrorist attack. Three people were killed and more than 170 others were injured.[1] In the aftermath of this disaster, law enforcement officials from the Boston division of the FBI and the Boston Police Department collaborated in the handling of the investigation and manhunt that led to one of the suspects being killed in a gunfight during a car chase and the other being wounded and apprehended later the next day. Boston Police Commissioner Edward F. Davis testified before the U.S. House of Representatives Homeland Security Committee, where he was subjected to intense questioning by lawmakers about perceived tensions between the FBI and the Boston Police Department in handling the case and a lack of information sharing between the two agencies that some felt could have resulted in potentially preventing the attack. After the hearing, Davis and Richard DesLauriers, the head of the Boston division of the FBI, issued a joint statement in which they emphasized that "our agencies have, and continue to have, a close, strong, and effective partnership."[2] This event provides an excellent example of how two law enforcement agencies needed to work together effectively in order to achieve a common objective.

Notes

1. See "An Overview of the Bombing at the Boston Marathon," April 16, 2003. http://www.abcactionnews.com/dpp/news/national/an-overview-of-the-bombing-at-the-boston-marathon.
2. A. Johnson. "FBI Head Richard DesLauriers Downplays Any Tension among Law Enforcement over Marathon Bombings." http://www.boston.com/metrodesk/2013/05/11/fbi-head-richard-deslauriers-downplays-any-tension-among-law-enforcement-over-marathon-bombings/IGRrkVeJfFwh2AraauKNUK/story.html.

While the majority of the discussion of managing teams focuses on how to create and manage an effective team as a distinct entity or system, it is also important for a team to understand how to "manage the boundary of a team."[35] The boundary refers to everything outside of a team yet inside the larger organization within which a team exists. This larger context comprises a variety of factors, including the strategy, structure, people, and processes of the organization as well as other teams that exist within that organization. It is the effective management of the relationships and interactions with these other teams that is referred to as interteam relations.

For example, suppose you are the chair of the events committee in a student organization in which you are a member. One of the ideas that you and your committee have come up with is to hold a networking event. For the event, you plan to invite business professionals and alumni from the local community where your university is located to come socialize and interact with your student members. All the members of your committee and the larger organization are enthusiastic about the event. However, as you proceed with planning for the event, you realize that your committee will need to work with the alumni and professional relations committees of your student organization to identify appropriate individuals to invite to the event. You will also need to work with the finance committee to develop a budget for the event that will use the organization's limited resources effectively.

Strategies for Enhancing Interteam Cooperation and Reducing Conflict

Team leaders must have the capacity to develop and to sustain effective relationships and partnerships with other teams. For instance, other teams in an organization may possess specific expertise or resources needed by the team to meet its objectives.

There are a number of strategies that leaders can use to manage interteam relations effectively and to prevent conflict between these teams.

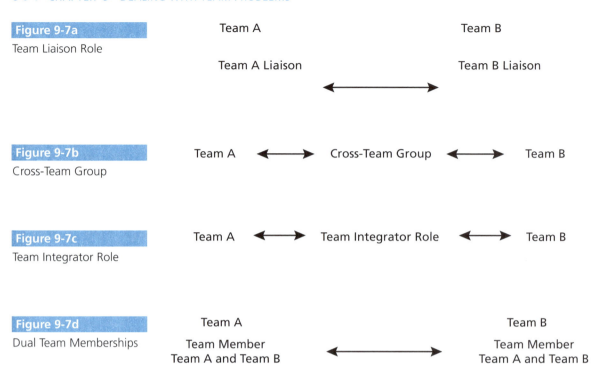

Figure 9-7a
Team Liaison Role

Figure 9-7b
Cross-Team Group

Figure 9-7c
Team Integrator Role

Figure 9-7d
Dual Team Memberships

These strategies involve the integration of various structures into a team's system.[36]

- **Team liaison roles.** This strategy involves having each team designate one member as the formal team liaison. The role of the liaison is to communicate with and to coordinate the team's planning and activities with the liaison from the other team(s). Figure 9-7a shows the basic structure of a team liaison role.

  Identifying and using team liaison roles help to ensure that teams keep each other in the loop and on the same page in terms of their respective processes.

- **Cross-team groups.** A **cross-team group** creates a separate formal group that is composed of multiple individuals from each team who work together to coordinate the activities of each team. Figure 9-7b shows the basic structure of a cross-team group.

  Cross-team groups can be effective when the nature of the task or project is highly complex and requires individuals from diverse backgrounds and expertise to represent the needs and interests of each team.

- **Team integrator roles**—A **team integrator role** involves the designation of one individual to facilitate the interaction and activities of two or more teams. This individual often is not a formal member of any of the teams involved, but rather is one who possesses strong team facilitation skills. Figure 9-7c shows the structure of the team integrator role.

  The team integrator must meet with each of the teams involved in the process and share information about the status and issues related to the other team's process. If there are disagreements, then the team integrator may negotiate or facilitate a joint meeting of the team leaders and/or members to resolve these issues.

- **Dual Team Memberships.** A dual membership structure gives membership on both teams to at least one member of each team. Figure 9-7d shows the structure of a dual membership.

    Dual team memberships can be effective in ensuring that there is at least one person on each team that possesses full knowledge and direct experience and involvement with the perspectives, issues, and activities of both teams involved in an overall project or initiative.

Turning around Failing Teams

Sometimes problems in teams are due to problem team members or to interpersonal conflict. In such cases, it may be possible to use corrective mechanisms such as those we've already discussed. In other cases, though, the team just seems to have come off the rails. Sometimes, things have just deteriorated. Here we consider three situations: when the problems are the result of apathy and lack of vigilance, when they are due to a crisis, and when they can be traced to deficiencies in team culture.

Reviving Zombie Teams

We said earlier in the chapter that teams sometimes become too comfortable with their situations and display apathy. They may become walking-dead **zombie teams** that fail to change as needed and begin to drag down other parts of the organization. As noted by Jake Breeden, "The last thing a successful leader wants is to be on a zombie team, aimlessly wandering around and snacking on the brains of more important resources."[37]

When teams become complacent, it is important to take steps to encourage them to challenge themselves, to scan new horizons, and to push themselves farther. For example, the team leader might use one of these strategies:

- **Challenge team members to discuss whether the team is on the right track and doing as well as it could.**
- **Use the devil's advocate, the nominal group technique, or other approaches to having the members question whether the team should be moving in new directions and, if so, what those directions might be.**
- **Employ stretch—difficult but not outrageous—goals to motivate team members to perform beyond their current levels.**
- **Tie rewards to improved performance.**

Team Crisis Management

Teams often face crises or are called on to help respond to crises.[38] Crises are defined as low-probability, high-impact events that are characterized by time pressure and ambiguity and have significant consequences. Researchers have described how even highly trained teams respond with varying degrees of effectiveness when dealing with crises such as cardiac arrest incidents and simulated neonatal resuscitation.[39]

Members of the NASA team worked together and used creative problem solving to guide Apollo 13 back to earth after an accident on the spacecraft in April 1970.

- **Develop contingency plans.** As discussed earlier, the book and movie *The Perfect Storm* describe a crisis situation in which a series of freakish weather conditions merged to create a perfect storm. Contingency planning identifies alternative courses of action that can be taken when unexpected events—perhaps even worst-case, perfect storms—occur. Contingency plans lay out potential courses of action and may reduce feelings of panic when crises occur.
- **Develop routines but emphasize flexibility of response.** Routines are important to deal with crises. For example, the Department of Homeland Security suggests that emergency response training should emphasize Incident Action Plans.[40] However, routines and plans can serve as chains if they are followed blindly. Alicia Stachowski, Seth Kaplan, and Mary Waller have studied how fourteen nuclear power plant control room crews responded to a simulated crisis.[41] They found that higher performing teams had routines but also had the flexibility to deviate from them as needed. Waller discusses insights into team crisis management and team mental models in this "Team Scholar" feature.

TEAM SCHOLAR

Dr. Mary J. Waller

Mary Waller is professor of organizational behavior in the Schulich School of Business at York University in Toronto, Canada. She earned her PhD from the University of Texas–Austin. Her research focuses on team dynamics during crisis situations and has appeared in the *Academy of Management Journal*, *Academy of Management Review*, *Journal of Applied Psychology*, and other academic outlets.

In this interview Professor Waller discusses her work on team crisis management.

What generated your interest in teams in crisis situations?

For the 10 years before I began doctoral-level studies, I worked in petroleum, aviation, and software development organizations. In each of these organizations, I witnessed remarkable team behaviors during very stressful, nonroutine, crisis situations. Team members' behaviors were so striking—in both good and bad ways—that these episodes made a lasting impression on me. As I learned more about research on group and team dynamics during graduate work at UT–Austin, I chose to focus my own research efforts on understanding more about team behaviors during crises.

You've done fascinating work on nuclear power plant control room crews in simulated crisis situations. What are some of your key findings?

My first study of control crews in nuclear power facilities, in 2004, focused on differences among crew behaviors and performance during routine and nonroutine situations. My coauthors and I found that these highly trained crews' behaviors did not differ significantly during routine situations; however, as the situation shifted to a crisis, higher performing crews engaged in more shared mental model development, shared more information, engaged in more face-to-face communication, and paid less attention to time as compared to the lower performing crews. So, although the teams were composed and trained similarly and behaved identically during routine situations, they behaved very differently in very specific ways when unexpected, critical events unfolded.

Given that these results concerning information sharing and shared mental model development mainly involved crew member interactions, my second study of nuclear power control crews, in 2009, focused more intently on the interaction patterns of high performing versus low performing crews. Using a pattern recognition algorithm, we found that high performing crews engaged in fewer interaction patterns than other crews; for those interactions that did fall into stable patterns, high performers' patterns were shorter and less complex than those of other crews. In other words, higher performing crews were not locked into standardized, procedural responses, but instead adaptively communicated when and where needed, and in very brief, straightforward interactions.

Some of your research has focused on shared mental models in teams. What are shared mental models? Why are they important in teams?

I have heard team members remark about playing off the same page countless times during my team observations; to me, these team members are referring to shared mental models. A mental model is a mental representation of knowledge, relationships, or systems; if a mental model is shared or similar among team members, individuals' efforts are more likely to contribute to the overall team goal. However, if a mental model is not shared among team members, individual efforts could work against each other, slowing team progress. Additionally, my 2013 coauthors and I found that in dynamic and changing situations, teams better at updating their shared mental models outperform other teams.

You've examined such time-related variables as deadlines, temporal entrainment, and team pacing behavior. What have you learned about the roles of time in teams?

Time is an incredible and sometimes invisible driver of team action. We see attention to time and time pressure motivating teams to make decisions and move forward in task progress. We also see powerful external pacers, such as the fiscal year or period review meetings, leading teams to pattern their behaviors over time in very predictable ways. And we know that teams with such patterns are susceptible to falling into routinized, habitualized behavior very easily—behavior that is very hard to change, even during crisis situations when it is obvious these old patterns will no longer be effective. So if you think of a team as a horse (and the organization as the carriage), time can be either the carrot or the stick—either way, a huge motivator and catalyst of action and task progress. However, time can also be the blinders, keeping teams stuck in habitualized routines and unable to adapt—and limiting effective team behavior in dynamic settings.

What do you see as some of the most important emerging issues regarding teams?

Some of the most important issues regarding teams have to do with emergent states. Emergent states are properties of teams that emerge over time as teams engage in various processes to do their work. For example, trust, cohesion, and a sense of efficacy among team members may emerge over time after individuals interact, work together, and receive performance feedback. We know that these emergent states are important factors in team effectiveness, but our understanding of both the trajectory of state emergence as well as state longevity once emerged is quite limited. Now that we know more about which emergent states have positive effects on team outcomes, we need more research regarding how to keep the states at optimum levels for sustained team effectiveness.

Sources: A. A. Stachowski, S. A. Kaplan, and M. J. Waller. "The Benefits of Flexible Team Interaction During Crises." *Journal of Applied Psychology*, 2009, *94*, 1536–1543; S. Uitdewilligen, M. J. Waller, and A. H. Pitariu. "Mental Model Updating and Team Adaptation. *Small Group Research*, 2013, *44*, 127–158; M. J. Waller, N. Gupta, and R. C. Giambatista. "Effects of Adaptive Behaviors and Shared Mental Models on Control Crew Performance." *Management Science*, 2004, *50*, 1534–1544.

To learn more about Professor Waller's research on teams, visit her website at http://teamwork.ssb.yorku.ca/Team_Dynamics_Research/Welcome.html/.

Team Culture Change

There is increasing recognition that culture of the organization or team may influence member satisfaction, performance, and other outcomes. In this context, culture refers to the values, symbols, stories, heroes, and rites that have special meaning for employees. While there is often a focus on organizational, or corporate, culture, there are in fact many subcultures operating in organizations. Different divisions, and different teams, may have unique subcultures.

Cultures serve many functions, including the following:[42]

- **Facilitate cooperation.** By providing shared values and assumptions, culture may enhance goodwill and mutual trust, encouraging cooperation on a team.
- **Enhance decision making.** Shared beliefs and values give team members a consistent set of basic assumptions and preferences. This may lead to a more efficient decision-making process since there are fewer disagreements about which premises should prevail.
- **Serve as a control mechanism.** Culture serves as a subtle control system, informally approving or prohibiting some patterns of behavior. This sort of control, called clan control (see Chapter 3), derives from culture and

relies on shared beliefs and values. These shared beliefs and values provide a map that members can rely on to choose appropriate courses of action.

- **Improve communication.** Culture reduces communication problems in teams in at least two ways. First, there is no need to communicate on matters for which shared assumptions already exist; such things go without saying. Second, shared assumptions provide guidelines and cues to help interpret messages that are received.
- **Increase commitment.** People feel committed to an organization when they identify with it and feel an emotional attachment to it. Strong cultures foster intense identification and feelings through beliefs and values that team members can share with others.
- **Provide shared interpretations of experience.** Organizational reality is socially constructed: what an individual sees is conditioned by what others sharing the same experience say they are seeing. Shared beliefs and values influence this process by providing organization members with shared perceptions of their experience.
- **Justify behavior.** Finally, culture helps organization members make sense of their behavior by providing justification for it. For example, it may be possible to justify expenditures on family-sensitive work practices on the basis of shared values relating to the value of people in the organization.

The team leader is a creator, shaper, guardian, and communicator of team and organizational culture. Team leaders play these roles through the behaviors they model, the things they expect and reward, the policies they set, and the cultural elements they employ. The following are some key elements of organizational culture.

- **Values are deep-seated, personal standards that influence our moral judgments, responses to others, and commitment to personal, team, and organizational goals.** A culture in which there is sharing and acceptance of core values is called a **strong culture.**
- **Symbols are things that stand for or suggest something else.** For example, symbolic team names containing metaphors such as "Olympians," "jugglers," "wolf pack," "explorers," and "jazz" may all reflect qualities team members are attempting to convey.
- **Narratives are written or spoken accounts used by members to make sense of their experiences and express their feelings and beliefs.** Narratives often focus on certain basis themes, such as whether the organization supports equality or inequality, security or insecurity, and control or lack of control.
- **Heroes are role models, people who behave in exemplary ways that others seek to emulate.** For instance, team members who spent weekends helping the team meet a deadline, who selflessly worked to support others in difficult times, or who provided many years of dedicated service may all be regarded as heroes.
- **Rites combine cultural forms into a public performance.** Rites can be important in signaling member transitions, celebrating accomplishments, or bringing team members together. Following are a few examples:

- **Rites of passage** mark important transitions. For example, employees who complete a rigorous off-site training program may be welcomed back with a speech, certificates, or party.
- **Rites of enhancement** celebrate accomplishments of members, enhancing their status. These rites provide public recognition of personal accomplishments and motivate others to similar efforts.
- **Rites of integration**—such as annual holiday parties or elaborate annual meetings—bring team members together by fostering shared feelings that bind and commit them to the team and organization.

- **Rituals** are relatively simple combinations of repetitive behaviors, often brief and carried out without much thought. For example, a special team handshake or hallway greeting may help cement team identity.

If the team leader chooses to attempt to change the team's culture, the change management steps outlined in Chapter 8 should be followed. For instance, successful change is fostered by using these approaches:

- *Logos*: convincing team members of the need for change through reason, logic, and data
- *Ethos*: encouraging change through the strength of your moral character and the trust others have in you
- *Pathos*: appealing to team members' emotional and psychological needs

In the case of major culture change, it is often possible to appeal to a burning platform—a clear and present danger if the situation does not change; additionally, it is important to emphasize key values and to use stories, symbols, heroes, and rites and ceremonies to facilitate and reinforce change. As with all change efforts, participation of team members in the change process is likely to be critical in ensuring acceptance of the change and motivation to enthusiastically implement the change and sell it to others.

TEAMS IN THE NEWS: Using Culture Change to Turn Around NCAA Teams

Coaches—especially of elite National Collegiate Athletic Association (NCAA) Division 1 teams—face tremendous pressure to lead their teams to success. Peter Schroeder interviewed ten Division 1 head coaches who had led previously unsuccessful teams to championship levels within 5 years. Interviews and other methods led Schroeder to conclude that such turnarounds featured changes in team culture. Coaches began the turnaround process by creating core sets of values specific to their teams. To reinforce those values coaches taught team members specific tactics, recruited athletes who would embrace the values, and then rewarded and punished athletes' actions on the basis of whether they were consistent with the values.

Source: This discussion is based on P. J. Schroeder, "Changing Team Culture: The Perspectives of Ten Successful Head Coaches," *Journal of Sport Behavior*, 2010, *33(1)*: pp. 63–88.

In this chapter we have addressed important topics in preventing, diagnosing, and alleviating or resolving team problems. In the next chapter we consider the important—and sometimes overlooked—issue of evaluating team effectiveness. We will discuss team dashboards, team process evaluation, PDCA and continuous improvement, and team action planning.

Summary and Integration

Here are the key takeaways for this chapter:

Problems may arise in teams for many reasons. Before trying to resolve problems, it is important to take the time and effort needed to properly define them.

Some team members create problems by freeloading, complaining, bullying, or acting as martyrs. Proper selection, training, evaluating, and rewarding may alleviate such problems, but the team leader will often have to take a strong role to resolve them.

Many perceptions and processes can cause serious, or even tragic, consequences for teams. It is important to take necessary action to understand, prevent, and/or ameliorate these potential dysfunctions.

Conflict is common both within and between teams. Although conflict may serve some useful functions, it often causes severe problems. It is important to understand the conflict process, team members' conflict styles, and when conflict styles are likely to be problematic. Proper management of interteam relations may require use of coordinating mechanisms.

Teams will sometimes fail to achieve their goals due to apathy, crises, or deficient cultures. These issues may require use of motivational techniques, crisis management tools, and culture change efforts.

Notes

1   M.C. Brown, "Administrative Succession and Organizational Performance: The Succession Effect," *Administrative Science Quarterly*, 1982, *27(1)*, pp. 1–16.
2   The term "self-fulfilling prophecy" was first coined by Robert Merton; see R.K. Merton, "The Self-Fulfilling Prophecy," *Antioch Review*, 1948, *8(2)*, pp. 193–210. See also D. Eden, "Self-Fulfilling Prophecy as a Management Tool: Harnessing Pygmalion," *Academy of Management Review*, 1984, *9(1)*, pp. 64–73; R. Rosenthal, "Critiquing Pygmalion: A 25-Year Perspective," *Current Directions in Psychological Science*, 2008, *4(6)*, pp. 171–172; and, V.V. Raman, "A Self-Fulfilling Prophecy: Linking Belief to Behavior," *Annals of the New York Academy of Sciences*, 2011, *1234(1)*, pp. 104–107.
3   For more on problem definition, see G.H. Wedberg, "But First, Understand the Problem," *Journal of Systems Management*, June 1990, pp. 20–28; S. Tomas, "Creative Problem-Solving: An Approach to Generating Ideas," *Hospital Materiel Management Quarterly*, May 1999, *20(4)*, pp. 33–45; and, T.L. Saaty & M.P. Niemira, "A Framework for Making a Better Decision," *Research Review*, 2006, *13(1)*, pp. 1–4.
4   For a good discussion of problem behaviors in teams, see D.S. Jalajas & R.I. Sutton, "Feuds in Student Groups: Coping with Whiners, Martyrs, Saboteurs, Bullies, and Deadbeats," *Journal of Management Education*, 1984, 9, pp. 94–102.

5 To learn more about social loafing, see M. Diehl, "Productivity Loss in Idea-Generating Groups: Tracking Down the Blocking Effect," *Journal of Personality and Social Psychology,* 1991, *61(3)*, pp. 392–403; S.J. Karau & K.D. Williams, "Social Loafing: A Meta-Analytic Review and Theoretical Integration," *Journal of Personality and Social Psychology,* 1993, *65(4)*, pp. 681–706; B. Latané, K. Williams, & S. Harkins, "Many Hands Make Light the Work," *Journal of Personality and Social Psychology,* 1979, *37(6)*, pp. 822–832; and, R. van Dick, P.A. Tissington, & G. Hertel, "Do Many Hands Make Light Work?: How to Overcome Social Loafing and Gain Motivation in Work Teams," *European Business Review*, 2009, *21(3)*, pp. 233–245.

6 These are based primarily on R. van Dick, P.A. Tissington, & G. Hertel, "Do Many Hands Make Light Work?: How to Overcome Social Loafing and Gain Motivation in Work Teams," *European Business Review*, 2009, *21(3)*, pp. 233–245. For more on ways to discourage social loafing, see C.J. Dommeyer, "Using the Diary Method to Deal with Social Loafers on the Group Project: Its Effects on Peer Evaluations, Group Behavior, and Attitudes," *Journal of Marketing Education,* 2007, *29(2),* pp. 175–188; and, C.J. Dommeyer, "A New Strategy for Dealing with Social Loafing on the Group Project: The Segment Manager Method," *Journal of Marketing Education*, 2012, *34(2)*, pp. 113–127.

7 S. Shellenbarger, "What to Do with a Workplace Whiner," *Wall Street Journal*, September 12, 2012, p. D1.

8 Ibid.

9 See R.L. Rapson, E. Hatfield, & J. Cacioppo, *Emotional Contagion* (Cambridge, UK: Cambridge University Press, 1993); and, S.G. Barsade & D.E. Gibson, "Group Affect: Its Influence on Individual and Group Outcomes," *Current Directions in Psychological Science*, 2012, *21(2)*, pp. 119–123.

10 Will Bowen, quoted in S. Shellenbarger, "What to Do with a Workplace Whiner," *Wall Street Journal*, September 12, 2012, p. D1.

11 S. Shellenbarger, "What to Do with a Workplace Whiner," *Wall Street Journal*, September 12, 2012, p. D1.

12 To learn more about bullying in teams, see E. Baillien, I. Neyens, & H. De Witte, "Organizational, Team Related and Job Related Risk Factors for Bullying, Violence and Sexual Harassment in the Workplace: A Qualitative Study," *International Journal of Organisational Behaviour*, 2008, *13(2)*, pp. 132–146; and, R.L. Dhar, "Why Do They Bully?: Bullying Behavior and Its Implication on the Bullied," *Journal of Workplace Behavioral Health*, 2012, *27(2)*, pp. 79–99.

13 For a discussion of the impact of team design features on team performance, see G.L. Stewart, "A Meta-Analytic Review of Relationships between Team Design Features and Team Performance," *Journal of Management*, 2006, *32(1)*, pp. 29–54; and, M.I.D. Piña, A.M.R. Martinez, & L.G. Martínez, "Teams in Organizations: A Review on Team Effectiveness," *Team Performance Management*, 2008, *14(1/2)*, pp. 7–21.

14 See L. Summers & B. Rosen, "Mavericks Ride Again," *Training and Development*, 1994, *48(5)*, pp. 119–123; and, T. Soika, "Addressing Problem Employees: Every Manager's Worst Headache," *Hearing Journal*, 2006, *59(2)*, pp. 31–32.

15 See W.F. Cascio, "Managing a Virtual Workplace," *Academy of Management Executive*, 2000, *14(3)*, pp. 81–90; and, P.A. Bamberger, I. Erev, M. Kimmel, & T. Oref-Chen, "Peer Assessment, Individual Performance, and Contribution to Group Processes: The Impact of Rater Anonymity," *Group & Organization Management*, 2005, *30(4)*, pp. 344–377.

16 To learn more about 360-degree feedback, see R. Lepsinger & A. Lucia, *The Art and Science of 360 Degree Feedback* (New York: John Wiley & Sons, 2009);

and, K. Nowack & S. Mashini, "Evidence-Based Answers to 15 Questions about Leveraging 360-Degree Feedback," *Consulting Psychology Journal: Practice and Research*, 2012, *64(3)*, pp. 157–182.

17 For a discussion of the "shadow of the future" see G. Dietz & D.N. Den Hartog, "Measuring Trust inside Organizations," *Personnel Review*, 2006, *35(5)*, pp. 557–588.

18 I.L. Janis, *Victims of Groupthink* (Boston: Houghton Mifflin, 1972), p. 9.

19 For discussions of evidence relating to groupthink, see R.J. Aldag & S.R. Fuller, "Beyond Fiasco: A Reappraisal of the Groupthink Phenomenon and a New Model of Group Decision Processes," *Psychological Bulletin*, 1993, *113(3)*, pp. 533–552; S.R. Fuller & R.J. Aldag, "Organizational Tonypandy: Lessons from a Quarter Century of the Groupthink Phenomenon," *Organizational Behavior and Human Decision Processes*, 1998, *73(2/3)*, pp. 163–184; and, P. 't Hart, E.K. Stern, & B. Sundelius, *Beyond Groupthink* (Ann Arbor, MI: University of Michigan Press, 1997).

20 I.L. Janis, *Crucial Decisions: Leadership in Policymaking and Crisis Management* (New York: Free Press: 1989), p. 60.

21 See, for example, J. Longley & D.G. Pruitt, "Groupthink: A Critique of Janis' Theory," in L. Wheeler (ed.), *Review of Personality and Social Psychology* (Newbury Park, CA: Sage, 1980), pp. 507–513; W. Park, "A Review of Research on Groupthink," *Journal of Behavioral Decision Making*, 3, pp. 229–245; and, R.J. Aldag & S.R. Fuller, "Beyond Fiasco: A Reappraisal of the Groupthink Phenomenon and a New Model of Group Decision Processes," *Psychological Bulletin*, 1993, *113(3)*, pp. 533–552.

22 For a more general model of group problem solving, termed the General Group Problem-Solving (GGPS) model, showing how the groupthink model is a simplified and deterministic model of group problem-solving processes, see S.R. Fuller & R.J. Aldag, "The GGPS Model: Broadening the Perspective on Group Problem Solving," in M. Turner (ed.), *Groups at Work: Advances in Theory and Research* (Lawrence Erlbaum Associates, 2001), pp. 3–24.

23 This model is based on L.R. Pondy, "Organizational Conflict: Concepts and Models," *Administrative Science Quarterly*, 1967, *12*, pp. 296–320. For a recent discussion of these issues, see K.J. Behfar, E.A. Mannix, R.S. Peterson, & W.M. Trochim, "Conflict in Small Groups: The Meaning and Consequences of Process Conflict," *Small Group Research*, 2011, *42*, pp. 127–176.

24 For a good discussion of conflict see C.K. De Dreu & L.R. Weingart, "Task versus Relationship Conflict, Team Performance, and Team Member Satisfaction: A Meta-Analysis," *Journal of Applied Psychology*, 2003, *88(4)*, pp. 741–749.

25 C. Bendarsky, K. Behfar, L. Weingart, G. Todorave, J. Bear, & K. Jehn, "Revisiting the Dimensions of Intra-Group Conflict: Theoretical and Psychometric Construct Refinement," paper presented at the 23rd Annual International Association of Conflict Management Conference, Boston, MA, June 24–27, 2010.

26 I.L. Janis & L. Mann, *Decision Making: A Psychological Analysis of Conflict, Choice, and Commitment* (New York: Free Press, 1977), p. 60.

27 For more on the need for vigilance in teams, see P.M. Fandt, "Encouraging Decision Vigilance through Increased Accountability," *Journal of Applied Business Research*, 2011, *9(3)*, pp. 129–135. For a discussion of the related issue of decision avoidance, see C.J. Anderson, "The Psychology of Doing Nothing: Forms of Decision Avoidance," *Psychological Bulletin*, 2003, *129(1)*, pp. 139–167.

28 See, for instance, K.M. Eisenhardt, J.L. Kahwajy, & L.J. Bourgeois III, "How Management Teams Can Have a Good Fight," *Harvard Business Review*, July/

August 1997, pp. 77–85; and, T.K. Capozzoli, "Conflict Resolution: A Key Ingredient in Successful Teams," *Supervision*, November 1999, pp. 14–16.

29   Various names have been used to describe these styles. As one example, one classification of styles is turtle (avoiding), shark (forcing), teddy bear (accommodating), fox (compromising), and owl (collaborating). See "Are You an Animal?" *Incentive*, September 1996, pp. 56–57.

30   The examples of actions associated with the various conflict styles are drawn from C.J. Riggs, "Dimensions of Organizational Conflict: A Functional Analysis of Communication Tactics," in R.N. Bostrom (ed.), *Communication Yearbook 7* (Beverly Hills, CA: Sage, 1983), pp. 517–531.

31   Use of these styles also appears to be related to personality, with preferred style varying depending on the degree to which the manager exhibits various combinations of the Big Five personality dimensions. See P.J. Moberg, "Linking Conflict Strategy to the Five-Factor Model: Theoretical and Empirical Foundations," *International Journal of Conflict Management*, 2001, *12(1)*, pp. 47–68.

32   For research linking collaborative style to job performance see, for instance, M.A. Rahim, D. Antonioni, & C. Psenicka, "A Structural Equations Model of Leader Power, Subordinates' Styles of Handling Conflict, and Job Performance," *International Journal of Conflict Management*, 2001, *12(3)*, pp. 191–211.

33   K.W. Thomas, "Toward Multidimensional Values in Teaching: The Example of Conflict Behaviors," *Academy of Management Review,* 1977, 2, p. 487.

34   R. Wageman & A. Donnenfeld, "Intervening in Intra-Team Conflict," in K.M. Behfar & L.L. Thompson (eds.), *Conflict in Organizational Groups: New Directions in Theory and Practice* (Evanston, IL: Northwestern University Press, 2007), pp. 261–280.

35   L.A. Hill, *Managing Your Team* (Boston: Harvard Business Publishing, 1995). The quote is from p. 366.

36   D.A. Nadler & M.L. Tushman, *Competing by Design* (New York: Oxford Press, 1997).

37   J. Breeden, *Tipping Sacred Cows: Kick the Bad Work Habits that Masquerade as Virtues* (New York: John Wiley & Sons, 2013), p. 67. See also H. Walk, "Beware the Zombie Team," http://www.linkedin.com/today/post/article/20121201221602–7298-beware-the-zombie-team. Walk discusses the zombie team in terms of teams that are so devoted to their current projects that they dwell on preserving and following up on those projects rather than considering new options.

38   See, for instance, C. Sapriel, "Effective Crisis Management: Tools and Best Practice for the New Millennium," *Journal of Communication Management*, 2003, *7(4)*, 348–355; and, A.A. Stachowski, S.A. Kaplan, & M.J. Waller, "The Benefits of Flexible Team Interaction during Crises," *Journal of Applied Psychology*, 2009, *94(6)*, pp. 1536–1543.

39   D. Carbine, N. Finer, E. Knodel, & W. Rich, "Video Recording as a Means of Evaluating Neonatal Resuscitation Performance," *Pediatrics*, 2000, 4, 654–659; and, F. Tschan, N.K. Semmer, D. Gautschi, P. Hunziker, M. Spychiger, & S.U. Marsch, "Leading to Recovery: Group Performance and Coordinative Activities in Medical Emergency Driven Groups," *Human Performance*, 19, 277–304.

40   U.S. Department of Homeland Security, *National Incident Management System [NIMS]: National Standard Curriculum Training Development Guidance, FY07.* https://www.dhs.gov/xlibrary/assets/foia/mgmt_directive_9500_national_incident_management_system_integration_center.pdf.

41   A.A. Stachowski, S.A. Kaplan, & M.J. Waller, "The Benefits of Flexible Team Interaction during Crises," *Journal of Applied Psychology*, 2009, *94(6)*, 1536–1543.

42   These functions are drawn primarily from V. Sathe, *Culture and Related Corporate Realities* (Homewood, IL: Richard D. Irwin, 1985), pp. 25–31; J. Martin &

C. Siehl, "Organizational Culture and Counterculture: An Uneasy Symbiosis," *Organizational Dynamics*, August 1983, pp. 52–64; and, J.C. Picken & G.G. Dess, "Out of (Strategic) Control," *Organizational Dynamics*, 1997, *26(1)*, pp. 35–48.

Bibliography

Aldag, R.J., & Fuller, S.R. "Beyond Fiasco: A Reappraisal of the Groupthink Phenomenon and a New Model of Group Decision Processes," *Psychological Bulletin*, 1993, *113(3)*, pp. 533–552.

"An Overview of the Bombing at the Boston Marathon." http://www.abcactionnews.com/dpp/news/national/an-overview-of-the-bombing-at-the-boston-marathon

Anderson, C.J. "The Psychology of Doing Nothing: Forms of Decision Avoidance," *Psychological Bulletin*, 2003, *129(1)*, pp. 139–167.

"Are You an Animal?" *Incentive*, September 1996, pp. 56–57.

Baillien, E., Neyens, I., & De Witte, H. "Organizational, Team Related and Job Related Risk Factors for Bullying, Violence and Sexual Harassment in the Workplace: A Qualitative Study," *International Journal of Organisational Behaviour*, 2008, *13(2)*, pp. 132–146.

Bamberger, P.A., Erev, I., Kimmel, M., & Oref-Chen, T. "Peer Assessment, Individual Performance, and Contribution to Group Processes: The Impact of Rater Anonymity," *Group & Organization Management*, 2005, *30(4)*, pp. 344–377.

Barsade, S.G., & Gibson, D.E. "Group Affect: Its Influence on Individual and Group Outcomes," *Current Directions in Psychological Science*, 2012, *21(2)*, pp. 119–123.

Behfar, K.J., Mannix, E.A., Peterson, R.S., & Trochim, W.M. "Conflict in Small Groups: The Meaning and Consequences of Process Conflict," *Small Group Research*, 2011, *42*, pp. 127–176.

Bendarsky, C., Behfar, K., Weingart, L., Todorave, G., Bear, J., & Jehn, K. "Revisiting the Dimensions of Intra-Group Conflict: Theoretical and Psychometric Construct Refinement." Paper presented at the 23rd Annual International Association of Conflict Management Conference, Boston, MA, June 24–27, 2010.

Breeden, J. *Tipping Sacred Cows: Kick the Bad Work Habits that Masquerade as Virtues* (New York: John Wiley & Sons, 2013).

Brown, M.C. "Administrative Succession and Organizational Performance: The Succession Effect," *Administrative Science Quarterly*, 1982, *27(1)*, pp. 1–16.

Capozzoli, T.K. "Conflict Resolution: A Key Ingredient in Successful Teams," *Supervision*, November 1999, pp. 14–16.

Carbine, D., Finer, N., Knodel, E., & Rich, W. "Video Recording as a Means of Evaluating Neonatal Resuscitation Performance," *Pediatrics*, 2000, *4*, 654–659.

Cascio, W.F. "Managing a Virtual Workplace," *Academy of Management Executive*, 2000, *14(3)*, pp. 81–90.

De Dreu, C.K., & Weingart, L.R, "Task versus Relationship Conflict, Team Performance, and Team Member Satisfaction: A Meta-Analysis," *Journal of Applied Psychology*, 2003, *88(4)*, pp. 741–749.

Dhar, R.L. "Why Do They Bully?: Bullying Behavior and Its Implication on the Bullied," *Journal of Workplace Behavioral Health*, 2012, *27(2)*, pp. 79–99.

Diehl, M. "Productivity Loss in Idea-Generating Groups: Tracking down the Blocking Effect," *Journal of Personality and Social Psychology*, 1991, *61(3)*, pp. 392–403.

Dietz, G., & Den Hartog, D.N. "Measuring Trust inside Organizations," *Personnel Review*, 2006, *35(5)*, pp. 557–588.

Dommeyer, C.J. "A New Strategy for Dealing with Social Loafing on the Group Project: The Segment Manager Method," *Journal of Marketing Education*, 2012, *34(2)*, pp. 113–127.

Dommeyer, C.J. "Using the Diary Method to Deal with Social Loafers on the Group Project: Its Effects on Peer Evaluations, Group Behavior, and Attitudes," *Journal of Marketing Education,* 2007, *29(2),* pp. 175–188.

Eden, D. "Self-Fulfilling Prophecy as a Management Tool: Harnessing Pygmalion," *Academy of Management Review,* 1984, *9(1),* pp. 64–73.

Eisenhardt, K.M., Kahwajy, J.L., & Bourgeois, L.J., III, "How Management Teams Can Have a Good Fight," *Harvard Business Review,* July/August 1997, pp. 77–85.

Fandt, P.M. "Encouraging Decision Vigilance through Increased Accountability," *Journal of Applied Business Research,* 2011, *9(3),* pp. 129–135.

Fuller, S.R., & Aldag, R.J. "The GGPS Model: Broadening the Perspective on Group Problem Solving." In M. Turner (ed.), *Groups at Work: Advances in Theory and Research* (Lawrence Erlbaum Associates 2001), pp. 3–24.

Fuller, S.R., & Aldag, R.J. "Organizational Tonypandy: Lessons from a Quarter Century of the Groupthink Phenomenon," *Organizational Behavior and Human Decision Processes,* 1998, *73(2/3),* pp. 163–184.

Hill, L.A. *Managing Your Team* (Boston: Harvard Business Publishing, 1995).

Jalajas, D.S., & Sutton, S.I. "Feuds in Student Groups: Coping with Whiners, Martyrs, Saboteurs, Bullies, and Deadbeats," *Journal of Management Education,* 1984, *9,* pp. 94–102.

Janis, I. L. *Victims of Groupthink* (Boston: Houghton Mifflin, 1972).

Janis, I.L. *Crucial Decisions: Leadership in Policymaking and Crisis Management* (New York: Free Press: 1989).

Janis, I.L., & Mann, L. *Decision Making: A Psychological Analysis of Conflict, Choice, and Commitment* (New York: Free Press, 1977).

Johnson, A. "FBI Head Richard DesLauriers Downplays Any Tension among Law Enforcement over Marathon Bombings." http://www.boston.com/metrodesk/2013/05/11/fbi-head-richard-deslauriers-downplays-any-tension-among-law-enforcement-over-marathon-bombings/IGRrkVeJfFwh2AraauKNUK/story.html

Karau, S.J., & Williams, K.D. "Social Loafing: A Meta-Analytic Review and Theoretical Integration," *Journal of Personality and Social Psychology,* 1993, *65(4),* pp. 681–706.

Krasikova, D.V., Green, S.G., & LeBreton, J.M. "Destructive Leadership: A Theoretical Review, Integration, and Future Research Agenda," *Journal of Management,* 2013, *39(5),* pp. 1308–1338.

Latané, B., Williams, K., & Harkins, S. "Many Hands Make Light the Work," *Journal of Personality and Social Psychology,* 1979, *37(6),* pp. 822–832.

Lepsinger, R., & Lucia, A. *The Art and Science of 360 Degree Feedback* (New York: John Wiley & Sons, 2009).

Longley, J. & Pruitt, D.G. "Groupthink: A Critique of Janis' Theory." In L. Wheeler (ed.), *Review of Personality and Social Psychology* (Newbury Park, CA: Sage, 1980), pp. 507–513.

Martin, J., & Siehl, C. "Organizational Culture and Counterculture: An Uneasy Symbiosis," *Organizational Dynamics,* August 1983, pp. 52–64.

Merton, R.K. "The Self-Fulfilling Prophecy," *Antioch Review,* 1948, *8(2),* pp. 193–210.

Moberg, P.J. "Linking Conflict Strategy to the Five-Factor Model: Theoretical and Empirical Foundations," *International Journal of Conflict Management,* 2001, *12(1),* pp. 47–68.

Nadler, D.A., & Tushman, M.L. *Competing by Design* (Oxford Press: New York, 1997).

Nowack, K., & Mashini, S. "Evidence-Based Answers to 15 Questions about Leveraging 360-Degree Feedback," *Consulting Psychology Journal: Practice and Research,* 2012, *64(3),* pp. 157–182.

Park, W. "A Review of Research on Groupthink," *Journal of Behavioral Decision Making,* 1990, *3,* 229–245.

Picken, J.C., & Dess, G.G. "Out of (Strategic) Control," *Organizational Dynamics*, 1997, *26(1)*, pp. 35–48.

Piña, M.I.D., Martinez, A.M.R., & Martínez, L.G. "Teams in Organizations: A Review on Team Effectiveness," *Team Performance Management*, 2008, *14(1/2)*, pp. 7–21.

Pondy, L.R. "Organizational Conflict: Concepts and Models," *Administrative Science Quarterly*, 1967, *12*, pp. 296–320.

Rahim, M.A., Antonioni, D., & Psenicka, C. "A Structural Equations Model of Leader Power, Subordinates' Styles of Handling Conflict, and Job Performance," *International Journal of Conflict Management*, 2001, *12(3)*, pp. 191–211.

Raman, V.V. "A Self-Fulfilling Prophecy: Linking Belief to Behavior," *Annals of the New York Academy of Sciences*, 2011, *1234(1)*, pp. 104–107.

Rapson, R.L., Hatfield, E., & Cacioppo, J. *Emotional Contagion* (Cambridge, UK: Cambridge University Press, 1993).

Riggs, C.J. "Dimensions of Organizational Conflict: A Functional Analysis of Communication Tactics." In R.N. Bostrom (ed.), *Communication Yearbook 7* (Beverly Hills, CA: Sage, 1983), pp. 517–531.

Rosenthal, R. "Critiquing Pygmalion: A 25-Year Perspective," *Current Directions in Psychological Science*, 2008, *4(6)*, pp. 171–172.

Saaty, T.L., & Niemira, M.P. "A Framework for Making a Better Decision," *Research Review*, 2006, *13(1)*, pp. 1–4.

Sapriel, C. "Effective Crisis Management: Tools and Best Practice for the New Millennium," *Journal of Communication Management*, 2003, *7(4)*, 348–355.

Sathe, V. *Culture and Related Corporate Realities* (Homewood, IL: Richard D. Irwin, 1985).

Schroeder, P.J. "Changing Team Culture: The Perspectives of Ten Successful Head Coaches," *Journal of Sport Behavior*, 2010, *33(1)*: pp. 63–88.

Shellenbarger, S. "What To Do With a Workplace Whiner," *Wall Street Journal*, September 12, 2012, p. D1.

Soika, T. "Addressing Problem Employees: Every Manager's Worst Headache," *Hearing Journal*, 2006, *59(2)*, pp. 31–32.

Stachowski, A.A., Kaplan, S.A., & Waller, M.J. "The Benefits of Flexible Team Interaction during Crises," *Journal of Applied Psychology*, 2009, *94(6)*, 1536–1543.

Stewart, G.L. "A Meta-Analytic Review of Relationships between Team Design Features and Team Performance," *Journal of Management*, 2006, *32(1)*, pp. 29–54.

Summers, L., & Rosen, B. "Mavericks Ride Again," *Training and Development*, 1994, *48(5)*, pp. 119–123.

't Hart, P., Stern, E.K., & Sundelius, B. *Beyond Groupthink* (Ann Arbor, MI: University of Michigan Press, 1997).

Thomas, K.W. "Toward Multidimensional Values in Teaching: The Example of Conflict Behaviors," *Academy of Management Review,* 1977, *2*, p. 484–490.

Tomas, S. "Creative Problem-Solving: An Approach to Generating Ideas," *Hospital Materiel Management Quarterly*, May 1999, *20(4)*, pp. 33–45.

Tschan, F., Semmer, N.K., Gautschi, D., Hunziker, P., Spychiger, M., & Marsch, S.U. "Leading to Recovery: Group Performance and Coordinative Activities in Medical Emergency Driven Groups," *Human Performance*, *19*, 277–304.

U.S. Department of Homeland Security. *National Incident Management System [NIMS]: National Standard Curriculum Training Development Guidance, FYO7.* https://www.dhs.gov/xlibrary/assets/foia/mgmt_directive_9500_national_incident_management_system_integration_center.pdf

van Dick, R., Tissington, P.A., & Hertel, G. "Do Many Hands Make Light Work?: How to Overcome Social Loafing and Gain Motivation in Work Teams," *European Business Review*, 2009, *21(3)*, pp. 233–245.

Wageman, R., & Donnenfeld, A. "Intervening in Intra-Team Conflict." In K.M. Behfar & L.L. Thompson (eds.), *Conflict in Organizational Groups: New Directions in Theory and Practice* (Evanston, IL: Northwestern University Press, 2007), pp. 261–280.

Walk, H. "Beware the Zombie Team." http://www.linkedin.com/today/post/article/20121201221602–7298-beware-the-zombie-team

Wedberg, G.H. "But First, Understand the Problem," *Journal of Systems Management*, June 1990, pp. 20–28.

CHAPTER 10

Teams
Evaluating Team Effectiveness

Learning Objectives

After reading this chapter, you should be able to do the following:

1. Identify and describe the various methods for evaluating team effectiveness.
2. Identify and discuss best practices for conducting an evaluation of team effectiveness.
3. Apply tools such as tree diagrams and accountability documents for linking team evaluation results to action plans for enhancing team effectiveness and performance.

IN THIS CHAPTER, WE FOCUS ON EVALUATING THE TEAM component of the High Performance Teams Model (see Chapter 1) and how to enhance team effectiveness. Evaluation is a critical aspect of team management, and this chapter provides tools, methods, and strategies for driving ongoing improvements in a team's effectiveness and performance in the short and long term. The content from Chapter 2 on designing a team system is relevant to the material in this chapter since a team charter, Gantt chart, and dashboard provide the foundation for developing an effective system for evaluating a team's effectiveness and performance.

Overview of Evaluating Team Effectiveness

Reflect on your past and current experiences such as working on various teams in school, internships, and jobs. Certainly, you have had some positive experiences working in teams, but in at least some cases you may have worked on a team that did not function effectively or perform well. This could have been due to any combination of classic problems working on and leading teams, including social loafing

> ### TEAM WORDS OF WISDOM
>
> "I think it's very important to have a feedback loop, where you're constantly thinking about what you've done and how you could be doing it better."
>
> ~
>
> ELON MUSK, CEO, TESLA MOTORS

Figure 10-1

Cycle of Dysfunctional Teams

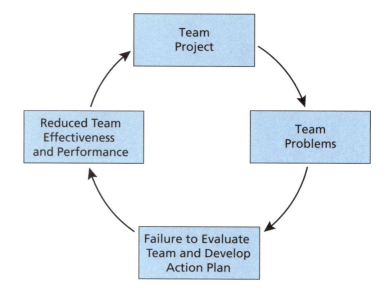

among some team members, personality clashes, lack of member engagement in the team process, lack of member commitment to the objectives of the team, and lack of clearly defined roles and decision-making processes.

It is frustrating that negative experiences tend to occur again and again across different teams and in working with different people. How can we break this dysfunctional cycle? Figure 10-1 displays a basic process model showing what typically occurs as part of this problem. In the first stage, a team launches a project and begins to engage in its various tasks and activities. In the second stage, the team starts to experience various problems with its functioning that the team and team leaders may or may not make any attempts to address. The critical part of this process is what does not occur in most teams: a systematic and in-depth evaluation of the team that identifies what it is doing well, its opportunities for improvement, and its need to develop an action plan for enhancing team effectiveness and performance moving forward. This gap in the basic team process continues to reduce the effectiveness and performance of the team as the root causes of the team's problems have not been addressed. It is this **cycle of dysfunctional teams** that we often experience over and over, despite the fact that we move on to other teams and work with other people.

One of the best options for addressing the fundamental problem of dysfunctional and/or underperforming teams is a rigorous process of ongoing team learning and evaluation that becomes institutionalized into a team's process for getting things done and for achieving results.

In this chapter we examine the issue of evaluating the effectiveness of a team in order to enhance its functioning and performance in terms of methods, tools, and strategies that you can use as a leader or team member to build great teams in the future.

Skills Practice 10.1 on the text website involves conducting some research on the Internet to find an example of a team's process for evaluating its performance and how it is implemented.

General Objectives of Traditional Performance Evaluations

Key objectives of a performance evaluation generally include the following:[1]

- **To enable a leader to communicate challenging yet realistic goals to direct reports**[2] (see the discussion of goal-setting theory in Chapter 4)
- **To increase productivity by providing timely feedback to direct reports**
- **To help an organization make decisions about the pay, promotions, and professional development of direct reports**

They don't actually assess employee performance	They are not based on effectiveness metrics	Each year's evaluation stands alone
The feedback provided is too infrequent	Managers are not held accountable for doing them	Assessments are kept a secret
Assessments are not based on data	They are disconnected from rewards	No second review is conducted
Cross-comparisons of employees are not conducted	There are no goals for the process	All performance criteria are weighted equally
Managers are not trained to do them	Inconsistency among managers	Managers are unwilling to give negative feedback
Managers don't know the employee well enough	Employees do not evaluate themselves	Communication and feedback are just one way

Figure 10-2

Common Problems with Traditional Performance Evaluation Methods

Challenges When Conducting Traditional Performance Evaluations[3]

Although there are many benefits associated with conducting traditional employee performance appraisals, there are many challenges inherent in designing and implementing an effective appraisal process. Figure 10-2 lists some common problems with performance appraisals. Performance appraisals do present problems and challenges; however, they are highly beneficial in achieving the objectives listed earlier as long as they are designed and implemented effectively. These issues will still be relevant as we turn our focus to performance evaluations for teams.[4]

Overview of Team-Based Performance Evaluation Systems

The evaluation of team effectiveness and performance shares many similarities with traditional employee performance evaluation approaches.

Potential Benefits

Potential benefits of team evaluation systems include the following:[5]

- **Team members know each other's performance better than managers and supervisors and therefore evaluate each other more accurately.**

> **TEAM WORDS OF WISDOM**
>
> "You've got to be rigorous in your appraisal system. The biggest cowards are managers who don't let people know where they stand."
>
> JACK WELCH, FORMER CEO, GENERAL ELECTRIC

- Peer pressure is a powerful motivator for team members.
- The team solicits and reviews numerous opinions within and outside the team and does not depend on one person's opinion.
- Team members see each other's work on a regular basis, improving the accuracy of their observations. This enhances the face validity of the feedback.
- Team evaluation supports the development of assessment skills among team members who are the evaluators.
- Since members recognize that team members will be evaluating their work, they often show increased commitment and productivity.
- Team members become more aware of performance standards and behavior requirements because they are accountable for maintaining them.

To secure these benefits, employers must now deal with generational challenges relating to the value of an effective performance appraisal process. Given the entrance of the Millennial Generation—those born between 1981 and 1999—into the workforce, employers and managers will increasingly need to develop effective strategies to engage them. This includes offering meaningful opportunities for collaboration and effective mechanisms for providing performance feedback on a regular basis.[6]

Potential Drawbacks

Potential drawbacks associated with conducting team performance evaluations include these:[7]

- **They are time consuming.** As a result, some managers and team members may resist participating in the process if they feel it is a waste of their time or that the amount of effort required does not justify the benefit.
- **It can be difficult to distinguish between the contributions of the team and those of individual members** since tasks are often interdependent and integrated with one another.
- **Some team members do not feel comfortable evaluating other team members.** Many workers have been conditioned to view the performance evaluation process in a more traditional sense, where managers evaluate team members individually without feedback from others.[8]
- **Extensive training is required for team members to develop the knowledge and skills required to provide feedback effectively.**

A key practical takeaway is that developing and implementing an effective team performance evaluation system requires substantial time and resources to design the system, achieve buy-in from team leaders and members about the benefits of evaluating team performance, and support the system with effective coaching and training.

Team Performance Evaluation Systems

Although various methods can be used to evaluate team performance, the methods typically involve collecting, analyzing, and acting on feedback from one or more stakeholders (those who are impacted by the work of a team or team member or have a vested interest in a team's activities) or customers (those who are end-users or consumers of what a team or team

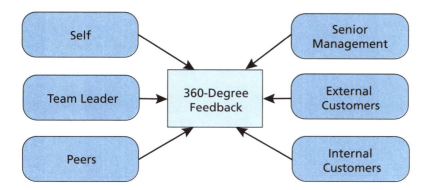

Figure 10-3

Sources of Feedback for
Team Evaluations

member does). Figure 10-3 presents a model that identifies the potential
sources of feedback used by teams to evaluate their performance. When
all or most of the sources of feedback are used, the process is oftentimes
referred to as a **360-degree feedback process** that can be used for team evaluations and leadership development.

General Characteristics of Effective Team Performance Evaluation Systems

In order to design and implement an effective team performance evaluation
system, it is important that the system possess the following characteristics:

- **Trust and respect between management and teams.** If trust and respect
  are missing, it will be difficult to obtain valid and useful feedback to
  enable teams to enhance their effectiveness. Team members may be more
  concerned with shielding themselves from managers who may take
  retaliatory action against them if their performance or other actions are
  viewed in a negative light by management.
- **Agreement about goals, procedures, and timing of the team evaluation
  process.** To ensure efficiency in implementation of the process, there must
  be a formal and systematic process defined for all parties involved.
- **Clear and well-defined performance objectives for the team and team
  members.**
- **Open and active exchange of information.** Open and honest discussion of
  issues, both positive and negative, will result in a clear understanding of
  the functioning of a team and how to enhance its effectiveness.
- **Respect between peers on a team.** Team members must respect and trust
  one another in order to gain buy-in for the team evaluation process.

In addition, an effective team performance evaluation system must be
based on clearly and explicitly defined performance criteria that are appropriate for the team, given its objectives and organizational context. One
good example of a set of performance criteria for teams comes from the
TEaM (Teamwork Excellence Modified) Model developed by Pavel Castka,
Christopher Bamber, and John Sharp, shown in Figure 10-4.[9]

T.J.B. Kline and J.-L. McGrath offer another set of criteria, shown in
Figure 10-5, for evaluating team performance.[10]

Figure 10-4

Key Areas and Critical Factors from the TEaM Model

Criterion	Examples of Key Factors
Leadership	• Leaders develop the teamwork culture in the organization. • Leaders are involved with team leaders and team members.
Policy and Strategy	• Policy and strategy are reviewed and updated. • Policy and strategy are implemented.
People and Teams	• People resources are planned, managed, and improved. • People are rewarded, recognized, and cared for according to their individual and team results.
Partnerships and Resources	• Partnerships among different teams are managed. • Information and knowledge are managed.
Team Factors	• Organizational impact. • Defined focus.
Team Processes	• Processes are systematically designed and managed. • Customer relationships are managed and enhanced.
People and Team Results	• Perceptual measures. • Performance indicators.
Customer Results	• Perceptual measures. • Performance indicators.
Society Results	• Perceptual measures. • Performance indicators.
Key Performance Results	• Key performance outcomes. • Key performance indicators.

Figure 10-5

Kline and McGrath Team Performance Criteria

Team Performance Criterion	Definition
Problem Solving	How well the team determines its goals and objectives and the alignment of the team's objectives with the organization's goals.
Quality of Work	The care that has gone into a team's work, the number of errors committed, satisfaction of the customer.
Workload Allocation	The degree of equitable distribution of the team's workload, the effective use of each team member's skill set.
Meeting Objectives	How well a team is able to meet its goals and objectives.
Team Attitude	The degree to which a team cooperates effectively, shares information, and is committed to team goals.

Source: Adapted from T.J.B. Kline and J.-L. McGrath, "Development and Validation of Five Criteria for Evaluating Team Performance." *Organizational Development Journal*, 1998, *16(3)*, pp. 9–28.

The practical takeaway from these examples is the need to develop a set of formal performance criteria that is appropriate for a given team in its unique context. However, this framework should not replace the need for a careful analysis of the tasks, processes, and outcomes for each team, involving team leaders, team members, and others such as internal and external customers and stakeholders.

Skills Practice 10.2 on the text website focuses on conducting an interview with a team leader and one or more team members regarding their views on team performance evaluation. This provides a useful comparative perspective on the team evaluation process.

TEAMS IN THE NEWS: "Microsoft Abandons 'Stack Ranking'"

The nature and uses of performance appraisal can have powerful effects on team cohesiveness and functioning. As an example, Microsoft announced in late 2013 that it was dumping its controversial "stack ranking" employee-review and compensation system. *Stack ranking*, sometimes derided as "rank and yank," requires managers to grade their employees and rank them against one another. It is used by about 30% of *Fortune 500* companies. Popularized by former GE CEO Jack Welch, stack ranking forces some team members to be designated as underperformers, and perhaps to be denied bonuses and promotions or even terminated. Critics say this fosters unhealthy competition in teams and erodes teamwork.

Following Microsoft's announcement and a flood of criticisms of stack ranking, Welch defended the approach, calling it "differentiation" and saying "now, one of the most common criticisms of differentiation is that it destroys teamwork. Nonsense. If you want teamwork, you identify it as a value. Then you evaluate and reward people accordingly. You'll get teamwork. I guarantee it."

Still, many firms are abandoning such performance appraisal systems, often turning instead to peer-evaluation systems.

Sources: S. Ovide & R. Feintzeig, "Microsoft Abandons 'Stack Ranking' of Employees," *Wall Street Journal*, November 12, 2013. http://online.wsj.com/news/articles/SB10001424052702303460004579193951987616572; J. Welch, "'Rank and Yank'? That's Not How It's Done," *Wall Street Journal*, November 14, 2013. http://online.wsj.com/news/articles/SB10001424052702303789604579198281053673534; R. A. Silverman & L. Kwoh, "Peer Performance Reviews Take Off," *Wall Street Journal*. http://online.wsj.com/news/articles/SB10000872396390444130304577561170001371712.

Common Mistakes When Using 360-Degree Feedback

Given the complexity of using 360-degree feedback for evaluating components of a team system, there are a variety of mistakes that are made in the design and/or implementation of such a feedback process. Being aware of these pitfalls can help management make more effective decisions about the system. Specifically, the most common mistakes made in relation to using a 360-degree feedback process are shown in Figure 10-6.

Within a team evaluation context, Figure 10-7 shows the typical types of feedback obtained for various elements of a team system. The logic of

Figure 10-6

Common Mistakes Associated with 360-Degree Feedback Systems

• Having no clear purpose	• Having insufficient communication to teams about the system	• Not clarifying who owns the feedback
• Using the process as a substitute for managing a team member	• Compromising confidentiality of feedback from raters	• Unfriendly administration and scoring of feedback for teams
• Not conducting a pilot test of the system	• Not clarifying the use of the feedback for teams	• Linking the system to other systems without a pilot test
• Not involving key stakeholders in the design of the system	• Not giving teams sufficient resources to make the process work	• Making it an event rather than a process
• Not evaluating effectiveness		

Figure 10-7

Typical Sources of Feedback for Elements of Team Systems

Feedback Source	Team Members	Team Leaders	Overall Team
Self	X	X	X
Immediate Supervisor	X	X	X
Peers	X	X	X
Direct Reports		X	X
Top Management		X	X
Customers (Internal and External)	X	X	X

360-degree feedback is that feedback from multiple sources provides the most comprehensive and valid understanding of the performance of team members, team leaders, and the overall team.

Put into a broader system, a 360-degree feedback approach for conducting a team evaluation is shown in Figure 10-8.

This process model must begin with management making fundamental decisions about appropriate performance measures and targets for teams. These decisions should be guided by an understanding of the organization's mission, vision, and strategic objectives. This understanding should serve as the basis for development of objectives that management hopes to achieve through the use of team 360-degree feedback. Next, decisions must be made about the structure of the feedback process in terms of which sources of feedback will be collected for team members, team leaders, and the overall team itself. While it may be tempting to include all relevant feedback sources in the process, be cautious because management often greatly underestimates the amount of time and resources that will be required to successfully implement a 360-degree feedback process. Sample self-evaluation questions are shown in Figure 10-9.

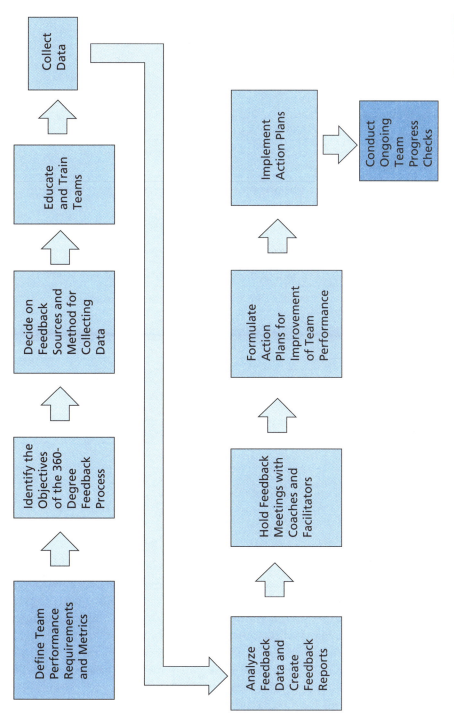

Figure 10-8

360-Degree Process
for Evaluating Team
Performance

Collect
Data

Educate
and Train
Teams

Decide on
Feedback
Sources and
Method for
Collecting
Data

Identify the
Objectives
of the 360-
Degree
Feedback
Process

Define Team
Performance
Requirements
and Metrics

Implement
Action Plans

Conduct
Ongoing
Team
Progress
Checks

Formulate
Action
Plans for
Improvement
of Team
Performance

Hold Feedback
Meetings with
Coaches and
Facilitators

Analyze
Feedback
Data and
Create
Feedback
Reports

Figure 10-9

Sample Self-Evaluation
Questions for Team
Evaluations

Evaluation Focus	Question
Team Member	I avoid blaming others for group problems.
Team Member	When team members contribute good ideas, I express my appreciation.
Team Member	I encourage the use of effective problem-solving and decision-making procedures.
Team Member	I act and encourage others to act in the best interests of the team.
Team Member	I encourage the use of effective conflict management strategies.
Team Leader	I come to early team meetings with a clear, written agenda.
Team Leader	I am motivated to act as the leader of the team.
Team Leader	I encourage the expression of different opinions on the team.
Team Leader	I set high performance standards for the team.
Team Leader	I review quality expectations with the team early and often.
Overall Team	Members of the team are clear about their roles.
Overall Team	The team implements its solutions and decisions.
Overall Team	Subgroups on the team are accepted and integrated in the team as a whole.
Overall Team	The team is highly cohesive and cooperative.
Overall Team	Team norms encourage innovative solutions to problems.

Source: Adapted from S. A. Wheelan. *Creating Effective Teams*. Thousand Oaks, CA: Sage, 1999.

In addition, Figure 10-10 shows a summary table indicating which raters should be used for different team members (such as managers and customers), the type of ratings that should be obtained (such as outcomes, behavior, competency), and how those rating should be used (such as development, evaluation, self-regulation) for different types of teams (e.g., project teams, service teams). While this table should not be used to make decisions without consideration of the particular team and context in question, it is still a valuable guide in the design of a team evaluation system.

Sample questions for direct report evaluations of their team leaders, peer evaluations, and customer evaluations are shown in Figure 10-11.[11]

Once the feedback questions and sources have been finalized, the questions are usually incorporated into an electronic survey, using tools such as SurveyMonkey (www.surveymonkey.com) and Qualtrics (www.qualtrics.com) that can be e-mailed directly to the feedback sources. E-surveys have become a very popular method for administering surveys due to their ease of development and administration relative to traditional paper-and-pencil methods.

Performance Appraisal Methods for Different Types of Teams

Team Type	Who is Being Rated	Who Provides Rating	What is Rated?			How Is the Rating Used?		
			Outcome	Behavior	Competency	Development	Evaluation	Self-Regulation
Work or Service Team	Team Member	Manager	✓	✓	✓	✓	✓	
		Other Team Members		✓	✓	✓		
		Customers		✓		✓		
		Self	✓	✓	✓	✓		✓
	Entire Team	Manager	✓	✓	✓	✓	✓	
		Other Teams		✓		✓		
		Customers	✓	✓		✓		
		Self	✓	✓	✓	✓		✓
Project Team	Team Member	Manager	✓		✓	✓	✓	
		Project Leaders		✓	✓	✓		
		Other Team Members		✓	✓	✓		
		Customers		✓	✓			
		Self	✓	✓	✓	✓		
	Entire Team	Customers	✓	✓			✓	
		Self	✓	✓	✓	✓		✓

Figure 10-10

Summary of Suggested Team Feedback Systems for Different Types of Teams

Figure 10-10
(continued)

Performance Appraisal Methods for Different Types of Teams

Team Type	Who is Being Rated	Who Provides Rating	What is Rated?			How Is the Rating Used?		
			Outcome	Behavior	Competency	Development	Evaluation	Self-Regulation
Network Team	Team Member	Manager		✓	✓	✓	✓	
		Team Leaders		✓	✓	✓		
		Coworkers		✓	✓	✓		
		Other Team Members		✓	✓	✓		
		Customers		✓	✓	✓		
		Self	✓	✓	✓	✓		✓
	Entire Team	Customers	✓				✓	

Note: These questions would be answered based on a 4-point scale with 1 = Strongly Disagree to 4 = Strongly Agree.
Source: S. G. Scott and W. O. Einstein. "Strategic Performance Appraisal in Team-Based Organizations: One Size Does Not Fit All." *Academy of Management Executive,* 2001, *15(2),* pp. 107–116.

Evaluator	Object of Evalution	Question
Direct Report	Team Leaders	My team leader provides effective direction and structure in terms of assigning tasks to the team.
Direct Report	Team Leaders	My team leader is fair and consistent when making decisions regarding the team.
Direct Report	Team Leaders	My team leader articulates a clear vision to our team.
Direct Report	Team Leaders	My team leader explains decisions that he/she makes to the team.
Direct Report	Team Leaders	My team leader solicits input from all team members before making a final decision.
Peer	Team Members	My associate is responsive to the needs I have on our team.
Peer	Team Members	My associate treats me like a valued partner in the work that we accomplish together on our team.
Peer	Team Members	My associate is open to new ideas and approaches for improving our performance as a team.
Peer	Team Members	My associate demonstrates high levels of professionalism in his/her work activities on our team.
Peer	Team Members	My associate demonstrates a high level of commitment to the achievement of our team's objectives.
Customer	Team Members	The team member understands my requirements as a customer.
Customer	Team Members	The team member consistently meets my expectations in terms of the actual service he/she provides to me as a customer.
Customer	Team Members	The team member solicits my feedback regarding how he/she can better serve me as a customer on a regular basis.
Customer	Team Members	The team member is responsive to my service requests as a customer.
Customer	Team Members	The team member is willing to work with me as a partner if I have concerns about the service I am receiving from him/her.

Figure 10-11

Sample Questions for Direct Report Evaluations, Peer Evaluations, and Customer Evaluations of Teams

Note: These questions are typically answered on a 5-point scale with 1 = Strongly Disagree to 5 = Strongly Agree.
For a discussion of perceived fairness in performance appraisals, see Palaiologos, A., Panagiotis, P., & Panayotopoulou, L. (2011). Organizational justice and employee satisfaction in performance appraisal. *Journal of European Industrial Training, 35*(8), pp. 826–840.

Those asked to provide feedback about a team leader, team member, or the overall team should be told to be as frank as possible in order to make the feedback useful to the recipient. It should also be emphasized that all responses will be completely confidential and anonymous.

Figure 10-12

Sample Excerpt from a 360-Degree Feedback Report

Rating Scales	1	2	3	4	5
Frequency-Based	Never	Rarely	Sometimes	Frequently	Always
Comparison-Based	Well Below Average (1st – 14th percentile)	Below Average (15th – 39th percentile)	Average (40th – 59th percentile)	Above Average (60th – 85th percentile)	Well Above Average (86th – 99th percentile)
Ability-Based	Very Weak	Weak	Satisfactory	Strong	Very Strong

My Report: Team Leadership Performance Dimension

Team Leader Sub-Dimensions	Self-Ratings	Stakeholder (Team Members) Feedback Average	Scores: Self: ☐ Team: ▨				
			1	2	3	4	5
Articulating a Vision To what extent do you effectively formulate and communicate the team's vision to followers?	4.0	3.2					
Inspiring Followers To what extent do you take action to energize and motivate team members to realize your vision?	3.0	4.1					
Empowering Others To what extent do you give team members the autonomy to make decisions and to take actions to support the achievement of your vision?	4.0	2.7					
Building a Team To what extent do you take action to build a cohesive team that leverages the capabilities of all members?	4.0	3.2					

All organization members—not just team leaders and team members—must be educated about the new system's objectives and benefits. This requires more than just an e-mail announcement or memo. A town hall meeting or webinar meeting led by the CEO or president should be held to thoroughly communicate and educate about the new system to all team members and the organization as a whole. Team leaders and members should receive in-depth training on how to interpret feedback, facilitate discussion of feedback with others, and develop action plans for using the feedback to enhance team effectiveness in the future.

Using the 360-degree feedback process leads to the generation of a formal analysis and report that provides comparisons between different sources of feedback. Figure 10-12 shows an excerpt from a feedback summary report.[12]

The most valuable information in such a summary report (which can sometimes exceed fifty pages in length) is the comparisons between self-ratings and the ratings given by others (called *feedback scores*). In this case, the individual's self-ratings are consistently higher than the scores received from others. In other cases, you might find the opposite scenario in which a team leader or team member scored himself or herself consistently lower than did others. Whatever the outcome, the power of such a gap analysis is in carefully examining discrepancies in ratings. Doing so stimulates discussion, evaluation, and potential changes in future behavior.

After the feedback reports for team leaders, members, and/or the overall team have been generated, trained facilitators from either the firm's organizational development or human resources function, or external consultants, need to meet with all teams to process the feedback to facilitate interpretation of results and to ensure that the teams develop a balanced perspective on the results.

Guidelines for Effective Team Feedback Sessions

Some guidelines for conducting feedback sessions include the following:[13]

- **Set a mutually agreeable time to hold a discussion after all materials have been received.**
- **Warmly greet the team member.** This is important in order for the facilitator to establish rapport with the team member and to hopefully reduce his or her anxiety about the process.
- **Explain how the feedback session will proceed**; ask for suggestions from the team member. This is important to do so that the team member understands how the process will be conducted. Providing an explanation will also help to reduce uncertainty about the process.
- **Ask open-ended questions to encourage a two-way discussion.**
- **Be willing to listen to the team member's explanations.**
- **Use concrete examples of the member's performance to explain reasons for the team's rating.** This is important in order to enhance the validity of the performance feedback.
- **In areas needing improvement, discuss behavior that can be changed and the specific improvements desired.**
- **Stress specific improvement goals rather than focusing on past mistakes.** Maintaining a positive focus in general will enhance the receptivity of the team member to performance feedback.
- **Reach agreement on specific performance-improvement goals.** It is important that the team member understands and buys into specific performance improvement goals.
- **Summarize discussion points.**
- **Explain the next steps in the process.**
- **Schedule follow-up coaching sessions to review the team member's progress.**

After the feedback sessions with teams have been completed, facilitators and teams need to develop action plans for addressing the strengths and opportunities for improvement identified in the feedback summary reports. These action plans need to include specific action steps that team leaders and team members can implement in order to enhance their individual effectiveness as well as that of the overall team. A sample action plan is shown in Figure 10-13.

Figure 10-13

Sample Action Plan
Worksheet Based on
360-Degree Feedback
Process

Performance Development Plan

Team Leader/Member:

Team Name:

Date:

Performance Outcomes	Objectives	Action Steps	Progress Check Dates

When using this action-planning template, a team leader or team member would work with a facilitator to complete a basic plan of action for performance improvement in the next year. Performance Outcomes list the key strengths and opportunities for improvement based on the discussion of the feedback summary report. Objectives include specific, measurable targets that the individual would work to achieve. Action Steps document what the team leader or member will do to move toward achieving the performance objectives. Finally, Progress Check Dates identify the specific dates when the team leader or member plan to meet with a facilitator to assess progress toward achieving objectives and to make adjustments to the action plan as necessary.

Regular progress-check meetings should be held to support the improvement efforts for team leaders, members, and teams in general. This part of the process is often overlooked, and failure to hold progress-check meetings is a major contributor to process failure.

Skills Practice 10.3 on the text website focuses on working through the basic steps in the process for conducting an actual team performance evaluation.

Insights and Advice

Terri Petmezas, associate consultant, ZS Associates

TEAM MANAGEMENT COACH

Based on your work experiences, what types of methods or processes have been used to evaluate team performance of the teams you have been a part of in the past? Which ones do you feel have been the most effective? The least effective? Why? Can you give us an example of one experience that you feel is particularly noteworthy?

At ZS, we have an extraordinarily rigorous review process. At the end of every project, each person gets both upward and downward feedback (as applicable), and everyone writes a self-review as well. Those above you on the team collaborate on the review that is typically written by your direct superior. And you submit feedback for anyone above you with whom you feel you worked closely enough to have worthwhile feedback to give. The reviews are based on ZS's competency model that includes things such as professionalism, quality of work, analytic capabilities, and communication, among others (the competency model is extremely detailed, but it's proprietary). Then, at the end of the project, everyone has a one-on-one with his or her direct superior to discuss the review. There is a fine line between review-worthy feedback, and just-in-time [JIT] feedback. In the past, I have received some constructive feedback during the review meeting that would have been really helpful had it been given earlier. As a result, it wasn't effective feedback for the project. I could only take it as an FYI for the future. I now tell my teams to please provide me with JIT feedback so that I can course-correct in real time.

Based on your work experiences, what types of methods or processes have been used to link team performance evaluations to specific actions to enhance the effectiveness of teams? Can you give an example of a team that did this especially well?

Because of the nature of our company, our teams change more frequently than they stay the same, so there's an inherent challenge in enhancing the effectiveness of teams. It's hard to tell if your current team functions better than your last team because you've improved certain skills with the specific goal of improving the functionality of the team, or if it's just because different personalities jive better together so the team works better as a whole. I have been in both of those situations. One of the competencies we review is teamwork and people management. In this part of the review, you get upward and downward feedback (as applicable) about interpersonal skills, mentoring, coaching, teaching, and more. You'll get feedback specific to a project during the project review, but twice a year, your professional development manager [PDM] compiles all of your reviews and sits down to discuss your overall review. During this meeting, your PDM will provide coaching on areas where you can grow on a more macro level, will help identify trends or patterns, and will answer any questions you may have.

What advice would you give to students to help them to learn how to evaluate team performance in organizations and to link these evaluations to action plans for enhancing team performance?

Keep notes throughout the project. In the example I just gave, when it came time to write the review for the associate I didn't get along with very well, my first draft was extremely negative. The manager had to help me make it more realistic because all that stuck out in my mind were the bad things. Had I kept notes, I would have remembered a lot of positive aspects about this person's performance on the project as well. And as a result, my review wasn't as detailed as it could have been. I recommend jotting down weekly notes about yourself and about each team member: something specific that went well, something specific that didn't, and an action-oriented piece of feedback.

Also, have a detailed project kickoff to set expectations. During this kickoff, let the team know specific areas where you're working to improve so that they can help keep an eye out for opportunities for you or provide real-time feedback in those areas. Discuss expectations about project work, quality, and work styles (for instance, can someone come in early and leave early to be with family, does someone prefer to work later in the evening to overlap with India, does anyone have a standing weekly commitment he or she needs to make time for, are any vacations planned). Even ask about communication preferences: e-mail, chat program, text, phone call, or a walk into an office. Knowing and using these small details can help team members work more smoothly together.

Team Audit Support from the Organization and Top Management

In addition to conducting a full 360-degree evaluation of a team, it is also helpful to conduct a team audit of the relationship between the team and its organizational environment. Completing both types of review results in a more holistic and comprehensive evaluation of the team. Thomas Keen and Cheri Keen suggest that the following issues be addressed when conducting a team audit:[14]

- **Did management demonstrate an understanding of how the team worked?**
- **Did management determine the impact across the organization of the changes associated with the team?**
- **Did management spend sufficient time to ensure that the organization was ready for the transition to teams?**
- **Did management help to develop a team vision that provided a specific endpoint?**
- **Does the team possess an effective culture based on evidence of satisfying team experiences; organization-wide success stories about teams; and team spirit, confidence, and a can-do attitude?**

Methods for Linking Team Evaluation to Performance Improvement

You should now have a basic understanding of the 360-degree feedback process and how it can be implemented to develop and evaluate teams.[15] A final topic to be addressed is how to support the implementation or execution of the action plans that team leaders, members, or teams as a whole develop to enhance their effectiveness and performance. Two tools—the tree diagram and the accountability document—can help teams execute action plans.

Tree Diagrams

A **tree diagram** lays out a roadmap of actions that can be taken to support the achievement of specific goals.[16] Figure 10-14 presents a tree diagram for improving customer service in a grocery store.[17] The logical flow of the tree diagram moves from the left to the right, with the goal stated in the box at the

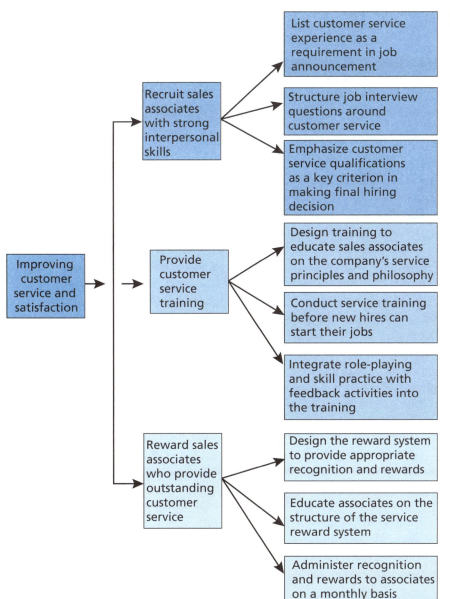

Figure 10-14

Sample Tree Diagram
Improving Customer
Service and Satisfaction at
a Retail Store

far left side of the diagram. After that, general action steps (e.g., reduce wait-ing) for improving customer service are listed. As you look farther to the right in the diagram, you see that each general action step has two to four additional specific action steps to support it. The value of a tree diagram is that it provides a roadmap of actions that will enable a team to achieve a desired objective.

Here are the steps for a team to follow to develop a tree diagram:

1. **State the desired goal of the team.** Write this in a box on the far left side of the diagram.
2. **Identify a set of general action steps that would help the team achieve the stated objective.** Write each of these general action steps in a box to the right of the goal box and draw lines connecting them.
3. **Now, list more specific action steps that the team could take to suc-cessfully implement each general action step.** Write each of these action steps in a box to the right of the general action steps and draw lines connecting them.

This process can continue, if desired, to drill down action steps to as much detail as is needed to enable the team to possess the clarity needed to be successful.

Skills Practice 10.4 on the text website illustrates the steps that need to be implemented to create a tree diagram that provides a visual representation of an action plan for achieving a targeted objective.

Accountability Documents

Although a tree diagram is useful to a team in developing a plan of action for achieving a desired objective, one issue that is still not addressed is who is accountable for implementing each of the action steps in the tree dia-gram. A tool that can be highly beneficial in ensuring the effective linkage between action plans and responsibilities is the **accountability document**. An accountability document is simply a summary table that lists the names of individuals who are responsible for the successful execution of each action step in a tree diagram.

Figure 10-15 is an example of a basic accountability document. The far left side of the document provides space to list action steps (again, these could be taken directly from the tree diagram). The figure also shows who is respon-sible for that action step, the resources needed to successfully implement the action step, evidence of actions taken and of impact, and a communication plan in relation to informing others about activities related to that action step.

Here are the steps for a team to follow to create an accountability document:

1. **List the action steps associated with the achievement of a desired team goal.**
2. **Decide who will be accountable for each action step.**
3. **Assess the resources team members will need to successfully implement their action steps.**
4. **Discuss the accountability document at team meetings on a regular basis.** Individuals who are accountable for each action step should provide brief progress reports to the rest of the team. The team leader should then document evidence of progress and impact associated with each team member's activities.

Accountability Document

Name of Team:

Project Name:

Project Objectives:

Strategy:

Action Steps	Person Responsible	Resources Needed	Timeline for Completion	Progress Made	Comments

Figure 10-15

Sample Accountability Document

TEAMS IN THE NEWS: Process Improvement Teams Add Value to Their Organizations

In Chapter 1, we introduced the International Team Excellence Award Program (ITEA) of the American Society for Quality. This program encourages teams from all types of organizations to demonstrate that they implement best practices for process improvement and for quality improvement teams. Participation in this program requires all teams to engage in an in-depth evaluation of their team structures and processes and how the team adds value to the success of their organizations. (Follow this link for a profile of the winning teams from the 2014 competition: http://asq.org/wcqi/team-award/case-studies-2014.aspx).

Source: American Society for Quality (ASQ). "The Global Impact of Quality," 2014 World Conference on Quality and Improvement, May 5–7, 2014. http://wcqi.asq.org/2013/team-competition/case-studies-2012.html.

Summary and Integration

Some key practical takeaways for team management from this chapter include the following:

To learn about and to enhance their effectiveness and performance, teams need a systematic process for obtaining feedback from relevant sources.

Many team performance evaluation systems use a 360-degree feedback process, or some variation of it, to capture the perspectives of many different raters.

Much of the power of a 360-degree feedback process is its ability to identify gaps in perceptions between self-ratings and others' ratings of team member effectiveness.

The facilitation of a discussion regarding the feedback summary reports for teams is critical to the success of the process as doing so enables team leaders and members to interpret the results and to link them to actions for improvement.

Tools such as tree diagrams and accountability documents help in the team evaluation process as they provide visual representations of a road map for achieving a desired objective and a system for assigning formal responsibility of action steps to team members.

Notes

1 K. Jordan, *Performance Appraisal* (Boston: Harvard Business School Press, 2009).
2 For a discussion of performance appraisal and goal setting, see O. Bouskila-Yam & A.N. Kluger, "Strength-Based Performance Appraisal and Goal Setting." *Human Resource Management Review*, 2011, *21(2)*, pp. 137–147.
3 J. Sullivan, "The Top 50 Problems with Performance Appraisals," 2011. http://www.tlnt.com/2011/01/31/the-top-50-problems-with-performance-appraisals/.

4 For another recent discussion of performance appraisal and its challenges, see S. Bach, "Performance Management," in S. Bach & M. Edwards (eds.), *Managing Human Resources: Human Resource Management in Transition* (Hoboken, NJ: John Wiley and Sons, 2012), pp. 221–242.

5 D. Harrington-Mackin, *The Team-Building Tool Kit: Tips, Tactics, and Rules for Effective Workplace Teams* (New York: AMACOM, 1994), pp. 52–58.

6 J. Gilbert, "The Millennials: A New Generation of Employees, a New Set of Engagement Policies," *Ivey Business Journal*, September-October 2011. http://www.iveybusinessjournal.com/topics/the-workplace/the-millennials-a-new-generation-of-employees-a-new-set-of-engagement-policies#.Uyx2Ul79oxN

7 D. Harrington-Mackin, *The Team-Building Tool Kit: Tips, Tactics, and Rules for Effective Workplace Teams* (New York: AMACOM, 1994), pp. 162–163.

8 For further discussion of rater discomfort in performance appraisals see M.C. Saffie-Robertson & S. Brutus, "The Impact of Interdependence on Performance Evaluations: The Mediating Role of Discomfort with Performance Appraisal," *International Journal of Human Resource Management*, 2014, *25(3)*, pp. 459–473.

9 P. Castka, C. Bamber, & J. Sharp, "Measuring Teamwork Culture: The Use of a Modified EFQM Model," *Journal of Management Development*, 2003, *22(2)*, pp. 149–170.

10 T.J.B. Kline & J.-L. McGrath, "Development and Validation of Five Criteria for Evaluating Team Performance," *Organizational Development Journal*, 1998, 16(3), pp. 9–28.

11 For a discussion of the impact of the source of the ratings, see G. Guenole, T. Cockerill, T. Chamorro-Premuzic, & L. Smillie, "Evidence for the Validity of 360 Dimensions in the Presence of Rater-Source Factors," *Consulting Psychology Journal: Practice and Research*, 2001, *63(4)*, pp. 203–218.

12 My Report Competence Summary. http://www.appraisal360.co.uk/uploads/online_report_summary.jpg.

13 D. Harrington-Mackin, *The Team-Building Tool Kit: Tips, Tactics, and Rules for Effective Workplace Teams* (New York: AMACOM, 1994).

14 T. Keen & C. Keen, "Conducting a Team Audit," *Training and Development*, 1998, *52(2)*, pp. 13–15.

15 For more on 360-degree feedback, see K.M. Nowack & S. Mashihi, "Evidence-Based Answers to 15 Questions about Leveraging 360-Degree Feedback," *Consulting Psychology Journal: Practice and Research*, 2012, *64(3)*, pp. 157–182; H. Aguinas, H. Joo, & R. Gottfredson, "Why We Hate Performance Management—And Why We Should Love It," *Human Performance*, 2011, *54(6)*, pp. 503–507; and, M.L. Collins, *The Thin Book of 360 Feedback* (Bend, OR: Thin Book Publishing, 2011).

16 S. Shiba, *Tree Diagrams* (Salem, NH: GOAL/QPC, 1997).

17 Tennessee Institute for Perinatal Quality Care, "Improving Customer Satisfaction in a Grocery Store." http://tipqc.org/qi/jit/tools/tree-diagram/.

Bibliography

Aguinas, H., Joo, H., & Gottfredson, R. "Why We Hate Performance Management—and Why We Should Love It," *Human Performance*, 2011, *54(6)*, pp. 503–507.

American Society for Quality (ASQ). "The Global Impact of Quality." 2014 World Conference on Quality and Improvement, May 5–7, 2014. http://wcqi.asq.org/2013/team-competition/case-studies-2012.html

Bach, S. "Performance Management." In S. Bach & M. Edwards (eds.), *Managing Human Resources: Human Resource Management in Transition.* (Hoboken, NJ: John Wiley and Sons, 2012), pp. 221–242.

Bouskila-Yam, O., & Kluger, A.N. "Strength-Based Performance Appraisal and Goal Setting," *Human Resource Management Review*, 2011, *21(2)*, pp. 137–147.

Castka, P., Bamber, C., & Sharp, J. "Measuring Teamwork Culture: The Use of a Modified EFQM Model," *Journal of Management Development*, 2003, *22(2)*, pp. 149–170.

Collins, M.L. *The Thin Book of 360 Feedback* (Bend, OR: Thin Book Publishing, 2011).

DecisionWise. "360 Degree Feedback Case Study." http://www.decision-wise.com/case-studies/general-mills-.360-degree-feedback.html

Gilbert, J. "The Millennials: A New Generation of Employees, a New Set of Engagement Policies," *Ivey Business Journal*, September-October 2011. http://www.iveybusinessjournal.com/topics/the-workplace/the-millennials-a-new-generation-of-employees-a-new-set-of-engagement-policies#.Uyx2Ul79oxN

Guenole, G., Cockerill, T., Chamorro-Premuzic, T., & Smillie, L. "Evidence for the Validity of 360 Dimensions in the Presence of Rater-Source Factors," *Consulting Psychology Journal: Practice and Research*, 2011, *63(4)*, pp. 203–218.

Harrington-Mackin, D. *The Team-Building Tool Kit: Tips, Tactics, and Rules for Effective Workplace Teams* (New York: AMACOM, 1994).

Jordan, K. *Performance Appraisal* (Boston, MA: Harvard Business School Press, 2009).

Keen, T., & Keen, C. "Conducting a Team Audit," *Training and Development*, 1998, *52 (2)*, pp. 13–15.

Kline, T.J.B., & McGrath, J.-L. "Development and Validation of Five Criteria for Evaluating Team Performance," *Organizational Development Journal*, 1998, *16(3)*, pp. 9–28.

Nowack, K.M., & Mashihi, S. "Evidence-Based Answers to 15 Questions about Leveraging 360-Degree Feedback," *Consulting Psychology Journal: Practice and Research*, 2012, *64(3)*, pp. 157–182.

Palaiologos, A., Panagiotis, P., & Panayotopoulou, L. "Organizational Justice and Employee Satisfaction in Performance Appraisal," *Journal of European Industrial Training*, 2011, *35(8)*, pp. 826–840.

Saffie-Robertson, M.C., & Brutus, S. "The Impact of Interdependence on Performance Evaluations: The Mediating Role of Discomfort with Performance Appraisal," *International Journal of Human Resource Management*, 2014, *25(3)*, pp. 459–473.

Scott, S.G., & Einstein, W.O. "Strategic Performance Appraisal in Team-Based Organizations: One Size Does Not Fit All," *Academy of Management Executive*, 2001, *15(2)*, pp. 107–116.

Shiba, S. *Tree Diagrams* (Salem, NH: GOAL/QPC, 1997).

Sullivan, J. "The Top 50 Problems with Performance Appraisals," 2011. http://www.tlnt.com/2011/01/31/the-top-50-problems-with-performance-appraisals

Tennessee Institute for Perinatal Quality Care. "Improving Customer Satisfaction in a Grocery Store." http://tipqc.org/qi/jit/tools/tree-diagram

Wheelan, S.A. *Creating Effective Teams* (Thousand Oaks, CA: Sage, 1999).

CHAPTER 11

The New Teams
Virtual, Global, Connected, and Self-Managing

Learning Objectives

After reading this chapter, you should be able to do the following:

1. Recognize key environmental, social, cultural, organizational, and other factors influencing future demands, needs, and developments in teams.
2. Understand and learn how to manage virtual teams.
3. Recognize key challenges and directions in managing global teams.
4. Recognize potential benefits, challenges, and consequences of use of group collaborative technology.
5. Develop skills for individual and team self-management.
6. See how these developments converge into a dynamic, integrative, mutually reinforcing complex.

. . . .

THROUGHOUT THIS TEXT WE ENDEAVOR TO COMMUNICATE THE MOST recent developments in teams. In this chapter we focus specifically on emerging issues that are now affecting teams and that will shape the ways teams will work in the future.

The Changing Environment for Teams

As we've seen throughout the text, the environment in which teams find themselves are changing, and changing with unprecedented speed. Consider the following:

Globalization

In Chapter 5 we discussed the importance of cross-cultural differences. Recognizing and dealing with cross-cultural differences are both critical in the domestic workforce. The relevance of cross-cultural differences is enhanced with globalization, including the growth of global teams.[1] We examine global teams in more depth later in the chapter.

Increased Turnover

Historically, many employees enjoyed the security of a stable job, and firms reaped the benefits of a well-trained, experienced, loyal workforce. The **psychological contract** was an implied contract between the employee and the organization: the employee would be loyal and work hard, and the company would provide rewards and security.[2] The traditional psychological contract is now dying, or being severely rewritten. About one-fifth of workers voluntarily leave their jobs each year, and another one-sixth are fired or otherwise turn over.[3] This turnover entails enormous costs, including those related to recruitment, training, lost productivity, new hiring, and lost sales. The increasingly fluid labor force challenges the continuity of teams.

Growing Computer Literacy and the Explosion of Information Technology

Employees are more computer literate, possessing the knowledge and ability to use computers and related technology efficiently, and are computer fluent, having a robust understanding of what is needed to use information technology effectively across a range of applications.[4] They routinely use information technology such as Facebook, Twitter, and Second Life. Recognizing this, some companies are now embracing such sites. For example, Cisco is among the firms that recruit in Linden Lab's Second Life. Linden Labs lets companies create private spaces in Second Life, and IBM now has the extra control of a Second Life space that will be located on its own website, out of the public environment.[5]

At the same time, information technology is becoming more sophisticated, pervasive, and applicable to many team-related tasks. We discuss group collaborative technology later in the chapter.

New Office Forms

Office workers in the past often expected to spend their time in offices, perhaps sitting in well-ordered rows of desks. At the very least, employees would expect to "own" a space—it was *their* office, or *their* desk. Further, they knew where they could expect to find others. Now, offices are taking many forms—if there are offices at all. Following are some examples of current work situations.

- **Office-less**. Web services company Automatic, Inc. has employees working in twenty-six countries, ninety-four cities, and twenty-eight U.S. states. Its offices are workers' homes. Work gets done wherever employees choose, and virtual meetings are conducted on Skype or over Internet chat.[6] However, some people hunger for face-to-face contact, and such contact is most critical for new employees or when people without a track record launch a new project.
- **Coworking**. Coworking is a style of work that involves a shared working environment, typically an office, and independent activity.[7] Employees in the same environment are often working for different organizations, or they may be freelancers or forming startups.[8] For those who might otherwise be working in isolation at home, the chance to participate in an active workspace may be invigorating. In some cases, a coworking community is formed to provide a social, collaborative environment. Coworking is very popular in Europe and is rapidly gaining adopters in the U.S.[9]
- **Stand-Up Meetings**. In some companies all meetings are now held standing up. The idea is that employees will be more attentive in these kinds of meetings. Holding stand-up meetings reminds people to keep the meeting short and to the point. More often, stand-up meetings last 5 to 15 minutes and are used at the start of the day to track progress and

Betahaus in Berlin

plan for the future. Typically, team members try in turn to stick to the following questions:

- **What did I accomplish yesterday?**
- **What will I do today?**
- **What obstacles are impeding my progress?**

The goal of these meetings is not to give a status update to management but to provide communication and coordination for team members.

Reduced Focus on Hierarchy

The traditional emphasis on a bureaucratic hierarchy with clear lines of authority and strict deference to those at higher levels has generally been eroded. Increasingly, hierarchies have flattened, and leadership styles have become more participative. At the extreme, some companies now have no titles except as required by law. For instance, see the "Teams in the News" feature about the lack of titles at the Nerdery.

TEAMS IN THE NEWS: Abandoning Job Titles at the Nerdery

The Nerdery is a fast-growing tech agency on *Inc. Magazine*'s Hire Power Awards list, Inc's "salute to the job creators who are restoring lives and rebuilding the economy by putting Americans back to work." The company states that the Nerdery "has a dog-friendly work-place, a perpetual chess tournament and a 250-seat Rock Band venue, but the most critical ingredient in keeping an army of technical

geniuses happy (other than caffeine) is compelling problems to solve. Luckily, our unique business model ensures that we never run short on interesting problems to sink our teeth into."

The Nerdery's co-founder, Luke Bucklin, sent many company-wide e-mails, designed as much to entertain as to inform and inspire.[1] One of the most important was sent on September 8, 2010, weeks before he died in a plane crash: "Our job titles are designed to empower us, not to limit us! Put your business card on the desk in front of you . . . This card does not define you. You are a Co-President. You are bigger than your defined role, and you are much more than your job title. Play your part—transcend your job title, be a hero."

Mike Derheim (pictured), cofounder and now CEO, took this message to heart. The hundreds of employees added since Bucklin's accident all have the title of co-president. According to Derheim, it means employees have the freedom and responsibility to do what's best for the business, regardless of rank. On day one, every employee learns about Bucklin's story and is trained on what it means to be co-president.

Note

1. I. Lapowski, "Why Everyone at My Company Has One Job Title," *Inc. Magazine*, http://www.inc.com/magazine/201212/issie-lapowsky/the-nerdery-mike-derheim-everyone-at-my-company-has-one-job-title.html.

Robotics

Modern workplaces are being transformed by robotics. One noteworthy development is the advent of telepresence robots.[10] With **telepresence robots** humans and robots directly interact.[11] For example, iRobot—the maker of the Roomba autonomous vacuum cleaner—has developed Ava, a telepresence robot that uses Cisco Systems' technology.[12] With Ava, executives can serve as robo-bosses in order to interact with workers or projects around the world. The mobile robot displays the user's image on a screen. Ava can learn an office layout so the boss can command it, through an app, to travel to a colleague's workspace. Once there, it uses a camera, speakers, and microphone to converse and observe, even hearing a speaker from half a mile away.[13]

Rate of Change

Heraclitus wrote in about 500 B.C. that "nothing endures but change."[14] This has never been truer. Not only is the rate of change increasing, but changes in technology, global interactions, and social mores and roles; increasing urbanization; rising education levels; and many other factors make change more rapid and more all pervasive.

In short, the world is quickly making new demands on teams, as well as providing emerging opportunities, and teams must be designed and managed to respond. In the following sections, we explore virtual teams, global teams, team collaborative technology, and self-managing teams.

Virtual Teams

Virtual teams are defined by N.A. Ebrahim, S. Ahmed, and Z. Taha as "small temporary groups of geographically, organizationally and/or time dispersed knowledge workers who coordinate their work predominantly with electronic information and communication technologies in order to accomplish one or more organization tasks."[15] While we don't think it is necessarily the case that virtual teams must be small or temporary, that is often the case. As noted by A. Powell, G. Piccoli, and B. Ives, "Virtual teams are often assembled in response to specific needs and are often short lived. . . . This is not a defining characteristic of the virtual team but a byproduct of the specialized function they often serve."[16] The other aspects of the definition are worth clarifying. Virtual teams share these characteristics:

- **Are dispersed on one or more dimensions: geographic, organizational, and/or time.** So, virtual teams may span three (and perhaps more) dimensions: space, organization, and time. We might expect that the more dimensions virtual teams traverse, the more potential difficulties and benefits they may present.
- **Coordinate their work predominantly through electronic and communication technologies.**
- **Work together to accomplish one or more organizational tasks.**

Virtual teams take many forms. For example, some are formed within the same organization and are used to connect team members operating in geographically dispersed locations. Others are used to connect different departments in the same organization.

The growing use of virtual teams is a result of the changing environment, as discussed previously. Figure 11-1 summarizes factors influencing the emergence of virtual teams.

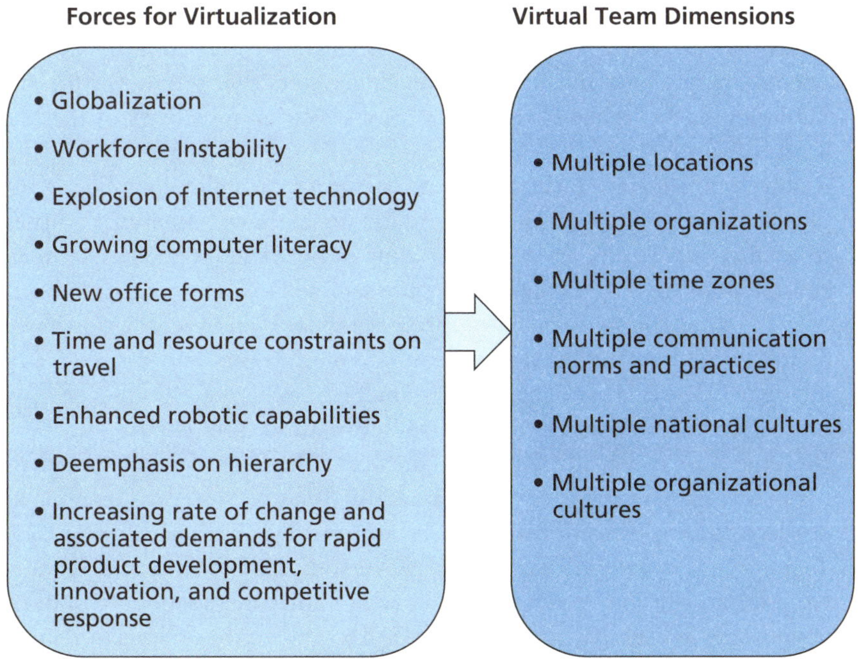

Forces for Virtualization

- Globalization
- Workforce Instability
- Explosion of Internet technology
- Growing computer literacy
- New office forms
- Time and resource constraints on travel
- Enhanced robotic capabilities
- Deemphasis on hierarchy
- Increasing rate of change and associated demands for rapid product development, innovation, and competitive response

Virtual Team Dimensions

- Multiple locations
- Multiple organizations
- Multiple time zones
- Multiple communication norms and practices
- Multiple national cultures
- Multiple organizational cultures

Figure 11-1

Virtual Teams

Benefits of Virtual Teams

Virtual teams offer several potential benefits.[17] As suggested earlier, they help transcend potential barriers of time, space, coordination, and even national culture.

In addition, they provide benefits in these ways:

- **Reduce the expenses associated with travel.**[18]
- **Permit access to needed talent worldwide.**
- **Reduce the need for face-to-face meetings.**
- **Potentially use the full 24-hour workday by traversing time zones.** For instance, teams or team members in Asia may work while those in North America are asleep.

Challenges of Virtual Teams

In general, virtual teams actualize the possibility of capturing team process gains but are potentially more vulnerable to process losses. Virtual teams offer special challenges[19] in that the various barriers they help transcend also all present unique issues.

- **Asynchronous communications may prove troublesome.** This challenge can occur when virtual-team members are in different time zones. Team members in one time zone may, for instance, chafe at having to wait for inputs or responses from their distant team members.
- **Communications are leaner.** The fact that face-to-face communication is minimized or eliminated in virtual teams is often cited as a severe limitation. Compared to face-to-face communications, communications via technologies such as e-mail are less rich. Substantial research shows that physical proximity enhances communication among employees, so separation across time and space may appear to be a critical weakness of virtual teams. Fortunately, though, technological advances are serving to narrow the psychological distance gap. As a dramatic example, researchers at the Human Media Lab at Queen's University, Canada, have developed a holographic 3D videoconferencing system that provides a life-size 3D holographic image of another person, evoking memories of the *Star Trek* holodeck.[20]
- **Reduced face-to-face interaction may encourage social loafing.** For example, in laboratory research, face-to-face teams have sometimes outperformed virtual teams, with social loafing in the virtual teams as a partial cause.[21] Some research suggests that any such social loafing may be a result of dehumanization—the lack of direct personal human interaction.[22]
- **Team members often have different reference points and norms.** Team members with varying backgrounds, interests, expertise, and perspectives may perceive, interpret, and evaluate information differently.
- **Building trust is a challenge.** This issue occurs because virtual-team members often have little history of interaction, don't personally interact, may have no expectations of future interaction, and often must form quickly. Teams must develop what Debra Meyerson, Karl Weick, and Rodney Kramer have termed swift trust.[23] They note that members in temporary systems are allowing themselves to be vulnerable to the actions of relative

strangers, often with little early opportunity for early and continuous monitoring. As such, members often input expectations for trust from other settings with which they are familiar.[24] One study of global virtual teams found that teams with the highest levels of trust shared three characteristics:[25]

1. They began their interactions with a series of social messages—introducing themselves and providing some personal background—before focusing on the task at hand.
2. They set clear roles for each team member, enabling members to identify with one another.
3. All team members demonstrated positive attitudes, displaying eagerness, enthusiasm, and an intense action orientation in all their messages.

As noted by Wayne Cascio, this suggests that first impressions are critical in virtual teams, the tone of messages should be upbeat and action oriented, and trust is critical.[26]

- **Turnover results in increased costs.** As indicated earlier, turnover is almost always very costly for organizations. However, turnover in virtual teams may be especially troublesome since team members must quickly learn about new, distant coworkers and their characteristics.
- **Cultural differences can affect team operation.** If virtual teams are cross-cultural, member differences on cultural dimensions such as individualism or collectivism, power distance, and uncertainty avoidance may play roles.[27] We consider such differences later in the chapter in the context of global teams.

Leading Virtual Teams

In Chapter 3 we discussed the stages of group development. Those stages—forming, storming, norming, performing, and adjourning—take on new forms and demands in virtual teams.[28] For one thing, the early stages must be traversed very quickly. For another, each of the stages presents specific difficulties relative to what happens in those same stages in traditional, face-to-face teams.

Managerial Interventions through the Virtual Team Life Cycle

To better understand contributors to virtual team effectiveness, Stacie Furst, Martha Reeves, Benson Rosen, and Richard Blackburn tracked six virtual teams from project inception to project delivery. They identified factors at each stage of the virtual team life cycle that affected team performance. Their results, summarized in Figure 11-2, identified specific managerial interventions to increase a virtual team's ability to fully develop and contribute to team performance.[29]

As shown in Figure 11-2, the forming stage requires the team leader and experienced team members, with support from top management, to quickly clarify the team's mission and to develop shared understanding and a sense of identity. In addition, **realistic virtual-team previews (RVTPs)**, give members an accurate picture of the nature of the virtual team's role and task, including the challenges it may face. With realistic job previews (**RJPs**), job candidates are given accurate

Figure 11-2

Managing the Life Cycle of Virtual Teams

Stage of Life Cycle			
Forming	**Storming**	**Norming**	**Performing**
• Realistic virtual team previews	• Face-to-face team building sessions	• Create customized templates or team charters specifying task requirements	• Ensure departmental and company supports virtual teamwork
• Coaching from experienced team members	• Training on conflict resolution	• Set individual accountabilities, completion dates, and schedules	• Provide sponsor support and resources for team to perform
• Develop shared understanding and sense of team identity	• Encourage conflicting employees to work together to find common ground	• Establish procedures for sharing information	
• Develop clear mission	• Shuttle diplomacy and mediation to create compromise solutions	• Distinguish task, social, and contextual information; design procedures appropriate for each	
• Acquire top management support		• Assign a team coach with skills for managing virtually	

Note: For another perspective on the life cycle of virtual teams, see G. Hertel, S. Geister, & U. Konradt, "Managing Virtual Teams: A Review of Current Empirical Research," *Human Resource Management Review*, 2005, *15*, pp. 69–95.
Source: S. Furst, M. Reeves, B. Rosen, and R. Blackburn. "Managing the Life Cycle of Virtual Teams." *Academy of Management Executive*, 2004, *18(2)*, pp. 6–20.

job-related information—both positive *and* negative. Research shows RJPs to promote accurate initial expectations, help newcomers develop coping mechanisms to manage workplace strain, and enhance perceptions of employer concern and honesty.[30] Meta-analyses show RJPs to lower initial expectations, reduce turnover, and increase job satisfaction and job performance.[31] Therefore, RVTPs should help inoculate team members to the trials that are likely to confront the virtual team.

At the storming stage team leaders (and members) must foster interaction to enhance mutual understanding, train and encourage reliance on effective conflict-resolution approaches, mediate member disagreements, and encourage focus on shared team goals.

The norming stage requires development of processes for customizing task requirements, specification of responsibilities and deadlines, designation of procedures for transfer of information, and (perhaps) assignment of a team coach.

Finally, the performing stage demands departmental and company support, including provision of needed resources.

Practices of Effective Virtual-Team Leaders

Figure 11-3 shows six practices of effective virtual-team leaders.[32] The leader behaviors shown in that figure—building trust, managing diversity, managing meetings, monitoring progress, reporting on team activities, and using rewards and recognition—are important in all team contexts, but their significance is amplified in virtual teams.

Since virtual team members may come from different cultures, may be unfamiliar with one another, may have different preferred communication

Leadership Practices of Virtual Team Leaders	Examples of How Virtual Team Leaders Do It
1. Establish and Maintain Trust Through the Use of Communication Technology	• Focusing the norms on how information is communicated • Revisiting and adjusting the communication norms as the team gets together ("virtual get-togethers") • Making progress explicit through use of team virtual workspace
2. Ensure That Diversity in the Team Is Understood, Appreciated, and Leveraged	• Prominent team expertise directory and skills matrix in the virtual workspace • Allowing diverse opinions to be expressed through use of asynchronous electronic means (e.g., electronic discussion threads)

3. Manage Virtual Work-Cycle and Meetings	• All idea convergence between meetings (asynchronous idea generation) and idea convergence and conflict resolution during virtual meetings (synchronous idea convergence)
	• Use:
	  • at the start of each virtual meeting for social relationship building
	  • during meetings to ensure through "check-ups" that everyone is engaged and heard from
	  • at the end of meetings to ensure that the minutes and future work plan are posted to team repository

4. Monitor Team Progress Through the Use of Technology	• Closely scrutinize asynchronous (electronic threaded discussion and document postings in the knowledge repository) and synchronous (virtual meeting participating and instant messaging) communication patterns • Make progress explicit through balanced scorecard measurements posted in the team's virtual workspace
5. Enhance External Visibility of the Team and its Members	• Frequent report-outs to a virtual steering committee (comprised of local bosses of team members)
6. Ensure Individuals Benefit from Participating in Virtual Teams	• Virtual reward ceremonies • Individual recognition at the start of each virtual meeting • Make sure each team member's "real location" boss is aware of the member's contribution

Figure 11-3

Practices of Effective Virtual-Team Leaders

Source: Based on A. Malhotra, A. Majchrzak, and B. Rosen. "Leading Virtual Teams." *Academy of Management Perspectives*, 2007, *21(1)*, p. 60.

Figure 11-4

Choosing When and How
to Use e-Communication
Methods

Sample Questions
• Can laptops, tablets, and other wireless devices be used during meetings? If so, when and for what purposes?
• When, if ever, is it appropriate to use cell phones during meetings?
• When is it appropriate to use e-mail rather than face-to-face meetings, phone calls, or other alternatives?
• What content is appropriate or inappropriate in e-mails? What are appropriate formats and size limits for e-mail attachments?
• How should e-mails and other forms of electronic messaging be used, distributed, and stored?
• How can members access common materials such as meeting agendas, slide presentations, videos, or blogs?
• Are there types of information that should be shared only face-to-face?
• Who are appropriate or inappropriate recipients of various forms of information?
• When should file transfer sites, intranets, or shared drives be used?

styles, and may fear that their contributions will not be recognized back home, it is important for team leaders to act quickly to build trust; clarify member roles and expertise; recognize and reward members' roles, expertise, and contributions; develop protocols for information exchange; and ensure the opportunity for full and equal member voice.[33]

Using e-Communications

Virtual teams obviously rely heavily on electronic communications. Especially since such reliance can lead to confusion, inconsistency, and even incivility, clarification of guidelines and expectations regarding e-communication is vital. Figure 11-4 presents some of the questions that must be addressed when using e-communications.

Global Teams

As we've said, one growing use of virtual teams is to permit global teams to function effectively.[34] Sujin Horwitz and Cecilia Santillan define **global virtual teams (GVTs)** as "globally dispersed, culturally diverse, and technologically connected individuals who work interdependently with a limited life span of membership in order to accomplish a common goal."[35]

In addition to the challenges generally posed by virtual teams, the fact that global teams are geographically diverse offers special difficulties. Consider potential difficulties resulting from culture clashes on the basis of Hofstede's dimensions, discussed in Chapter 5:

- **Team members from individualistic cultures may feel less comfortable working in teams than do members in collectivist cultures.** They may also want less emphasis on team rewards.
- **Team members in high power distance cultures may be reluctant to communicate with, and to respect the inputs of, members in low power**

distance cultures who are below their rank. They may also be relatively more comfortable with autocratic decisions.

- Team members in high uncertainty avoidance cultures may be much more risk averse than members in low uncertainty avoidance cultures.
- Team members in high quantity of life cultures may be more concerned with achieving goals and less with the process of goal attainment than those in high quality of life cultures. The former may also focus relatively more on performance outcomes and less on affective outcomes such as job satisfaction and intrinsic feelings of accomplishment.
- Team members in cultures with long-term time orientation may want to emphasize long-term outcomes, rather than focus on short-term gains, relative to members in cultures with short-term time orientations.

In addition, as we discussed in Chapter 5, cultures may be high context or low context. Those in high context cultures, such as most Asian, Hispanic, African, and Arab countries, depend heavily on the context in which communication occurs (such as the social setting, use of nonverbal cues, and the person's history and status), while those in low context cultures, such as Germany and the United States, rely primarily on the words themselves. As such, team members in high context cultures will likely feel less comfortable with relatively impersonal forms of communication in virtual teams than will those in low context cultures. They may also feel constrained by the relative inability to use, and respond to, nonverbal cues. Conversely, members in high context cultures may be frustrated by their inability to decipher meaning from the words themselves as used by their counterparts.

While such cultural differences are generally seen as problems, they may also offer a valuable source of heterogeneity, with differences serving as complements. For example, team members in or from cultures differing on key dimensions may be able to help their counterparts understand how policies and practices may be problematic in their cultures. Having team members from different cultures may also serve to moderate the various perspectives, providing a balancing of views.

With global teams, the development of trust becomes more complicated since not just levels of trust but also the nature and meaning of trust may vary across cultures.[36] National differences in value systems, culture, and institutions are likely to influence initial trust between partners.[37] Some research shows that that the Japanese trust strangers less than do Americans.[38] Team members may also trust those from some nations more than others. In addition, for countries such as Germany that have strong institutional systems to govern business relationships, such as technical standards, market rules, and legal norms, personal trust plays a secondary role. Conversely, when institutional supports are weak, personal trust and relationships are more important.[39] Further, in virtual global teams, in which there is often little time or direct interaction to develop trust, the impact of these complexities is amplified.[40]

With global teams it is important not just to give a realistic team preview but also to provide a **realistic living conditions preview**.[41] That is, team members who are transferred from their native cultures may need accurate, favorable and unfavorable, information on the general living environment in the host country.[42]

As we also discussed in Chapter 5, the development of cultural intelligence is important for any cross-cultural dealings. In the context of team members working together, it is especially vital. Therefore, assigning members with high **motivational cultural intelligence (MCI)** to global teams can be critical. MCI "is conceptualized as an individual's intrinsic motivation and specific self-efficacy to engage in cross-cultural experiences and master its nuances."[43] That is, it is desirable to assign members to global teams who are motivated to try new things and feel they are competent to do so.

Team Collaborative Technology

We said in Chapter 7 that new electronic tools promise to make group brainstorming, and group decision processes in general, more effective. These tools generally are forms of **group decision support systems (GDSS)**. According to Daniel Power, whose "Team Scholar" profile is included later in this chapter, "In general, group decision support systems (GDSS) are interactive, computer-based systems that facilitate solution of semi-structured and unstructured problems by a designated set of decision-makers working together as a group. . . . GDSS include structured decision tools like brainstorming, commenting on ideas, and rating and ranking of alternatives (cf., DeSanctis & Gallupe, 1987)."[44] Increasingly, "working together" is not limited by proximity.

GDSS are a subset of the broader category of group support software and tools called *groupware*. In addition to GDSS, groupware (now sometimes called *collaborative software*) includes any software designed to support more than one person working on a shared task by allowing multiple users to access the same data. It also typically provides a mechanism to help users coordinate and track ongoing projects or decision processes. Thus, groupware helps people work together through computer-supported communication, collaboration, and coordination. Examples of groupware include IBM Notes (formerly IBM Lotus Notes) and Microsoft SharePoint. We provide links to information about these and other groupware tools on the text website.

One form of GDSS is a **collaboratory**.[45] Collaboratories are used to conduct and facilitate research across geographical distances. A collaboratory is defined as a network-based facility and organizational entity that spans distance; supports rich and recurring human interaction oriented to a common research area; fosters contact between researchers who are both known and unknown to each other; and provides access to data sources, artifacts, and tools required to accomplish research tasks.[46] Collaboratories, sometimes referred to as virtual research environments, connect shared resources with research and social practices that prevail in its research community.[47] In other words, collaboratories are centers without walls in which participants make use of computing and communication technologies to access shared instruments and data, as well as to communicate with others.

One popular electronic tool for facilitating brainstorming and other team decision processes is a GDSS called ThinkTank, described on the text website.[48] IBM's electronic brainstorming teams, described in Chapter 7, use a version of ThinkTank. Research shows that when ThinkTank or other tools

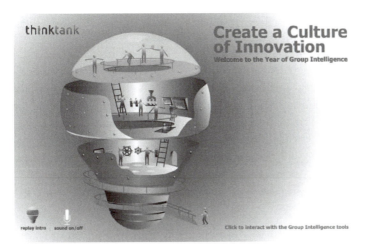

that permit electronic brainstorming are used, the performance of brainstorming groups improves dramatically. Some research shows that when ideas of individuals generating ideas alone are combined, they outperform the output of brainstorming groups. That research is controversial and sidesteps the fact that it is rare to ask many individuals to separately generate ideas for subsequent combination (the nominal group technique discussed in Chapter 7 is an exception). However, it is clear that, especially with large groups, electronic brainstorming teams outperform the aggregated output of individuals generating ideas separately.[49] ThinkTank includes tools not just for electronic brainstorming but also for organizing ideas, analyzing alternatives, generating and sharing reports, and other processes. In general, as detailed by GroupSystems CEO and President Luis Solis, these tools address the following:[50]

- **Discovery.** Uncovering who knows what, who knows whom, and who knows how to do tasks or projects better, anywhere in the world and outside the native organization.
- **Ideation.** Generating ideas and ways to innovate, grow, or solve problems, thus projecting the possibilities for the future.
- **Teaming.** Converging on a few important choices or possibilities that the group may be capable of developing further and supporting.
- **Leading.** Achieving high levels of consensus by means of voting so that group members are confident that their voices have been heard, their votes counted, and that an effective voting methodology was employed.
- **Learning.** Documenting group work or group memory for subsequent work for members unable to attend work sessions or for inclusion in other materials.

Group collaborative support systems such as ThinkTank are potentially useful throughout the stages of team decision making, and they may facilitate group processes more generally. ThinkTank has been employed by a wide array of organizations. As some representative examples, ThinkTank has been used by these companies or organizations:[51]

- An independent investigative board authorized by NASA to determine causes of the Columbia Accident

- The Environmental Protection Agency to conduct future trends analysis, pollution prevention and radiation protection
- DynTek, a professional technology services firm, to create and monitor critical success factors important to its growth as a company
- The Air Force Manpower Agency (AFMA) to examine and evaluate all aspects of the agency's operation, including best practices, manpower standards, performance management, activity-based costing and competitive sourcing procedures
- The Sun Microsystems Global Vodafone team to remain unified and cohesive
- Agilent Technologies to achieve distributed collaboration and knowledge automation

A challenge is that when virtual teams are using group decision support tools, various members may have difficulty deciding which tools to use, how to use them, in which order, and so on. These are likely to be exacerbated by difficulties in communication, coordination, and collaboration. As a result, companies often use facilitators to coordinate and expedite the process.[52] Facilitators configure technologies to support the process and help lead teams through the process. They monitor and intervene as needed to improve communication, information access, goal focus, and the team's overall process.

However, firms often find it not feasible or too expensive to use facilitators.[53] In such cases, collaboration engineering is often helpful. According to Sujin Horwitz and Cecila Santillan, **collaboration engineering (CE)** "is a research-based approach to designing and deploying collaboration processes for high value recurring team tasks, and thinkLets within CE are the units of facilitation which can be integrated into groupware tools in order to develop streamlined activities for a given team task (Briggs et al., 2003; Bragge et al., 2009)."[54] CE is concerned with patterns of deliberation and collaboration. It is essentially a replacement for a human facilitator. Robert Briggs et al. label such an approach *facilitator-in-a-box*.[55]

CE identifies the following **patterns of collaboration:**

- **Diverge.** Move toward having more concepts with which to work.
- **Converge.** Move toward narrowing the number of concepts deemed worthy of attention.
- **Clarify.** Move toward greater shared understanding of concepts.
- **Organize.** Derive understanding of relationships among concepts.
- **Evaluate.** Increase understanding of the value of concepts.
- **Build consensus.** Move toward greater agreement among stakeholders.

To facilitate use of GDSS such as ThinkTank, Briggs and his colleagues have developed **thinkLets**. Each thinkLet includes information on when to use or not to use that thinkLet, an overview, inputs and outputs, setup, steps, insights, and success stories.[56] thinkLets are available for several patterns of collaboration. Figure 11-5 presents a thinkLet, called LeafHopper, for divergent thinking.

Select this thinkLet . . .	When you know in advance that the team must brainstorm on several topics at once.
	When different participants will have different levels of interest or expertise in the different topics.
	When it is not important to assure that every participant contributes to every topic.
Do not select this thinkLet . . .	When it is important to assure that every person addresses each topic.
Overview	Participants start with an electronic list of several discussion topics; each item on the list links to an instance of a simultaneous comment window; each participant hops among the topics to contribute as dictated by interest and expertise.
	Inputs: A list of topics that must be addressed by the team.
	Outputs: A set of comments organized by discussion topic.

How to use LeafHopper	*Tool:* **GroupSystem Topic Commenter**
	Configuration:
	1. Participants may contribute comments under each topic.
	2. Participants may not contribute new topics.
	3. Contributions will be anonymous.
	4. Create one topic card for each brainstorming question in Topic Commenter or one of the other list/comments tools.
	Script:
	5. Explain the topics to the team and verify that the participants understand them.
	6. Explain the kinds of ideas that the team must contribute.
	7. Explain how to open the comment window under each discussion item.
	8. Say this:
	a. Start working on the topics in which you have the most interest or the most expertise. If you have time, move on to each of the other topics to read and comment on the contributions of others.
	b. You may not have time to work on every topic; so work first on the topics that are most important to you.

Figure 11-5

LeafHopper: A thinkLet Example for Divergent Thinking

Source: S. K. Horwitz & S. Santillan. "Knowledge Sharing in Global Virtual Team Collaboration: Application of CE and thinkLets." *Knowledge Management Research & Practice*, 2012, *10*, p. 348, as adapted from R. O. Briggs et al., "ThinkLets: Achieving Predictable, Repeatable Patterns of Group Interaction with Group Support Systems (GSS)," *Proceedings of the 34th Hawaii International Conference on System Sciences*, IEEE Computer Society, Los Alamitos, CA, 2001. R. O. Briggs et al., "Collaboration Engineering with thinkLets to Pursue Sustained Success with Group Support Systems." *Journal of Management Information Systems*, 2003, *19(4)*, pp. 31–64.

The thinkLet in Figure 11-5, LeafHopper, suggests potential benefits of a GDSS. In this case, where the team is brainstorming ideas, these benefits relative to traditional brainstorming include the following:

- **Team members can make anonymous inputs.**
- **Team members can contribute simultaneously, not just sequentially.**
- **No team member can dominate the process.**
- **Team members can address many issues at once.**
- **Team members can all feel they are contributing since they can select topics for which they have the greatest interest and expertise.**
- **There is a detailed external group memory.** Since everything is stored electronically, minutes are easily produced and are available for subsequent meetings. Moreover, the meeting record is unbiased and complete, and the team's evolution over time can be tracked.

As shown in Figure 11-6, thinkLets can be used at each stage of the problem solving process.

Figure 11-6

Examples of thinkLets

Name	Purpose	Specific Use
LeafHopper	• Use divergent thinking to generate concepts	• To have a group brainstorm ideas regarding a number of topics simultaneously
Pin The Tail On The Donkey	• Use convergent thinking to identify important concepts	• To have a group identify important concepts that warrant future deliberation
RichRelations	• Organize concepts into categories	• To have a group uncover possible categories in which the number of existing concepts can be organized
StrawPoll	• Evaluate concepts in terms of a criterion	• To have a group evaluate a number of concepts regarding a single criterion
MoodRing	• Track degree of consensus	• To continuously track the level of consensus within the group regarding a certain issue

Source: Based on S.K. Horwitz & S. Santillan. "Knowledge Sharing in Global Virtual Team Collaboration: Application of CE and thinkLets." *Knowledge Management Research & Practice*, 2012, *10*, p. 349, as adapted from R.O. Briggs et al. "ThinkLets: Achieving Predictable, Repeatable Patterns of Group Interaction with Group Support Systems (GSS)." *Proceedings of the 34th Hawaii International Conference on System Sciences*, IEEE Computer Society, Los Alamitos, CA, 2001. R.O. Briggs et al. "Collaboration Engineering with thinkLets to Pursue Sustained Success with Group Support Systems." *Journal of Management Information Systems*, 2003, *19(4)*, 31–64.

TEAM SCHOLAR

Daniel J. Power, University of Northern Iowa

Daniel J. Power is professor of management and information systems at the College of Business Administration at the University of Northern Iowa, Cedar Falls, Iowa and the editor of DSSResources.com. Since completing his PhD in 1982,

he has published more than forty articles, book chapters and Proceedings papers. His articles have appeared in leading journals. He has published five books, the latest of which is *Decision Support, Analytics, and Business Intelligence* (Business Expert Press, 2013).

Why is computerized decision support important?

Both individuals and groups use computerized decision support. This field continues to grow and evolve. As new computing technologies are developed, there are often opportunities to expand the scope and capabilities for human-computer interaction and hence more and better decision support.

You developed and tested an early decision support system, DECAID. What was its purpose? How has it evolved?

DECision AID, or the shortened form DECAID, was a collection of heuristic programs that helped an individual complete a systematic decision process, including categorizing the decision situation, defining a decision question, evaluating goals and alternatives, and collecting information. Applications for the system were in teaching managerial decision making. The system was further developed in 2005 as a Planning DSS that could be used by individuals or a team. That Web-based system needs further refinement, and development has been suspended.

What do you see as the current status of Group Decision Support Systems (GDSS)?

In my decision support system taxonomy, group DSS may be either primarily communication driven—supporting collaboration—or model driven—helping a team apply a tool such as brainstorming or the nominal group technique (NGT). Communication technology has improved significantly for groups and team communication-driven decision support. In 2001 we really lacked low-cost interactive video, whiteboards, and screening sharing needed for effective global collaboration and decision support. In 2013 managers and individuals have those capabilities and much more, including social networking capabilities, telepresence, high-definition videoconferencing and collaborative word processing. Not as much progress has occurred with model-driven group DSS. Most of the client-server implementations such as GroupSystems migrated to the Web, but the features have stayed fairly static. There are opportunities for innovation using smart phones and new tools such as Google Glass.

Can you cite any especially interesting/noteworthy examples of GDSS use?

At my website, DSSResources.com, there are a number of case studies related to various types of decision support, including traditional GDSS. Mike McCall and Julia Young described an example of how they use GDSS for strategic planning in their consulting at facilitate.com. Facilitate claims to "change the way you run meetings." There is also a classic case by John Wasyluk and Dan Saaty. Their Expert Choice (http://expertchoice.com/) product has evolved from an individual decision-aiding tool first developed in the 1980s to a team decision-support tool. GroupSystems.com is another collaborative tool.

What are some new directions you see GDSS evolving toward in the future?

Specialized decision rooms have become largely obsolete. Team rooms and corporate boardrooms are, however, increasingly computing-intensive spaces, and the computing technologies have become more mobile and more ubiquitous for supporting teams and group decision making. People bring tablets to decision meetings and use a wide array of collaborative technologies for both synchronous and asynchronous distance meetings and team-decision support. Groups probably need more decision support because teams are more distributed, more information is available, and choices are perhaps more complicated. The developments in handheld devices and cellular technologies provide many opportunities to support team information sharing and collaborative decision making. At the personal, social network level, you can get quick feedback from friends. At the individual and group level in organizations, decision makers are immersed in a web of information. Videoconferencing is almost commonplace, and rich media collaboration penetrates most homes and offices in developed countries. Global communications networks have changed the discussion about group decision support systems.

You are the editor of DSSResources.com, a Web-based knowledge repository about computerized decision-support systems, the editor of PlanningSkills.com, and the editor of DSS News, a bi-weekly e-newsletter. What are their contents and purposes?

DSSResources.com (Decision Support Systems Resources) is a Web-based knowledge repository. The mission of this site is to help people who are interested in learning about how to use information technologies and software to improve decision making. The site was started in 1999. *Decision Support News* is a bi-weekly e-newsletter that I write and edit. It was started in May 2000.

Team collaboration is also facilitated by the emergence of Web 2.0. **Web 2.0** refers to cumulative changes in the way Web pages are developed and used. A Web 2.0 site may let users interact and collaborate in a social media dialogue as creators in a virtual community. This is in contrast to websites where users simply passively view content. Social networking sites and hosted sites are examples of Web 2.0.[57]

Self-Managing Teams

The first-century Roman philosopher, author, and statesman Lucius Annaeus Seneca wrote, "He is most powerful who has power over himself."[58] As a team member and in other roles in organizations, you must increasingly be able to motivate yourself and to teach others this critical skill. **Self-management** is the process of managing oneself. Instead of relying solely on others to reward and punish, to direct, to set goals, and to provide feedback, we must learn to use these tools to manage our own behavior.

Complete Self-Assessment 11.1 on the text website to get baseline information as a foundation for your later self-management goals. The self-assessment gauges the degree to which you currently set goals for yourself, monitor your progress toward goal attainment, seek feedback concerning your performance, manage your time, appropriately allocate your time, reward yourself for goal attainment, and commit to your goals.[59]

The Need for Self-Management

Self-management is needed particularly when employees are relatively isolated, such as with telecommuting or virtual teams. It may also be useful when supervision is lacking or when employees must be self-directing, as with enriched jobs and in self-managed work teams.[60] In such cases, self-management may serve as a potent "substitute for leadership."[61] The movement in organizations toward what has been called **self-organization**—freeing employees to figure out how to get the job done without central planning or control—assumes that employees will have the skills to proactively deal with workplace uncertainties and demands.[62] Many companies are working toward abandoning traditional top-down organization and moving toward self-organization.[63]

In addition, self-management may be less expensive than reliance on organizational reward-and-control systems: once self-management skills have been learned, they are transferable across a vast array of tasks and settings. Finally, self-reinforced behavior is generally maintained more effectively than if it had been externally regulated.[64] In view of all these potential benefits, it isn't surprising that self-management is often presented as a distinguishing characteristic of "best" and "most admired" firms.[65] Self-motivation is among the key characteristics sought by employers.

As we discuss later in this chapter, self-management is important both at the individual and team level. We first discuss individual self-management and then consider how it applies to teams.

Consequences of Self-Management

Self-management works. Early evidence came from clinical settings, where self-management techniques have been very successful in programs dealing with weight loss, smoking cessation, and phobia reduction.[66] In academic settings, they have led to improved study habits and enhanced academic performance. In organizational settings, they have reduced absenteeism, increased satisfaction with work, enhanced commitment to the organization, and improved task performance.[67]

Forms of Self-Management

There are two broad approaches to self-management. The first, termed **behavioral self-management**, is based on learning to manage our own behaviors; deciding what we want to achieve; and setting up appropriate systems of goals, rewards, and controls. The second, termed **cognitive self-management**, involves the development of effective thinking patterns.

These approaches can best be used together to achieve effective and satisfying patterns of thought and behavior.

Guidelines for Behavioral Self-Management

Here are concrete steps to take to change or maintain behaviors:

- **Pinpoint the specific behavior you want to change or maintain.** One way to do this is through self-observation. You may decide, for instance, that you are working on jobs that you should delegate to others, that you need to lose weight, or that you spend too much time chatting with people who walk into your office.

- **Set specific goals for behavioral change.** As discussed in Chapter 4, effective goals should be specific, difficult, and measurable. Further, if the goals are to be effective, our acceptance of and commitment to them must be sincere. Some specific goals might include the following:
  - Exercise at least 4 days a week for at least 30 minutes per day.[68]
  - Quit smoking for 3 months.

- **Keep track of the frequency, duration, and any other dimensions of interest, such as the time and place at which the behavior occurs.** Use diaries, graphs, or timing devices as needed. Sometimes, self-monitoring itself is sufficient to change the behavior. For instance, if you identify how much time you spend watching television, you may simply watch less. Here are some examples of monitoring techniques:
  - Weigh in once a week at the gym.
  - Each time I eat fast food, write down what I ate and how much the meal cost me.

- **Modify cues.** Sometimes the behavior we want to change is preceded by other events that serve as cues or signals for the behavior. By altering or controlling the cues, you may be able to change the behavior. For example, you may find that you can't get your work done because you're constantly answering the phone. A solution might be to activate your voice mail or have an assistant hold calls. Or, you may increase desired behaviors by as simple a prompt as a to-do list. Some cue modifications might include the following:
  - Plan a menu for the week ahead.
  - Study on the second floor of the library so I don't see my friends who study on the first floor.

- **Modify consequences.** This can involve self-reward or self-punishment (or both). You might, for example, reward yourself for quitting smoking by spending the savings on purchases of musical CDs. Or, you may decide that you'll skip a concert if you don't meet your goal. Here are some consequences that may serve as rewards or punishments:
  - Each time I complete a project before it's due, I'll buy myself a new CD.
  - I will save the money I would have spent on cigarettes for 6 months and apply it to a trip to Negril, Jamaica.

- Some consequences, such as the CD purchase, are relatively immediate whereas others, such as the trip to Jamaica, must wait until the behavior has been exhibited for a lengthy period of time. It is generally best to use a combination of such consequences, such as a reward for each week you don't smoke plus a longer-term reward, such as the Jamaica trip.

- **Reorder behavior.** We often do relatively enjoyable tasks in order to put off others we don't care for.[69] As a result, the things we put off may never get done or may get done poorly. To prevent this, make pleasant behaviors depend on completion of the noxious task. For instance, if you enjoy reading your mail but find writing reports to be unpleasant, put off reading the mail until you have finished the project reports. Here are additional examples:
  - Exercise before dinner rather than after.
  - Eat the vegetables before I eat the meat. This way, I should be more full before I eat the meat.

- **Write a contract with yourself** (see Skills Practice 11.1 on the text website to develop a sample contract). In the contract, specify the behavior you will change, the length of the contract, how you will monitor progress, the rewards or punishments you will use, and so on. Write the contract clearly and post it in a conspicuous spot. Have others witness the contract, sign it, and agree to help to monitor your behaviors.
- **Rehearse.** Physically or mentally practice activities before you actually perform them. Rehearsal may suggest that you should rethink your goals or your approaches to attaining them.
- **Check your progress on a regular basis.** If you're not doing as well as you'd like, take corrective action, such as changing prompts or rewards or making sure that you are rewarding yourself promptly.
- **Plan strategies to maintain a successful change.** If not, you may fall back into your old habits. But don't become wedded to the same system of rewards and punishments on which you relied to bring about the change. Consider something such as a maintenance diet or give yourself a bit more slack regarding leisure activities.

Use Skills Practice 11.1 on the text website to apply self-management to your own behaviors. Try it first with a behavior that you can easily observe and in which you may quickly see results, such as an exercise schedule or a program to cut down on distractions at work. Then, apply it to a longer-term goal, such as learning a new skill. Once you master these techniques, you can draw on them to help with almost any task.

Cognitive-Focused Strategies for Self-Management

Behavioral self-management works best when accompanied by effective thinking.[70] One step to effective thinking is to physically and mentally redesign tasks to make them more naturally rewarding. This involves creating ways to do tasks so that the enjoyment of performing the task itself creates significant natural reward value. Natural rewards come from performing tasks in a way that allows us to experience a sense of competence, a sense of self-control, and a sense of purpose. In addition, effective thinking is fostered by establishment of constructive and effective habits of thinking, such as opportunity thinking as opposed to obstacle thinking. By studying and managing our beliefs and assumptions, we can begin to develop the ability to find opportunities in new work challenges. Use of mental imagery techniques and positive internal self-talk aids this process. Effective, positive thinking patterns are necessary for successful self-management and helpful in effectively dealing with stress.[71]

Self-Leadership in Teams

As noted by Chris Neck and Chuck Manz, "Self-leadership is just as important when you are working in a team as when you are working alone. To reach your individual potential while working within a team, you still must lead yourself. In fact, only by effectively leading yourself as a team member can you help the team lead itself, reach *its* potential, and thus achieve synergy. The act of the team leading itself describes the concept of team self-leadership." They go on to define team self-leadership as "the application of mental and behavioral self-leadership strategies that enable team members to provide themselves with self-direction and self-motivation, and ultimately to become effective, personally empowered contributors to the team."[72]

Behavioral Aspects of Team Self-Leadership

Team Self-Observation

Self-observation represents the team's collective effort to observe and record its behavior and performance, as well as the effort to try to understand the antecedents and consequences of those actions.

Team Self–Goal Setting

While individual team members may have personal goals that are necessary to achieve team goals, the focus for teams is on the shared goals of the team as a whole. This requires the group as a collective (not an individual leader) to establish the goals. Doing so represents an element of team self-leadership.

Team Cue Modification

Teams can remove things that cue undesirable behaviors or increase exposure to cues for desirable behavior. These efforts to modify cues are collectively performed by the team, not just initiated by the team leader or another individual.

Team Self-Reward and Self-Punishment

Teams can reinforce their own behaviors by giving rewards to one another or to the team as a whole. Rewards may be tangible, such as monetary bonuses or time off, or intangible, such as the feeling of accomplishment from the work completed by the team, pleasure from working in the team, or increased satisfaction from participation. Punishments might include things such as requiring the team to work extra hours to make up for time spent socializing rather than focusing on the task. To be considered a team self-influence, the team, not an individual, must administer and receive sanctions as a group.

Team Rehearsal

Just as individuals may rehearse before actually engaging in behaviors, teams may rehearse. For example, a team may practice a presentation it will make to upper management.

Cognitive Aspects of Team Self-Leadership

Effective thinking is also important at the team level. For example, teams can develop opportunity thinking as opposed to obstacle thinking. They can try to build natural rewards into the task to enhance a common sense of competence, self-control, and purpose. Teams may employ mental imagery to enhance team performance by establishing a common vision. Members of teams facing strategic decisions should benefit from interactively crafting a common image regarding what they wish to accomplish, and jointly visualizing effective means for doing so.

The Convergence

Based on our discussion to this point in the chapter, it becomes clear that many common forces are now shaping, and will be shaping, the nature of teams, how team members will interact, potential team benefits and challenges, and other processes and outcomes. Further, it should be apparent that there is a convergence of mutually reinforcing developments. Teams are increasingly global, requiring virtual teams. Group collaborative technology facilitates virtual global teams. With differences across time, space, organizations, and cultures, hierarchical control will often be less feasible, and self-management will be increasingly vital. These are all symbiotic, mutually reinforcing, and mutually dependent forces.

Summary and Integration

Key takeaways for this chapter include the following:

Many forces are reshaping the environment and team challenges, opportunities, and characteristics.

Virtual teams, facilitated by new collaborative technologies, can help transcend boundaries of time, space, organizations, and even national cultures.

Teams are increasingly global, with the corresponding promise and perils of cross-cultural diversity.

Group collaborative technology supports virtual and global teams, providing key tools for effective team decision making.

Teams are increasingly self-managing, or will at least benefit from adoption of behavioral and cognitive self-management techniques.

The forces we've considered in this chapter and throughout the text are fostering a convergence of developments: teams are increasingly virtual, global, technology dependent, and self-managing.

Notes

1 R. Wageman, H. Gardner, & M. Mortensen, "Teams Have Changed: Catching up to the Future," *Industrial & Organizational Psychology*, 2012, *5(1)*, pp. 48–52.

2 D.M. Rousseau, "Psychological and Implied Contracts in Organizations," *Employee Responsibilities and Rights Journal*, 1989, 2, pp. 121–139.

3 Bureau of Labor Statistics, *Job Openings and Labor Turnover–January 2012* (U.S. Department of Labor, 2012). http://www.bls.gov/news.release/archives/jolts_03132012.htm

4 L. Snyder, *Fluency with Information Technology* (Boston: Addison-Wesley, 2003).

5 R. King, "The (Virtual) Global Office," *Businessweek*, May 2, 2008. http://www.businessweek.com/stories/2008-05-02/the-virtual-global-officebusinessweek-business-news-stock-market-and-financial-advice. See also, G. Salmon, "The Future for (Second) Life and Learning," *British Journal of Educational Technology*, 2009, *40(3)*, pp. 526–538.

6 R.E. Silverman, "Step into the Office-Less Company," *Wall Street Journal*, September 5, 2012, p. B6.

7 D. Fost, "They're Working on Their Own, Just Side by Side," *New York Times*, February 20, 2008. http://www.nytimes.com/2008/02/20/business/businessspecial2/20cowork.html?pagewanted=all.

8 C. Spinuzzi, "Working Alone Together: Coworking as Emergent Collaborative Activity," *Journal of Business and Technical Communication*, 2012, *26(4)*, pp. 399–441.

9 C. Rushby, "Europe's Capital of Co-Working: Is Sharing Desks Worth It?" *Silicon Allee*, November 28, 2012. http://siliconallee.com/silicon-allee/editorial/2012/11/28/europes-capital-of-co-working-is-sharing-desks-worth-it?

10 R.E. Silverman, "My Life as a Telecommuting Robot," *Wall Street Journal*, August 8, 2012, p. B1.

11 P. Olson, "Rise of the Telepresence Robots," *Forbes*, July 15, 2013. http://www.forbes.com/sites/parmyolson/2013/06/27/rise-of-the-telepresence-robots/

12 J. Hicks, "i-Robot's New Ava 500 Puts Robotics in Heart of the Enterprise," *Forbes*, June 10, 2013. http://www.forbes.com/sites/jenniferhicks/2013/06/10/irobots-new-ava-500-puts-robotics-in-heart-of-the-enterprise/. To learn about another telepresence robot, Baxter, see J. Markoff, "A Robot with a Reassuring Touch," *New York Times*, September 18, 2012, p. D1.

13 C. Matthews, "Talking Heads; The Maker of Roomba Creates a Roboboss: There's No Place to Hide," *Time*, June 24, 2013, p. 12.

14 Heraclitus, *Fragments: The Collected Wisdom of Heraclitus*, trans. Brooks Haxton (New York: Viking, 2001).

15 N. A. Ebrahim, S. Ahmed, & Z. Taha, "Virtual Teams: A Literature Review," *Australian Journal of Basic and Applied Sciences*, 2009, *3(3)*, p. 2655. See also F. Siebdrat, M. Hoegl, & H. Ernst, "How to Manage Virtual Teams," *MIT Sloan Management Review*, 2009, *50(4)*, pp. 63–68.

16 A. Powell, G. Piccoli, & B. Ives, "Virtual Teams: Review of Current Literature and Directions for Future Research," *DATA BASE for Advances in Information Systems*, 2004, *35(1)*, p. 7.

17 M. LaBrosse, "Managing Virtual Teams," *Employment Relations Today*, 2008, *35(2)*, pp. 81–86.

18 P. Bjorn & O. Ngwenyama, "Virtual Team Collaboration: Building Shared Meaning, Resolving Breakdowns and Creating Translucence," *Information Systems Journal*, 2009, *19(3)*, pp. 227–253.

19 B.L. Kirkman, B. Rosen, C.B. Gibson, P.E. Tesluk, & S.O. McPherson, "Five Challenges to Virtual Team Success: Lessons from Sabre, Inc.," *Academy of Management Executive*, 2002, *16(3)*, pp. 67–79.

20 K. Kim, J. Bolton, A. Girouard, J. Cooperstock, & R. Vertegaal, "TeleHuman: Effects of 3D Perspective on Gaze and Pose Estimation with a Life-Size Cylindrical Telepresence Pod." *Proceedings of CHI'12 Conference on Human Factors in Computing Systems*. ACM Press, 2012, pp. 2531–2540.

21 A.L. Blaskovich, "Exploring the Effect of Social Distance: An Experimental Investigation of Virtual Collaboration, Social Loafing, and Group Decisions," *Journal of Information Systems*, 2008, *22(1)*, pp. 27–46.

22 O.A. Alnuaimi, L.P. Robert, & L.M. Maruping, "Team Size, Dispersion, and Social Loafing in Technology-Supported Teams: A Perspective on the Theory of Moral Disengagement," *Journal of Management Information Systems*, 2010, *27(1)*, pp. 203–230.

23 D. Meyerson, K.E. Weick, & R.M. Kramer, "Swift Trust and Temporary Groups," in R.M. Kramer & T.R. Tyler (eds.), *Trust in Organizations: Frontiers of Theory and Research* (Thousand Oaks, CA: Sage, 1996), pp. 166–195.

24 See also S. Jarvenpaa & D.E. Leidner, "Communication and Trust in Global Virtual Teams," *Organization Science*, 1999, *10(6)*, pp. 791–815.

25 D. Coutu, "Trust in Virtual Teams," *Harvard Business Review*, 1998, 76, pp. 20–21.

26 W.F. Cascio, "Managing a Virtual Workplace," *Academy of Management Executive*, 2000, *14(3)*, pp. 81–90.

27 A. Powell, G. Piccoli, & B. Ives, "Virtual Teams: Review of Current Literature and Directions for Future Research," *DATA BASE for Advances in Information Systems*, 2004, *35(1)*, pp. 6–36.

28 S. Furst, M. Reeves, B. Rosen, & R. Blackburn, "Managing the Life Cycle of Virtual Teams," *Academy of Management Executive*, 2004, *18(2)*, pp. 6–20.

29 Ibid.

30 P.W. Hom, R.W. Griffeth, L.E. Palich, & J.S. Bracker, "Revisiting Met Expectations as a Reason Why Realistic Job Previews Work," *Personnel Psychology*, 1999, *52*, pp. 97–112.

31 See, for instance, J.M. Phillips, "Effects of Realistic Job Previews on Multiple Organizational Outcomes: A Meta-Analysis," *Academy of Management Journal*, 1988, *41*, pp. 673–690.

32 A. Malhotra, A. Majchrzak, & B. Rosen, "Leading Virtual Teams," *Academy of Management Perspectives*, 2007, *21(1)*, pp. 60–70.

33 R. Lyons, H.A. Priest, J.L. Wildman, E. Salas, & D. Carnegie, "Managing Virtual Teams: Strategies for Team Leaders," *Ergonomics in Design*, 2009, *17(8)*, pp. 8–13.

34 L. Zander, M.I. Mochaitis, & C.L. Butler, "Leading Global Teams," *Journal of World Business*, 2012, *47(4)*, pp. 592–603.

35 S.J. Horwitz & C. Santillan, "Knowledge Sharing in Global Virtual Team Collaboration: Applications of CE and thinkLets," *Knowledge Management Research & Practice*, 2012, *10*, p. 343.

36 S. Zaheer & A. Zaheer, "Trust across Borders," *Journal of International Business Studies*, 2006, *37*, pp. 21–29.

37   A. Ariño, J. de la Torre, & P.S. Ring, "Relational Quality: Managing Trust in Corporate Alliances," *California Management Review*, 2001, *44(1)*, pp. 109–131.

38   T. Yamagishi, K.S. Cook, & M. Watabe, "Uncertainty, Trust, and Commitment Formation in the United States and Japan," *American Journal of Sociology*, 1998, *104(1)*, pp. 165–194.

39   F. Welter, T. Kautonen, A. Chepurenko, E. Malieva, & U. Venasaar, "Does Trust Matter?: A Cross-Cultural View of Entrepreneurship in Different Trust Milieus," *Frontiers of Entrepreneurship Research, Proceedings of the 23rd Annual Entrepreneurship Research Conference* (Babson Park, MA: Babson College), p. 230.

40   M.T. Maynard, J.E. Mathieu, T.L. Rapp, & L.L. Gilson, "Something(s) Old and Something(s) New: Modeling Drivers of Global Virtual Team Effectiveness," *Journal of Organizational Behavior*, 2012, *33*, pp. 342–365.

41   K.J. Templer, C. Tay, & N.A. Chandrasekar, "Motivational Cultural Intelligence, Realistic Job Preview, Realistic Living Conditions Preview, and Cross-Cultural Adjustment," *Group & Organization Management*, 2006, *31*, pp. 154–173.

42   K.J. Templer, C. Tay, & N.A. Chandrasekar, "Motivational Cultural Intelligence, Realistic Job Preview, Realistic Living Conditions Preview, and Cross-Cultural Adjustment," *Group & Organization Management*, 2006, *31*, pp. 154–173.

43   Ibid., p. 156.

44   D.J. Power, "What Are Group Decision Support Systems and How Do They Work?" *DSS News*, 2001, *2(7)*. See also G. DeSanctis & R. Gallupe, "A Foundation for the Study of Group Decision Support Systems," *Management Science*, 1987, *33(5)*, pp. 589–609.

45   T.A. Finholt & G.M. Olson, "From Laboratories to Collaboratories: A New Organizational Form for Scientific Collaboration," *Psychological Science*, 1997, *8(1)*, pp. 28–36.

46   Science of Collaboratories Project, *Workshop on the Social Underpinnings of Collaboration*, Final Summary, 2003. http://www.scienceofcollaboratories.org/Workshops/WorkshopJune42001/index.php?FinalSummary (Archived by WebCite® at http://www.webcitation.org/5sjUuZBHZ)

47   Finholt, T.A., "Collaboratories," in B. Cronin (ed.), *Annual Review of Information Science and Technology*, 2002, *36*, pp. 73–107.

48   See W.H. Cooper, R.B. Gallupe, & S. Pollard, "Some Liberating Effects of Anonymous Electronic Brainstorming," *Small Group Research*, 1998, *29*, pp. 147–178; and, D.M. DeRosa, C.L. Smith, & D.A. Hantula, "The Medium Matters: Mining the Long-Promised Merit of Group Interaction in Creative Idea Generation Tasks in a Meta-Analysis of the Electronic Group Brainstorming Literature," *Computers in Human Behavior*, 2007, *23*, pp. 1549–1581.

49   See also A.R. Dennis, R.K. Minas, & A.P. Bhagwatwar, "Sparking Creativity: Improving Electronic Brainstorming with Individual Cognitive Priming," *Journal of Management Information Systems*, 2013, *29(4)*, pp. 195–215.

50   L. Solis, *How to Improve Your Organization's Group Intelligence*. http://www.sterlinghoffman.com/newsletter/articles/article271b.html

51   These examples, as well as others, can be seen on the GroupSystems website: http://www.groupsystems.com/what-clients-say

52   D. Pauleen & P. Yoong, "Facilitating Virtual Team Relationships via Internet and Conventional Communication Channels," *Electronic Networking Applications and Policies*, 2001, *11(3)*, pp. 190–202.

53   J.F. Nunamaker, Jr., B.A. Reinig, & R.O. Briggs, "Principles for Effective Virtual Teamwork," *Communications of the ACM*, 2009, *52(4)*, pp. 113–117.

54   S.K. Horwitz & C. Santillan, "Knowledge Sharing in Global Virtual Team Collaboration: Applications of CE and thinkLets," *Knowledge Management*

Research & Practice, 2012, *10*, pp. 342–353; the quote is from pages 342–343. See also R.O. Briggs, G.-J. de Vreede, & J.F. Nunamaker, "Collaboration Engineering with thinkLets to Pursue Sustained Success with Group Support Systems," *Journal of Management Information Systems,* 2003, *19(4),* pp. 31–64; and J. Bragge, T. Tuunanen, & P. Martiin, "Inviting Lead-users from Virtual Communities to Co-create Innovative IS Services in a Structured Groupware Environment," *Service Science,* 2009, *1(4),* pp. 241–255.

55 R.O. Briggs, S.L. Kolfshoten, G.-J. de Vreede, S. Lukosch, & C.C. Albrecht, "Facilitator-In-a-Box: Process Support Applications to Help Practitioners Realize the Potential of Collaboration Technology," *Journal of Management Information Systems,* 2013, *29(4),* pp. 159–193.

56 R.O. Briggs, G.-J. de Vreede, J.F. Nunamaker, and D. Tobey, "ThinkLets: Achieving Predictable, Repeatable Patterns of Group Interaction with Group Support Systems (GSS)," *Proceedings of the 34th Hawaii International Conference on System Sciences,* IEEE Computer Society, Los Alamitos, CA, 2001; and, R.O. Briggs & G.-J. de Vreede, *ThinkLets: Building Blocks for Concerted Coordination* (Omaha, NE: Center for Collaboration Science, 2009).

57 X.-L. Shen, M.K.O. Lee, & C.M.K. Cheung, "Harnessing Collective Intelligence of Web 2.0: Group Adoption and Use of Internet-Based Collaboration Technologies," *Knowledge Management Research & Practice,* 2012, *10,* pp. 301–311; M. Schumacher, M. Divine, J.S.-L. Cardinal, & J.-C. Bocquet, "Virtual Teams Challenging Human and Technical Web 2.0 Dimensions," *International Journal of Networking and Virtual Organisations,* 2012, *10(2),* pp. 210–228; and, M. London, "Generative Team Learning in Web 2.0 Environments," *Journal of Management Development,* 2013, *32(1),* pp. 73–95.

58 L.A. Seneca, *Moral Epistles,* translated by R.M. Gummere. The Loeb Classic Library, 3 volumes, Volume II, Epistle XC (Cambridge, MA: Harvard University Press, 1917–1925), http://www.stoics.com/seneca_epistles_book_2.html

59 This scale is based on M. Castaneda, T.A. Kolenko, & R.J. Aldag, "Self-Management Perceptions and Practices: A Structural Equations Analysis," *Journal of Organizational Behavior,* 1999, *20,* pp. 101–120.

60 M. Castaneda, T.A. Kolenko, & R.J. Aldag, "Self-Management Perceptions and Practices: A Structural Equations Analysis," *Journal of Organizational Behavior,* 1999, *20,* pp. 101–120. See also, J.E. Mathieu, L.L. Gilson, & T.M. Ruddy, "Empowerment and Team Effectiveness: An Empirical Test of an Integrated Model," *Journal of Applied Psychology,* 2006, *91(1),* pp. 97–108.

61 See S. Kerr & J.M. Jermier, "Substitutes for Leadership: Their Meaning and Measurement," *Organizational Behavior and Human Performance,* 1978, 22, pp. 375–403; P.M. Podsakoff, S.B. McKenzie, & W.H. Bommer, "Meta-Analysis of the Relationships Between Kerr and Jermier's Substitutes for Leadership and Employee Job Attitudes, Role Perceptions, and Performance," *Journal of Applied Psychology,* 1996, *81,* 380–399; and, S.D. Dionne, F.J. Yammarino, J.P. Howell, & J. Villa, "Substitutes for Leadership, or Not," *Leadership Quarterly,* 2005, *16(1),* pp. 169–193.

62 T. Petzinger, Jr., "Self-Organization Will Free Employees to Act Like Bosses," *Wall Street Journal,* January 3, 1997, p. B1; and, J.P. Walsh, A.D. Meyer, & C.B. Schoonhoven, "A Future for Organization Theory: Living in and Living with Changing Organizations," *Organization Science,* 2006, *17(5),* pp. 657–671.

63 See T.A. Stewart, "Looking Ahead: The Search for the Organization of Tomorrow," *Fortune,* May 18, 1992, pp. 92–98; J.J. Laabs, "Ben & Jerry's Caring Capitalism," *Personnel Journal,* November 1992, pp. 50–57; R. Wageman,

"Case Study: Critical Success Factors for Creating Superb Self-Managing Teams at Xerox," *Compensation and Benefits Review*, September/October 1997, pp. 31–41; and, A.B. Jambekar & K.I. Pelc, "Improvisation Model for Team Performance Enhancement in a Manufacturing Environment," *Team Performance Management*, 2007, *13(7/8)*, pp. 259–274.

64 D.B. Jeffrey, "A Comparison of the Effects of External Control and Self-Control on the Modification and Maintenance of Weight," *Journal of Abnormal Psychology*, 1974, *83*, pp. 404–410; and, R.M. Ryan & E.L. Deci, "Self-Regulation and the Problem of Human Autonomy: Does Psychology Need Choice, Self-Determination, and Will?" *Journal of Personality*, 2006, *74(6)*, pp. 1557–1586.

65 T.M. Hout & J.C. Carter, "Getting It Done: New Roles for Senior Executives," *Harvard Business Review*, November/December 1995, pp. 133–141; "New *Fortune*/Hay Group Ranking of 'The World's Most Admired Companies' Published," *PR Newswire*, November 30, 1999; and, M. Ezzamel, H. Willmott, & F. Worthington, "Manufacturing Shareholder Value: The Role of Accounting in Organizational Transformation," *Accounting, Organizations, and Society*, 2008, *33(2/3)*, pp. 107–140.

66 For reviews, see F. Andrasik & J.S. Heimberg, "Self-Management Procedures," in L.W. Frederiksen (ed.), *Handbook of Organizational Behavior Management* (New York: Wiley-Interscience, 1982), pp. 219–247; and, J.H. Barlow, D.R. Ellard, J.M. Hainsworth, F.R. Jones, & A. Fisher, "A Review of Self-Management Interventions for Panic Disorders, Phobias, and Obsessive-Compulsive Disorders," *Acta Psychiatrica Scandinavica*, 2005, *111(4)*, pp. 272–285.

67 See, for instance, M.E. Gist, A.G. Bavetta, & C.K. Stevens, "Transfer Training Method: Its Influence on Skill Generalization, Skill Repetition, and Performance Level," *Personnel Psychology*, 1990, *43*, pp. 501–523; G.P. Latham & C.A. Frayne, "Self Management Training for Increasing Job Attendance: A Follow-Up and a Replication," *Journal of Applied Psychology*, 1989, *74*, pp. 411–416; and, J.B. Vancouver & D.V. Day, "Industrial and Organisation Research on Self-Regulation: From Constructs to Applications," *Applied Psychology*, 2005, *54(2)*, pp. 155–185.

68 The examples of self-management goals, monitoring, modifying of cues and consequences, and reordering of behaviors are from former students' self-management exercises.

69 The idea of making a more preferred activity a reward for completing a less preferred activity is called the Premack Principle. See, for instance, "Making a Difference: Motivating Gifted Students Who Are Not Achieving," *Teaching Exceptional Children*, September/October 2005, pp. 22–31.

70 This section is based on C.C. Manz & H.P. Sims, Jr., "SuperLeadership: Beyond the Myth of Heroic Leadership," *Organizational Dynamics*, Spring 1991, pp. 18–35. See also D. Sullivan, "Clear Thinking for Scary Times," *Advisor Today*, September 2002, *97(9)*, p. 108; and, R. Jones & G. Kriflik, "Strategies for Managerial Self-Change in a Cleaned-Up Bureaucracy: A Qualitative Study," *Journal of Managerial Psychology*, 2005, *20(5)*, pp. 397–416.

71 For instance, see K.M. Richardson & H.R. Rothstein, "Effects of Occupational Stress Management Intervention Programs: A Meta-Analysis," *Journal of Occupational Health Psychology*, 2008, *13(1)*, pp. 69–93.

72 C.P. Neck & C.C. Manz, *Mastering Self-Leadership: Empowering Yourself for Personal Excellence*, 6th ed. (Upper Saddle River, NJ: Pearson, 2103). The quote is from page 90.

Bibliography

Alnuaimi, O.A., Robert, L.P., & Maruping, L.M. "Team Size, Dispersion, and Social Loafing in Technology-Supported Teams: A Perspective on the Theory of Moral Disengagement," *Journal of Management Information Systems*, 2010, *27(1)*, pp. 203–230.

Andrasik, F., & Heimberg, J.S. "Self-Management Procedures." In L.W. Frederiksen (ed.), *Handbook of Organizational Behavior Management* (New York: Wiley-Interscience, 1982), pp. 219–247.

Ariño, A., de la Torre, J., & Ring, P.S. "Relational Quality: Managing Trust in Corporate Alliance," *California Management Review*, 2001, *44(1)*, pp. 109–131.

Barlow, J.H., Ellard, D.R., Hainsworth, J.M., Jones, F.R., & Fisher, A. "A Review of Self-Management Interventions for Panic Disorders, Phobias, and Obsessive-Compulsive Disorders," *Acta Psychiatrica Scandinavica*, 2005, *111(4)*, pp. 272–285.

Bjorn, P., & Ngwenyama, O. "Virtual Team Collaboration: Building Shared Meaning, Resolving Breakdowns and Creating Translucence," *Information Systems Journal*, 2009, *19(3)*, pp. 227–253.

Blaskovich, A.L. "Exploring the Effect of Social Distance: An Experimental Investigation of Virtual Collaboration, Social Loafing, and Group Decisions," *Journal of Information Systems*, 2008, *22(1)*, pp. 27–46.

Bragge, J., Tuunanen, T., & Martiin, P. "Inviting Lead-users from Virtual Communities to Co-create Innovative IS Services in a Structured Groupware Environment," *Service Science, 1(4)*, pp. 241–255.

Briggs, R.O., & de Vreede G.-J. *ThinkLets: Building Blocks for Concerted Coordination* (Omaha, NE: Center for Collaboration Science, 2009).

Briggs, R.O., de Vreede, G.-J., & Nunamaker, J.F. "Collaboration Engineering with thinkLets to Pursue Sustained Success with Group Support Systems," *Journal of Management Information Systems*, 2003, *19(4)*, pp. 31–64.

Briggs, R. O., de Vreede, G.-J., Nunamaker, J.F., & Tobey, D. "ThinkLets: Achieving Predictable, Repeatable Patterns of Group Interaction with Group Support Systems (GSS)." *Proceedings of the 34th Hawaii International Conference on System Sciences*, IEEE Computer Society, Los Alamitos, CA, 2001.

Briggs, R.O., Kolfshoten, S.L., de Vreede, G.-J., Lukosch, S., & Albrecht C.C. "Facilitator-In-a-Box: Process Support Applications to Help Practitioners Realize the Potential of Collaboration Technology," *Journal of Management Information Systems*, 2013, *29(4)*, pp. 159–193.

Bureau of Labor Statistics. *Job Openings and Labor Turnover–January 2012* (U.S. Department of Labor, 2012). http://www.bls.gov/news.release/archives/jolts_03132012.htm

Cascio, W.F. "Managing a Virtual Workplace," *Academy of Management Executive*, 2000, *14(3)*, pp. 81–90.

Castaneda, M., Kolenko, T.A., & Aldag, R.J. "Self-Management Perceptions and Practices: A Structural Equations Analysis," *Journal of Organizational Behavior*, 1999, *20*, pp. 101–120.

Castaneda, M., Kolenko, T.A., & Aldag, R.J. "Self-Management Perceptions and Practices: A Structural Equations Analysis," *Journal of Organizational Behavior*, 1999, *20*, p. 297.

Cooper, W.H., Gallupe, R.B., & Pollard, S. "Some Liberating Effects of Anonymous Electronic Brainstorming," *Small Group Research*, 1998, 29, pp. 147–178.

Coutu, D. "Trust in Virtual Teams," *Harvard Business Review*, 1998, 76, pp. 20–21.

Dennis, A.R., Minas, R.K., & Bhagwatwar, A.P., "Sparking Creativity: Improving Electronic Brainstorming with Individual Cognitive Priming," *Journal of Management Information Systems*, 2013, *29(4)*, pp. 195–215.

DeRosa, D.M., Smith, C.L., & Hantula, D.A. "The Medium Matters: Mining the Long-Promised Merit of Group Interaction in Creative Idea Generation Tasks in a Meta-Analysis of the Electronic Group Brainstorming Literature," *Computers in Human Behavior*, 2007, *23*, pp. 1549–1581.

DeSanctis G., & Gallupe, R. "A Foundation for the Study of Group Decision Support Systems," *Management Science*, 1987, *33(5)*, pp. 589–609.

Dionne, S.D., Yammarino, F.J., Howell, J.P., & Villa, J. "Substitutes for Leadership, or Not," *Leadership Quarterly*, 2005, *16(1)*, pp. 169–193.

Ebrahim, N.A., Ahmed, S., & Taha, Z. "Virtual Teams: A Literature Review," *Australian Journal of Basic and Applied Sciences,* 2009, *3(3),* pp. 2653–2669.

Ezzamel, M., Willmott, H., & Worthington, F. "Manufacturing Shareholder Value: The Role of Accounting in Organizational Transformation," *Accounting, Organizations, and Society*, 2008, *33(2/3)*, pp. 107–140.

Finholt, T.A., "Collaboratories." In B. Cronin (ed.), *Annual Review of Information Science and Technology*, 2002, *36*, pp. 73–107.

Finholt, T.A., & Olson, G.M. "From Laboratories to Collaboratories: A New Organizational Form for Scientific Collaboration," *Psychological Science*, 1997, *8(1)*, 28–36.

Fost, D. "They're Working on Their Own, Just Side by Side," *New York Times*, February 20, 2008. http://www.nytimes.com/2008/02/20/business/businessspecial2/20cowork.html?pagewanted=all

Furst, S.A., Reeves, M., Rosen, B., & Blackburn, R. "Managing the Life Cycle of Virtual Teams," *Academy of Management Executive*, 2004, *18(2)*, pp. 6–20.

Gist, M.E., Bavetta, A.G., & Stevens, C.K. "Transfer Training Method: Its Influence on Skill Generalization, Skill Repetition, and Performance Level," *Personnel Psychology*, 1990, *43*, pp. 501–523.

GroupSystems. *How to Improve Your Organization's Group Intelligence.* http://groupsystems.com/wp-content/uploads/2012/02/GroupIntelligence.pdf

Heraclitus. *Fragments: The Collected Wisdom of Heraclitus*, trans. Brooks Haxton (New York: Viking, 2001).

Hertel, S., Geister, S., & Konradt, U. "Managing Virtual Teams: A Review of Current Empirical Research," *Human Resource Management Review*, 2005, *15*, pp. 69–95.

Hicks, J. "i-Robot's New Ava 500 Puts Robotics in Heart of the Enterprise," *Forbes*, June 10, 2013. http://www.forbes.com/sites/jenniferhicks/2013/06/10/irobots-new-ava-500-puts-robotics-in-heart-of-the-enterprise

Hom, P.W., Griffeth, R.W., Palich, L.E., & Bracker, J.S. "Revisiting Met Expectations as a Reason Why Realistic Job Previews Work," *Personnel Psychology*, 1999, *52*, pp. 97–112.

Horwitz, S.J., & Santillan, C. "Knowledge Sharing in Global Virtual Team Collaboration: Applications of CE and thinkLets," *Knowledge Management Research & Practice*, 2012, *10*, pp. 342–353.

Hout, T.M., & Carter, J.C. "Getting It Done: New Roles for Senior Executives," *Harvard Business Review*, November/December 1995, pp. 133–141.

Jambekar, A.B., & Pelc, K.I. "Improvisation Model for Team Performance Enhancement in a Manufacturing Environment," *Team Performance Management*, 2007, *13(7/8)*, pp. 259–274.

Jarvenpaa, S., & Leidner, D.E. "Communication and Trust in Global Virtual Teams," *Organization Science*, 1999, *10(6)*, pp. 791–815.

Jeffrey, D.B. "A Comparison of the Effects of External Control and Self-Control on the Modification and Maintenance of Weight," *Journal of Abnormal Psychology*, 1974, *83*, pp. 404–410.

Jones, R., & Kriflik, G. "Strategies for Managerial Self-Change in a Cleaned-Up Bureaucracy: A Qualitative Study," *Journal of Managerial Psychology*, 2005, *20(5)*, pp. 397–416.

Kerr, S., & Jermier, J.M. "Substitutes for Leadership: Their Meaning and Measurement," *Organizational Behavior and Human Performance*, 1978, *22*, pp. 375–403.

Kim, K., Bolton, J., Girouard, A., Cooperstock, J. & Vertegaal, R. "TeleHuman: Effects of 3D Perspective on Gaze and Pose Estimation with a Life-Size Cylindrical Telepresence Pod." *Proceedings of CHI'12 Conference on Human Factors in Computing Systems* (ACM Press, 2012), pp. 2531–2540.

King, R. "The (Virtual) Global Office," *Businessweek*, May 2, 2008. http://www.businessweek.com/stories/2008-05-02/the-virtual-global-officebusinessweek-business-news-stock-market-and-financial-advice

Kirkman, B.L., Rosen, B., Gibson, C.B., Tesluk, P.E., & McPherson, S.O. "Five Challenges to Virtual Team Success: Lessons from Sabre, Inc.," *Academy of Management Executive*, 2002, *16(3)*, pp. 67–79.

Laabs, J.J. "Ben & Jerry's Caring Capitalism," *Personnel Journal*, November 1992, pp. 50–57.

LaBrosse, M. "Managing Virtual Teams," *Employment Relations Today*, 2008, *35(2)*, pp. 81–86.

Lapowski, I. "Why Everyone at My Company Has One Job Title," *Inc. Magazine*. http://www.inc.com/magazine/201212/issie-lapowsky/the-nerdery-mike-derheim-everyone-at-my-company-has-one-job-title.html

Latham, G.P., & Frayne, C.A. "Self Management Training for Increasing Job Attendance: A Follow-Up and a Replication," *Journal of Applied Psychology*, 1989, *74*, pp. 411–416.

London, M. "Generative Team Learning in Web 2.0 Environments," *Journal of Management Development*, 2013, *32(1)*, pp. 73–95.

Lyons, R., Priest, H.A., Wildman, J.L., Salas, E., & Carnegie, D. "Managing Virtual Teams: Strategies for Team Leaders," *Ergonomics in Design*, 2009, *17(8)*, pp. 8–13.

"Making a Difference: Motivating Gifted Students Who Are Not Achieving," *Teaching Exceptional Children*, September/October 2005, pp. 22–31.

Malhotra, A., Majchrzak, A., & Rosen, B. "Leading Virtual Teams," *Academy of Management Perspectives*, 2007, *21(1)*, pp. 60–70.

Manz, C.C., & Sims, H.P., Jr., "SuperLeadership: Beyond the Myth of Heroic Leadership," *Organizational Dynamics*, Spring 1991, pp. 18–35.

Markoff, J. "A Robot with a Reassuring Touch," *New York Times*, September 18, 2012, p. D1.

Mathieu, J.E., Gilson, L.L., & Ruddy, T.M. "Empowerment and Team Effectiveness: An Empirical Test of an Integrated Model," *Journal of Applied Psychology*, 2006, *91(1)*, pp. 97–108.

Matthews, C. "Talking Heads; The Maker of Roomba Creates a Roboboss: There's No Place to Hide," *Time*, June 24, 2013, p. 12.

Maynard, M.T., Mathieu, J.E., Rapp, T.L., & Gilson, L.L. "Something(s) Old and Something(s) New: Modeling Drivers of Global Virtual Team Effectiveness," *Journal of Organizational Behavior*, 2012, *33*, pp. 342–365.

Meyerson, D., Weick, K.E., & Kramer, R.M. "Swift Trust and Temporary Groups." In R.M. Kramer & T.R. Tyler (eds.), *Trust in Organizations: Frontiers of Theory and Research* (Thousand Oaks, CA: Sage, 1996), pp. 166–195.

Neck, C.P., & Manz, C.C. *Mastering Self-Leadership: Empowering Yourself for Personal Excellence*, 6th ed. (Upper Saddle River, NJ: Pearson, 2013).

"New *Fortune*/Hay Group Ranking of 'The World's Most Admired Companies' Published," *PR Newswire*, November 30, 1999.

Nunamaker, J.F., Jr., Reinig, B.A., & Briggs, R.O. "Principles for Effective Virtual Teamwork," *Communications of the ACM*, 2009, *52(4)*, pp. 113–117.

Olson, P. "Rise of the Telepresence Robots," *Forbes*, July 15, 2013. http://www.forbes.com/sites/parmyolson/2013/06/27/rise-of-the-telepresence-robots

Pauleen, D., & Yoong, P. "Facilitating Virtual Team Relationships via Internet and Conventional Communication Channels," *Electronic Networking Applications and Policies*, 2001, *11(3)*, pp. 190–202.

Petzinger, T., Jr., "Self-Organization Will Free Employees to Act Like Bosses," *Wall Street Journal*, January 3, 1997, p. B1.

Phillips, J.M. "Effects of Realistic Job Previews on Multiple Organizational Outcomes: A Meta-Analysis," *Academy of Management Journal*, 1988, *41*, pp. 673–690.

Podsakoff, P.M., McKenzie, S.B., & Bommer, W.H. "Meta-analysis of the Relationships between Kerr and Jermier's Substitutes for Leadership and Employee Job Attitudes, Role Perceptions, and Performance," *Journal of Applied Psychology*, 1996, *81*, pp. 380–399.

Powell, A., Piccoli, G., & Ives, B. "Virtual Teams: Review of Current Literature and Directions for Future Research," *DATA BASE for Advances in Information Systems*, 2004, *35(1)*, pp. 6–36.

Power, D.J. "What Are Group Decision Support Systems and How Do They Work?" *DSS News*, 2001, *2(7)*.

Richardson K.M., & Rothstein, H.R. "Effects of Occupational Stress Management Intervention Programs: A Meta-Analysis," *Journal of Occupational Health Psychology*, 2008, *13(1)*, pp. 69–93.

Rousseau, D.M. "Psychological and Implied Contracts in Organizations," *Employee Responsibilities and Rights Journal*, 1989, 2, pp. 121–139.

Rushby, C. "Europe's Capital of Co-Working: Is Sharing Desks Worth It?" *Silicon Allee*, November 28, 2012. http://siliconallee.com/silicon-allee/editorial/2012/11/28/europes-capital-of-co-working-is-sharing-desks-worth-it?

Ryan, R.M., & Deci, E.L. "Self-Regulation and the Problem of Human Autonomy: Does Psychology Need Choice, Self-Determination, and Will?" *Journal of Personality*, 2006, *74(6)*, pp. 1557–1586.

Salmon, G. "The Future for (Second) Life and Learning," *British Journal of Educational Technology*, 2009, *40(3)*, pp. 526–538.

Schumacher, M., Divine, M., Cardinal, J.S.-L., & Bocquet, J.-C., "Virtual Teams Challenging Human and Technical Web 2.0 Dimensions," *International Journal of Networking and Virtual Organisations*, 2012, *10(2)*, pp. 210–228.

Science of Collaboratories Project. Workshop on the Social Underpinnings of Collaboration. *Final Summary*, 2003. http://www.scienceofcollaboratories.org/Workshops/WorkshopJune42001/index.php?FinalSummary (Archived by Web-Cite® at http://www.webcitation.org/5sjUuZBHZ)

Seneca, L. A. *Moral Epistles*. Translated by R. M. Gummere. The Loeb Classic Library, 3 Volumes. Volume II (Cambridge, MA: Harvard University Press, 1917–1925). http://www.stoics.com/seneca_epistles_book_2.html

Shen, X.-L., Lee, M.K.O., & Cheung, C.M.K. "Harnessing Collective Intelligence of Web 2.0: Group Adoption and Use of Internet-Based Collaboration Technologies," *Knowledge Management Research & Practice*, 2012, *10*, pp. 301–311.

Siebdrat, F., Hoegl, M., & Ernst, H. "How to Manage Virtual Teams," *MIT Sloan Management Review*, 2009, *50(4)*, pp. 63–68.

Silverman, R.E. "My Life as a Telecommuting Robot," *Wall Street Journal*, August 8, 2012, p. B1.

Silverman, R.E. "Step into the Office-Less Company," *Wall Street Journal*, September 5, 2012, p. B6.

Snyder, L. *Fluency with Information Technology* (Boston: Addison-Wesley, 2003).

Solis, L. *How to Improve Your Organization's Group Intelligence*. http://www.sterlinghoffman.com/newsletter/articles/article271b.html

Spinuzzi, C. "Working Alone Together: Coworking as Emergent Collaborative Activity," *Journal of Business and Technical Communication*, 2012, *26(4)*, pp. 399–441.

Stewart, T.A. "Looking Ahead: The Search for the Organization of Tomorrow," *Fortune*, May 18, 1992, pp. 92–98.

Sullivan, D. "Clear Thinking for Scary Times," *Advisor Today*, September 2002, *97(9)*, p. 108.

Templer, K.J., Tay, C., & Chandrasekar, N.A. "Motivational Cultural Intelligence, Realistic Job Preview, Realistic Living Conditions Preview, and Cross-Cultural Adjustment," *Group & Organization Management*, 2006, *31*, pp. 154–173.

Vancouver, J.B., & Day, D.V. "Industrial and Organisation Research on Self-Regulation: From Constructs to Applications," *Applied Psychology*, 2005, *54(2)*, pp. 155–185.

Wageman, R. "Case Study: Critical Success Factors for Creating Superb Self-Managing Teams at Xerox," *Compensation and Benefits Review*, September/October 1997, pp. 31–41.

Wageman, R., Gardner, H., & Mortensen, M. "Teams Have Changed: Catching up to the Future," *Industrial & Organizational Psychology*, 2012, *5(1)*, pp. 48–52.

Walsh, J.P., Meyer, A.D., & Schoonhoven, C.B. "A Future for Organization Theory: Living in and Living With Changing Organizations," *Organization Science*, 2006, *17(5)*, pp. 657–671.

Welter, F., Kautonen, T., Chepurenko, A., Malieva, E., & Venasaar, U. "Does Trust Matter? A Cross-Cultural View of Entrepreneurship in Different Trust Milieus," *Frontiers of Entrepreneurship Research. Proceedings of the 23rd Annual Entrepreneurship Research Conference* (Babson Park, MA: Babson College), p. 230.

Yamagishi, T., Cook, K.S., & Watabe, M. "Uncertainty, Trust, and Commitment Formation in the United States and Japan," *American Journal of Sociology*, 1998, *104(1)*, pp. 165–194.

Zaheer, S., & Zaheer, A. "Trust across Borders," *Journal of International Business Studies*, 2006, *37*, pp. 21–29.

Zander, L., Mochaitis, M.I., & Butler, C.L. "Leading Global Teams," *Journal of World Business*, 2012, *47(4)*, pp. 592–603.

Designing and Implementing Team-Based Organizations

Learning Objectives

After reading this chapter, you should be able to do the following:

1. Define a team-based organization.
2. Discuss the objectives of a team-based organization.
3. Understand how to conduct a readiness review for the potential implementation of team-based organizations.
4. Identify and describe the challenges associated with implementation of team-based organizations.
5. Identify and describe the elements of a team-based organization.
6. Identify and describe the steps in creating a team-based organization.
7. Identify and describe best practices for creating organizations that support teams.

I N THIS CHAPTER WE FOCUS ON THE TEAM CONTEXT component of our High Performance Teams Model. As you have seen, many factors influence team effectiveness and success. Much of our focus has been on the team itself—such as its structures and processes, leaders and members, and group culture and dynamics. Other important factors, often overlooked or underemphasized, include the team's context and environment.

It is critical to recognize that team and organizational leaders must also build an overall organizational system that supports team formation, development, and performance. Those who address such contextual factors in building team support systems will more successfully leverage team contributions to organizational success.

This quotation from Stephen Covey, a motivational speaker and consultant, indicates that talented and motivated teams can do the right things but still fail because of their organizational environment. As an organizational leader, you must think not only about the functioning of a team itself, but also about the environment, which you influence, and the degree to which it supports the team.

In **team-based organizations** the team, rather than an individual, is the fundamental

> **TEAM WORDS OF WISDOM**
>
> "If you put good people in bad systems you get bad results. You have to water the flowers you want to grow."
>
> STEPHEN R. COVEY,
> AUTHOR OF *SEVEN HABITS OF HIGHLY EFFECTIVE PEOPLE*

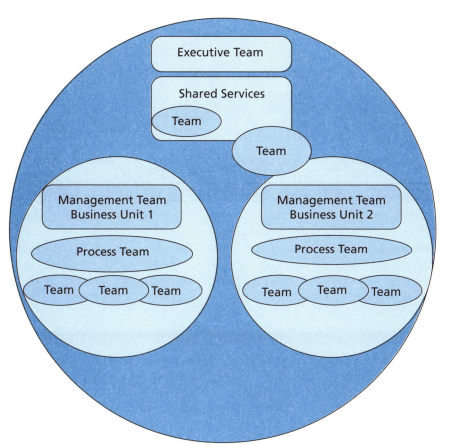

Figure 12-1

A Team-Based Organization

Source: Based on S. Mohrman, C. Cohen, and A. Mohrman, Jr.. *Designing Team-Based Organizations* (San Francisco: Jossey-Bass, 1995), p. 49.

work unit.[1] Team-based organizations focus on designing an infrastructure that will support the development and deployment of teams throughout an organization. Susan Mohrman et al. contrast a team-based organization, such as shown in Figure 12-1, with a traditional functional organization.[2]

For comparison purposes, Figure 12-2 shows a traditional organizational chart depicting a functional design. Under this structure, organization is based on functional area, such as finance or marketing. For example, a financial analyst may have little interaction with, or knowledge of, the marketing function. In such a design the functional areas are sometimes described as silos, self-contained and isolated from other functions. As a result, coordination, learning, and cooperation suffer.[3]

In a team-based organization as shown in Figure 12-1, however, teams are the building blocks. They manage work processes (e.g., process teams), facilitate interteam coordination of activities and communications (e.g., teams linking the shared service unit with the business unit), and provide leadership for the overall organization (e.g., executive teams). Reporting relationships between units and functional unit leaders/executives are less hierarchical, and in the team-based organization some teams (such as Business Unit 1) operate with considerable autonomy.

Figure 12-2

A Traditional Functional
Organizational Design

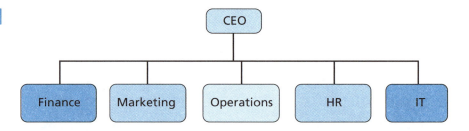

TEAMS IN NEWS: The Google Garage

Google, the search and Internet behemoth, uses the Google Garage to promote collaboration and cross-functional interaction among employees by having fun and creating a playground-like environment. The Google Garage (its title reflecting the fact that Google was born—like Apple and Hewlett-Packard—in a garage) is a commons area where employees of different backgrounds, interests, and roles come together to learn and create.[1]

Google program manager Mamie Rheingold says, "We packed too many people into this space; they were literally elbow to elbow. What happened was they kind of just had to collaborate. If you can't ignore the person next to you, you might as well collaborate with them."[2] This kind of interaction helps Google teams develop novel products and services that expand the company's presence in new markets. The Google Garage illustrates how the organizational context can shape and support worker interaction.[3] Frederik Pferdt, Google's program manager for innovation and creativity, says, "If you want to encourage creativity, and wild ideas, and moonshot thinking, you should create that exact environment that helps you achieve that."[4] (Follow this link to learn more: http://www.fastcompany.com/3017824/work-smart/how-googles-flexible-workspace-ignites-creative-collaboration-on-wheels?partner=newsletter/.)

Notes

1. M. Kohrman, "How Google's Flexible Workspace Ignites Creative Collaboration (on Wheels)." *Fast Company*, September 26, 2013. http://www.fastcompany.com/3017824/work-smart/how-googles-flexible-workspace-ignites-creative-collaboration-on-wheels?partner=newsletter.
2. Ibid.
3. For more on the Google Garage, see M. Kohrman, "Go Inside Google Garage, the Collaborative Workspace That Thrived on Crazy, Creative Ideas," *Fast Company*, September 19, 2013. https://www.google.com/search?q=%-22google+garage%22&ie=utf-8&oe=utf-8&aq=t&rls=org.mozilla:en-US:official&client=firefox-a&channel=sb. See also V. Taylor, "Inside Google's Amsterdam Office: Waffle Ceiling Panels, Exposed Brick and a Caravan Meeting Room," *New York Daily News*, March 26, 2014. http://www.nydailynews.com/life-style/google-garage-meets-dutch-pride-amsterdam-office-article-1.1735871.
4. Ibid.

Characteristics of Team-Based Organizations

Attributes distinguishing team-based organizations from those with traditional organizational structures include the following transitions:[4]

Transition 1: Managers into leaders. Rather than focusing on tactics and operations, managers engage in strategic planning (vision and mission) and empowering followers to help achieve business objectives.

Transition 2: Employees into teammates. The basic defining element is the team rather than the individual. All members of the organization participate in teams, and teams are the primary mechanism for getting work done.

Transition 3: A hierarchical organization into one of empowerment. Rather than focusing on layers of hierarchy and authority that centralize power at top organizational levels, create bureaucracy, and underuse the knowledge and skills of lower-level workers, team-based organizations emphasize the empowerment of semi-autonomous teams to make strategic decisions.

Skills Practice 12.1 on the text website involves conducting research on the Internet to identify an example of a team-based organization and how it is structured and implemented.

Importance of Team-Based Organizations

Research tends to support the value of team-based organizations. A study of the 100 most innovative companies in the United States found that, while compensation, organizational change and restructuring, training, and labor management relations were important, senior management's key concern was how to create and sustain team-based organizations to support innovation as the organization's competitive advantage.[5]

As an example, a large insurance company wanted to increase its emphasis on workforce diversity. Consumers had successfully sued it, alleging that it was discriminatory when judging the insurability of members of particular racial or ethnic groups. The lawsuit settlement required the company to launch a formal diversity initiative to enhance employee sensitivity to diversity issues and to change the company's culture.

A team of members of the company's marketing department was assembled to lead the initiative. Management emphasized race and ethnicity in composing the team and launched the team with great fanfare and excitement. However, as the team began to plan and execute monthly diversity events, it encountered financial and support barriers. Management committed to only a very small budget of about $1,000 to support the team's activities. There was also little support from IT, HR, operations, legal, and even senior management. Within a year, the team had lost its momentum and stopped meeting on a regular basis. In large part, the team failed due to lack of organizational support.

Skills Practice 12.2 on the text website involves conducting an interview with a team leader about his or her perspective regarding team-based organizations and how to function effectively within this type of system.

Factors Driving the Movement toward Team-Based Organizations[6]

Many environmental factors have contributed to the increasing emphasis on team-based organizations, including the following:

- **Growing focus on quality and customer satisfaction.** Teams are now viewed as the preferred approach for empowering workers to understand and satisfy customer needs and to meet quality requirements for products and services.
- **Shift from a homogeneous to a diverse workforce.** The continuing diversity of the U.S. workforce along dimensions such as race, ethnicity, gender, age, lifestyle, and personal values presents opportunities for new strategies to harness this rich array of attributes.
- **Need to reengineer organizations to drive continuous improvement and increase long-term performance.** The saying "Two heads are better than one" applies as members of organizations working together to diagnose and solve problems tend to produce better results than those working in isolation.
- **Philosophy that emphasizes supporting employees.** Organizational leaders increasingly recognize that if workers are to be successful in supporting business objectives, the firm must provide a supportive culture, work processes, and methods.
- **Worker values reflecting a need for meaningful work.** Employees prefer to have challenging and meaningful jobs that keep them engaged, motivated, and performing at a high level. Opportunities to work on a greater variety of tasks and assume more responsibility make teams an attractive option for satisfying workers' higher–level needs. This issue was discussed in more detail in our coverage of Maslow's hierarchy of needs and the Job Characteristics Model in Chapter 4.
- **Increased awareness that employee involvement enhances productivity.** Employers increasingly understand that workers support practices and projects in which they participate; they better understand them and feel a sense of ownership for ensuring their success.
- **Increased recognition that a project manager cannot plan and control a project by himself or herself.** As project size and complexity increase, a project manager's job can become overwhelming. Using teams can help empower others to take on responsibility for many aspects of a project.

Benefits of Team-Based Organizations[7]

The factors driving the movement toward team-based organizations are also closely related to the benefits of this approach. Specifically, team-based organizations enhance an organization's capacity to achieve in these ways:

- Improved product and service quality
- Increased flexibility and adaptability to changes in the external environment
- **Coordination of activities and work processes among different parts of an organization**
- **Greater employee satisfaction, engagement, and development of broader knowledge and skills**
- **Increased productivity, streamlining of work processes, elimination of waste, and reduction in operating costs**

- **Improved accountability**
- **Greater operational flexibility**

These factors may help an organization achieve a sustainable competitive advantage in terms of innovation in product development (e.g., Apple), service processes (e.g., Amazon), and/or product quality (e.g., Toyota).

Challenges Associated with Implementing Team-Based Organizations[8]

When creating effective teams we tend to focus on internal factors, such as defining team objectives, specifying members' roles of team members, deciding how to manage teamwork, and determining how to make decisions. However, development of effective team-based organizations also requires attention to organizational-level factors, such as organization structure, culture, and environment.

Implementation of team-based organizations may require massive organizational change, potentially endangering the long-term chances of successful implementation and sustenance. John Kotter estimates that 70% of changes in organizations, both small and large, will fail to achieve their objectives.[9] Successful transitions to team-based organizations require understanding the challenges likely to be encountered and the strategies that can be deployed to overcome them. Common barriers in such transitions include the following:

- **Resistance to change.** As discussed in greater detail in Chapter 8, people generally dislike change that takes them outside their comfort zones. Pushback associated with change may come from fear of loss of things of value (such as jobs, reporting relationships, or responsibilities). Managers should not underestimate the degree to which employees may resist even seemingly small changes. Reactions to larger (paradigm-shifting) changes such as movement toward team-based organizations are understandably especially subject to resistance.[10]
- **Avoidance of the team coordinator role.** The team coordinator typically provides oversight and facilitation support for teams in a team-based organization. Since this position does not entail the management of a team in the traditional, hierarchical sense, it may be difficult to find individuals who are willing to take on the role and/or who have the skill set and experiential foundation to be effective in it.
- **Fear of blame.** In team-based organizations, accountability for achieving the objectives of specific business units is clearly assigned to individual self-managing teams. This helps ensure team accountability for results, whether those results are positive or negative. Some people find such autonomy, responsibility, and accountability uncomfortable.
- **Limited skills and abilities**. A team-based organizational system requires workers who can function in a cross-functional manner and make decisions without supervision. These skills may be scarce in a traditional organization. If so, successful implementation of a team-based organization will be difficult.
- **Pay distribution.** In a team-based organization, compensation systems are often based on team rather than individual performance. Those who believe they contribute relatively more to the team's success may not view equal distribution as fair.

TEAM MANAGEMENT COACH

Insights and Advice

Tim Hallock, director of quality management, Central Wisconsin Center

How would you define a team-based organization? What specific actions does management need to take to create an organization that truly supports working in teams?

In my opinion, a team-based organization is defined not by the number or types of teams it has, but rather by how engaged employees are in achieving its mission. It is important to engage employees not just in doing their work but also in thinking and contributing to how that work could be done better and support a higher purpose (mission). This often requires the involvement of workers in various types of teams. Team-based organizations believe that quality is achieved through the people who do the work, and they give those people an opportunity to learn and drive results. Leaders see the need to manage key functions not just within a hierarchical, top-down, departmental structure but also in a cross-departmental or cross-functional way.

What are the most common mistakes you have seen managers and management make in building organizations that support teams?

- They do not support teams with resources (such as training, coaching, and direction).
- They form teams with no clear aim or purpose.
- They set unrealistic timeframes, if any, for completion.
- They have limited or no project management and reporting requirements.
- They believe people are too busy doing their regular jobs to have time for teams.
- They believe teams are not appropriate for front-line employees.
- They have teams but maintain a status quo management style, unwilling to change or even test a change. Teams get discouraged and lose the curiosity to improve.

What advice would you give to students regarding strategies they should use to create team-based organizations after graduation?

Students need to clearly examine their management philosophy. If they believe results will come by engaging employees in the overall mission of the organization, they will need principles and practices that support that belief, including these:

- People will be rewarded by being part of something good.
- Quality requires involving people.
- We have time to improve.
- Continuous improvement is better than delayed perfection—so try things.
- I need to get dirty—to get out to the front line and do a Gemba Walk. (Note: In Japan the front-line is called *Gemba*, the real place, and in a Gemba Walk the manager goes to the front line to see the actual work, ask questions, and learn.)[1]
- Have a personal curiosity for improvement.
- Consider that all work is part of a process and that neither I, nor anyone else, is an expert in everything.

Note

1. See M. Imai, *Genba Kaizen: A Commonsense Low-Cost Approach to Management* (New York: McGraw-Hill Professional, 1997); and, J. Womack, *Gemba Walks* (Lean Enterprise Institute, 2011).

Good Reasons for Converting to a Team-Based Organization	Poor Reasons for Converting to a Team-Based Organization
• Total quality management efforts and employee involvement processes have shown the power of teamwork	• The organization has downsized and lacks supervisors to effectively supervise everyone
• Competition has increased in the industry	• The boss, headquarters, or the corporate executives told us to start self-directed work teams
• Potential in the workforce is being wasted or used inefficiently	• Management believes that members are already self-directed
• There is a visible need for stronger management-employee partnerships	• The transition to teams may prevent unionization of the company's workforce

Figure 12-3

Readiness Review Assessment Questions for Team-Based Organizations

Source: Adapted from D. Ray & H. Bronstein. *Teaming Up*. New York: McGraw-Hill, 1995, pp. 23–29.

Readiness to Become a Team-Based Organization

When considering whether to create a team-based organization, leaders should conduct in-depth assessments of the readiness for transition of their organizational strategy, operations, culture, practices, and employee relations. Taking the time to do this analysis is critical since successful movement to team-based organizations depends on the fit between requirements of the new approach and the ability of organization members and the organization's culture and structure to support the change.

Such a formal assessment is sometimes called a **readiness review**. Conducting such a review involves collection of in-depth data regarding the functioning and effectiveness of an organization. These data may be based on quarterly financial reports, the strategic plan, stakeholder information (both from and about suppliers and partner organizations), customer satisfaction, employee satisfaction and engagement, industry and competitors, and other indices. As part of the process of analyzing and discussing the data collected, leaders should attempt to identify reasons why team-based organizations may or may not be a good fit, as shown in Figure 12-3.[11]

Management should also assess the organization's status and history to determine its readiness to transition to a team-based organization. Doing so requires a systematic and evidence-based approach and a willingness on the part of managers to conduct an open and honest assessment of an organization's strengths and weaknesses. Figure 12-4 shows key positive and negative indicators of readiness.[12]

Skills Practice 12.3 on the text website illustrates the steps associated with assessing the readiness of an organization to implement a team-based system. This is a useful assessment to conduct as it helps to gauge the likelihood of the success of a team-based organization in a specific situation.

Models of Team-Based Organizations

So far, we have considered the nature of a team-based organization, its differences from a traditional organization, and its potential benefits. However, problems are often encountered in the transition to team-based

Figure 12-4

Figure 12-4

Indicators of Readiness for
Team-Based Organizations

Positive Indicators of Readiness for Team-Based Organizations	Negative Indicators of Readiness for Team-Based Organizations
• A recent history of positive and improving labor conditions	• A continuing history of management-labor strife
• A history of management's flexibility and willingness to implement employee empowerment processes	• A recent downsizing
• A history of management's ability to stick with a process for long periods of time	• A history of top management inability to stay focused on change long enough to see results
• A strong new management team at the local level that has no history with the workforce and has previously demonstrated skills in employee involvement	• Key local managers are known by the work force to be unsupportive of employee involvement
• An already functioning pay for performance, pay for knowledge, or skill-based compensation system	• Strong objections by corporate headquarters to allocating the full estimated resources required to implement self-directed work teams successfully
• A management group that has consistently involved the workforce in strategic planning, workplace training, or multilevel problem solving	• Weak or unsupportive human resources or labor relations departments

Source: Adapted from D. Ray & H. Bronstein. *Teaming Up.* New York: McGraw-Hill, 1995.

organizations. To better understand these issues, we next present conceptual models identifying key elements of team-based organizations, the relationships among their elements, and their impacts on organizational outcomes and performance. Each model observes team-based organizations through a unique and complementary lens.

The Mohrman, Cohen, and Mohrman Team-Based Organization Model[13]

The Mohrman, Cohen, and Mohrman model, shown in Figure 12-5, views team-based organizations as team systems embedded in a larger organizational context, including the organization's strategy and external environment (such as the market, customers, competitors, and the legal and economic environment). The Nature of Task factor is at the core of the model since it ultimately determines whether consideration of a team-based organization is advantageous. For example, if an organization's basic tasks are simple, routine, and not interdependent, a team-based organization may not be appropriate.

Within the team system, several design factors must be addressed and incorporated into an integrated team structure. Figure 12-5 shows that the Key Design features include combining *clustering* decisions regarding organizing tasks and activities (such as team attributes, management structure and roles) with *linking* decisions regarding how teams will work with each other and coordinate their communications and activities (e.g., multiteam linkages, integration processes). The model also views Facilitators as playing

Figure 12-5

Mohrman, Cohen, and Mohrman Effectiveness Framework for Team-Based Knowledge Organizations

Source: Based on S. A. Mohrman, S. G. Cohen, and A. M. Mohrman. *Designing Team-Based Organizations: New Forms of Knowledge Work*. San Francisco, CA: Jossey-Bass, 1995, p. 63.

a key role in ensuring coordination and integration of activities, enabling teams to make decisions effectively and providing general support for teams to enhance their effectiveness and overall performance. Finally, the model shows Effectiveness measures that can be enhanced through the use of a team-based organization. These include macro-level measures such as business unit and team performance but also micro-level measures such as team member satisfaction and learning.

The Design Sequence model shown in Figure 12-6 links the general team-based organization framework to a process for creating a team-based organization.[14]

The five steps in the Design Sequence model and the key tasks and actions for each step are shown in Figure 12-7. That figure demonstrates the need for a systematic and disciplined process for transitioning to a team-based organization.[15]

Skills Practices 12.4, 12.5, and 12.6 on the text website focus on the implementation of various aspects of the overall process for transitioning to a team-based organization, including responsibility charting, a job-skills matrix, and a cross-training matrix.

The Forrester and Drexler Team-Based Organization Model[16]
The Forrester and Drexler model, shown in Figure 12-8, is particularly useful in identifying the critical issues team-based organizations must address to be successful, the crucial factors required for success (*keys*), and potential barriers or issues that may be encountered at various landmarks during the process (*off/keys*). It also specifies a roadmap for leaders and managers of team-based organizations to follow by specifying the order in which the critical issues need to be addressed (e.g., formation comes first, then dependability, and so on).

Figure 12-6

Mohrman, Cohen,
and Mohrman Design
Sequence for Transition
to a Team-Based
Organization

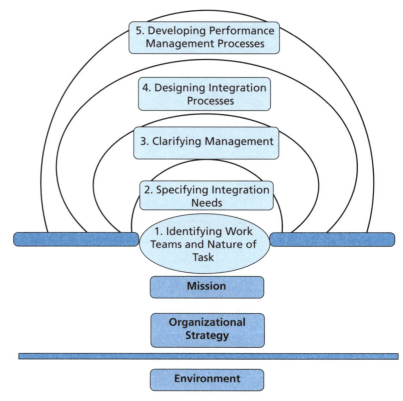

5. Developing Performance
Management Processes

4. Designing Integration
Processes

3. Clarifying Management

2. Specifying Integration
Needs

1. Identifying Work
Teams and Nature of
Task

Mission

**Organizational
Strategy**

Environment

Source: Based on S. A. Mohrman, S. G. Cohen, & A. M. Mohrman. *Designing Team-Based Organizations: New Forms of Knowledge Work*. San Francisco, CA: Jossey-Bass, 1995, p. 72.

Figure 12-7

Key Tasks or Activities at
Each Step in the Design
Sequence Model

Step	Key Tasks or Activities
1: Identifying Work Teams and Nature of Task	• The teams should be relatively self-contained. • Support services are in place for the team. • Individuals are cross-trained to facilitate flexibility and cross-coordination between members. • Members are dedicated so that they don't have split priorities. • The team reports as a unit to the organization. • The team decides how it wants to handle task management, boundary management, and performance management on its own.
2: Specifying Integration Needs	• Use formal mechanisms such as liaison roles, overlapping membership, cross-team integrating teams (teams that coordinate two other teams) to support the integration of work between two or more teams. • Use formal mechanisms to integrate multiple teams and business units such as management teams, and representative integrating teams.
3: Clarifying Management Structure and Roles	• Use responsibility charting to determine appropriate roles for team members and managers and how they will change over time. • Determine management structure, reporting structure, and roles based on amount of task interdependence, size of the team, functional discipline diversity of members, technical experience and skills, life span of teams, and amount of change.

CHAPTER 12   DESIGNING TEAM-BASED ORGANIZATIONS

4: Designing Integration Processes	• Define a strategy, communicate it, and operationalize it at all systemic levels. • Align goals vertically and laterally. • Choose goals that are measurable. • Assign rewards in accordance with organizational goals. • Facilitate flexibility and responsiveness. • Plan collectively. • Clarify decision-making authority. • Create common systematic decision making processes that provide a foundation for collaboration.
5: Designing Performance Management Processes	• Align performance goals and criteria for individuals, teams, business units, and the overall organization. • Have team members, manager, external stakeholders (e.g., suppliers, customers) participate in providing performance feedback. • Establish direction and role for all team members. • Identify needs of team members. • Clarify deliverables, services, and tasks. • Establish goals, objectives, and metrics. • Identify necessary skills, tools, and resources. • Make teamwork and contributions to the team more important in evaluating and rewarding team member performance. • Tie together the fates of people who must work together. • Have special team awards.

Figure 12-7

(continued)

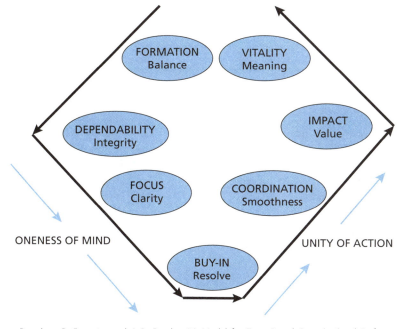

Figure 12-8

The Forrester and Drexler Team-Based Organization Model

Source: Based on R. Forrester and A.B. Drexler. "A Model for Team-Based Organizational Performance." *Academy of Management Executive*, 1999, *13(3)*, p. 38.

The model suggests seven critical issues that need to be addressed to successfully create a team-based organization:

• **Formation.** The establishment of needed teams, the settings in which they will work, and provision of appropriate support. The objective is to give teams the grounding they need to be successful.

- **Dependability.** How well teams can count on one another and on the organization. This includes teams consistently doing what they are supposed to do and keeping their commitments to each other and to the organization.
- **Focus.** The organization's clarity of vision and its precision and accuracy in marking progress. Focus also includes how goals are assigned to teams as well as the goals' clarity and coherence.
- **Buy-in.** The commitment that teams and individuals have to the goals and direction the organization has set or allowed to be set. Team and individual buy-in also includes the determination to do what it takes to realize their goals.
- **Coordination.** The mechanisms in place to make the entire organization act in unison.
- **Impact.** The potential to affect the organization by making a difference in terms of the outcomes that are most important to an organization.
- **Vitality.** The processes through which an organization sustains itself, finds and maintains its energy level, and taps the motivation of its members to serve the purposes of the organization as well as those of the members.

Figure 12-9 shows the keys to success and the off/keys, or potential barriers to success for each stage. For example, focus requires the keys of clear direction, measurable goals, and accountability. However, the off/keys of aimlessness, uncertainty, and freelancing (when the team strikes out on its own, regardless of the interests of the organization) detract from focus. As

Figure 12-9

Keys and Off/Keys in the Team-Based Organizational Performance Model

Keys	Stage	Off/Keys
• Composition • Coherence • Supportive Systems	• Formation	• Incongruence • Organizational Barriers • Team Isolation
• Information Sharing • Follow Through • Give and Take	• Dependability	• Secrecy • Skepticism • Self-Interest
• Clear Direction • Measurable Goals • Accountability	• Focus	• Aimlessness • Uncertainty • Freelancing
• Balanced Power • Sufficient Resources • Connecting Values	• Buy-In	• Powerlessness • Frustration • Alienation
• Operational Planning • Communications • Integrating Mechanisms	• Coordination	• Redundancy • Shortfalls • Disjointedness
• Innovation • Flexibility • Outstanding Results	• Impact	• Status Quo • Rigidity • Mediocrity
• Enthusiasm • Openness • Learning	• Vitality	• Apathy • Defensiveness • Complacency

Source: Based on R. Forrester and A. B. Drexler. "A Model for Team-Based Organization Performance." *Academy of Management Executive*, 1999, *13(3)*, p. 38.

another example, enthusiasm, openness, and learning enhance vitality while apathy, defensiveness, and complacency diminish it.

Best Practices for the Successful Implementation of Team-Based Organizations

Now that we have covered several models of team-based organizations, you should have an understanding of the process associated with creating a team-based organization and some of the key actions needed in each stage of the process. Our final topic relates to best practices associated with the creation and implementation of team-based organizations.

James Shonk developed a framework (see Figure 12-10) identifying keys to success for team-based organizations.[17] The model shows that alignment between the organization's philosophy, overall business strategy, and the

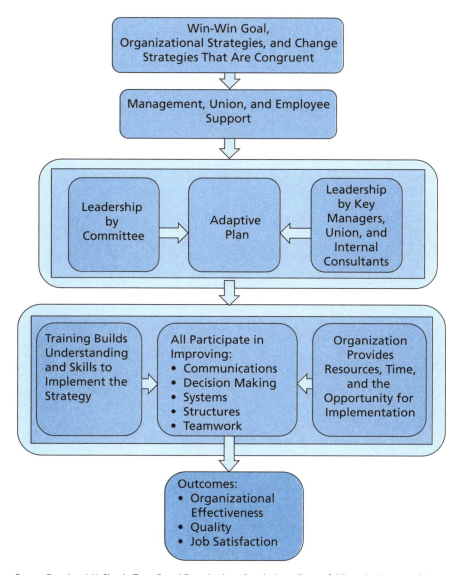

Figure 12-10

Key Elements for Success of Team-Based Organizations

Source: Based on J. H. Shonk. *Team-Based Organizations: Developing a Successful Team Environment.* (Homewood, IL: Business One Irwin, 1992), p. 11.

Figure 12-11

Best Practices for Team-Based Organizations

Best Practice	Description
Organizational Support	Teams need support of their leaders, sponsors, and top management.
Process Focus	Teams should focus on how things get done in order to add value and yield positive results.
Role Clarity	Each team and its members must be clearly delineated and member roles communicated to all relevant parties in the organization.
Continuous Learning	Teams must focus on learning in order to drive continuous improvement in their processes and performance outcomes.
Systems Alignment	Team structures and processes must support and/or be aligned with the objectives, strategies, and processes of its organization.
Communicating Business Objectives	Team leaders and top management must clearly and effectively articulate business objectives of the team on an ongoing basis.
Implementing Solutions Quickly	Teams must be agile in identifying issues or problems and in developing and implementing solutions that will meet or exceed the requirements of internal or external customers.
Building Internal Expertise	Teams should implement an ongoing evaluation and learning process to enhance the team's capacity to perform its tasks and achieve its objectives.
Involving Key Stakeholders	Teams need to understand their stakeholders (those affected by the team's work) and how to engage them in the team's activities and drive team effectiveness.
Applying Integrative Solutions	Teams must see problems from a cross-functional perspective and leverage this perspective to develop and implement effective solutions to complex problems facing the team.

Source: Based on L. D. Kricher. *Best Practices of Team-Based Organizations*. White Paper, Development Dimensions International, 1997.

goals of the team-based strategy is crucial, as is support of all key stakeholders. Finally, the organization must provide training and resources to facilitate the success of a team-based strategy.

Other best practices for team-based organizations are shown in Figure 12-11.

Many of these best practices reflect factors in the Shonk model (such as providing organizational support, aligning systems, applying integrated solutions, and involving stakeholders). Team-based organizations should also emphasize continuous learning and development of internal expertise to build the capacity of the organization and workforce to use self-directed teams effectively.

The Trent Model for Becoming an Effective Teaming Organization[18]

Robert Trent developed a comprehensive model for becoming a team-based organization. The model outlines a formal, integrated process for designing and implementing a team-based organization, including specific diagnostic questions and strategies to support the process. It also addresses the importance of the long-term maintenance of teams in organizations once they have been established because this is a common problem with most change initiatives.

The Trent Model consists of four phases—Plan, Perform, Evaluate, and Maintain—and key actions to be taken in each phase. Many strategies identified in this model reinforce the importance of the actions needed to create a team-based organization, including assessing the readiness of an organization for teams (Phase 1), establishing formal goals and structures to support teams (Phase 2), evaluating teams based on performance feedback and providing appropriate rewards based on team performance (Phase 3), and using those team evaluations to determine what is working and not working and sharing these key insights with other teams and the organization as a whole (Phase 4).

The Plan Phase

In the Plan phase, shown in Figure 12-12, the foundation for the design of a team-based organization is created. Two things should be emphasized. First, management needs to assess its readiness for moving to a team-based approach. This assessment should include management's willingness to provide long-term support for teams and the degree to which the organization's culture supports teams.

Organizations ready for teams have cultures valuing open communication, trust, employee empowerment, collaboration, and good relations between management and the workforce.[19] Second, the selection of team tasks should align with the overall objectives of the organization. In addition, the tasks assigned to teams require cross-functional involvement and coordination from different parts of the organization (such as marketing, manufacturing, design, research and development, and information technology). As in the

Phase	Diagnostic Questions
Assess Organizational Readiness	• Are we a team-oriented organization? • Will our culture support team interaction? • Do our employees possess team skills?
Select Appropriate Tasks	• Use teams for assignments that directly support organizational objectives. • Use teams for major decisions that require buy-in from different functional groups. • Use teams for complex or large-scale projects that no single functional unit can manage.
Form Teams	• Determine functional representation and team size given the assigned task. • Establish formal team member roles. • Identify qualified team leaders and team members.
Evaluate Additional Preparation Issues	• Establish reporting links to executive leadership. • Identify and provide required resources. • Create a team charter detailing mission, tasks, and objectives.

Figure 12-12
The Plan Phase of the Trent Model

Source: Robert J. Trent, "Becoming an Effective Teaming Organization," *Business Horizons*, 2004, *47(2)*, p. 35.

Mohrman, Cohen, and Mohrman model, the Plan phase of the Trent Model emphasizes realigning the rest of the organization to support teams in the Evaluate Additional Preparation Issues step of the process. This is done by establishing reporting relationships between teams and leadership and by connecting team performance with organizational reward systems.

The Perform Phase

In the second phase of the process—the Perform phase— (see Figure 12-13), the emphasis is more on the internal development and functioning of teams through enhancing team commitment and motivation and facilitating team communication, consensus, and a positive team culture. This phase corresponds with our coverage of the design, development, and leadership of effective teams in earlier chapters.

Figure 12-13

The Perform Phase of the Trent Model

Phase	Diagnostic Questions
Establish Team-Based Performance Goals	• Executive leadership establishes targets and objectives. • Team members establish specific goals that are measurable and objective.
Promote Member Effort and Commitment	• Motivate members by assigning a meaningful and challenging task. • Hold teams and individuals accountable for achieving measurable goals. • Evaluate and reward individual and team performance.
Facilitate Internal Team Interaction	• Develop shared team performance norms and performance strategies. • Manage internal conflict and the dynamics of group interaction. • Understand how to reach consensus on major decisions and issues.

Source: Robert J. Trent, "Becoming an Effective Teaming Organization," *Business Horizons*, 2004, *47(2)*, pp. 37.

The Evaluate Phase

In the Evaluate phase of the process (see Figure 12-14), management needs to conduct an in-depth and systematic evaluation of teams through the use

Figure 12-14

The Evaluate Phase of the Trent Model

Phase	Diagnostic Questions
Assess Progress toward Stated Goals	• Measure and report progress to executive sponsors and clients on a regular basis. • Self-assess the quality of internal interaction and progress toward stated goals.
Provide Feedback and Rewards	• Provide timely feedback to team members. • Include participation as part of each team member's formal performance evaluation. • Make rewards available for superior effort and performance.

Source: Robert J. Trent, "Becoming an Effective Teaming Organization," *Business Horizons*, 2004, *47(2)*, pp. 38.

Phase	Diagnostic Questions
Maintain Team Performance	• Continue to evaluate performance and hold members accountable for goal attainment. • Take corrective action as required to maintain effectiveness and intensity, including rotating members and leaders. • Disband nonperforming teams or teams whose assignments are complete.

Figure 12-15

The Maintain Phase of the Trent Model

Source: Robert J. Trent, "Becoming an Effective Teaming Organization," *Business Horizons*, 2004, *47(2)*, p. 40.

of a formal, multifaceted assessment process. Meaningful and specific feedback must be provided to teams, and rewards should be linked to team performance. Much of the focus of this phase relates to concepts and methods for evaluating team performance discussed in Chapter 10.

The Maintain Phase

In the fourth and final phase of the process—the Maintain phase (shown in Figure 12-15)—management must remain committed to evaluating and enhancing the effectiveness of teams and sharing best practices with all teams in the organization. The learning aspect of this phase is the primary mechanism through which an organization enhances its ability to use teams to support the achievement of key objectives. Management can support sharing and learning by blogs and newsletters, company intranets, brown bag lunches, workshops and conferences, and other methods focused on team best practices.[20]

TEAMS VIDEO: Whole Systems Team Approach at Topeka Pet Food Manufacturing

This classic video profiles one of the earliest attempts to create a team-based organizational system. The Topeka System, based on cooperative systems, learning, flexibility, broad skills, cross-functional teams, and self-regulation, was implemented at a pet food manufacturing company, Topeka Pet Food Manufacturing, in Topeka, Kansas, that had been in turmoil. The approach was viewed as revolutionary at the time. The resulting productivity gains became well known, prompting other organizations to emulate the system. (Follow this link to view the video: http://www.youtube.com/watch?v=ml4QPrnBUN4/.)

Source: For a discussion of the Tokepa system, see R.E. Walton, "Work Innovations at Topeka: After Six Years," *Journal of Applied Behavioral Science*, 1977, *13(3)*, pp. 422–433. For a follow up, see D.A. Whitsett & L. Yorks, "Looking Back at Topeka: General Foods and the Quality-of-Work-Life Experiment," *California Management Review*, 1983, *25(4)*, pp. 93–109. See also, J.D. Houghton, C.P. Neck, & C.C. Manz, "We Think We Can, We Think We Can: The Impact of Thinking Patterns and Self-Efficacy on Work Team Sustainability," *Team Performance Management*, 2003, *9(1/2)*, pp. 31–41; and, W.W. Burke & D.L. Bradford, "The Crisis in OD," in D.L. Bradford & W.W. Burke (eds.), *Reinventing Organization Development: New Approaches to Change in Organizations* (Hoboken, NJ: John Wiley & Sons, 2005), pp. 7–14.

Summary and Integration

Practical takeaways for team management from this chapter include the following:

A team-based organization leverages the power of teams to drive innovation and superior business results.

In a team-based organization, the team is the basic unit for accomplishing work.

Management must conduct a readiness review before making a decision about whether to pursue the transition to a team-based organization.

The transition to a team-based organization represents a huge change in the structure and operations of most organizations. An organization needs to be sure to have a comprehensive action plan to address resistance to team-based organizations.

Organizational and management support are critical if teams are to be successful in team-based organizations.

Management should review the status of the movement to a team-based organization to make adjustments to the overall operating system in order to drive improvements in performance.

Notes

1   J.H. Shonk, *Team-Based Organizations: Developing a Successful Team Environment* (Chicago: Irwin, 1997). For a good discussion of team-based organizations see C.L. Harris & M.M. Beyerlein, "Team-Based Organization: Creating an Environment for Team Success," in M.A. West, D. Tjosvold, & K.G. Smith, *The Essentials of Teamworking: International Perspectives* (Hoboken, NJ: John Wiley & Sons, 2005), pp. 149–171.

2   S. Mohrman, S. Cohen, & A. Mohrman, *Designing Team-Based Organizations: New Forms of Knowledge Work* (San Francisco, CA: Jossey-Bass, 1995).

3   For discussions of the dangers of a silo mentality, see T.L. Pittinsky, "Softening Silos: The Nuts and Bolts of Leading Amid Difference," *Leader to Leader*, 2010, *57*, pp. 18–23; and, F. Cilliers & H. Greyvenstein, "The Impact of Silo Mentality on Team Identity: An Organisational Case Study," *S.A. Journal of Industrial Psychology*, 2012, *38(2)*, pp. 75–84.

4   J. Dement, "Managers, Leaders, and Teams in a Team-Based Environment," *Hospital Materiel Management Quarterly*, 1996, *18(1)*, pp. 1–9.

5   Anonymous. "Organizations Strive for Dream Team Success." *IIE Solutions*, December, 1998, *30(12)*, p. 11.

6   D. Kezsbom, "Team-Based Organizations and the Changing Role of the Project Manager," *Transactions of the AACE International*, 1994.

7   J.H. Shonk, *Team-Based Organizations: Developing a Successful Team Environment* (Chicago: Irwin, 1992).

8   R.Y. Chang & M.J. Curtin, *Succeeding as a Self-Managed Team* (Irvine, CA: Richard Chang Associates, 1997).

9   J. Kotter, "The 8-Step Process for Leading Change," (Cambridge, MA: Kotter International, 2012). http://www.kotterinternational.com/our-principles/changesteps

10 For discussions of resistance to major change, see C. Laszio & J.J.-F. Laugel, *Large-Scale Organizational Change* (Woburn, MA: Butterworth-Heinemann, 2012); S. Oreg, M. Vakola, & A. Armenakis, "Change Recipients' Reactions to Organizational Change: A 60-Year Review of Quantitative Studies." *Journal of Applied Behavioral Science*, 2011, *47(4)*, pp. 461–524; and, R. Thomas & C. Hardy, "Reframing Resistance to Organizational Change" *Scandinavian Journal of Management*, 2011, *27(3)*, pp. 322–331.

11 D. Ray & H. Bronstein, *Teaming Up* (New York: McGraw-Hill, 1995).

12 Ibid. For more on change readiness see M. Vakola, "Multilevel Readiness to Organizational Change: A Conceptual Approach," *Journal of Change Management*, 2013, *13(1)*, pp. 96–109; and, A.E. Rafferty, N.J. Jimmieson, & A.A. Armenakis, "Change Readiness: A Multilevel Review," *Journal of Management*, 2013, *39(1)*, pp. 110–135.

13 S.A. Mohrman, S.G. Cohen, & A.M. Mohrman. *Designing Team-Based Organizations.* (San Francisco, CA: Jossey-Bass, 1995).

14 For more on building a team-based organization, see M.A. West & L. Markiewicz, *Building Team-Based Organizations: A Practical Guide to Organizational Transformation* (Walden, MA: Blackwell Publishing, 2004).

15 For further discussion of Step 5, see K. Mendibil & J. MacBryde, "Factors That Affect the Design and Implementation of Team-Based Performance Measurement Systems," *International Journal of Productivity and Performance Management,* 2006, *55(2)*, pp. 118–142.

16 R. Forrester and R. Drexler, "A Model for Team-Based Organization Performance." *Academy of Management Executive*, 1999, *13(3)*, pp. 36–49.

17 J. Shonk, *Team-Based Organizations: Developing a Successful Team Environment* (Chicago: Irwin, 1997).

18 R.J. Trent, "Becoming an Effective Teaming Organization," *Business Horizons*, 2004, *47(2)*, pp. 33–40.

19 For discussions of the role of organizational culture in transforming and maintaining team-based organizations, see R.A. Jones, N.L. Jimmieson, & A. Griffiths, "The Impact of Organizational Culture and Reshaping Capabilities on Change Implementation Success: The Mediating Role of Readiness for Change," *Journal of Management Studies*, 2005, *42(2)*, pp. 361–386; and, S.W. Yoon, J.H. Song, D.H. Lim, & B.-K. Joo, "Structural Determinants of Team Performance: The Mutual Influences of Learning Culture, Creativity, and Knowledge," *Human Resource Development International*, 2010, *13(3)*, pp. 249–264.

20 For more on sustaining change in team-based organizations, see D. Buchanan, L. Fitzgerald, D. Ketley, R. Gollop, J.L. Jones, S.S. Lamont, A. Neath, & E. Whitby, "No Going Back: A Review of the Literature on Sustaining Organizational Change," *International Journal of Management Reviews*, 2005, *7(3)*, pp. 189–205.

Bibliography

Anonymous. "Organizations Strive for Dream Team Success." *IIE Solutions*, December, 1998, *30(12)*, p. 11.

Buchanan, D., Fitzgerald, L., Ketley, D., Gollop, R., Jones, J.L., Lamont, S.S., Neath, A., & Whitby, E. "No Going Back: A Review of the Literature on Sustaining Organizational Change," *International Journal of Management Reviews*, 2005, *7(3)*, pp. 189–205.

Burke, W.W., & Bradford, D.L. "The Crisis in OD." In D.L. Bradford & W.W. Burke (eds.), *Reinventing Organization Development: New Approaches to Change in Organizations* (Hoboken, NJ: John Wiley & Sons, 2005), pp. 7–14.

Chang, R.Y., & Curtin, M.J. *Succeeding as a Self-Managed Team* (Irvine, CA: Richard Chang Associates, 1997).

Cilliers, F., & Greyvenstein, H. "The Impact of Silo Mentality on Team Identity: An Organisational Case Study," *S.A. Journal of Industrial Psychology*, 2012, *38(2)*, pp. 75–84.

Dement, J. "Managers, Leaders, and Teams in a Team-Based Environment," *Hospital Materiel Management Quarterly*, 1996, *18(1)*, pp. 1–9.

Forrester, R., & Drexler, A.B. "A Model for Team-Based Organization Performance," *Academy of Management Executive*, 1999, *13(3)*, pp. 36–49.

Harris, C.L., & Beyerlein, M.M. "Team-Based Organization: Creating an Environment for Team Success." In M.A. West, D. Tjosvold, & K.G. Smith, *The Essentials of Teamworking: International Perspectives* (Hoboken, NJ: John Wiley & Sons, 2005), pp. 149–171.

Houghton, J.D., Neck, C.P., & Manz, C.C. "We Think We Can, We Think We Can: The Impact of Thinking Patterns and Self-Efficacy on Work Team Sustainability," *Team Performance Management*, 2003, *9(1/2)*, pp. 31–41.

Imai, M. *Genba Kaizen: A Commonsense Low-Cost Approach to Management* (New York: McGraw-Hill Professional, 1997).

Jones, R.A., Jimmieson, N.L., & Griffiths, A. "The Impact of Organizational Culture and Reshaping Capabilities on Change Implementation Success: The Mediating Role of Readiness for Change," *Journal of Management Studies*, 2005, *42(2)*, pp. 361–386.

Kezsbom, D. "Team-Based Organizations and the Changing Role of the Project Manager," *Transactions of the AACE International*, 1994.

Kohrman, M. "Go Inside Google Garage, the Collaborative Workspace That Thrived on Crazy, Creative Ideas," *Fast Company*, September 19, 2013. https://www.google.com/search?q=%22google+garage%22&ie=utf-8&oe=utf-8&aq=t&rls=org.mozilla:en-US:official&client=firefox-a&channel=sb

Kohrman, M. "How Google's Flexible Workspace Ignites Creative Collaboration (on Wheels)," *Fast Company*, September 26, 2013. http://www.fastcompany.com/3017824/work-smart/how-googles-flexible-workspace-ignites-creative-collaboration-on-wheels?partner=newsletter

Kotter, J. "The 8-Step Process for Leading Change," (Cambridge, MA: Kotter International, 2012). http://www.kotterinternational.com/our-principles/changesteps

Kricher, L.D. *Best Practices of Team-Based Organizations*. White Paper, DDI Dimensions International, 1997.

Laszio, C., & Laugel, J.J.-F. *Large-Scale Organizational Change*. (Woburn, MA: Butterworth-Heinemann, 2012).

Mendibil, K., & MacBryde, J. "Factors That Affect the Design and Implementation of Team-Based Performance Measurement Systems," *International Journal of Productivity and Performance Management,* 2006, *55(2)*, pp. 118–142.

Mohrman, S., Cohen, S., & Mohrman, A., Jr. *Designing Team-Based Organizations: New Forms of Knowledge Work.* (San Francisco, CA: Jossey-Bass, 1995).

Oreg, S., Vakola, M., & Armenakis, A. "Change Recipients' Reactions to Organizational Change: A 60-Year Review of Quantitative Studies," *Journal of Applied Behavioral Science*, 2011, *47(4)*, pp. 461–524.

Pittinsky, T.L. "Softening Silos: The Nuts and Bolts of Leading amid Difference," *Leader to Leader*, 2010, *57*: 18–23.

Rafferty, A.E., Jimmieson, N.J., & Armenakis, A.A. "Change Readiness: A Multilevel Review," *Journal of Management*, 2013, *39(1)*, pp. 110–135.

Ray, D., & Bronstein, H. *Teaming Up* (New York: McGraw-Hill, 1995).

Shonk, J. *Team-Based Organizations: Developing a Successful Team Environment* (Chicago: Irwin, 1992).

Taylor, V. "Inside Google's Amsterdam Office: Waffle Ceiling Panels, Exposed Brick and a Caravan Meeting Room," *New York Daily News*, March 26, 2014. http://www.nydailynews.com/life-style/google-garage-meets-dutch-pride-amsterdam-office-article-1.1735871

Thomas, R., & Hardy, C. "Reframing Resistance to Organizational Change," *Scandinavian Journal of Management*, 2011, *27(3)*, pp. 322–331.

Trent, R.J. "Becoming an Effective Teaming Organization," *Business Horizons*, 2004, *47(2)*, pp. 33–40.

Vakola, M. "Multilevel Readiness to Organizational Change: A Conceptual Approach," *Journal of Change Management*, 2013, *13(1)*, pp. 96–109.

Walton, R.E. "Work Innovations at Topeka: After Six Years," *Journal of Applied Behavioral Science*, 1977, *13(3)*, pp. 422–433.

West, M.A., & Markiewicz, L. *Building Team-Based Organizations: A Practical Guide to Organizational Transformation* (Walden, MA: Blackwell Publishing, 2004).

Whitsett, D.A., & Yorks, L. "Looking Back at Topeka: General Foods and the Quality-of-Work-Life Experiment," *California Management Review*, 1983, *25(4)*, pp. 93–109.

Womack, J. *Gemba Walks* (Lean Enterprise Institute, 2011).

Yoon, S.W., Song, J.H., Lim, D.H., & Joo, B.-K. "Structural Determinants of Team Performance: The Mutual Influences of Learning Culture, Creativity, and Knowledge," *Human Resource Development International*, 2010, *13(3)*, pp. 249–264.

CHAPTER 13

Teams Summary and Integration

Learning Objectives

After reading this chapter, you should be able to do the following:

1. Understand team management from an integrated perspective based on the High Performance Teams Model.
2. Identify and describe opportunities to develop teamwork and team management skills before graduation.
3. Identify and describe opportunities to develop teamwork and team management skills after graduation.
4. Develop and execute a formal action plan for developing your teamwork and team management skills.

Coming Full Circle: Revisiting the High Performance Teams Model

As we move into this last chapter, we want to reconnect you with the High Performance Teams Model introduced in Chapter 1. We discuss here how the key concepts, frameworks, methods, and tools from each chapter align with the phases of the High Performance Teams Model and with one another. Reviewing these connections should help you develop an overall perspective on your future teamwork and team leadership endeavors to enhance your capacity to diagnose, lead, manage, and develop effective teams in your job and career. Figure 13-1 again shows the interconnections among the elements of a comprehensive approach to managing teams. It illustrates the links between designing the team system, developing the team, facilitating the team, and evaluating the team and notes the importance of the team context.

Phase 1: Designing the Team System
This first phase of the High Performance Team Models addressed in several chapters in this text, focused on how to structure teams to support their long-term success.

- Chapter 1: Teams: Opportunities and Challenges
- Chapter 2: Designing the Team System
- Chapter 10: Evaluating Team Effectiveness
- Chapter 11: The New Teams: Virtual, Global, Connected, and Self-Managing
- Chapter 12: Team-Based Organizations

Figure 13-1

The High Performance
Teams Model

Chapter 1 considered attributes of different types of teams, characteristics of effective and ineffective teams (for instance, the Scholtes Team Model and the Five Dysfunctions of a Team), and a systems model for analyzing teams (the Hill and Anteby Model). Chapter 2 discussed the importance of creating a team infrastructure for success that included a team charter to define the scope and objectives of a team's work or project, a Gantt chart to provide a roadmap and timeline for achieving a team's objectives, a role responsibilities matrix to assign responsibility for tasks to team subgroups, and a team dashboard to provide a formal measurement system for evaluating team performance. Together, these tools help ensure that a team possesses a formal structure as a foundation for the next phase of the High Performance Teams Model.

Chapter 11 discussed contemporary types of team structures such as global teams, virtual teams, and self-managing teams. Organizations are increasingly using these forms to maintain flexibility and efficiency and to leverage the talents and experiences of their members, some of whom may work in different parts of the overall organization or even the world.

Some issues discussed in Chapters 10 and 12, included in Phase 4, are also relevant in this phase. These include the Chapter 10 discussion of processes and strategies, such as 360-degree feedback, that can be deployed to evaluate and enhance team effectiveness. Moreover, team design issues ultimately align with and support the models for organizations that support the extensive use of teams for work activities and projects (Chapter 12).

Phase 2: Developing the Team

This second phase of the High Performance Teams Model, including Chapters 3, 4, 5, and 6, examined a wide range of strategies for building effective teams.

- Chapter 3: Building and Developing a Team
- Chapter 4: Socializing, Building Trust, Training, Motivating, and Leading Teams
- Chapter 5: Managing Team Diversity
- Chapter 6: Fostering Effective Communication in Teams

Chapter 3 reinforced the team design content from Chapter 2 by emphasizing the importance of effective planning for team efforts by defining a team's assignment (its charter) and team roles (its role responsibility matrix). Once the basic structural issues were addressed, the chapter covered the stages of team development. Consideration of those stages provided a formal process model for diagnosing team functioning (such as identifying the team's current stage of team development) and for offering strategies to facilitate movement of a team through the forming (i.e., breaking the ice), storming (i.e., working through differences), norming (i.e., the emergence of a cohesive team with a strong team culture) and performing (i.e., a high-functioning team that is able to manage itself) stages as longer-term goals.

Chapter 4 explored the role of people and culture in developing high performance teams. It emphasized the importance of building trust among team members; socializing members into a team's culture; and training members to enhance their task-related knowledge, skills, and abilities. Models for effectively leading teams (such as consideration and initiating structure, substitutes and neutralizers of leadership, and transformational leadership) were presented. These models reflect, among other things, a leader's focus on concern for people (consideration) and concern for the task (initiating structure), as well as his or her attempts to inspire followers and organizations to achieve fundamental transformation. Approaches to motivating team members to increase their effort and channel it toward appropriate behaviors and desired objectives, such as learning theory and goal-setting theory, were also explained.

Chapter 5 further explored people issues with a focus on personality factors and other individual differences as they shape decisions regarding development of a proper mix of capabilities to achieve team objectives. It also discussed how teams can leverage diversity to enhance creativity and effectiveness. As the general population and workforce become more diverse on many dimensions (such as age, race, ethnicity, gender, and sexual orientation), and economy and business in general become increasingly global, leveraging team diversity offers both major opportunities and challenges for leaders of teams and organizations.

Since communication is a foundation for effective team coordination, Chapter 6 addressed the communication process (e.g., message encoding and decoding), emphasizing the importance of getting everyone on the same page and actively listening to others in order to demonstrate empathy and enhance understanding of team issues and concerns. Leaders who use active listening effectively are better able to build trust with their team members.[1]

Phase 3: Facilitating the Team
Chapters 7, 8, and 9 covered the third stage of the High Performance Teams Model.

- Chapter 7: Facilitating Team Processes
- Chapter 8: Managing Change in Teams
- Chapter 9: Dealing with Team Problems

This section extended our discussion by addressing ongoing team process issues and strategies to support continuous team improvement. Chapter 7 discussed the critical topic of how to effectively plan and conduct team meetings through using tools such as meeting agendas and assigning formal roles to team members (e.g., timekeeper, scribe, facilitator) during meetings to keep a team on task during meetings, finish meetings on time, and document activities and decisions for future meetings. We also discussed practical strategies that leaders can use to effectively facilitate team meetings to ensure balanced participation of team members, effective communication, systematic decision making, and constructive conflict resolution.[2]

In Chapter 8, we focused on the issue of effective change management. This is an ongoing concern for most teams that may need to modify their focus and approaches in response to increasingly complex and dynamic operating environments in which they exist. We also discussed a process for planning and implementing changes with the unfreezing (establishing the need for change), changing (supporting the change), and refreezing (institutionalizing change) stages from the Lewin Change Process Model. Further, we addressed strategies for overcoming team member resistance to change (such as education, communication, participation, and involvement) and contingencies for their use.

In Chapter 9, we discussed team problems and strategies for dealing with them. The latter included conflict management styles (such as compromising, competing, and avoiding) and contingencies for their use. We emphasized the importance of conflict management. For example, failure to properly manage conflict aftermath in teams may result in low team morale, damaged working relationships, and reduced team cohesion. We also discussed team decision making and problem solving, including the use of practical tools for solving problems. For example, the affinity technique is useful due to its ease of use and effectiveness in overcoming problems of traditional brainstorming. Further, we addressed the groupthink phenomenon, which is often seen as undermining a team's decision-making processes and outcomes. We noted that Janis's prescriptions for overcoming difficulties in groups are very useful, but that the overall groupthink model does not appear to be valid. Finally, we noted common problems with interteam relationships and coordination and proposed strategies for supporting effective coordination of multiple teams (such as integrating and coordinating mechanisms).

Phase 4: Evaluating the Team

• Chapter 10: Evaluating Team Effectiveness

While earlier chapters addressed the design, development, and facilitation of teams, this fourth phase of the High Performance Teams Model focuses on approaches for systematically assessing team effectiveness and performance (such as using 360-degree feedback). In Chapter 10 we emphasized that rigorous evaluation of team effectiveness requires addressing issues related to team design, development, and facilitation early in the team process. We also presented tools and strategies for supporting the implementation of changes to enhance team effectiveness. These included tree diagrams to provide a visual roadmap of an action plan for implementing a strategy or initiative and accountability documents to integrate formal progress checks, deadlines, and member accountability for tasks.

The Team Context: Organizational and External Environments

- Chapter 12: Team-Based Organizations

Chapter 12 addressed this final element of the High Performance Teams Model. We emphasized that team success requires that top management create an organizational system defined in terms of teamwork. As such, an organization's processes, structures, culture, and people must all view the team as the core mode for accomplishment and support using a strategic approach for the development and use of teams. We also discussed how design elements, such as integrating and coordinating mechanisms (see Chapter 9 for managing interteam relations), are essential in the design of a team-based organization.

Moving Forward: Opportunities to Develop Teamwork and Team Management Skills as a Student

Skills Practice 13.1 on the text website provides an opportunity for you to assess the degree to which you have achieved your learning objectives regarding team management based on reading this textbook. This should be reviewed as a basis for considering the key takeaways discussed in the remainder of this chapter.

Our goal for this book has been to provide you with a rich and valuable overview of team management concepts, models, strategies, and tools and to help apply this knowledge to your future professional development and job/career success. We now discuss options to support development of teamwork and team management skills before graduation. These include the following:

- Academic coursework and workshops
- Student organizations
- Case competitions
- Books, newsletters, and other publications
- Volunteering and service learning
- Networking
- Internships

Take Academic Coursework and Participate in Workshops on Teams

Check course offerings at your college or university to see if they include additional courses on teams or group dynamics. You may find these kinds of courses in the management departments in your school of business (e.g., leadership of teams courses), psychology departments (e.g., group dynamics or group facilitation courses), or communication departments (e.g., group communications courses).

Another attractive option is to find a professor knowledgeable regarding teams and teamwork who would be willing to serve as your academic advisor as well as other students to work with on a consulting or field project related to a shared interest. An independent study lets you earn credit while working with a team on an interesting project. This could be a consulting project working with a local company or a nonprofit organization. Alternatively, you could even focus your independent study team project on issues related to team effectiveness in the form of a more traditional research project.

Your college or university may offer short workshops or programs on team issues. A student leadership office or center on your campus could be a good source of such programs.

Join Student Organizations to Obtain Teamwork and Team Management Experience

Most colleges and universities have many options for involvement in student organizations to learn more about majors or intended careers, to network with professionals, and to develop leadership skills. Consider finding an organization that interests you and join it not just to be a general member but to really get involved by taking on leadership roles. Most organizations have opportunities to join committees and to become executives each semester. By joining a committee, you will have an opportunity to work with others and to develop your teamwork skills. Take the initiative to get involved and to invest in your development.

Some popular business student organizations that offer opportunities to develop your teamwork and team leadership skills include the following:

- **Enactus (enactus.org).** "An international non-profit organization that brings together student, academic and business leaders who are committed to using the power of entrepreneurial action to improve the quality of life and standard of living for people in need."[3] Enactus encourages college students to work in teams to identify opportunities to bring about positive change in people, communities, and organizations.
- **DECA (deca.org),** "Prepares emerging leaders and entrepreneurs for careers in marketing, finance, hospitality and management in high schools and colleges around the globe."[4] DECA uses a competition format for a wide range of topics (e.g., customer service, human resources, ethics) that provides students with opportunities to formulate solutions to problems and to present and defend them to panels of managers and practitioners.
- **Future Business Leaders of America (fbla-pbl.org).** The world's oldest and largest student organization. "A quarter of a million high school and middle school students, college and university students, faculty, educators, administrators, and business professionals have chosen to be members of the premier business education association preparing students for careers in business."[5] This organization promotes the development of leadership skills through conferences, events, networking, and other activities.
- **Collegiate Entrepreneurs' Organization (www.c-e-o.org/).** "The premier entrepreneurship network with chapters on university campuses across North America and beyond. CEO currently supports entrepreneurship on over 240 chapters in over 43 states."[6] Collegiate Entrepreneurs' Organization promotes entrepreneurship through a national conference, business plan case competitions, networking, educational programs, and other activities.

There are many other excellent organizations to consider. The text website offers more information about student organizations and updates on website information provided in the text.

Join Student Competition Teams

Many schools provide opportunities to join teams to represent your college or university, typically along with two to four other students, and compete against teams from other schools[7]. These competitions may focus on analyzing case studies written either by business school professors (such as Harvard Business School cases) or developed by a major corporation based on its experiences and needs. Other competitions might include a computer simulation (such as of impacts of strategies) in which teams make decisions about running a company, such as athletic shoe manufacturer; the simulation gives performance data after each round and ranks each team based on its performance.[8] Most competitions require a team presentation that is used as the basis for judging the quality of each team's case analysis and recommendations. Competitions generally use corporate executives to serve as judges and offer awards for the top-performing teams.

These competitions may be intense, but most students feel they are valuable and enjoyable experiences.[9] The competitions strengthen your teamwork skills since they generally require teams to work together under time pressure to analyze a case and formulate a presentation. Ask your student activities office, your academic or career advisor, your professors, or the leaders of student organizations in which you may be involved about such competitions. The text website provides more information regarding student competition teams.

Read Books, Newsletters, and Other Publications

An excellent—and critical—opportunity to learn about teams is to keep up with current real-world events, business trends, and other developments. For students, one excellent source of business news is the ***Wall Street Journal*** (*WSJ*). Many recruiters believe that every student, especially if majoring in business, should develop the daily habit of reading the *WSJ*. It isn't necessary to read the entire issue, but scanning the headlines and reading through articles that seem especially relevant to you is valuable. Although articles focusing specifically on teams may not be found in every issue, team-related articles are pervasive. For example, a few of the team-related articles published in March and April 2014 were titled "What the Best C-suites and Basketball Teams Have in Common,"[10] "CEOs Must Demand Teamwork,"[11] and "For Team-Building Events, a New Ingredient: Fun."[12]

In reading the *WSJ* and other publications, remember that your overall goal is to increase your knowledge of business issues and trends and to understand how teams fit and function in larger organizational and environmental contexts. The text website offers information about additional news-based websites with information about teams.

Engage in Volunteer/Service Learning Team Experiences

Many nonprofit organizations provide opportunities for volunteer involvement. Your college or university may even sponsor a volunteer fair and post specific volunteer opportunities on its websites. These opportunities may involve working with others in teams to handle fund-raising, marketing, and event planning. Many nonprofit organizations may be willing to design volunteer opportunities around the interests of student volunteers since the experience itself is the compensation. If you are interested in developing teamwork or team management skills, tell your volunteer coordinator or supervisor. He or she may be able to integrate appropriate responsibilities and activities into your volunteer experience.

Join LinkedIn and Build Your Teamwork Network

LinkedIn is a professional networking website (www.linkedin.com) used by millions of students and professionals to contact others in their fields, industries, or alma maters to learn about opportunities for professional development, conferences and events, or the latest thinking about key issues of interest.[13] In addition to being able to make contact with your current or past team members, you can also join a variety of groups for professionals interested in ideas for building or leading effective teams. Once you have a LinkedIn account, search for "teamwork" and you will see numerous matches for related interest groups. This is an excellent way to network and ask questions about team issues you are experiencing.

Obtain Internships That Provide Opportunities for Teamwork or Team Management

Internships provide practical experience to develop knowledge and skills.[14] A wide variety of internships may provide opportunities to work in teams with other professionals. This experience is invaluable in helping students learn to develop self-confidence in working with professionals and being part of a team with specific business objectives. One highly recommended strategy for interns, as we discussed earlier under volunteer work, is to inform your supervisor of your interest in working in teams on special projects and even your willingness to lead a committee, task force, or project team. Although doing so may seem intimidating, being proactive and taking initiative may create opportunities to demonstrate your team leadership capabilities and potential to your boss and employer.

Opportunities to Develop Teamwork and Team Management Skills as a Working Professional

Some of the recommended strategies for developing teamwork and team management skills for students, such as joining LinkedIn and reading books and other publications on teams, also apply after you graduate. Here are a few additional strategies to consider once you are a working professional.

- **Volunteer for teamwork and team management committees, task forces, and projects in your work unit and organization.** As we suggested for students engaged in internships, it is also important for professionals to be proactive and give themselves opportunities to demonstrate their abilities to add value. A first step is to inform your boss that you are not only seeking opportunities to develop your collaborative skills as a team member, but also opportunities to step into a team leadership role at some point. In many companies, committees addressing issues such as loss prevention, safety, and cost containment seek volunteers from throughout the organization. Special task forces are frequently commissioned to address issues such as competition in the company's industry, evaluation of vendors or suppliers, and ways to foster workplace enhancement.

- **Join professional associations in your field.** There are many professional associations in which individuals can participate after graduation to develop teamwork and leadership skills. These often have local professional chapters with their own members and often offer events such as conferences at the state, regional, and national levels. They seek motivated volunteers to serve on committees and in executive or board positions.

- **Seek leadership positions on boards of directors with nonprofit organizations.** Nonprofit organizations may also provide opportunities to work in and lead teams. Such organizations include the American Red Cross, the Make a Wish Foundation, Habitat for Humanity, the American Cancer Society, and the Humane Society. The text website offers information regarding these and other national nonprofit organizations providing local volunteer opportunities.

- **Obtain an MBA or other advanced business degree.** Many of you are currently pursuing an MBA or other advanced business degree. However, if you are an undergraduate, while you may choose to work before pursuing a graduate degree, earning an MBA will provide additional formal training in teamwork and opportunities to work with other bright, motivated, and experienced professionals in teams. Research shows that managers who received MBAs believe they have gained valued competencies and skills through the training, and they have experienced higher self-perceptions and heightened career success.[15] Other research links receipt of the MBA to career success[16] as well as to success of the graduates' organizations.[17] Some MBA programs include a formal teams class in their core foundation, others may offer teams classes as options, and yet others may include non-credit teamwork modules for incoming students during orientation week.

Key Practical Takeaways for You as a Team Member

One of the goals of this textbook is to provide practical takeaways for team members and team leaders. We first address takeaways for team members and then for team leaders.

- **Go into each new team opportunity with a positive attitude.** In order to demonstrate that you are an effective team player, maintain a positive attitude about the team, the nature of its work, and the people involved with the team. Try to focus on the positive aspects of what the team is doing, and try not to dwell on things that you do not like about the team or its members. People often pick up on the negative vibes that tend to manifest themselves in a team member's negative attitude. Such attitudes are often contagious, leading to a negative team culture. Instead, give the new team a fresh chance for a positive experience.[18]

- **Break the ice with your team members and leader.** Take the time to introduce yourself to every team member at the start of a team process. Invite some team members to have coffee or lunch to get to know one another. Show up 5 to 10 minutes early for team meetings and engage in small talk with other team members. Schedule a meeting with your team leader to get acquainted and ask about his or her expectations of you.

- **Be a team player.** Show your teammates and team leader that you are willing and able to work with them and to take on at least some responsibilities and activities to help them be successful. Work to understand your team's overall objectives and approaches rather than thinking strictly in terms of your role on the team. Show willingness to help other team members even if doing so is not your own formal responsibility. Such behaviors, termed organizational citizenship behaviors, are increasingly important in organizations.[19]

- **Be aware of how you are perceived by your team members and team leader.** Managing your personal brand is an important aspect of being an effective team member. That is, what attributes do the team members and leader attribute to you as a team member? Are you seen as you would hope—as a team player, dependable, trustworthy, and hard working? Or, are you seen more as selfish, dogmatic, and inflexible? The best strategy is to understand what teamwork means in the context of your team and to take actions that reflect being a good team player in that context. Asking a trusted teammate or your leader for feedback on your effectiveness as a team member can also yield valuable developmental observations and insights.

- **Engage in constructive politics.** Many students are turned off by a discussion of being political. However, to be an effective team player you must work proactively to build support from your teammates and team leader for your contributions to the team.[20] Maintain open communications with others by sharing information about team issues and providing constructive feedback to resolve problems. Don't engage in less appropriate political activities such as gossiping or spreading rumors about team members or the team leader, undermining the credibility of other team members through comments made at meetings or through e-mail, or intentionally excluding targeted teammates from important discussions about team issues and decisions.

- **Consider stepping into an emergent leadership role.** Emergent leadership refers to leadership demonstrated by team members who may not have formal leadership authority but assume a leadership role when the needs of a particular team-related situation or issue present an opportunity.[21] Team members should be careful not to engage in actions that may be viewed by their teammates and/or team leader as overstepping their boundaries. Tread lightly by asking others questions about what they think should be done to handle an issue and offering to take the lead on a course of action if it is acceptable to the team and team leader.

- **Manage up and help your team leader succeed.** Finally, it is important to develop and maintain an effective working relationship with your team leader. This does not mean that you have to be best friends with your team leader, but you need to demonstrate proper respect for your team leader's authority. It is also important to understand your team leader's priorities, decision-making and communication styles, and hot buttons that elicit a strong negative reaction. Address these aspects at the beginning of the working relationship with a team leader either by asking teammates who know the team leader to share information about their views of the team leader's style or by simply asking your team leader directly.

Key Practical Takeaways for You as a Team Leader

Now, let's discuss some key takeaways for formal leaders of teams.

- **Create a high performance team, starting with good design.** Use team charters to define the scope and objectives of the team's task, creating a Gantt chart, role responsibilities matrix, and team dashboard. These tools help to define the team discipline and approach needed for long-term team success.
- **Give staffing the team system the attention it deserves.** Carefully address team composition to ensure that knowledge, skill, and experience requirements are met given the team's task. Employ an effective process to socialize new members so that they embrace the team's culture. Provide training to enable team members to acquire the knowledge, skills, and abilities needed to work together effectively and meet the team's task requirements.
- **Plan and facilitate effective meetings.** Plan team meetings in advance by creating formal agendas. Facilitate meetings by assigning team members to formal roles, such as facilitator, timekeeper, and scribe. Ensure that the scribe provides members with meeting summaries to serve as external memory and as input for planning future meetings.
- **Demonstrate effective team leadership.** Model appropriate behaviors that demonstrate support for teamwork. Provide appropriate incentives and rewards to motivate team members to engage in positive behaviors that reinforce teamwork and align with team goal attainment. Remember that some of the most basic and least costly rewards, such as verbal or written forms of recognition, can be among the most effective motivators for team members.
- **Open up the communication process.** Devote significant time and resources to ensure the proper sharing of information and coordination of activities through an open communication process using active listening. Foster a culture that embraces openness as a core value and work to build trust among team members and overall team cohesion.
- **Proactively manage change as an ongoing process.** Achieve and maintain your team's readiness for change by building a culture that embraces change. When implementing change, achieve buy-in from team members by using education and communication, participation, and involvement. Provide support for change and work to reinforce changes through rewards and the redesign of processes, jobs, policies, and systems.
- **Establish effective interteam relations**. Use formal design mechanisms to ensure that interteam relationships are effective and to avoid the emergence of silos between teams that may inhibit task coordination.
- **Build the context for teams.** Work to build a larger organizational context that supports and reinforces team activities. This may require meetings with your own managers and perhaps even upper management to discuss the structures, processes, and resources needed for teams to successfully add value to the organization's long-term success.

Skills Practice 13.2 on the text website is a useful activity to help prepare for job interviews that may include questions about working on teams and team leadership.

Journey's End

We conclude our journey through the world of teams with a few quotations:

> Creating a better world requires teamwork, partnerships, and collaboration, as we need an entire army of companies to work together to build a better world within the next few decades. This means corporations must embrace the benefits of cooperating with one another.[22]
>
> Simon Mainwaring, CEO, We First

> Never doubt that a small group of thoughtful, committed people can change the world. Indeed, it is the only thing that ever has.[23]
>
> Margaret Mead, cultural anthropologist, writer, and speaker

> In the long history of humankind (and animal kind, too) those who learned to collaborate and improvise most effectively have prevailed.[24]
>
> Charles Darwin, naturalist and geologist

We have enjoyed being your partners in this journey. Good luck with your future teaming endeavors.

Notes

1 For additional discussions of active listening, see H. Weger, Jr., G.C. Bell, E.M. Minei, & M.C. Robinson, "The Relative Effectiveness of Active Listening in Initial Interactions," *International Journal of Listening*, 2014, *28(1)*, pp. 13–31; and, S.S. Taylor & D. Ladkin, "Leading as Craft-Work: The Role of Studio Practices in Developing Artful Leaders," *Scandinavian Journal of Management*, 2014, *30(1)*, pp. 95–103.

2 For a discussion of how team meeting processes impact on team and organizational success, see S. Kauffeld & N. Lehmann-Willinbrock, "Meetings Matter: Effects of Team Meetings on Team and Organizational Success," *Small Group Research*, 2012. *43(2)*, pp. 130–158.

3 Enactus Organization Home Page: http://enactus.org/who-we-are/our-story/.

4 DEA Organization Home Page: http://www.deca.org/about/.

5 FBLA/PBL National website: http://www.fblapbl.org/web/page/614/sectionid/614/pagelevel/1/main_interior.asp.

6 Collegiate Entrepreneurs' Organization national website: http://www.c-e-o.org/about-us.

7 See M.M. van Wyk , "The Effects of Teams-Games-Tournaments on Achievement, Retention, and Attitudes of Economics Education Students," *Journal of Social Science*, 2011, *26(3)*, pp. 183–193; and, F. Hoy, "Team Approaches to Entrepreneurship and Family Business Education," in J. Katz & A.C. Corbett, *Entrepreneurship and Family Business*: *Advances in Entrepreneurship, Firm Emergence and Growth*, vol. 12 (Bingley, UK: Emerald Group Publishing, 2010), pp. 349–357.

8 For a discussion of use of simulations in team competitions, see R.W. Hornaday & M. Ensley, "Teamwork Attributes in Classwork Simulation," *Developments in Business Simulation and Experiential Learning*, 2000, *27*, pp. 195–200.

9   For a discussion of pressures associated with such competitions, see M.P. Dargnies, "Men Too Sometimes Shy Away from Competition: The Case of Team Competition," *Management Science*, 2012, *58(11)*, pp. 1982–2000.

10 R.A. Howell, "What the Best C-Suites and Basketball Teams Have in Common," *Wall Street Journal*, March 14, 2014. http://blogs.wsj.com/experts/2014/03/10/what-the-best-c-suites-and-basketball-teams-have-in-common

11 R.M. Kanter, "CEOs Must Demand Teamwork," *Wall Street Journal*, March 14, 2014. http://blogs.wsj.com/experts/2014/03/14/ceos-must-demand-teamwork

12 T. Gutner, "For Team-Building Events, a New Ingredient: Fun," 2014. http://online.wsj.com/news/articles/SB1000142405270230451250457943510133477106

13 See J.G. Gerard, "Linking in with LinkedIn®: Three Exercises That Enhance Professional Social Networking and Career Building," *Journal of Management Education*, 2012, *36*, pp. 866–897; J. Crant, "Using LinkedIn to Boost Top Financial Careers," *Journal of Corporate Accounting & Finance*, 2014, *25(3)*, pp. 19–23; and, M. Huston, "Get Social: Build Your Career with Facebook? Yes, Really," *ASHA Leader*, 2013, *18*. http://leader.pubs.asha.org/article.aspx?articleid=1788381

14 For discussions of the value of internships, see S. Richardson & M. Scott, "Preparing for Practice: How Internships and Other Practice-Based Learning Exchanges Benefit Students, Industry Hosts and Universities," *AICCM Bulletin*, 2011, *32*, pp. 73–79; C. Westerberg & C. Wickersham, "Internships Have Value, Whether or Not Students Are Paid," *Chronicle of Higher Education*, April 24, 2011. http://chronicle.com/article/Internships-Have-Value/127231/; and, J. Gault, E. Leach, & M. Duey, "Effects of Business Internships on Job Marketability: The Employers' Perspective," *Education + Training*, 2010, *52(1)*, pp. 76–88.

15 Y. Baruch & A. Leeming, "The Added Value of MBA Studies: Graduates' Perceptions," *Personnel Review*, 2001, *30(5/6)*, pp. 589–602.

16 Y. Baruch & M. Peiperl, "The Impact of an MBA on Graduate Careers," *Human Resource Management Journal*, 2000, *10(2)*, pp. 69–90.

17 A. Gupta & S.E. Bennett, "An Empirical Analysis of the Effect of MBA Programs on Organizational Success," *International Journal of Educational Management*, 2014, *28(4)*, pp. 451–460.

18 To learn more about the nature and importance of emotional dynamics and emotional contagion in organizations and teams, see F. Liu & S. Maitlis, "Emotional Dynamics and Strategizing Processes: A Study of Strategic Conversations in Top Team Meetings," *Journal of Management Studies*, 2012, *52*, pp. 202–234; J. Volmer, "Catching Leaders' Mood: Contagion Effects in Teams," *Administrative Sciences*, 2012, *2*, pp. 203–220; and, C. Emery, T.S. Calvard, & M.E. Pierce, "Leadership as an Emergent Group Process: A Social Network Study of Personality and Leadership," *Group Processes & Intergroup Relations*, 2013, *16*, pp. 28–45.

19 See, for instance, M.E. Arthaud-Day, J.C. Rode, & W.H. Turnley, "Direct and Contextual Effects of Individual Values on Organizational Citizenship Behaviors in Teams," *Journal of Applied Psychology*, 2012, *97(4)*, pp. 792–807; and, J.Y.M. Lai, L.W. Lam, & S.S.K. Lam, "Organizational Citizenship Behaviors in Work Groups: A Team Cultural Perspective," *Journal of Organizational Behavior*, 2013, *34(7)*, pp. 1039–1056.

20 For discussions of the importance of politics in organizations and for career progress, see G.R. Ferris & D.C. Treadway, (eds.), *Politics in Organizations: Theory and Research Contributions* (New York: Taylor & Francis Group, 2012); Y. Liu, "Are You Willing and Able?: Roles of Motivation, Power, and

Politics in Career Growth," *Journal of Management*, 2010, *36(6)*, pp. 1432–1460; and, C. Spinosa, C. Davis, & B. Glennon, "Transforming Crippling Company Politics," *Organizational Dynamics* 2014, *43(2)*, pp. 88–95.

21 To learn more about emergent leadership and when it is appropriate, see S.G. Barsade, "The Ripple Effect: Emotional Contagion and Its Influence on Group Behavior," *Administrative Science Quarterly*, 2002, 47, pp. 644–675; C. Emery, T.S. Calvard, & M.E. Pierce, "Leadership as an Emergent Group Process: A Social Network Study of Personality and Leadership," *Group Processes and Intergroup Relations*, 2013, *16(1)*, pp. 28–45; and, L. D'Innocenzo, J.E. Mathieu, & M.R. Kukenberger, "A Meta-Analysis of Different Forms of Shared Leadership-Team Performance Relations," *Journal of Management*, 2014 (in press).

22 S. Mainwaring, *We First* (Basingstoke, UK: Palgrave Macmillan, 2013).

23 The original source of this quotation is uncertain. For a good discussion of Margaret Mead's views on the place of small groups in cultural change and innovation, see M. Mead, *Continuities in Cultural Evolution* (New Brunswick, NJ: Transaction Publishers, 1964).

24 This is the introductory quotation on the website of the Darwin Center for Geobiology and is widely attributed to Darwin's *On the Origin of Species* (London: John Murray, 1859). However, it does not appear in that book, and its origins are controversial.

Bibliography

Arthaud-Day, M.E., Rode, J.C., & Turnley, W.H. "Direct and Contextual Effects of Individual Values on Organizational Citizenship Behaviors in Teams," *Journal of Applied Psychology*, 2012, *97(4)*, pp. 792–807.

Barsade, S.G. "The Ripple Effect: Emotional Contagion and Its Influence on Group Behavior," *Administrative Science Quarterly*, 2002, 47, pp. 644–675.

Baruch, Y., & Leeming, A. "The Added Value of MBA Studies: Graduates' Perceptions," *Personnel Review*, 2001, *30(5/6)*, pp. 589–602.

Baruch, Y., & Peiperl, M. "The Impact of an MBA on Graduate Careers," *Human Resource Management Journal*, 2000, *10(2)*, pp. 69–90.

Crant, J. "Using LinkedIn to Boost Top Financial Careers," *Journal of Corporate Accounting & Finance*, 2014, *25(3)*, pp. 19–23.

Dargnies, M.P. "Men Too Sometimes Shy Away from Competition: The Case of Team Competition," *Management Science*, 2012, *58(11)*, pp. 1982–2000.

D'Innocenzo, L., Mathieu, J.E., & Kukenberger, M.R. "A Meta-Analysis of Different Forms of Shared Leadership-Team Performance Relations," *Journal of Management*, 2014 (in press).

Emery, C., Calvard, T.S., & Pierce, M.E. "Leadership as an Emergent Group Process: A Social Network Study of Personality and Leadership," *Group Processes & Intergroup Relations*, 2013, 16, pp. 28–45.

Ferris, G.R., & Treadway, D.C. (eds.). *Politics in Organizations: Theory and Research Contributions* (New York: Taylor & Francis Group, 2012).

Gault, J., Leach, E., & Duey, M. "Effects of Business Internships on Job Marketability: The Employers' Perspective," *Education + Training*, 2010, *52(1)*, pp. 76–88.

Gerard, J.G. "Linking in with LinkedIn®: Three Exercises That Enhance Professional Social Networking and Career Building," *Journal of Management Education*, 2012, 36, pp. 866–897.

Gupta, A., & Bennett, S.E. "An Empirical Analysis of the Effect of MBA Programs on Organizational Success," *International Journal of Educational Management*, 2014, *28(4)*, pp. 451–460.

Gutner, T. "For Team-Building Events, a New Ingredient: Fun," 2014. http://online. wsj.com/news/articles/SB10001424052702304512504579493510133477106

Hornaday, R.W., & Ensley, M. "Teamwork Attributes in Classwork Simulation," *Developments in Business Simulation and Experiential Learning*, 2000, 27, pp. 195–200.

Howell, R.A. "What the Best C-Suites and Basketball Teams Have in Common," *Wall Street Journal*, March 14, 2014. http://blogs.wsj.com/experts/2014/03/10/what-the-best-c-suites-and-basketball-teams-have-in-common

Hoy, F. "Team Approaches to Entrepreneurship and Family Business Education." In J. Katz & A.C. Corbett, *Entrepreneurship and Family Business*: *Advances in Entrepreneurship, Firm Emergence and Growth*, vol. 12 (Bingley, UK: Emerald Group Publishing, 2010), pp. 349–357.

Huston, M. "Get Social: Build Your Career with Facebook? Yes, Really," *ASHA Leader*, 2013, *18*. http://leader.pubs.asha.org/article.aspx?articleid=1788381

Kanter, R.M. "CEOs Must Demand Teamwork," *Wall Street Journal*, March 14, 2014. http://blogs.wsj.com/experts/2014/03/14/ceos-must-demand-teamwork

Kauffeld, S., & Lehmann-Willinbrock, N. "Meetings Matter: Effects of Team Meetings on Team and Organizational Success," *Small Group Research*, 2012, *43(2)*, pp. 130–158.

Lai, J.Y.M., Lam, L.W., & Lam, S.S.K. "Organizational Citizenship Behaviors in Work Groups: A Team Cultural Perspective," *Journal of Organizational Behavior*, 2013, *34(7)*, pp. 1039–1056.

Liu, F., & Maitlis, S. "Emotional Dynamics and Strategizing Processes: A Study of Strategic Conversations in Top Team Meetings," *Journal of Management Studies*, 2012, *52*, pp. 202–234.

Liu, Y. "Are You Willing and Able?: Roles of Motivation, Power, and Politics in Career Growth," *Journal of Management*, 2010, *36(6)*, pp. 1432–1460.

Mainwaring, S. *We First* (Basingstoke, UK: Palgrave Macmillan, 2011).

Mead, M. *Continuities in Cultural Evolution* (New Brunswick, NJ: Transaction Publishers, 1964).

Richardson, S., & Scott, M. "Preparing for Practice: How Internships and Other Practice-Based Learning Exchanges Benefit Students, Industry Hosts and Universities," *AICCM Bulletin*, 2011, *32*, pp. 73–79.

Spinosa, C., Davis, C., & Glennon, B. "Transforming Crippling Company Politics," *Organizational Dynamics*, 2014, *43(2)*, pp. 88–95.

Taylor, S.S., & Ladkin, D. "Leading as Craft-Work: The Role of Studio Practices in Developing Artful Leaders," *Scandinavian Journal of Management*, 2014, *30(1)*, pp. 95–103.

van Wyk, M.M. "The Effects of Teams-Games-Tournaments on Achievement, Retention, and Attitudes of Economics Education Students," *Journal of Social Science*, 2011, *26(3)*, pp. 183–193.

Volmer, J. "Catching Leaders' Mood: Contagion Effects in Teams," *Administrative Sciences*, 2012, 2, pp. 203–220.

Weger, H., Jr., Bell, G.C., Minei, E.M., & Robinson, M.C. "The Relative Effectiveness of Active Listening in Initial Interactions," *International Journal of Listening*, 2014, *28(1)*, pp. 13–31.

Westerberg, C. & Wickersham, C. "Internships Have Value, Whether or Not Students Are Paid," *Chronicle of Higher Education*, April 24, 2011. http://chronicle.com/article/Internships-Have-Value/127231/

GLOSSARY

A

Accommodating Conflict Style
Conflict style used by individuals who are cooperative without being assertive, thus satisfying the other party's needs while neglecting their own. The accommodating party may thus be taken advantage of, losing stature and self-esteem. This result creates a win-lose situation, with the accommodating party being the loser.

Accountability Document
A summary table listing the names of individuals who are responsible for the successful execution of each action step in a tree diagram.

Action Forums
Broadly inclusive corporate meetings that involve key players from management, the workforce, and even outside suppliers and customers. By bringing these players together, using action forums leads to faster and better decisions and helps ensure the commitment of those who will implement the decisions.

Active Listening
Careful listening to more than just the content of a message. With active listening, such as is needed in counseling situations and conflict interviews, it is important to pay attention to nonverbal cues, to convey to the speaker a sense of trust, identify with the speaker's feelings and thoughts, and encourage the speaker to be as specific as possible about feelings and concerns.

Adjourning
The final stage of team development, in which the team dissolves after accomplishing its purpose or breaks up because of internal or external issues.

Affinity Technique
Decision-making technique used to identify creative solutions to a problem. The affinity technique achieves its purpose by requiring a team to systematically generate potential solutions to a problem, cluster them in terms of their similarities, name the clusters, and then use a voting procedure to identify which ideas should be given the highest priority.

American Society for Quality (ASQ)
The world's largest professional association for students, academics, and business professionals who are interested in enhancing the quality of the work processes, products, and services of all types of organizations.

Amplifying Values

The process of identifying and elevating certain values as basic to the overall mission; an element of framing.

Amygdala

A set of neurons in the brain's limbic system. Its chemical surges produce everything from blind rage to fear to avoidance of pain to euphoria. It is the integrative center for emotions, emotional behavior, and motivation.

ASQ International Team Excellence Award

A formal program developed by the American Society for Quality (ASQ) to promote and recognize team performance excellence. The program evaluates the effectiveness of problem-solving and process improvement teams using formal criteria that trained examiners apply as part of an in-depth evaluation process.

Attributed Charisma

Transformational leader behavior resulting from leader's display of a sense of power and confidence, ability to remain calm during crisis situations, and provision of reassurance that obstacles can be overcome.

Authoritarianism

A trait of individuals who believe that power and status should be clearly defined and that there should be a hierarchy of authority. Such individuals feel that authority should be concentrated in the hands of a few leaders and that this authority should be obeyed. They expect unquestioning obedience to their commands; authoritarian-submissive subordinates willingly give it.

Autocratic Leader

A leader who makes decisions himself or herself without input from others.

Avoidance Learning

Operant learning strategy based on learning that a desired behavior will enable an individual to prevent or avoid a negative consequence.

Avoiding Conflict Style

Conflict style used by parties who are neither assertive nor cooperative, neglecting the interests of both parties by trying to sidestep the conflict or put off making a decision. Regular use of this strategy may lead to frustration, uncertainties, and stalemates, yielding a lose-lose outcome, with neither party's needs being satisfied.

B

Behavioral Self-Management

Use of learning theory principles to manage our own behaviors, deciding what we want to achieve and setting up appropriate systems of goals, rewards, cues, and controls.

Belief Amplification

The process of emphasizing factors that support or impede actions taken to achieve desired values; an element of framing.

Big Five Personality Dimensions

Five sets of personality characteristics that categorize the hundreds of personality traits that have been identified. The so-called Big Five are extraversion, agreeableness, conscientiousness, emotional stability, and openness to experience.

Bullies

Team members who actively disrupt the team by pushing their opinions on others and seem to revel in making others feel inadequate or unintelligent. They may feel they are better prepared or more knowledgeable than others and are anxious to display their expertise, or they may use bullying to cover up their inadequacies.

Burning Platform

A dramatic, vivid demonstration that the current situation is unacceptable.

C

Cafeteria-Style Benefit Plans

Plans in which employees can choose from a range of alternative benefits to best fit their needs.

Catalytic Mechanisms

Mechanisms that help translate objectives into performance by making stretch goals reachable. These mechanisms generally involve a dramatic policy that turns normal corporate practice on its head, requiring people to act in new ways that further the overarching corporate goal.

Category-Based Trust

Trusting others because we see them as somehow similar to us in terms of social (e.g., gender, age group, race) or organizational (e.g., team membership, level, tenure, functional area) category. We see others who seem similar to us as members of our in-group and tend to attribute positive characteristics such as honesty, cooperativeness, and trustworthiness to them.

Changing

The second phase in Lewin's change model, in which changes are made to people, structures, or tasks and ongoing support is provided.

Check-In

A simple activity that asks each team member to share how he or she is doing or anything that is new. This is usually done in a round-robin fashion, going around the table.

Check-Out

An activity that goes around the table, with each team member being asked to comment on his or her thoughts about the meeting, what was accomplished, and how he or she feels about the meeting and the overall direction of the team.

Clan Control

Norm-based control resulting from a desire to meet the expectations of one's team members.

Classical (or Pavlovian) Conditioning

The process of conditioning that relies on pairing of a stimulus (e.g., food) that leads to some response (e.g., salivation) with another stimulus (e.g., ringing of a bell) that doesn't normally lead to the response. Through such pairing, the response is transferred to the new stimulus (e.g., ringing the bell results in salivation).

Coercive Power

Power based on one person's perceived ability to affect punishment that another receives.

Cognitive Resource Diversity Theory

A theory stating that diversity should enhance performance by bringing more perspectives and a wider range of knowledge to bear on problems, thereby increasing creativity and decision-making effectiveness.

Cognitive Self-Management

Self-management approach involving the development of effective thinking patterns.

Collaboration Engineering (CE)

A research-based approach to designing and deploying collaboration processes for high-value recurring team tasks. ThinkLets within CE are the units of facilitation that can be integrated into groupware tools in order to develop streamlined activities for a given team task.

Collaborative Conflict Style

Conflict style that is both cooperative and assertive, focusing on satisfying the needs of both parties. Sometimes called a problem-solving style, it has the potential for yielding win–win outcomes.

Collaboratory

A network-based facility and organizational entity that spans distance; supports rich and recurring human interaction oriented to a common research area; fosters contact between researchers who are both known and unknown to each other; and provides access to data sources, artifacts, and tools required to accomplish research tasks.

Collective Efficacy

A group's shared belief in its capabilities to organize and execute the courses of action required to produce given levels of attainment.

Collegiate Entrepreneurs' Organization (CEO)

The premier entrepreneurship network, with chapters on university campuses across North America and beyond. CEO, a nonprofit organization, currently supports entrepreneurship in over 240 chapters in more than forty-three states in the United States.

Communication

The transfer of information from one person to another. Communication may serve several important functions, including information, motivation, control, and emotive.

Communication Functions

Communication serves four key functions: (1) providing information for decision making; (2) encouraging commitment to organizational objectives, thus enhancing motivation; (3) clarifying duties, authority, and responsibilities, thereby permitting control; and (4) permitting the expression of feelings and the satisfaction of social needs. Communication may also help people vent frustrations.

Competing (or Forcing) Conflict Style

Conflict style used by a party who is assertive and uncooperative, attempting to satisfy his or her own needs at the expense of those of the other party. If the party is successful, this results in a form of win-lose outcome, with a clear winner and loser.

Complainers

Members who constantly complain about the team's scheduling, activities, progress, or other matters. They see the project as a waste of time, feel they aren't being treated well, or simply hate to work in teams.

Compromising Conflict Style

Conflict style used by a party who shows moderate levels of both assertiveness and cooperation. The compromise doesn't fully satisfy the needs of either party, but the pain is shared.

Confirmation Bias

The tendency to seek, interpret, and recall information in ways that confirm one's preconceptions. That is, we attempt to confirm our prior views, often leading us to avoid, ignore, and distort warning signs.

Conflict Aftermath

The residue of manifest conflict, conflict aftermath is likely to breed more conflict and, when it does, that conflict is likely to take on a life of its own. Examples are feuds for which the original insult, misdeed, or misunderstanding has been long forgotten but for which bitterness and even hatred are unabated. Failure to address the situation after a conflict has theoretically been resolved may result in damaged or destroyed working relationships between team members or between teams.

Conservatism in Information Processing

The tendency to underrevise past estimates in the face of new information. That is, we tend to give less weight to new information than we should.

Consideration Leadership Behavior

Leader behavior that shows friendship, mutual trust, respect, and warmth. Considerate leaders are friendly and approachable, look out for the personal welfare of team members, back up the members in their actions, and find time to listen to others.

Content Theories of Motivation

Theories of motivation that help us understand what people want and why they want it, typically in terms of various active needs and the motivations that people have to satisfy these needs. Maslow's Hierarchy of Needs is an example.

Context
Relevant factors in the larger organization in which a team exists as well the external environment of the organization.

Contingency Planning
The process of developing alternative courses of action that can be followed if a decision, perhaps because of unexpected events, does not work out as planned. Contingency plans ensure that backups are available, and they help remove the panic element in unforeseen situations.

Convergent Thinking
A process that emphasizes narrowing in on a solution to a problem.

Coworking
A style of work that involves a shared working environment, typically an office, and independent activity. Employees in the same environment are often working for different organizations, or they may be acting as freelancers or forming startups.

Critical Psychological State
In the Job Characteristics Model, the psychological states of experienced meaningfulness of work, experienced responsibility for work outcomes, and knowledge of the actual results of work activities.

Cross-Functional Team
Team composed of individuals from multiple functions in an organization (e.g., finance, marketing, engineering, manufacturing) that has the objective of bringing together and leveraging relevant knowledge and experience from individuals working in multiple functional areas in order to enhance the efficiency, quality, and user satisfaction of the outcome of the process (such as new products or improved customer service).

Cross-Team Groups
A separate formal group that is composed of multiple individuals from each team who work together to coordinate the activities of the teams.

Cross-Training
An instructional strategy in which each team member is trained in the duties of his or her teammates.

Cultural Intelligence
Intelligence that focuses on the ability to understand and manage culture and cultural differences in the workplace.

Cultural Intelligence Stages of Development
A process model that specifies five stages in development of cultural intelligence. The five stages are, respectively, (1) reactivity to external stimuli; (2) recognition of other cultural norms and motivation to learn about them; (3) accommodation of other cultural norms and rules in one's own mind; (4) assimilation of diverse cultural norms into alternative behaviors; and

(5) proactivity in cultural behavior based on recognition of cultural cues that others do not perceive.

Cycle of Dysfunctional Teams
A basic process model that identifies a failure to evaluate team effectiveness as a major cause of team failure.

D

DECA
A nonprofit organization that prepares emerging leaders and entrepreneurs for careers in marketing, finance, hospitality, and management in high schools and colleges around the globe.

Decision Making
The first three stages of the problem-solving process—problem definition, alternative generation, and alternative evaluation and choice.

Deep-Level Diversity
Diversity based on factors such as attitudes, values, beliefs, information, and opinions. We sometimes infer deep-level diversity from surface-level diversity.

Defense Mechanisms
Ways in which an individual may try to reduce the tensions caused by frustration, such as by physically leaving the source of frustration, mentally leaving, or striking back.

Democratic Leader
A leader who permits followers to participate in making decisions.

Devil's Advocate
An individual or group given the responsibility for challenging a proposal. The idea is to find flaws while they may still be remedied, or to recognize that the flaws are fatal before competitors, customers, or others become aware of them.

Dispositional Trust
Trait-like trust in others. Dispositional trust may result from early trust-related experiences that develop general beliefs about others' trustworthiness that translate to a personality characteristic.

Distraction
The condition occurring when a recipient does not understand the sender's message because he or she is thinking about something else.

Distributive Approach
An approach to negotiation that focuses on getting as much as possible from the other party (taking the biggest possible slice of the pie).

Distributive Fairness
The perception that an individual is getting what he or she deserves—not less, but *not more either*.

Divergent Thinking

A process emphasizing that problem solvers must stretch their minds and seek new possibilities. Creativity is especially important at the alternative-generation stage.

Dogmatism

The degree to which individuals are closed minded, have rigid belief systems and doggedly stick to their opinions, refusing to revise them in the face of conflicting evidence. Dogmatic individuals make decisions quickly, based on relatively little information, and are confident in those decisions. They like to follow the rules and are unlikely to consider novel alternatives.

Dual Team Memberships

A team membership structure that gives membership on two teams to at least one member of each team.

E

Effectiveness

The degree to which a team achieves goals related to performance and other measures of success.

Emotional Contagion

The transference of emotions across team members.

Emotional Intelligence

Intelligence reflected in how someone does in life, manages feelings, gets along with others, and is empathetic and motivated. Emotional intelligence is composed of interpersonal intelligence—the ability to understand other people: what motivates them, how they work, and how to work cooperatively with them—and intrapersonal intelligence—the capacity to form an accurate model of oneself and to be able to use that model to operate effectively in life.

Enactive Attainment

Individual self-efficacy resulting from successful task performance.

Enactus

"An international nonprofit organization that brings together student, academic, and business leaders who are committed to using the power of entrepreneurial action to improve the quality of life and standard of living for people in need" (http://enactus.org/who-we-are/our-story/).

Equity Theory

A process theory of motivation that addresses what causes a person to see his or her work environment as fair or unfair, and how this perception influences motivation. Equity theory is based on comparing the ratio of one's perceived rewards and contributions to those of significant others. Equity theory stresses that equity, rather than overreward or underreward, is desired.

Escalation of Commitment

The tendency to throw good money after bad, or continue to pour more time and resources into a failing project.

Escape Learning

An operant learning strategy based on learning that a desired behavior will enable an individual to escape from or remove a negative stimulus.

Exception Principle

A principle stating that only exceptions should be reported. It is a way to reduce information overload.

Expectancy Perception

The belief that one is able to effectively perform a task.

Expectancy Theory

A process theory of motivation that addresses the elements that must be present in a situation if a person is to be motivated to pursue a desired outcome. These include expectancy (the perception that greater effort will lead to heightened performance), valence (the degree to which outcomes of behavior are desired), and instrumentalities (the perceived linkages between enhanced performance and desired outcomes).

Expert Power

Power based on one person's perception that another has needed relevant knowledge in a given area. For instance, doctors, lawyers, and computer specialists may all have expert power.

Extrinsic Motivation

Motivation based on use of externally administered rewards, such as pay and benefits.

F

Fault Lines

Hypothetical dividing lines that may split a group into subgroups, generally based on multiple attributes such as age, gender, and race.

Felt Conflict

Conflict experienced as discomfort and tension. The party experiencing felt conflict is motivated to reduce those negative feelings. Felt conflict may be heightened by other tensions inside or outside the organization.

Five Dysfunctions of a Team Model

A framework for major causes of ineffective teams, arranged in a hierarchy. Causes include inattention to results, avoidance of responsibility, lack of commitment, fear of conflict, and absence of trust.

Force Field Analysis

A perspective that sees the success of change attempts as depending on whether forces in support of change are greater than those opposing change. Many factors, varying in strength and duration, oppose and support change. To develop a successful change effort, it is important to anticipate and manage potential sources of resistance to the change as well as potential forces favoring the change

Forming Stage of Group Development

The first stage of the stages of group development model, in which team members are getting acquainted and becoming oriented to the task.

Framing

Presenting the message—defining the purpose in a meaningful way. Framing is one of two critical aspects of the language of leadership (along with rhetorical crafting).

Framing Effects

The fact that the way information is framed can influence choices.

Freeloaders

Team members who don't carry their fair share of the team's workload; they engage in social loafing. Such freeloaders detract directly from team performance by their lack of contribution. In addition, they may provoke conflict in the team as other members refuse to carry an unproductive member.

Frustration Regression

A potential refinement of Maslow's Hierarchy of Needs theory. Frustration regression asserts that if needs at one level of the hierarchy are continually frustrated, individuals may revert their focus to needs lower on the hierarchy.

Functional Team

A team composed of individuals from within a common function (such as finance or marketing) whose objective is to bring together individuals with relevant knowledge and experience to handle operations or to achieve objectives related primarily to a single functional area.

Fundamental Attribution Error

The tendency to overattribute both praise and blame to people rather than to situations.

Future Business Leaders of America

A nonprofit organization that is the world's oldest and largest student organization. "A quarter of a million high school and middle school students, college and university students, faculty, educators, administrators, and business professionals have chosen to be members of the premier business education association preparing students for careers in business" (http://www.fbla-pbl.org/web/page/614/sectionid/614/pagelevel/1/main_interior.asp).

G

Gaming

Use of games, often computer-based, for training and enhancing employee engagement.

Gantt Chart

One of the most common types of project timelines, it shows the relationship between tasks that need to be performed over time, typically measured in weeks or months.

Global Virtual Team (GVT)

Globally dispersed, culturally diverse, and technologically connected individuals who work interdependently with a limited life span of membership in order to accomplish a common goal.

Goal Acceptance

The degree to which individuals or teams accept particular goals as their own.

Goal Commitment

The degree to which individuals or teams are dedicated to trying to reach the goals they have adopted.

Goal-Setting Theory

A process theory of motivation that addresses how goals can be set to properly motivate behavior and how to manage the process of attaining goals.

Ground Rules

Basic rules that are typically established early in the existence of a team to communicate expectations for appropriate team member behavior and performance.

Group

Two or more individuals working together as a unit that is characterized by a strong, clearly focused leader, individual accountability, a purpose that is the same as that of the larger organization, individual work products, and measurement of performance indirectly based on the unit's influence on others.

Group Brainstorming

A creativity enhancement technique that seeks to create the right atmosphere for relaxed, spontaneous thinking. A small group of employees is brought together, presented with the problem, and told to follow four rules: don't criticize any ideas, freewheel, try to come up with as many ideas as possible, and try to combine ideas and improve on them. Hitchhiking on others' ideas may create a chain of inspiration.

Group Decision Support Systems (GDSS)

Interactive, computer-based systems that facilitate solution of semistructured and unstructured problems by a designated set of decision makers working together as a group. GDSS include structured decision tools such as brainstorming, commenting on ideas, and rating and ranking of alternatives.

Group Mood

An internal, subjective, emotional state at the level of the group.

Group Potency

A group's shared belief—generalized across tasks—in its ability to organize and execute the courses of action required to produce given levels of attainment. While collective efficacy is task specific, group potency is a broader view of the group's general capabilities.

Groupthink

Janis's description of the mode of thinking that persons engage in when concurrence seeking becomes so dominant in a cohesive in-group that it tends to override realistic appraisals of alternative courses of action. According to Janis, groupthink refers to thinking characterized by deteriorating mental efficiency, reality testing, and moral judgment that results from in-group pressures. While research fails to support aspects of the groupthink model, Janis' prescriptions for improvement of group decision processes are valuable.

H

Heroes
Role models, people who behave in exemplary ways that others seek to emulate.

High Context Culture
A culture in which the context of communication is just as important as the words that are actually spoken, and cultural clues are important in understanding what is being communicated.

High Performance Teams Model
The integrative framework for this textbook that shows how all of the major topics covered fit together into a system that team leaders and members can use to create and sustain effective work teams.

Hindsight Bias
Also called Monday morning quarterbacking, this bias is the phenomenon of "I knew it all along." Hindsight bias is the tendency for people who learn of the outcome of an event to believe falsely that they would have predicted the reported outcome.

History-Based Trust
Trust developed as team members or others interact over time and learn more about one another's dispositions, intentions, and motives. Such interaction provides a basis for drawing inferences about trustworthiness.

Hofstede's Cultural Dimensions
Five important dimensions of national culture identified by Hofstede: individualism versus collectivism, power distance, uncertainty avoidance, quality versus quantity of life, and time orientation.

Hot Group
Group characterized by extremely high levels of team spirit, excitement, and energy. The hot group state of mind is task obsessed and full of passion, coupled with a distinctive way of behaving; a style that is intense, sharply focused, and full bore.

I

Icebreaker
Exercises used to help team members get acquainted and help overcome any initial discomfort.

Idealized Influence
Transformational leader behavior characterized by leaders talking about their important values and beliefs; consider the moral and ethical consequences

of their decisions; display conviction in their ideals, beliefs, and values; and model values in their actions.

Identity Fusion
Condition experienced by team members who fully identify with the team. When this happens, they feel fused, or one, with the group. Rather than their properties and the team's properties being distinct, the self-other barrier is blurred. The team is seen as equivalent with the personal self.

Illusory Correlation
The tendency to see relationships between variables that do not in fact exist, perhaps because of stereotypes or expectations.

Individualism versus Collectivism
The degree to which society believes that the individual or the collective is paramount. In individualistic cultures the cultural belief is that the individual comes first—social frameworks are loosely knit and people are chiefly expected to look after their own interests and those of their immediate families. There is an emphasis on individual achievement. Society offers individuals a great amount of freedom, and people are accustomed to making independent decisions and taking independent action. In collectivist cultures there are tight social frameworks in which people expect the groups of which they are members to look after them and protect them in times of trouble. In exchange for security, loyalty is expected.

Individualized Consideration
Transformational leader behavior showing personal interest and concern in individual followers and promoting followers' self-development through coaching, mentorships, and focus on development of followers' strengths.

Information Retention
The withholding of information, often because it is a valuable resource and source of power.

Initiating Structure Leadership Behavior
Behavior that helps clarify the task and get the job done. Initiating leaders provide definite standards of performance, set goals, organize work, emphasize meeting deadlines, and coordinate the work of team members.

Inspirational Leadership
Transformational leader behavior that gives followers hope, energizing them to pursue a vision. Such behavior envisions exciting new possibilities, talks optimistically about the future, expresses confidence that goals can be met, and articulates a compelling vision of the future.

Instrumentality
The perception that effective performance will be tied to task outcomes.

Integrative Approach
An approach to negotiation that seeks to get as large a total as possible for the bargaining parties (enlarging the pie) rather than just maximizing one's own gains.

Intellectual Stimulation
Transformational leader behavior that helps followers recognize problems and find ways to solve them. Such behaviors encourage followers to challenge the status quo, champion change, and foster creative deviance.

Interpersonal Distance
Comfortable distances for particular types of interactions. When people are too close to us or too far away, we tend to feel uneasy. Put another way, we have a sense of personal space, an area around us that we treat as an extension of ourselves, and we want people to be in specific parts—or zones—of that personal space for particular activities. The four zones are intimate, personal, social, and public.

Interteam Conflict
Conflict between teams.

Intrateam Conflict
Conflict within a team.

Intrinsic Motivation
Motivation to perform a job based on the job itself, rather than on externally administered rewards. This may result from job dimensions such as task significance, autonomy, and skill variety.

J

Job Characteristics Model
A model illustrating the elements of job characteristics theory. It depicts core job dimensions, critical psychological states, and personal and work outcomes, and it shows employee growth-need strength as a moderator of the impacts of the core job dimensions.

Job Characteristics Theory
A process theory of motivation that addresses how jobs can be designed to make them intrinsically motivating without the use of external rewards.

Job Enrichment
An approach to job design that emphasizes that the job itself can be designed in ways to motivate without use of externally administered rewards and punishments.

L

Language of Leadership
Language transformational leaders' use to inspire others, communicate their vision, ideal, and beliefs, provide compelling reassurance, and challenge team members to think in new ways. Framing and rhetorical crafting are two key aspects of the language of leadership.

Latent Conflict
Essentially, conflict waiting to happen; conditions are right for open conflict to develop. Latent conflict is influenced by the aftermath of preceding conflict situations and by environmental effects.

Law of Effect

The principle that behavior that is rewarded will tend to be repeated; behavior that is not rewarded will tend not to be repeated.

Leadership

The ability to influence others toward the achievement of goals. Leadership, then, relates to the ability to influence others toward desired outcomes.

Learning Theory

A theory of motivation that addresses how valued outcomes can be tied to behaviors in order to reinforce desired behaviors and eliminate undesired behaviors that are not related to the achievement of an organization's objectives.

Legitimate Power

Power resulting when one person thinks it is legitimate, or right, for another to give orders or otherwise exert force.

Lewin's Change Model

A three-stage model of the change process, including unfreezing, changing, and refreezing.

LinkedIn

An online, global website that supports professional networking and job searching activities of its users.

Locus of Control

The degree to which individuals believe that the things that happen to them are the result of their own actions. Those who believe that such things are within their own control have an internal locus of control. Those with an external locus of control see their lives as being controlled by fate, circumstance, or chance.

Low Context Culture

A culture in which the words used by the speaker explicitly convey the speaker's message to the listener.

M

Machiavellianism

Personality characteristic in which individuals think any behavior is acceptable if it achieves their goals (i.e., the ends justify the means). Machiavellians try to manipulate others. They are unemotional and detached, look out for Number One, and are unlikely to be good team players.

Martyrs

Team members who feel (whether correctly or not) that they are carrying the load for the team. They see themselves as being forced to cover for incompetent team members, as having all the worst assignments, and as doing far more than their fair share. Unlike complainers, they really don't want anything to change; they just want others to feel guilty and to acknowledge their burden. This often creates conflict as other team members chafe at the martyr's claims, attributions, and attitudes.

Maslow's Hierarchy of Needs

The theory that people seek to satisfy needs at the lowest level of the hierarchy before trying to satisfy needs on the next-higher level. The need that motivates a person depends on where that person is on the hierarchy at that time. In particular, Maslow believed that motivation could be examined in terms of five sets of needs: physiological, security, social, esteem, and self-actualization.

Maxwell's "17 Indisputable Laws of Teamwork"

- Law of the Bad Apple: rotten attitudes ruin a team
- Law of the Bench: good teams have great depth
- Law of Big Picture: the team's goal is more important than the role
- Law of the Catalyst: winning teams have players who make things happen
- Law of the Chain: the strength of a team is impacted by its weakest link
- Law of Communication: creating positive change in an organization requires communication
- Law of Compass: vision gives team members direction and confidence
- Law of Countability: teammates must be able to count on each other when it counts
- Law of Dividends: investment in the team compounds over time
- Law of the Edge: the difference between two equally talented teams is leadership
- Law of High Morale: when you're winning, nothing hurts
- Law of Identity: shared values define the team
- Law of Mt. Everest: as challenge escalates so does the need for teamwork
- Law of the Niche: all players have a place where they can add the most value
- Law of the Price Tag: a team fails to reach its potential when it fails to pay the price
- Law of the Scoreboard: the team can make adjustments when it knows where it stands
- Law of Significance: one is too small a number to achieve greatness as a team

Misrepresentation

Distortion of communicated information, often for the sender's benefit.

Motivation

Moving ourselves and others toward some goal. It requires arousal to initiate behavior toward a goal, direction to properly focus that behavior, and persistence to ultimately attain the goal.

Motivational Cultural Intelligence (MCI)

Especially applicable to global teams, it refers to an individual's intrinsic motivation and specific self-efficacy to engage in cross-cultural experiences and master their nuances. That is, it is desirable to assign members to global teams who are motivated to try new things in cross-cultural settings and who feel they are competent to do so.

Myers-Briggs Type Indicator (MBTI)

A tool for assessing personalities and forming teams. The MBTI gauges personality along four dimensions, yielding sixteen ($2 \times 2 \times 2 \times 2$) types. The MBTI gauges preferences for the dimensions, not necessarily their levels. The dimensions are these:

- **Extraversion (E) vs. Introversion (I).** Extraverts are outgoing, are energized by people and things, and don't like to be isolated from others. Introverts prefer to spend time alone and are energized by concepts and ideas.
- **Sensing (S) vs. Intuition (N).** Sensing types prefer to be precise and concrete. They like specific, detailed information and prefer to develop a single idea in depth. Intuitive types like to see the big picture. They are imaginative, like to explore what is new, and look to the future.
- **Thinking (T) vs. Feeling (F).** Thinking types prefer to be rational and systematic. They prefer to use careful analysis, logic, and hard facts to reach conclusions. Feeling types prefer to rely on their feelings and to go with their gut.
- **Perception (P) vs. Judgment (J).** Perception types enjoy a variety of frequent changes, learn by exploring what engages curiosity, and are casual and easy-going. Judgment types prefer schedules, routines, and systems, like to plan in advance, and are orderly and systematic.

N

Narratives

Written or spoken accounts used by members to make sense of their experiences and express their feelings and beliefs. Narratives often focus on certain basis themes, such as whether the organization supports equality or inequality, security or insecurity, and control or lack of control.

Need and Need Theories of Motivation

Something people require, such as food, security, social interaction, esteem, and self-actualization. Need theories posit that unsatisfied needs are the source of motivation.

Neocortex

The so-called rational brain. It is responsible for the sorts of intelligence gauged by IQ tests.

Neutralizer of Leadership

Something in the context, followers, or elsewhere, that minimizes the effect of leader behavior.

Nominal Group

A group, also called a coacting group, in which members work together without directly interacting.

Nominal Group Technique

A group decision-making technique that uses a blend of coacting (or nominal) stages, in which members act together without interacting, and interacting stages to capture the benefits of groups while minimizing potential problems. It seeks to encourage all members to make inputs, to prevent dominant members from controlling the process, to ensure that all ideas get a fair hearing, and to allow members to evaluate alternatives without fear of retribution. It has, successively, nominal, interacting, and nominal stages.

Nonreinforcement
An operant learning strategy that results in the elimination of an undesired behavior based on a lack of positive or negative consequences linked to the behavior.

Norming Stage of Group Development
The third stage of group development, in which a team becomes cohesive, members settle into their roles, and norms develop.

O

Operant (or Skinnerian) Conditioning
A process theory of motivation that deals with ways to increase desired behaviors and to decrease undesired behaviors based on the type of consequences that are linked with behaviors.

Organizational Behavior Modification
The systematic process of applying operant learning principles to the management of behavior in organizational settings.

Overconfidence Bias
Bias occurring when people's subjective confidence in their judgments is greater than their objective accuracy. It often results from hindsight bias, confirmation bias, and other factors.

P

Paralanguage
How something is said rather than what is said. It includes all vocal aspects of speech other than words. For example, voice qualities—such as pitch, rhythm, tempo, and volume—influence interpretation of a verbal message.

Participation
Involvement in a decision-making or other process; especially important when planning and implementing changes since it enriches people's work, raises self-esteem and self-confidence, and hones problem-solving skills.

Patterns of Collaboration
In collaboration engineering (CE), patterns of deliberation and collaboration, including diverge, converge, clarify, organize, evaluate, and build consensus.

PDCA Cycle
A problem-solving and continuous improvement process that involves four steps: Plan, Do, Check, and Act.

Performing Stage of Group Development
The fourth stage of group development, in which a team reaches maturity and focuses on performance.

Personal Space

An area around their bodies that people treat as an extension of themselves. They want people to be in specific parts—or zones—of that personal space for particular activities.

Personality

The organized and distinctive pattern of behavior that characterizes an individual's adaptation to a situation and endures over time.

Planned Change

Change that occurs when team leaders or others develop and install programs or other activities to alter processes or systems in a timely and orderly way.

Polarization

The tendency of group attitudes and decisions to be more extreme than those of the individual members before interaction.

Positive Reinforcement

An operant learning strategy that reinforces desired behaviors with rewards.

Power Distance

The degree to which a society accepts the fact that power in institutions and organizations is distributed unequally. A high power distance society accepts wide differences in power in organizations. Employees show great respect for authority, titles, status, and rank. Titles are important in bargaining. A low power distance society plays down inequalities as much as possible.

Proactivity

The extent to which people take action to influence their environments. Proactive individuals look for opportunities, show initiative, take action, and persevere until they are able to bring about change. They engage in high levels of entrepreneurial activities and have relatively high levels of job performance.

Problem-Solving Process

A five-stage process used to make and implement effective decisions. The stages are problem definition, alternative generation, alternative evaluation and choice, decision implementation, and monitoring and control of decision outcomes.

Problem-Solving Team

Team composed of individuals who possess relevant knowledge and experience related to resolving an undesirable condition or level of performance. Its purpose is to bring together and to leverage the knowledge and experience of individuals who can analyze a problem; identify its root cause; and identify and implement opportunities to enhance efficiency, effectiveness, and performance.

Process Conflict

Conflict regarding things such as how a project should be addressed and who should do what.

Process Improvement Team

A team typically composed of individuals who possess relevant knowledge and experience related to a specific key business process. Its purpose is to bring together and to leverage the knowledge and experience of individuals who can evaluate a process and identify and implement opportunities to enhance its efficiency, effectiveness, and performance.

Process Theories of Motivation

Theories of motivation that focus on how a person becomes motivated as part of an overall process rather than just acting on needs. Process theories include equity theory, operant learning theory, goal-setting theory, and expectancy theory.

Profit Sharing

A reward system in which employees receive payments, in addition to their regular salary and bonuses, tied to the company's profitability.

Proxemics

The use of interpersonal space (that is, proximity) to convey status or degree of intimacy.

Psychological Contract

An implied contract between the employee and the organization: the employee will be loyal and work hard, and the company will provide rewards and security.

Q

Quality versus Quantity of Life

The degree to which a culture values assertiveness and the acquisition of money and material things (quantity of life) or emphasizes the quality of life and the importance of relationships, showing sensitivity and concern for the welfare of others. In quality of life cultures, people stop to smell the roses. In quantity of life cultures, people try to get as many roses as possible. Quantity and quality of life were originally labeled masculinity and femininity respectively.

R

Reactive Change

Change that occurs when team leaders or others simply respond to pressure for change when it comes to their attention.

Readiness Review

A formal assessment of the organization's readiness for transition to a team-based organization.

Realistic Job Preview (RJP)

Accurate job information—both positive and negative—given to job candidates.

Realistic Living Conditions Preview

Giving team members who are transferred from their native cultures accurate information, favorable and unfavorable, on the general living environment in the host country

Realistic Virtual-Team Preview (RVTP)

Information that gives members an accurate picture of the nature of the virtual team's role and task, including the challenges it may face.

Referent Power

Power derived from the feeling of identity, or oneness, that one person has for another, or the desire for such identity. The commercial picturing Michael Jordan and saying, "Be like Mike," was a concise and direct appeal to referent power.

Refreezing

The third and final phase in Lewin's change model, in which outcomes are reinforced and constructive modifications are made.

Relationship Conflict

Sometimes called emotional conflict or affective conflict, it results from things such as personality clashes; anger; tension; annoyance; and conflict about personal taste, values, and interpersonal styles.

Relations-Oriented Roles

Roles needed to keep the team healthy and its members satisfied. Team members who help keep the group harmonious, assist in helping members resolve disputes, and encourage members as they face barriers are engaging in relations-oriented roles.

Reward Power

Power based on the perceived ability to reward. It depends on one person's ability to administer desired outcomes to another and to decrease or remove outcomes that are not desired.

Rhetorical Crafting

Use of symbolic language to give emotional power to a message. That is, the message provides a sense of direction, and rhetoric heightens its emotional appeal and makes it memorable.

Rhetorical Triangle

Aristotle's argument that all attempts to encourage others to change their minds, feelings, and behavior can be summarized in the context of the rhetorical triangle for which the axes are logos, ethos, and pathos. Logos refers to convincing others to accept a change through reason, logic, and data; ethos through the strength of one's moral character and followers' trust; and pathos through appeals to one's target audience's emotional and psychological needs.

Risk-Taking Propensity

Tendency to prefer gambles rather than playing it safe. Risk takers tend to make fast decisions based on relatively little information.

Rites

Combinations of cultural forms into a public performance. They can be important in signaling member transitions, celebrating accomplishments, or bringing team members together.

Rites of Enhancement

Rites celebrating accomplishments of members, enhancing their status. These rites provide public recognition of personal accomplishments and motivate others to similar efforts.

Rites of Integration

Rites, such as annual holiday parties or elaborate annual meetings, that bring team members together by fostering shared feelings that bind and connect them to the team and organization.

Rites of Passage

Rites marking important transitions. For example, employees who complete a rigorous off-site training program may be welcomed back with a speech, certificate, or party.

Rituals

Relatively simple combinations of repetitive behaviors, often brief and carried out without much thought.

Role

A set of expectations associated with a "hat" (such as team member, student, and friend) that one "wears."

Role Ambiguity

Condition in which the duties and responsibilities associated with a team member's role are not clear.

Role-Based Trust

Trust emanating from roles others hold. We often put our lives in the hands of others—such as airplane pilots or surgeons—who we may hardly know because we recognize the various hurdles—training, education, certification, and so on—they have surmounted to achieve their positions.

Role Conflict

The condition in which the duties and responsibilities of two or more different roles create conflicting expectations for a team member.

Role Overload

The condition in which the duties and responsibilities associated with a role or roles are overwhelming to a team member.

Role Responsibilities Matrix

A formal tool used to support the structure of a team that shows how different tasks that need to be completed have been assigned to various team members. Responsibility for tasks can be individual or shared.

Role Stress

Stress resulting from conflicting, ambiguous, and/or overwhelming role demands.

Round-Robin Process

A process asking members to give their comments in turn. For example, the leader may say, "Let's go around the table and see what each of us has to say." Sometimes, as when team members have made up lists of ideas, the round-robin technique may be used to have each member in turn give his or her first idea, then in turn give his or her second idea, and so on.

Rule-Based Trust

Trust based on shared understandings regarding the system of formal and informal rules governing appropriate behavior. Rule-based trust is sustained within an organization by ensuring that newcomers are aware of rules for appropriate behavior.

S

Satisfaction

The condition of need fulfillment. Need theories of motivation posit that a satisfied need is not a motivator.

Satisfaction Progression

Part of Maslow's Hierarchy of Needs theory: when needs at one level of the hierarchy are met, we move on to the next higher level in the hierarchy.

Scientific Approach

A team's use of a systematic process to collect data to analyze problems, generate problem solutions, make decisions, and enhance effectiveness.

Scoring Approaches

Choice-making approaches that assign a total score to each alternative. The alternative with the best score can then be chosen.

Screening Approaches

Approaches by which each alternative is identified as satisfactory or unsatisfactory. Unsatisfactory alternatives are screened out, leaving only those that can clear all hurdles.

Self-Efficacy

An individual's appraisal of his or her task-specific capability to achieve a particular level of performance in goal accomplishment.

Self-Fulfilling Prophecy

Also known as Pygmalion Effect, the situation in which our expectations shape reality. That is, our expectations cause us to see others in ways consistent with those expectations, to behave accordingly, and to cause others to then behave according to our expectations.

Self-Management

The process of managing oneself. Self-management may involve use of behavioral and cognitive approaches.

Self-Managing Work Team

Team composed of individuals who possess responsibilities related to managing an overall product or service business unit that has the objective of empowering members of a team to take full responsibility for designing and managing all aspects of operations for a specific product or service unit without a formal team leader.

Self-Monitoring

The extent to which people vary their behavior to match the situation and to make the best possible impression on others.

Self-Organization

The movement in organizations toward freeing employees to figure out how to get the job done without central planning or control.

Self-Oriented Roles

Roles team members adopt for personal gain. These roles may often hamper team performance and cohesiveness. For instance, some team members gain a sense of power by dominating others or blocking others' attempts to get things done.

Semantics

The situation in which the meaning of a message to the sender differs from its meaning to the recipient; also called code noise.

Similarity-Attraction Paradigm

The perspective that people's perceptions of others, often inferred on the basis of demographic similarity, lead to attraction among team members.

Social Learning

Learning that occurs through any of a variety of social channels—newspapers, books, television, conversations with family members, friends, teammates, and so on.

Social Loafing

The situation in which team members don't carry their fair share of the team's workload; also called freeloading.

Social Reciprocity

The principle that you get back what you give to others: what goes around, comes around.

Spontaneous Sociability

The willingness of team members to engage in cooperative, altruistic, extrarole behaviors that further attainment of collective goals.

Stopping Rules

Rules specifying the conditions under which a project should be abandoned.

Storming Stage of Group Development

The second stage of group development, in which conflict and disagreement among team members is likely.

Strong Culture

A culture characterized by sharing and acceptance of core values.

Strong Situation Hypothesis

A hypothesis asserting that factors such as personality and trust are important in weak situations (when demands from the situation are minimal) but less so in strong situations (when demands from the situation are powerful).

Substitute for Leadership

Something in the context, followers, or elsewhere that substitutes for formal leader behavior, making that behavior less necessary.

Surface-Level Diversity

Diversity in terms of features that are readily apparent, such as gender, race, and age. The workforce has become, and will continue to become, more diverse in each of these features.

Swift Trust

Trust developed quickly, as opposed to trust developed over time as team members interact and learn about one another. Swift trust is needed, for instance, in temporary teams, which are formed around a common task with a finite life span.

Symbols

Things that stand for or suggest something else. For example, symbolic team names containing metaphors such as "Olympians," "jugglers," and "wolf pack" may all reflect qualities team members are attempting to convey.

T

Task Conflict

Disagreement over ideas and opinions pertaining to the team's task; also called cognitive conflict.

Task-Oriented Roles

Roles needed to get a job done. Team members who initiate tasks, gather information for use by the team, offer suggestions, and help motivate others would be performing task-oriented roles.

Taskwork-Focused Team Training

Team training targeting taskwork to enhance the knowledge, skills, and abilities necessary to develop technical competencies of team members.

Team

A group of individuals working together that is characterized by shared leadership roles, individual and mutual accountability, a specific purpose, collective work outputs, open discussions and active problem-solving meetings, and measurement of performance based on collective work outputs.

Team-Based Rewards

Rewards directly tied to team performance as opposed to more general indices such as plant productivity or company profitability.

Team-Based Organization

Organization in which the team, rather than an individual, is the fundamental work unit. Team-based organizations focus on designing an infrastructure that will support the development and deployment of teams throughout an organization.

Team Charter
A basic tool for defining the objective and scope of a team project. The charter is a document developed by a team leader, usually with input from team members, that addresses basic planning issues such as resources required, identifying sponsors for a project, and so on.

Team Cohesiveness
The degree to which a team sticks together and possesses a strong team spirit.

Team (Collective) Efficacy
Team members' appraisal of the team's capacity to achieve a particular level of performance in goal accomplishment. It is essentially self-efficacy at the team level.

Team Dashboard
A formal measurement system that is used to evaluate the effectiveness of a team's functioning in terms of process and outcomes measures. It typically presents each performance measure using a gauge that provides a color-coded system (red, yellow, and green zones) for evaluating team performance.

Team-Focused Team Training
Interventions designed to improve how team members work together effectively.

Team Insurrection
Change driven through a grassroots, bottom-up effort led by a work team.

Team Integrator Role
Role involving the designation of one individual to facilitate the interaction and activities of two or more teams. This individual often is not a formal member of any of the teams involved, but rather is an individual who possesses strong team facilitation skills.

Team Liaison Role
The role of a team member that involves communication with and coordination of the team's planning and activities with the liaison from the other team(s).

Team Mental Models
Organized knowledge frameworks that allow team members to describe, explain, and predict behavior.

Team Norms
The unwritten rules of a team. Team norms are shared expectations about how team members should behave.

Team Socialization
The process by which new members develop into full, participative membership in the team and move from outsiders to insiders. During this process, new members may seek information in order to understand their roles in the team, to develop confidence that they can be successful on the job, and to gain a sense of social acceptance.

Team System

A perspective that views a team as being composed of multiple interrelated elements that must function together effectively in order for a team to be effective.

Teamwork-Focused Team Training

Interventions focused on teamwork that seek to improve how team members work together effectively.

Telepresence Robots

Mobile robots permitting humans to interact by using a camera, speakers, and a microphone to permit conversation and observation.

thinkLet

A unit of facilitation that can be integrated into groupware tools in order to develop streamlined activities for a given team task. An element of Collaboration Engineering (CE), it includes information on when to use or not to use the thinkLet, an overview, inputs and outputs, setup, steps, insights, and success stories.

Third-Party Trust

Third parties in organizations may convey trust-related information. For instance, team members may gossip about others' trustworthiness, recounting stories or evidence that allow others to infer whether an individual or subgroup can be trusted.

360-Degree Feedback Process

A comprehensive process for evaluating teams and team leaders that collects feedback from a variety of sources (e.g., peers, customers, followers) in order to understand the strengths and weaknesses of a team or team leader.

Time Orientation

A society's relative focus on the present or the long term. A long-term orientation is derived from values that include thrift (saving) and persistence in achieving goals. A short-term orientation is derived from values that express a concern for maintaining personal stability or happiness and living for the present.

Tolerance for Ambiguity

The degree to which individuals welcome uncertainty and change. Those with low tolerance for ambiguity see such situations as threatening and uncomfortable. Since teams are increasingly facing dynamic, unstructured situations, high tolerance for ambiguity is clearly an important characteristic of team members.

Transactive Memory System (TMS)

A form of cognitive architecture that encompasses both the knowledge held by particular group members and a collective awareness of who knows what.

Transformational Leadership

Leadership based on the personal values, beliefs, and qualities of the leader. Transformational leaders broaden and elevate the interests of their followers, generate awareness and acceptance of the purposes and mission of the group, and stir followers to look beyond their own interests to the interests of others.

Tree Diagram
A roadmap of actions that can be taken to support the achievement of specific goals.

Trust
Willingness to put oneself in a position of vulnerability, but with confidence that others will not take advantage of that vulnerability

Type A/B Behavior Patterns
Behavior characterized by differing approaches to perceived pressure. Type A's tend to work aggressively, speak explosively, and find themselves constantly struggling with feelings of great time pressure and impatience. Type B's — the opposite pattern—tend to be relaxed, steady paced, and easygoing.

U

Uncertainty Avoidance
The way societies deal with risk and uncertainty. In low-uncertainty-avoidance countries people are relatively comfortable with risks and tolerate behaviors and opinions that differ from their own. In high-uncertainty-avoidance countries there is a high level of anxiety among the people. Formal rules and other mechanisms are used to provide security and reduce risk. There is less tolerance for deviant ideas and behaviors, and people strive to believe in absolute truths.

Unconflicted Adherence
The condition in which the team continues to engage in past practices even though they are no longer appropriate. Because there is no manifest conflict, the team lacks vigilance and becomes apathetic.

Unfreezing
The first phase of Lewin's change model, in which a high felt need for change is created and resistance to change is minimized.

V

Valence
The value of an outcome.

Values
Deep-seated, personal standards that influence our moral judgments; responses to others; and commitment to personal, team, and organizational goals.

Verbal Persuasion
Individual self-efficacy resulting from receiving others' positive feedback and encouragement.

Verbal Qualifiers
Variations in tone or intensity of speech. For example, increases in rate or volume may indicate impatience or anger, respectively.

Vicarious Experience

Individual self-efficacy resulting from seeing similar others mastering the task.

Virtual Team

Team composed of individuals who are asked to collaborate on a task or project in which they will have little or no face-to-face interaction; the purpose is to enable individuals who are separated by physical distance to work together to achieve a desired objective.

Vocal Characterizers

In nonverbal communications, vocal characterizers are a form of paralanguage. They are sounds that can stand alone as symbols because they can be interpreted as having a specific meaning (e.g., laughing, yelling, crying, grunting).

W

Wall Street Journal (WSJ)

The leading source of business and economic news both in the United States and around the world. The *WSJ* is published 6 days a week and covers news stories related to business, politics, the economy, sports, arts and entertainment, culture and lifestyle, and more.

Web 2.0

The cumulative changes in the way webpages are developed and used. A Web 2.0 site may let users interact and collaborate in a social media dialogue as creators in a virtual community.

X

X-Team

An externally active team. X-Team members engage in (1) scouting to keep on top of what is going on in the external environment—how technologies are changing, markets are shifting, and competitors are behaving; (2) ambassadorship to align team activities to strategic priorities and to advocate for team goals; and (3) task coordination to manage the interdependencies between the team and other groups that provide inputs or that will complete team tasks.

Z

Zombie Team

A team that fails to change as needed and begins to drag down other parts of the organization.

Zones of Personal Space

So-called bubbles around people's bodies in which they prefer certain types of interaction. These zones, or bubbles, are—in increasing distances from the body—the intimate zone, personal zone, social zone, and public zone.

SUBJECT INDEX

AUTHOR INDEX